Realism and Reason

Philosophical Papers, Volume 3

Realism and Reason

Philosophical Papers, Volume 3

HILARY PUTNAM

Walter Beverly Pearson Professor of
Mathematical Logic, Harvard University

CAMBRIDGE
UNIVERSITY PRESS

Published by the Press Syndicate of the University of Cambridge
The Pitt Building, Trumpington Street, Cambridge CB2 1RP
40 West 20th Street, New York, NY 10011–4211, USA
10 Stamford Road, Oakleigh, Victoria 3166, Australia

First published 1983
Reprinted 1985, 1986, 1987, 1989, 1992

Printed in the United States of America

Library of Congress catalog card number: 82-12903

British Library cataloguing in publication data

Putnam, Hilary
Philosophical papers.
Vol. 3: Realism and reason
I. Philosophy
I. Title   II. Realism and reason
191 B945.P/

ISBN 0-521-24672-5 hardback
ISBN 0-521-31394-5 paperback

Contents

To the memory of my father,
Samuel Putnam

Introduction: An overview of the problem

The essays collected in this volume were written in a period of rethinking and reconsidering much of my philosophical position. A look at the introduction to the second volume of my *Philosophical Papers*, and at the essay titled 'Language and reality' in that volume, will reveal that in 1975 I thought that the errors and mistakes I detected in analytical philosophy were occasioned by 'naive verificationism' and 'sophisticated verificationism'. I described myself as a 'realist' (without any qualifying adjective), and I chiefly emphasized the importance of reference in determining meaning in opposition to the idea, traditional among both realists and idealists, that it is *meaning* that determines *reference*. Reference itself I described as a matter of causal connections. The following quotation (from 'Language and reality') illustrates these themes at work:

As language develops, the causal and noncausal links between bits of language and aspects of the world become more complex and more various. To look for any one uniform link between word or thought and object of word or thought is to look for the occult; but to see our evolving and expanding notion of reference as just a proliferating family is to miss the essence of the relation between language and reality. The essence of the relation is that language and thought do asymptotically correspond to reality, to some extent at least. A theory of reference is a theory of the correspondence in question.   (p. 290)

Nothing in this quotation strikes me as exactly wrong even now; but what does strike me is that I was walking on a razor's edge without knowing it. In the intervening years I have come to see that one cannot come to grips with the real problems in philosophy without being more sensitive to the epistemological position of the philosopher than I was willing to be when I wrote those words. Becoming more sensitive to that position had consequences which I did not expect. It led me to think about questions which are thought to be more the province of 'continental philosophy' than of 'analytical philosophy', for instance, to think about the fact that our notions of rationality evolve in history (see, e.g., Putnam, 1981), and about the fact that one's own philosophical tradition has both a past and a future. Some of the resulting reflections appear in this volume ('Convention: a theme in philosophy', and 'Beyond historicism', for example).

The problems with the idea of truth as correspondence

The issue that first made me uncomfortable with my hard-line 'realist' position was one with which every philosopher is familiar: *the notion that our words 'correspond' to determinate objects* (where the notion of an 'object' is thought to have a determinate reference which is independent of conceptual scheme) *had long seemed problematical*, although I did not see any alternative to accepting it. By the time I had to give my Presidential Address (Putnam, 1976) to the Eastern Division of the American Philosophical Association in 1976 the problems with the notion had come to strike me as insuperable, and I finally began to search for an alternative view. What are those problems?

As far back as Berkeley and Kant it had been pointed out that *the notion of a 'correspondence' is difficult once one becomes even a little bit psychologically sophisticated*. If one is not psychologically sophisticated, then it appears easy to say how we 'put our words in correspondence with objects'. We teach a child a word, say 'table', by showing him the object and by using the word in various ways in the presence of that object (or, rather, kind of object) until the child comes to 'associate' the word with the object. In some sense, this is undeniably true. (As an ordinary language remark about, say, pedagogy, it is unproblematical; for, in such a context, the notions of an 'object' and of 'showing someone an object' and of 'associating a sound with a kind of object' are all taken for granted, as part of the linguistic background we assume.)

However, psychology is something that came on the scene at the same time as modern philosophy. Early philosophical psychologists – for example, Hume – pointed out that we do not literally have the object in our minds. The mind never compares an image or word with an object, but only with other images, words, beliefs, judgments, etc. The idea of a comparison of words or mental representations with objects is a senseless one. So how can a determinate correspondence between words or mental representations and external objects ever be singled out? How is the correspondence supposed to be fixed?

It is important to recognize that the problem does *not* depend upon the acceptance of any particular theory of mental phenomena such as Hume's theory of 'ideas and impressions', or the so-called 'sense datum theory', or the 'Gestalt' theory, etc. On any theory, when the child learns the use of the word 'table', what happens is that the word is linked in certain complex ways ('associations') to certain mental phenomena (not all of them conscious, according to contemporary theory). Even if we replace mind talk with brain talk, and talk of 'mental phenomena' with talk of 'representations', 'information', computer programs, etc., as contemporary 'cognitive' psychologists do, the point remains: the functionally organized information-processing brain can manipulate 'perceptions' of tables, 'information' about tables, 'representations', etc., but not tables themselves. If we limit psychology, for the moment, to 'solipsistic' description, description of what happens in the individual considered in isolation from his environment, then no psychological facts in this narrow sense, no facts about introspectible mental phenomena (or even unconscious mental phenomena) and no facts about brain processing can fix any correspondence between a word or 'represen-tation' and anything external to the mind or brain.

The only paper in this book that makes serious use of technical logic ('Models and reality') is not an attempt to *solve* this problem (how the 'correspondence' is fixed), but rather a verification that the problem really exists. What I show is that no matter what operational and theoretical constraints our practice may impose on our use of a language, there are always *infinitely many different reference relations* (different 'satisfaction relations', in the sense of formal semantics, or different *correspondences*) which satisfy all of the constraints.† A parable may explain the significance of this bit of logic.

The Parable: According to a famous passage in *Either/Or*, God is subject to recurrent boredom. (He created the world because He was bored; then He created Adam because He was bored with the world; then Adam was bored with Eve...) Not only is this correct, but, in fact, at the time of the Tower of Babel episode, God became bored again. Not only did He cause us to start speaking different languages, but He started to play around with the satisfaction relations, the 'correspondences', upon which the words–world connection depends.

To understand what He did, pretend that English was one of the languages in existence back then. Imagine that C_1 and C_2 are two

---

† The argument does *not* assume that we can *know* what operational and theoretical constraints our practice imposes on our use of the language, or know what constraints it would impose on that use if we knew all observational facts, or know which theory is the 'ideal theory': the theory, or set of theories that satisfy those constraints, as some of my critics have mistakenly taken it to do.

admissible 'correspondences' (satisfaction relations), i.e., that C_1 (respectively, C_2) is the satisfaction relation that one gets if M_1 (respectively, M_2) is the model that one uses to interpret English, where M_1 and M_2 are both models which satisfy all the operational and theoretical constraints that our practice imposes. Then what He did (to Hebrew, to Assyrian, to Coptic, . . .) was to specify that when a *man* used a word, the word would stand for its image or images under the correspondence C_1, and that when a *woman* used a word, the word would stand for its image or images under the correspondence C_2.†

This situation continues to the present day. Thus, there is one set of things – call it the set of *cats* – such that, when a man uses the word 'cat' it stands for that set (in a God's eye view), and a different set of things – call it the set of *cats** – such that when a woman uses the word 'cat' it stands for *that* set (in a God's eye view); there is a relation between events – call it the relation of causation – such that, when a man uses the word 'causes' it stands for that relation (in a God's eye view), and a different relation such that when a woman uses the word 'causes' it stands for *that* relation (in a God's eye view); and so on.

Notice that the same sentences are true under both of His reference-assignments, the sentences we accept generate the same experiential expectations under both schemes, the behavior that is associated with believing-true or desiring-true particular sentences is the same under both schemes, and if the expectations we have or the things we do are successful (respectively, unsuccessful) the sentences we are *then* required to accept by our operational and theoretical criteria are the same and their truth values are the same.

It amused God for a while to see men and women talking to each other, never noticing that they were almost never referring to the same objects, properties and relations, but then, once again, inevitably, He became bored, so He invented philosophers. (Here caution compels me to end the parable.)

There are a number of stock 'easy answers' to the problems of the determination of reference (most of them are discussed in 'Why there isn't a ready-made world'). Thus, a philosopher might say, 'When the child comes to "associate" the word *table* with certain perceptions, images, etc., he is "associating" it not in the semantical sense

† This was suggested by Bob Nozick. If you don't believe that it is operational and theoretical constraints that determine the class of 'true' sentences, then just let T be the class of true sentences, *however* that is determined, and let M_1 and M_2 be two extremely different models for T which agree on the interpretation of 'psychological' predicates (e.g., 'It looks to X exactly as if he is seeing a table') but not on the interpretation of 'external' predicates ('X is a table').

(*table* doesn't *refer* to the visual impressions which trigger the utterance *there is a table in front of me*, or whatever), but in a causal sense. He is *caused* to have certain beliefs, partly by the fact that certain visual impressions occur. But those visual impressions, "mental representations", or whatever, are in turn caused by certain external events. Normally, they are caused by the presence of a table, in fact. So, indirectly, the word *table* comes to be associated with external tables.'

To see why this answer isn't a solution to the problem, imagine it being said first by a woman philosopher and then by a man philosopher. When the woman says this (now we are inside the parable again), she is pointing out that the child's belief *there is a table in front of me* is in a certain relation – the relation of effect* – to certain visual impressions, and that these are in relation *effect** to certain external events. In fact they are caused* by the presence* of a table*. So indirectly the word *table* has come to be associated with tables*. When the man says this, he is pointing out that the same visual impressions are caused by the presence of a table. So the word *table* has come to be associated with tables. Of course they are both right. The word *table* is 'indirectly associated' with tables* (in the way pointed out by the woman) and also 'indirectly associated' with tables (in the way pointed out by the man). It doesn't follow that there is such a thing as *the* correspondence (the One, metaphysically singled out correspondence) between words and things.

At this point in the dialogue, there is an argument that I invariably get from causal realists. This runs somewhat like this: 'You are caricaturing our position. A realist does not claim that reference is fixed by the conceptual connection (i.e., the connection in our theory) between the *terms* "reference", "causation", "sense impression", etc.; the realist claims that reference is fixed by causation itself.'

Here the philosopher is ignoring his own epistemological position. He is philosophizing as if naive realism were true of him (or, equivalently, as if he and he alone were in an *absolute* relation to the world). What *he* calls 'causation' really is causation, and *of course* there is a fixed, somehow singled-out, correspondence between the word and one definite relation in *his* case. Or so he assumes. But how this can be so was just the question at issue. (If this isn't clear, just imagine the words said first by a woman and then by a man, as before.)

A more sophisticated form of the same argument is this: 'Your argument only shows that reference is not fixed by anything psychological, anything "inside the head". But that is no problem: why can't reference be fixed by something non-psychological?'

The answer, quite simply, is that the idea that the 'non-psychological' fixes reference – i.e., that *nature itself* determines what our words stand for – is totally unintelligible. At bottom, to think that a sign-relation is *built into nature* is to revert to medieval essentialism, to the idea that there are 'self-identifying objects' and 'species' out there. (This is discussed at length in 'Why there isn't a ready-made world'.) Such an idea made sense in the context of a medieval world view, which had not only an elaborate ontology (essence and existence, substantial form, etc.) to back it up, but also an elaborate psychology (e.g., Aquinas' distinction between the 'passive imagination' and the 'productive imagination' as well as his 'phantasms', 'intellectual species', etc.) and an elaborate correspondence between the two (God had arranged it so that the 'intellectual species' produced by the productive imagination acting on the phantasms would have a pre-established correspondence to the substantial forms). In the context of a twentieth-century world view, by contrast, to say in one's most intimidating tone of voice 'I believe that causal connections determine what our words correspond to' is only to say that one believes in a *one-knows-not-what* which solves our problem *one-knows-not-how*.

Ontological relativity?

A solution that has occurred to some philosophers is to keep the idea of 'correspondence', but simply to abandon the idea that there is *one* correspondence that is 'fixed', one intended reference-relation. If we take this line, then the word 'table' refers to one definite set of things in an ordinary 'empirical' sense, but not in a 'transcendental' sense (not from the standpoint of the metalanguage). When we say that there is one set which is the set of tables and a different set which is the set of chairs, that statement is *true* (construed as an ordinary first-order statement). There *is* just one set which is the set of chairs and just one set which is the set of tables *in each model*, and the set of tables *in a model* is a different set from the set of chairs *in that same model*. But that does not mean that there is one set which is the set of chairs *in every admissible model*. The set of chairs in one model may be a subset or a superset of the set of tables in a different model. How we imagine tables and chairs, what experiences we have when we see and touch tables and chairs, what we do in their presence, etc., are all unaffected by the lack of a *unique* assignment of objects and sets of objects to our words; the words 'see', 'touch', 'sit down', etc., simply change *their* reference from model to model in such a way that nothing we can notice is ever affected.

The doctrine just described has been called 'ontological relativity'. It was suggested by Quine (generally he suggests this is the stance to take to all languages *other* than one's own, although there are places where he speaks of the reference of even his own terms as 'free floating'.) The doctrine that Davidson calls 'the empty reference theory' is, perhaps, the same doctrine.

This doctrine cannot, however, be accepted. I cannot accept it for my own language, because to do so would turn the notion of an object into a totally metaphysical notion. I know what tables are and what cats are and what black holes are. But what am I to make of the notion of an X which is a table *or* a cat *or* a black hole (or the number three *or*...)? An object which has *no* properties at all in itself and any property you like 'in a model' is an inconceivable *Ding an sich*. The doctrine of ontological relativity avoids the problems of medieval philosophy (the problems of classical realism) but it takes on the problems of Kantian metaphysics in their place. Nor can the doctrine be accepted for languages other than my own; the human situation is symmetrical. If other people's words do not determinately refer, then neither do my own. (Quine's view is discussed in 'Why reason can't be naturalized'.)

Disquotational theories of truth and reference

If the picture of the language user that we have thus far discussed – the picture of (there being) one particular correspondence between what is 'inside' the mind or brain (include language) and what is 'outside' – leads to the metaphysical fantasy of a 'ready-made world', with self-identifying objects, 'built-in' structure, essences, or whatever, and the modified picture of the mind or brain simply accepting a whole lot of different correspondences, without trying to 'fix' any particular one as *the* intended correspondence between word and object, leads to the metaphysical fantasy of a 'noumenal' world, with no determinate relation to our experiential world, then the trouble with this entire discussion must lie at a deeper level. It must lie, in fact, in the common assumption of both pictures: that we understand such notions as 'refers to' and 'corresponds to' *by associating these notions with Platonic objects* ('correspondences') – either unique objects or else whole batches of objects. Once this assumption has been made (usually uncritically and inexplicitly) then the entire system of competing philosophical theories and arguments unwinds itself with a sort of inevitability. But can we *avoid* this common assumption?

One attempt to do this is the 'disquotational' theory of truth. On this theory, we understand the word 'true' *not* by associating that word with a property, or a correspondence, but by learning such facts as the obvious fact that

(1) 'Snow is white' is true if and only if snow is white.

Learning such 'T-sentences' (sentences of the form '"*P*" is true if and only if *P*') is (in a rational reconstruction, at least) the process of coming to understand the word 'true'. Since associating the word 'true' with an 'object' (a property or correspondence) need not be involved at any stage in acquiring these facts, the whole idea of 'correspondence' is misleading. (Alternatively: (1) does say, in a way, that 'Snow is white' is true if and only if it corresponds to what is the case; so the disquotation theory *is* the correspondence theory, 'properly understood'.)

An objection to the disquotation theory which is still occasionally heard is that the understanding of the truth-functional connective 'if and only if' *presupposes* the very notions of truth and falsity which are being explained. This objection misses the thrust of the theory, however: the theory is *not* that we understand 'true' by learning that '"Snow is white" is true' is *true* if and only if it is true that snow is white, but that we understand 'true' by being trained to *assert* '"Snow is white" is true' when (and only when) we are prepared to *assert* 'Snow is white', and similarly in similar cases. The disquotational view is at home in a larger view on which our understanding of our first language comes about through the internalization of *assertibility conditions* and not through the learning of truth conditions in the realist sense.

If such a theory is to have any explanatory power, then something must be said about the notion of *assertion*. It seems to me that the theory does not work at all if assertion is taken in a 'thin' (or merely behavioral) sense, as it is, for example, by Quine. If 'asserting' *p* is merely *uttering p* (or subvocalizing 'yes' when another utters *p*), then all the theory tells us is that we are disposed to utter the *noise* '... is true' when we are prepared to utter certain other noises. If assertion is to be taken in a suitably 'thick' sense, however, then we have to recognize that asserting is guided by notions of *correctness* and *incorrectness*. But then the problem of truth reappears when we ask for an account of what it is for an assertion to be correct and what it is for it to be incorrect.

But why shouldn't the disquotationalist reply that 'correct' is just a synonym for 'true', and that he has already explained how 'true' works? A comparison with the case of an ordinary first-order scientific sentence, say, 'there is electric current flowing through this wire' may clarify the issue. An assertibility condition (a probabilistic one, within a scientific theory) for the sentence 'there is electric current flowing through this wire' is that the needle of a suitably attached voltmeter be deflected. But describing, as well as one can, what the assertibility conditions for this sentence are does not *preempt* the question 'What *is* electric current?'. Answering *that* question calls for a theory of electricity, not for 'transcendental' remarks about assertibility conditions for 'electricity talk'. Similarly, I suggest, describing assertibility conditions for 'This sentence is true' (or 'That is *right*', or 'That is correct', etc.) does not preempt the question 'What is the nature of truth?' (or rightness, or correctness etc.). If a philosopher says that *truth* is different from *electricity* in precisely this way: that there is room for a theory of electricity but *no room* for a theory of truth, that knowing the assertibility conditions is *knowing all there is to know* about truth, then, in so far as I understand him at all, he is denying that there is a *property* of truth (or a property of rightness, or correctness), not just in the realist sense, but in *any* sense. But this is to deny that our thoughts and assertions are *thoughts* and *assertions*. (This is discussed in 'Vagueness and alternative logic' and also figures in my criticism of naturalized epistemology in 'Why reason can't be naturalized'.)

A disquotational theory of *reference* holds that we understand 'refers to' *not* by associating the phrase 'refers to' with a 'correspondence', but by learning such assertibility conditions as the following:

(2) 'Cat' refers to an object X if and only if X is a cat.

Interpreted as an assertibility condition, what (2) tells us is to assert 'That sentence refers to (contains a word which refers to) cats' when and only when a sentence has been used which contains the word 'cat' or some word W such that one is prepared to assert

(3) Something is a W if and only if it is a cat.

Once again, the view finds its home in a larger view according to which the understanding of our language is through the internalization of assertibility conditions, and not through the learning of truth conditions in the realist sense. And once again, the tenability of the view will depend upon the availability of a sufficiently substantial notion of *assertibility*.

The views of Michael Dummett

If neither a correspondence theory nor a pure disquotational theory of truth is of much help, the situation is reminiscent of a common predicament in philosophy. As Strawson remarked many years ago, we are constantly being asked to choose between *metaphysical* positions on the one hand and *reductionist* positions on the other, and what is terribly difficult (but what makes the game of philosophy worth the candle) is to show that the metaphysical mystery is not the only alternative to the simplistic position of the reductionist (and, of course, vice versa).

During the years that I was wrestling with the problems I have just described, the first clear indication that a coherent alternative to both the correspondence theory and the pure disquotational theory might be available came from the writings of Michael Dummett. Dummett considers the learning of a language to be the learning of a practice and not of a set of correspondences; he considers the speaker's knowledge of his native language to consist in the implicit knowledge of the conditions under which the sentences of that language are *assertible* (a sort of *recognition ability*); but he rejects the physicalist identification of asserting with uttering, or with uttering plus a particular schedule of conditioning or a particular causal history. Rather, he identifies knowing when a sentence is assertible with *knowing when it would be justified.*

The use of the word 'true' is not, on this theory, a mere sign that a sentence is being 'reaffirmed', as it is on the disquotation theory. To be true is to be justified. Reference, however, is not something prior to truth; rather, knowing the conditions under which sentences about, say, tables, are true is knowing what 'table' refers to (as on a disquotational theory of *reference*). Indeed this idea – that objects and reference arise out of discourse rather than being prior to discourse – is rather widespread in twentieth-century philosophy, in both its analytical and 'continental' varieties. (Gadamer, for example, speaks of objects as 'emerging' from discourse.)

Truth as justification

The formula 'truth is justification' is misleading in a number of ways, however, which is why I have avoided it in my own writings, in spite of the inspiration I received from Dummett's work. For one thing, it suggests something which Dummett indeed believes and I do not (see 'Reference and truth'): that one can *specify* in an effective way what the justification conditions for all the sentences of a natural language are. Secondly, it suggests something on which Dummett's writing is rather ambiguous: that there is such a thing as *conclusive* justification, even in the case of empirical sentences.

My own view (for which I have suggested the name 'internal realism') is that truth is to be identified with justification in the sense of *idealized* justification, as opposed to justification-on-present-evidence.† Sometimes this seems to be Dummett's view too (at such times he speaks of a 'gap between justification and truth'); at other times he writes as if ordinary-language-sentences about material objects outside of theoretical science could be conclusively verified.

Consider the sentence 'There is a chair in my office right now.' Under sufficiently good epistemic conditions any normal person could verify this, where sufficiently good epistemic conditions might, for example, consist in one's having good vision, being in my office now with the light on, not having taken a hallucinogenic agent, etc. How do I know *these* are better conditions for this sort of judgment than conditions under which one does not have very good vision, or in which one is looking into the room through a telescope from a great distance, or conditions in which one has taken LSD? Partly by knowing how talk of this sort operates (what the 'language game' is, in Wittgenstein's sense), and partly by having a lot of empirical information. There is no single general rule or universal method for knowing what conditions are better or worse for justifying an arbitrary empirical judgment.

On this view (mine), then, 'truth' (idealized justification) is as vague, interest relative, and context sensitive as *we* are. The 'truth conditions' for an arbitrary sentence are not *surveyable* in Dummett's sense. I reject 'meaning theories'.‡

If truth conditions and assertibility conditions are not surveyable,

---

† If one accepts this account of truth, then (as Michael Dummett has pointed out in connection with his, related, account) the question of the status of some of the traditional laws of logic must be reopened, notably that of the status of the principle of bivalence (every statement is determinately true or false). This connection between the philosophy of language and the choice of a logic is a fascinating one; it is commented on in two of the papers in this volume, 'Vagueness and alternative logic', and 'Quantum mechanics and the observer'. The wider question of the 'apriority' of the laws of logic is also discussed in a series of papers in this volume.

‡ Of course it is possible to survey the *surface* truth conditions for the sentences of a language (if the language has been canonically formalized), e.g., '*snow is white*' *is true if and only if snow is white*, and even to write down a theory which has them all as theorems. This is what Donald Davidson calls a 'meaning theory' for the language. Where I differ from Davidson is in not attaching any philosophical significance to the surface truth conditions in the absence of an account of what it is for a native speaker to *know* them. (Cf. 'Reference and truth'.)

how do we learn them? We learn them just the way Dummett thinks, at least in the case of the less theoretical parts of the language, by acquiring a practice. What Dummett misses, in my view, is that what we acquire is not a knowledge that can be applied as if it were an algorithm. We do learn that in certain circumstances we are supposed to accept 'There is a chair in front of me' (normally). *But we are expected to use our heads.* We can refuse to accept 'There is a chair in front of me' even when it looks to us exactly as if there is a chair in front of us, if our general intelligence screams '*override*'. The impossibility (in practice at least) of formalizing the assertibility conditions for arbitrary sentences is just the impossibility of formalizing general intelligence itself.

If assertibility (in the sense of *warranted* assertibility) is not formalizable, idealized warranted assertibility (truth) is even less so, for the notion of better and worse epistemic conditions (for a particular judgment) upon which it depends is revisable as our empirical knowledge increases. That it is, nevertheless, a meaningful notion; that there *are* better and worse epistemic conditions for most judgments, and a fact of the matter as to what the verdict would be if the conditions were sufficiently good, a verdict to which opinion would 'converge' if we were reasonable, is the heart of my own 'realism'. It *is* a kind of realism, and I mean it to be a *human* kind of realism, a belief that there is a fact of the matter as to what is rightly assertible for us, as opposed to what is rightly assertible from the God's eye view so dear to the classical metaphysical realist. (On this, see 'Reflections on Goodman's *Ways of Worldmaking*'.)

I

Models and reality*

In 1922 Skolem delivered an address before the Fifth Congress of Scandinavian Mathematicians in which he pointed out what he called a 'relativity of set theoretic notions'. This 'relativity' has frequently been regarded as paradoxical; but today, although one hears the expression 'The Löwenheim–Skolem paradox', it seems to be thought of as only an *apparent* paradox, something the cognoscenti enjoy but are not seriously troubled by. Thus van Heijenoort writes, 'The existence of such a "relativity" is sometimes referred to as the Löwenheim–Skolem paradox. But, of course, it is not a paradox in the sense of an antinomy; it is a novel and unexpected feature of formal systems.' In this paper I want to take up Skolem's arguments, not with the aim of refuting them but with the aim of extending them in somewhat the direction he seemed to be indicating. It is not my claim that the 'Löwenheim–Skolem paradox' is an antinomy *in formal logic*; but I shall argue that it *is* an antinomy, or something close to it, in *philosophy of language*. Moreover, I shall argue that the resolution of the antinomy – the only resolution that I myself can see as making sense – has profound implications for the great metaphysical dispute about realism which has always been the central dispute in the philosophy of language.

The structure of my argument will be as follows. I shall point out that in many different areas there are three main positions on reference and truth: there is the extreme Platonist position, which posits non-natural mental powers of directly 'grasping' forms (it is characteristic of this position that 'understanding' or 'grasping' is itself an irreducible and unexplicated notion); there is the verificationist position which replaces the classical notion of truth with the notion of verification or proof, at least when it comes to describing how the language is understood; and there is the moderate realist position which seeks to preserve the centrality of the classical notions of truth and reference without postulating non-natural mental

* Presidential Address delivered before the Winter Meeting of the Association for Symbolic Logic in Washington, D.C., 29 December 1977. I wish to thank Bas van Fraassen for valuable comments on and criticisms of an earlier version.

powers. I shall argue that it is, unfortunately, the *moderate* realist position which is put into deep trouble by the Löwenheim–Skolem theorem and related model-theoretic results. Finally I will opt for verificationism as a way of preserving the outlook of scientific or empirical realism, which is totally jettisoned by Platonism, even though this means giving up *metaphysical* realism.

The Löwenheim–Skolem theorem says that a satisfiable first-order theory (in a countable language) has a countable model. Consider the sentence:

(i) $\sim(\exists R)$ (R is *one-to-one*. The domain of $R \subset N$. The range of values of R is S)

where 'N' is a formal term for the set of all whole numbers and the three conjuncts in the matrix have the obvious first-order definitions.

Replace 'S' with the formal term for the set of all real numbers in your favorite formalized set theory. Then (i) will be a *theorem* (proved by Cantor's celebrated 'diagonal argument'). So your formalized set theory *says* that a certain set (call it 'S') is non-denumerable. So S must *be* non-denumerable in all *models* of your set theory. So your set theory – say ZF (Zermelo–Fraenkel set theory) – has only non-denumerable models. But this is impossible! For, by the Löwenheim–Skolem theorem, *no* theory can have *only* non-denumerable models; if a theory has a non-denumerable model, it must have denumerably infinite ones as well. Contradiction.

The resolution of this apparent contradiction is not hard, as Skolem points out (and it is not this apparent contradiction that I referred to as an antinomy, or close to an antinomy). For (i) only 'says' that S is non-denumerable when the quantifier $(\exists R)$ is interpreted as ranging over *all* relations on $N \times S$. But when we pick a *denumerable* model for the language of set theory, '$(\exists R)$' does not range over *all* relations; it only ranges over relations *in the model*. (i) only 'says' that S is non-denumerable in a *relative* sense: the sense that the members of S cannot be put in one-to-one correspondence with a subset of N by any R *in the model*. And a set S can be 'non-denumerable' in this *relative* sense and yet be denumerable 'in reality'. This happens when there *are* one-to-one correspondences between S and N but all of them lie outside the given model. What is a 'countable' set from the point of view of one model may be an uncountable set from the point of view of another model. As Skolem sums it up, 'even the notions "finite", "infinite", "simply infinite sequence", and so forth turn out to be merely relative within axiomatic set theory'.

The philosophical problem

Up to a point all commentators agree on the significance of the existence of 'unintended' interpretations, for example, models in which what are 'supposed to be' non-denumerable sets are 'in reality' denumerable. All commentators agree that the existence of such models shows that the 'intended' interpretation, or, as some prefer to speak, the 'intuitive notion of a set', is not 'captured' by the formal system. But if *axioms* cannot capture the 'intuitive notion of a set', what possibly could?

A technical fact is of relevance here. The Löwenheim–Skolem theorem has a strong form (the so-called 'downward Löwenheim–Skolem theorem'), which requires the axiom of choice to prove, and which tells us that a satisfiable first-order theory (in a countable language) has a countable model which is a submodel of any given model. In other words if we are given a non-denumerable model M for a theory, then we can find a countable model M' of that same theory in which the predicate symbols stand for the same relations (restricted to the smaller universe in the obvious way) as they did in the original model. The only difference between M and M' is that the 'universe' of M' – i.e., the totality that the variables of quantification range over – is a proper subset of the 'universe' of M.

Now the argument that Skolem gave, and that shows that 'the intuitive notion of a set' (if there is such a thing) is not 'captured' by any formal system, shows that even a *formalization of total science* (if one could construct such a thing), or even a *formalization of all our beliefs* (whether they count as 'science' or not), could not rule out denumerable interpretations, and, *a fortiori*, such a formalization could not rule out *unintended* interpretations of this notion.

This shows that 'theoretical constraints', whether they come from set theory itself or from 'total science', cannot fix the interpretation of the notion *set* in the 'intended' way. What of 'operational constraints'?

Even if we allow that there might be a *denumerable infinity* of measurable 'magnitudes', and that each of them might be measured to *arbitrary rational accuracy* (which certainly seems a utopian assumption), it wouldn't help. For, by the 'downward Löwenheim–Skolem theorem', we can find a countable submodel of the 'standard' model (if there is such a thing) in which countably many predicates (each of which may have countably many things in its extension) have their extensions preserved. In particular, we can fix the values of countably many magnitudes at all rational space–time points, and still

3

find a countable submodel which meets all the constraints. In short, there certainly seems to be a *countable* model of our *entire body of belief* which meets all operational constraints.

The philosophical problem appears at just this point. If we are told 'axiomatic set theory does not capture the intuitive notion of a set', then it is natural to think that *something else* – our 'understanding' – does capture it. But what can our 'understanding' come to, at least for a naturalistically minded philosopher, which is more than *the way we use our language*? And the Skolem argument can be extended, as we have just seen, to show that the *total use of the language* (operational plus theoretical constraints) does not 'fix' a unique 'intended interpretation' any more than axiomatic set theory by itself does.

This observation can push a philosopher of mathematics in two different ways. If he is inclined to Platonism, he will take this as evidence that the mind has mysterious faculties of 'grasping concepts' (or 'perceiving mathematical objects') which the naturalistically minded philosopher will never succeed in giving an account of. But if he is inclined to some species of verificationism (i.e., to identifying truth with verifiability, rather than with some classical 'correspondence with reality') he will say, 'Nonsense! All the "paradox" shows is that our understanding of "The real numbers are non-denumerable" consists in our knowing *what it is for this to be proved*, and not in our "grasp" of a "model".' In short, the *extreme* positions – Platonism and verificationism – seem to receive comfort from the Löwenheim–Skolem paradox; it is only the 'moderate' position (which tries to avoid mysterious 'perceptions' of 'mathematical objects' while retaining a classical notion of truth) which is in deep trouble.

An epistemological/logical digression

The problem just pointed out is a serious problem for any philosopher or philosophically minded logician who wishes to view set theory as the description of a determinate independently existing reality. But from a mathematical point of view, it may appear immaterial: what does it matter if there are many different models of set theory, and not a unique 'intended model' *if they all satisfy the same sentences*? What we want to know as mathematicians is which sentences of set theory are true; we don't want to have the sets themselves in our hands.

Unfortunately, the argument can be extended. First of all, the

4

theoretical constraints we have been speaking of must, on a naturalistic view, come from only two sources: they must come from something like human decision or convention, whatever the source of the 'naturalness' of the decisions or conventions may be, or from human experience, both experience with nature (which is undoubtedly the source of our most basic 'mathematical intuitions', even if it be unfashionable to say so), and experience with 'doing mathematics'. It is hard to believe that either or both of these sources together can ever give us a *complete* set of axioms for set theory (since, for one thing, a complete set of axioms would have to be non-recursive, and it is hard to envisage coming to have a non-recursive set of axioms in the literature or in our heads even in the unlikely event that the human race went on forever doing set theory). And if a complete set of axioms is impossible, and the intended model*s* (in the plural) are singled out only by theoretical plus operational constraints then sentences which are independent of the axioms which we shall arrive at in the limit of set-theoretic inquiry really have *no* determinate truth value; they are just true in some intended models and false in others.

To show what bearing this fact may have on actual set-theoretic inquiry, I shall have to digress for a moment into technical logic. In 1938 Gödel put forward a new axiom for set theory: the axiom '$V = L$'. Here L is the class of all constructible sets, i.e., the class of all sets which can be defined by a certain constructive procedure if we pretend to have names available for all the ordinals, however large. (Of course, this sense of 'constructible' would be anathema to constructive mathematicians.) V is the universe of all sets. So '$V = L$' just says *all sets are constructible*. By considering the inner model for set theory in which '$V = L$' is true, Gödel was able to prove the relative consistency of ZF and ZF *plus* the axiom of choice and the generalized continuum hypothesis.

'$V = L$' is certainly an important sentence, mathematically speaking. Is it *true*?

Gödel briefly considered proposing that we *add* '$V = L$' to the accepted axioms for set theory, as a sort of meaning stipulation, but he soon changed his mind. His later view was that '$V = L$' is *really* false, even though it is consistent with set theory, if set theory is itself consistent.

Gödel's intuition is widely shared among working set theorists. But does this 'intuition' make sense?

Let MAG be a countable set of physical magnitudes which includes all magnitudes that sentient beings in this physical universe can actually measure (it certainly seems plausible that we cannot hope to

5

measure more than a countable number of physical magnitudes). Let OP be the 'correct' assignment of values; i.e., the assignment which assigns to each member of MAG the value that that magnitude actually has at each rational space–time point. Then all the information 'operational constraints' might give us (and, in fact, infinitely more) is coded into OP.

One technical term: an ω-*model* for a set theory is a model in which the *natural numbers* are ordered as they are 'supposed to be'; i.e., the sentence of 'natural numbers' of the model is an ω-sequence.

Now for a small theorem.†

Theorem: ZF *plus* $V = L$ *has an* ω-*model which contains any given countable set of real numbers.*

Proof

Since a countable set of reals can be coded as a single real by well-known techniques, it suffices to prove that *For every real s, there is an M such that M is an* ω-*model for ZF plus* $V = L$ *and s is represented in M.*

By the 'downward Löwenheim–Skolem theorem', this statement is true if and only if the following statement is:

For every real s, there is a countable M such that M is an ω-*model for ZF plus* $V = L$ *and s is represented in M.*

Countable structures with the property that the 'natural numbers' of the structure form an ω-sequence can be coded as reals by standard techniques. When this is properly done, the predicate '*M is an* ω-*model for ZF plus* $V = L$ *and s is represented in M*' becomes a two-place *arithmetical* predicate of reals M, s. The above sentence thus has the logical form (*For every real s*) (*There is a real M*) (...$M, s, ...$). In short, the sentence is a Π_2-sentence.

Now, consider this sentence *in the inner model* $V = L$. For every *s in the inner model* – i.e., for every s in L – there is a model – namely L itself – which satisfies '$V = L$' and contains s. By the downward Löwenheim–Skolem theorem, there is a countable submodel which is elementary equivalent to L and contains s. (Strictly speaking, we need here not just the downward Löwenheim–Skolem theorem, but the 'Skolem hull' construction which is used to prove that theorem.) By Gödel's work, this countable submodel itself lies in L, and as is easily verified, so does the real that codes it. So the above Π_2-sentence is true in the inner model $V = L$.

But Schoenfield has proved that Π_2-sentences are *absolute*: if a

† Barwise (1971) has proved the much stronger theorem that every countable model of ZF has a proper end extension which is a model of ZF plus $V = L$. The theorem in the text was proved by me before 1963.

Π_2-sentence is true in L, then it must be true in V. So the above sentence is true in V. $\square$

What makes this theorem startling is the following reflection: suppose that Gödel is right, and '$V = L$' is *false* ('in reality'). Suppose that there is, in fact, a *non-constructible real number* (as Gödel also believes). Since the predicate 'is constructible' is absolute in *β-models* – i.e., in models in which the 'well orderings' *relative to the model* are well orderings 'in reality' (recall Skolem's 'relativity of set theoretic notions'!), no model containing such a non-constructible s can satisfy 's is constructible' and be a *β-model*. But, by the above theorem, a model containing s *can* satisfy 's is constructible' (because it satisfies '$V = L$', and '$V = L$' says *everything* is constructible) and be an *ω-model*.

Now, suppose we formalize *the entire language of science* within the set theory ZF *plus* $V = L$. Any model for ZF which contains an abstract set isomorphic to OP can be extended to a model for this formalized language of science which is *standard with respect to OP*; hence, even if OP is non-constructible 'in reality', we can find a model *for the entire language of science* which satisfies '*everything is constructible*' and which assigns the correct values to all the physical magnitudes in MAG at all rational space–time points.

The claim Gödel makes is that '$V = L$' is false 'in reality'. But what on earth can this mean? It must mean, at the very least, that in the case just envisaged, the model we have described in which '$V = L$' holds would not be *the intended model*. But why not? It satisfies all theoretical constraints; and we have gone to great length to make sure it satisfies all operational constraints as well.

Perhaps someone will say that '$V \neq L$' (or something which implies that V does not equal L) should be added to the axioms of ZF as an additional 'theoretical constraint'. (Gödel often speaks of new axioms someday becoming evident.) But, while this may be acceptable from a non-realist standpoint, it can hardly be acceptable from a realist standpoint. For the realist standpoint is that there is *a fact of the matter* – a fact independent of our legislation – as to whether $V = L$ or not. A realist like Gödel holds that we have access to an 'intended interpretation' of ZF, where the access is not simply by linguistic stipulation.

What the above argument shows is that if the 'intended interpretation' is fixed only by theoretical plus operational constraints, then if '$V \neq L$' does not follow from those theoretical constraints – if we do not *decide* to make $V = L$ true or to make $V = L$ false – then there will be 'intended' models in which $V = L$ is *true*. If I am right, then the 'relativity of set-theoretic notions' extends to a *relativity of the truth value of* '$V = L$' (and, by similar arguments, of the axiom of choice and the continuum hypothesis as well).

Operational constraints and counterfactuals

It may seem to some that there is a major equivocation in the notion of what *can* be measured, or observed, which endangers the apparently crucial claim that the evidence we *could* have amounts to at most denumerably many facts. Imagine a measuring apparatus that simply detects the presence of a particle within a finite volume d*v* around its own geometric center during each full minute on its clock. Certainly it comes up with at most denumerably many reports (each *yes* or *no*) even if it is left to run forever. But how many are the facts it *could* report? Well, if it were jiggled a little, by chance let us say, its geometric center would shift *r* centimeters in a given direction. It would then report totally different facts. Since for each number *r* it could be jiggled that way, the number of reports it could produce is non-denumerable – and it does not matter to this that we, and the apparatus itself, are incapable of distinguishing every real number *r* from every other one. The problem is simply one of scope for the modal word 'can'. In my argument, I must be identifying what I call operational constraints, not with the totality of facts that could be registered by observation – i.e., ones that either will be registered, or would be registered if certain chance perturbations occurred – but with the totality of facts that will in actuality be registered or observed, whatever those be.

In reply, I would point out that even if the measuring apparatus *were* jiggled *r* centimeters in a given direction, we could only know the real number *r* to some rational approximation. Now, if the intervals involved are all rational, there are only *countably* many facts of the form: *if action A* (an action described with respect to place, time, and character up to some finite 'tolerance') *were performed, then the result* $r \pm \varepsilon$ (a result described up to some rational tolerance) *would be obtained with probability in the interval* (*a*, *b*). To know all facts of this form would be to know the *probability distribution* of all possible observable results of all possible actions. And our argument shows that a model could be constructed which agrees with all of these facts.

There is a deeper point to be made about this objection, however. Suppose we 'first orderize' counterfactual talk, say, by including *events* in the ontology of our theory and introducing a predicate ('subjunctively necessitates') for the counterfactual connection between unactualized event types at a given place–time. Then our

8

argument shows that a model exists which fits all the facts that will actually be registered or observed and fits our theoretical constraints, and this model *induces* an interpretation of the counterfactual idiom (a 'similarity metric on possible worlds', in David Lewis' theory) which renders true just the counterfactuals that are true according to some completion of our theory. Thus appeal to counterfactual observations cannot rule out any models at all unless the interpretation of the counterfactual idiom itself is *already* fixed by something beyond operational and theoretical constraints.

(A related point is made by Wittgenstein in his *Philosophical Investigations*: talk about what an ideal machine – or God – could compute is talk *within* mathematics – in disguise – and cannot serve to fix the interpretation of mathematics. 'God', too, has many interpretations.)

'Decision' and 'convention'

I have used the word 'decision' in connection with open questions in set theory, and obviously this is a poor word. One cannot simply sit down in one's study and 'decide' that '$V = L$' is to be true, or that the axiom of choice is to be true. Nor would it be appropriate for the mathematical community to call an International Convention and legislate these matters. Yet, it seems to me that if we encountered an extra-terrestrial species of intelligent beings who had developed a high level of mathematics, and it turned out that they *rejected* the axiom of choice (perhaps because of the Tarski–Banach theorem)†, it would be wrong to regard them as simply making a *mistake*. To do *that* would, on my view, amount to saying that acceptance of the axiom of choice is built in to our notion of rationality itself; and that does not seem to me to be the case. To be sure, our acceptance of choice is not arbitrary; all kinds of 'intuitions' (based, most likely, on experience with the finite) support it; its mathematical fertility supports it; but none of this is *so* strong that we could say that an equally successful culture which based *its* mathematics on principles *incompatible* with choice (e.g., on the so-called 'axiom of determinacy')‡ was *irrational*.

† This is a very counterintuitive consequence of the axiom of choice. Call two objects A, B 'congruent by finite decomposition' if they can be divided into finitely many disjoint point sets $A_1, \ldots, A_n$, $B_1, \ldots, B_n$, such that $A = A_1 \cup A_2 \cup \ldots \cup A_n$, $B = B_1 \cup B_2 \cup \ldots \cup B_n$, and (for $i = 1, 2, \ldots, n$) A_i is congruent to B_i. Then Tarski and Banach showed that *all spheres are congruent by finite decomposition*.

‡ This axiom, first studied by J. Mycielski (1963) asserts that infinite games with perfect information are determined, i.e., there is a winning strategy for either the first or second player. The axiom of determinacy implies the existence of a non-trivial countably additive two-valued measure on the real numbers, contradicting a well-known consequence of the axiom of choice.

9

But if both systems of set theory – ours and the extra-terrestrials' – count as *rational*, what sense does it make to call one *true* and the others *false*? From the Platonist's point of view there is no trouble in answering this question. 'The axiom of choice is true – true in *the* model', he will say (if he believes the axiom of choice). 'We are right and the extra-terrestrials are wrong.' But what is *the* model? If the intended model is singled out by theoretical and operational constraints, then, firstly, 'the' intended model is plural not singular (so the 'the' is inappropriate; our theoretical and operational constraints fit many models, not just one, and so do those of the extra-terrestrials as we saw before). And, secondly, the intended models for us do satisfy the axiom of choice and the extra-terrestrially intended models do not; we are not talking about the same models, so there is no question of a 'mistake' on one side or the other.

The Platonist will reply that what this really shows is that we have some mysterious faculty of 'grasping concepts' (or 'intuiting mathematical objects') and it is *this* that enables us to fix a model as *the* model, and not just operational and theoretical constraints; but this appeal to mysterious faculties seems both unhelpful as epistemology and unpersuasive as science. What neural process, after all, could be described as the perception of a mathematical object? Why of *one* mathematical object rather than another? I do not doubt that *some* mathematical axioms are built in to our notion of rationality ('every number has a successor'); but, if the axiom of choice and the continuum hypothesis are not, then, I am suggesting, Skolen's argument, or the foregoing extension of it, casts doubt on the view that these statements have a truth value independent of the theory in which they are embedded.

Now, suppose this is right, and the axiom of choice is true when taken in the sense that it receives from *our* embedding theory, and false when taken in the sense that it receives from extra-terrestrial theory. Urging this relativism is not advocating *unbridled* relativism; I do not doubt that there are some objective (if evolving) canons of rationality; I simply doubt that we would regard them as settling this sort of question, let alone as singling out *one* unique 'rationally acceptable set theory'. If this is right, then one is inclined to say that the extra-terrestrials have decided to let the axiom of choice be false and we have decided to let it be true; or that we have different 'conventions'; but, of course, none of these words is literally right. It may well be the case that the idea that statements have their truth values *independent* of embedding theory is so deeply built in to our ways of talking that there is simply no 'ordinary language' word or short phrase which refers to the theory-dependence of meaning and truth. Perhaps this is why Poincaré was driven to exclaim 'Convention, yes! Arbitrary, no!' when he was trying to express a similar idea in another context.

Is the problem a problem with the notion of a 'set'?

It would be natural to suppose that the problem Skolem points out, the problem of a surprising 'relativity' of our notions, has to do with the notion of a 'set', given the various problems which are *known* to surround *that* notion, or, at least, has to do with the problem of reference to 'mathematical objects'. But this is not so.

To see why it is not so, let us consider briefly the vexed problem of reference to theoretical entities in physical science. Although this may seem to be a problem more for philosophers of science or philosophers of language than for logicians, it is a problem whose logical aspects have frequently been of interest to logicians, as is witnessed by the expressions 'Ramsey sentence', 'Craig translation', etc. Here again, the realist – or, at least, the hard-core metaphysical realist – wishes it to be the case that *truth* and *rational acceptability* should be *independent* notions. He wishes it to be the case that what, for example, electrons *are* should be distinct (and possibly different) from what we believe them to be or even what we would believe them to be given the best experiments and the epistemically best theory. Once again, the realist – the hard-core metaphysical realist – holds that our intentions single out 'the' model, and that our beliefs are then either true or false in 'the' model *whether we can find out their truth values or not*.

To see the bearing of the Löwenheim–Skolem theorem (or of the intimately related Gödel completeness theorem and its model-theoretic generalizations) on this problem, let us again do a bit of model construction. This time the operational constraints have to be handled a little more delicately, since we have need to distinguish operational concepts (concepts that describe what we see, feel, hear, etc., as we perform various experiments, and also concepts that describe our acts of picking up, pushing, pulling, twisting, looking at, sniffing, listening to, etc.) from non-operational concepts.

To describe our operational constraints we shall need three things. First, we shall have to fix a sufficiently large 'observational vocabulary'. Like the 'observational vocabulary' of the logical empiricists, we shall want to include in this set – call it the set of 'O-terms' – such words as 'red', 'touches', 'hard', 'push', 'look at', etc. Second, we shall assume that there *exists* (whether we can define it or not) a set of S which can be taken to be the set of macroscopically observable things and events (observable with the human sensorium, that means). The notion of an observable thing or event is surely vague; so we shall want S to be a generous set, i.e., God is to err in the direction of counting too many things and events as 'observable for humans' when he defines the set S (if it is necessary to err in either direction), rather than to err in the direction of leaving out some things that might be counted as borderline 'observables'. If one is a realist, then such a set S must exist, of course, even if our knowledge of the world and the human sensorium does not permit *us* to define it at the present time. The reason we allow S to contain events (and not just things) is that, as Richard Boyd has pointed out; some of the entities we can directly observe are *forces* – we can *feel* forces – and forces are not objects. But I assume that forces can be construed as predicates of either objects, e.g. our bodies, or of suitable events.

The third thing we shall assume given is a valuation (call it, once again 'OP') which assigns the correct truth value to each n-place O-term (for $n = 1, 2, 3, \ldots$) on each n-tuple of elements of S on which it is defined. O-terms are in general also defined on things not in S; for example, two molecules too small to see with the naked eye may touch, a dust-mote too small to see may be black, etc. Thus OP is a *partial* valuation in a double sense; it is defined on only a subset of the predicates of the language, namely the O-terms, and even on these it only fixes a part of the extension, namely the extension of $T \restriction S$ (the restriction of T to S), for each O-term T.

Once again, it is the valuation OP that captures our 'operational constraints'. Indeed, it captures these 'from above', since it may well contain *more* information than we could actually get by using our bodies and our senses in the world.

What shall we do about 'theoretical constraints'? Let us assume that there exists a possible formalization of present-day total science, call it 'T', and also that there exists a possible formalization of *ideal* scientific theory, call it 'T_I'. T_I is to be 'ideal' in the sense of being *epistemically* ideal *for humans*. Ideality, in this sense, is a rather vague notion; but we shall assume that, when God makes up T_I, He constructs a theory which it would be rational for scientists to accept, or which is a limit of theories that it would be rational to accept, as more and more evidence accumulates, and also that he makes up a theory which is compatible with the valuation OP.

Now, the theory T is, we may suppose, well confirmed at the present time, and hence rationally acceptable on the evidence we *now* have; but there is a clear sense in which it may be false. Indeed, it may well lead to false predictions, and thus conflict with OP. But T_I, by hypothesis, does not lead to any false predictions. Still, the metaphysical realist claims – and it is just this claim that makes him a *metaphysical* as opposed to an empirical realist – that T_I may be, in reality, false. What is not knowable as true may none the less be true; what is epistemically most justifiable to believe may none the less be false, on this kind of realist view. The striking connection between issues and debates in the philosophy of science and issues and debates in the philosophy of mathematics – is that this sort of realism runs into *precisely* the same difficulties that we saw Platonism run into. Let us pause to verify this.

Since the ideal theory T_I must, whatever other properties it may or may not have, have the property of being *consistent*, it follows from the Gödel completeness theorem (whose proof, as all logicians know, is intimately related to one of Skolem's proofs of the Löwenheim–Skolem theorem), that T_I has models. We shall assume that T_I contains a primitive or defined term denoting each member of S, the set of 'observable things and events'. The assumption that we made, that T_I agrees with OP, means that all those sentences about members of S which OP requires to be true are theorems of T_I. Thus if M is any model of T_I, M has to have a member corresponding to each member of S. We can even replace each member of M which corresponds to a member of S by that member of S itself, modifying the interpretation of the predicate letters accordingly, and obtain a model M' in which each term denoting a member of S in the 'intended' interpretation does denote that member of S. Then the extension of each O-term in that model will be partially correct to the extent determined by OP: i.e., everything that OP 'says' is in the extension of P is in the extension of P, and everything that OP 'says' is in the extension of the complement of P is in the extension of the complement of P, for each O-term P, in any such model. In short, such a model is standard with respect to $P \restriction S$ (P restricted to S) for each O-term P.

Now, such a model satisfies all operational constraints, since it agrees with OP. And it satisfies those theoretical constraints we would impose in the ideal limit of inquiry. So, once again, it looks as if any such model is 'intended' – for what else could single out a model as 'intended' than this? But if this is what it *is* to be an 'intended model', T_I must be *true*: true in all intended models! The metaphysical realist's claim that even the ideal theory T_I might be false 'in reality' seems to collapse into unintelligibility.

Of course, it might be contended that 'true' does not follow from 'true in all intended models'. But 'true' is the same as 'true in the intended *interpretation*' (or 'in *all* intended interpretations', if there may be more than one interpretation intended – or permitted – by the speaker), on any view. So to follow this line – which is, indeed, the right one, in my view – one needs to develop a theory on which interpretations are specified *other* than by specifying models.

Once again, an appeal to mysterious powers of the mind is made by some. Chisholm (following the tradition of Brentano) contends that the mind has a faculty of *referring to external objects* (or perhaps to external properties) which he calls by the good old name 'intentionality'. And once again most naturalistically minded philosophers (and, of course, psychologists), find the postulation of unexplained mental faculties unhelpful epistemology and almost certainly bad science as well.

There are two main tendencies in the philosophy of science (I hesitate to call them 'views', because each tendency is represented by many different detailed views) about the way in which the reference of theoretical terms gets fixed. According to one tendency, which we may call the Ramsey tendency, and whose various versions constituted the received view for many years, theoretical terms come in batches or clumps. Each clump – for example, the clump consisting of the primitives of electromagnetic theory – is defined by a theory, in the sense that all the models of that theory which are standard on the observation terms count as intended models. The theory is 'true' just in case it has such a model. (The 'Ramsey sentence' of the theory is just the second-order sentence that asserts the existence of such a model.) A sophisticated version of this view, which amounts to relativizing the Ramsey sentence to an open set of 'intended applications' has recently been advanced by Joseph Sneed.

The other tendency is the realist tendency. While realists differ among themselves even more than proponents of the (former) received view do, realists unite in agreeing that a theory may have a true Ramsey sentence and not be (in reality) true.

The first of the two tendencies I described, the Ramsey tendency, represented in the United States by the school of Rudolf Carnap, accepted the 'relativity of theoretical notions', and abandoned the realist intuitions. The second tendency is more complex. Its, so to speak, conservative wing, represented by Chisholm, joins Plato and the ancients in postulating mysterious powers wherewith the mind 'grasps' concepts, as we have already said. If we have more available with which to fix the intended model than merely theoretical and operational constraints, then the problem disappears. The radical pragmatist wing, represented, perhaps, by Quine, is willing to give up the intuition that T_I might be false 'in reality'. This radical wing is 'realist' in the sense of being willing to assert that present-day science, taken more or less at face value (i.e., without philosophical reinterpretation) is at least roughly true; 'realist' in the sense of regarding reference as trans-theoretic (a theory with a true Ramsey sentence may be false, because later inquiry may establish an incompatible theory as better); but not *metaphysical* realist. It is the moderate 'center' of the realist tendency, the center that would like to hold on to metaphysical realism *without* postulating mysterious powers of the mind that is once again in deep trouble.

Pushing the problem back: the Skolemization of absolutely everything

We have seen that issues in the philosophy of science having to do with reference of theoretical terms and issues in the philosophy of mathematics having to do with the problem of singling out a unique 'intended model' for set theory are both connected with the Löwenheim–Skolem theorem and its near relative, the Gödel completeness theorem. Issues having to do with reference also arise in philosophy in connection with sense data and material objects, and, once again, these connect with the model-theoretic problems we have been discussing. (In some way, it really seems that the Skolem paradox underlies the *characteristic* problems of twentieth-century philosophy.)

Although the philosopher John Austin and the psychologist Fred Skinner both tried to drive sense data out of existence, it seems to me that most philosophers and psychologists think that there are such things as *sensations*, or *qualia*. These may not be objects of perception, as was once thought (it is becoming increasingly fashionable to view them as states or conditions of the sentient subject, as Reichenbach long ago urged we should); we may not have incorrigible knowledge concerning them; they may be somewhat ill-defined entities rather than the perfectly sharp particulars they were once taken to be; but it seems reasonable to hold that they are part of the legitimate subject matter of cognitive psychology and philosophy, and not mere pseudo-entities invented by bad psychology and bad philosophy.

Accepting this, and taking the operational constraint this time to be that we wish the ideal theory to correctly predict all sense data, it is easily seen that the previous argument can be repeated here, this time to show that (if the 'intended' models are the ones which satisfy the operational and theoretical constraints we now have, or even the operational and theoretical constraints we would impose in some limit) then, either the present theory is 'true', in the sense of being 'true in all intended models', provided it leads to no false predictions about sense data, or else the ideal theory is 'true'. The first alternative corresponds to taking the theoretical constraints to be represented by current theory; the second alternative corresponds to taking the theoretical constraints to be represented by the ideal theory. This time, however, it will be the case that even terms referring to ordinary material objects – terms such as 'cat' and 'dog' – are interpreted differently in the different 'intended' models. It seems, this time, as if we cannot even refer to ordinary middle-sized physical objects except as formal constructs variously interpreted in various models.

Moreover, if we agree with Wittgenstein that the *similarity relation* between sense data we have at different times is not itself something present to my mind – that 'fixing one's attention' on a sense datum and thinking 'by "red" I mean whatever is like *this*' doesn't really pick out any relation of similarity at all – and make the natural move of supposing that the intended models of my language when I now and in the future talk of the sense data I had at some past time t_0 are singled out by operational and theoretical constraints, then, again, it will turn out that my *past* sense data are mere formal constructs which are interpreted differently in various models. And if we further agree with Wittgenstein that the notion of truth requires a *public* language (or requires at least states of the self at more than one time: that a 'private language for one specious present' makes no sense), then even my *present* sense data are in this same boat... In short, one can 'Skolemize' absolutely everything. It seems to be absolutely impossible to fix a determinate reference (without appeal to non-natural mental powers) for *any* term at all. And if we apply the argument to the very metalanguage we use to talk about the predicament...?

The same problem has even surfaced recently in the field of cognitive psychology. The standard model for the brain/mind in this field is the modern computing machine. This computing machine is thought of as having something analogous to a formalized language in which it computes. (This hypothetical brain language has even received a name: 'mentalese'.) What makes the model of cognitive psychology a *cognitive* model is that 'mentalese' is thought to be a medium whereby the brain constructs an *internal representation* of the external world. This idea runs immediately into the following problem: if 'mentalese' is to be a vehicle for describing the external world, then the various predicate letters must have extensions which are sets of external things (or sets of n-tuples of external things). But if the way 'mentalese' is 'understood' by the deep structures in the brain that compute, record, etc. in this 'language' is *via* what Artificial Intelligence people call 'procedural semantics' – i.e., if the brain's *program for using* 'mentalese' comprises its entire 'understanding' of 'mentalese', where the program for using 'mentalese', like any program, refers only to what is *inside* the computer – then how do *extensions* ever come into the picture at all? In the terminology I have been employing in this paper, the problem is this: if the extension of predicates in 'mentalese' is fixed by the theoretical and operational constraints 'hard wired in' to the brain, or even by theoretical and operational constraints that it evolves in the course of inquiry, then these will not fix a *determinate* extension for any predicate. If thinking is ultimately done in 'mentalese', then *no concept we have will have a determinate extension*. Or so it seems.

The bearing of causal theories of reference

The term 'causal theory of reference' was originally applied to my theory of the reference of natural kind terms and to Kripke's theory (see pp. 70–5 for an account). These theories did not attempt to *define* reference, but rather attempted to say something about how reference is fixed, if it is not fixed by associating definite descriptions with the terms and names in question. Kripke and I argued that the intention to preserve reference through a historical chain of uses and the intention to cooperate socially in the fixing of reference make it possible to use terms successfully to refer although no one definite description is associated with any term by all speakers who use that term. These theories assume that individuals can be singled out for the purpose of a 'naming ceremony' and that inferences to the existence of definite theoretical entities (to which names can then be attached) can be successfully made. Thus these theories did not address the question as to how any term can acquire a determinate reference (or any gesture, such as pointing – of course, the 'reference' of gestures is just as problematic as the reference of terms, if not more so). Recently, however, it has been suggested by various authors that some account can be given of how at least some basic sorts of terms refer in terms of the notion of a 'causal chain'. In one version (Evans, 1973), a version strikingly reminiscent of the theories of Ockham and other fourteenth-century logicians, it is held that a term refers to 'the

17

dominant source' of the beliefs that contain the term. Assuming we can circumvent the problem that the dominant cause of our beliefs concerning *electrons* may well be *textbooks*,† it is important to notice that even if a *correct* view of this kind can be elaborated, it will do nothing to resolve the problem we have been discussing.

The problem is that adding to our hypothetical formalized language of science a body of theory entitled 'Causal theory of reference' *is* just adding more *theory*. But Skolem's argument, and our extensions of it, are not affected by enlarging the theory. Indeed, you can even take the theory to consist of *all true sentences*, and there will be many models – models differing on the extension of every term not fixed by OP (or whatever you take OP to be in a given context) – which satisfy the entire theory. If 'refers' can be defined in terms of some causal predicate or predicates in the metalanguage of our theory, then, since each model of the object language extends in an obvious way to a corresponding model of the metalanguage, it will turn out that, *in each model M, reference$_M$* is definable in terms of *causes$_M$*; but, unless the word 'causes' (or whatever the causal predicate or predicates may be) is already glued to one definite relation with metaphysical glue, this does not fix a determinate extension for 'refers' at all.

This is not to say that the construction of such a theory would be worthless as philosophy or as natural science. The program of cognitive psychology already alluded to, the program of describing our brains as computers which construct an 'internal representation of the environment', seems to require that 'mentalese' utterances be, in some cases at least, describable as the causal product of devices in the brain and nervous system which 'transduce' information from the environment, and such a description might well be what the causal theorists are looking for. And the program of realism in the philosophy of science – of *empirical* realism, not metaphysical realism – is to show that scientific theories can be regarded as better and better representations of an objective world with which we are interacting; and if such a view is to be part of science itself, as empirical realists contend it should be, then the interactions with the world by means of which this representation is formed and modified must themselves be part of the subject matter of the representation. But the problem as to how the *whole representation*, including the empirical theory of knowledge that is a part of it, can determinately refer is not a problem that can be solved by developing more and better empirical theory.

---

† Evans handles this case by saying that there are appropriateness conditions on the type of causal chain which must exist between the item referred to and the speaker's body of information.

Ideal theories and truth

One reaction to the problem I have posed would be to say: there are many ideal theories in the sense of theories which satisfy the operational constraints, and in addition have all the virtues (simplicity, coherence, containing the axiom of choice, whatever) that humans like to demand. But there are no 'facts of the matter' not reflected in constraints on ideal theories in this sense. Therefore, what is really true is what is common to all such ideal theories; what is really false is what they all deny; and all other statements are neither true nor false.

Such a reaction would lead to too few truths, however. It may well be that there are rational beings – even rational human species – which do not employ our color predicates, or who do not employ the predicate 'person', or who do not employ the predicate 'earthquake'.† I see no reason to conclude from this that *our* talk of red things, or of persons, or of earthquakes, lacks truth value. If there are many ideal theories (and if 'ideal' is itself a somewhat interest-relative notion), if there are many theories which (given appropriate circumstances) it is perfectly rational to accept, then it seems better to say that, in so far as these theories say different (and sometimes, apparently incompatible) things, some facts are 'soft' in the sense of depending for their truth value on the speaker, the circumstances of utterance, etc. This is what we have to say in any case about cases of ordinary vagueness, about ordinary causal talk, etc. It is what we say about apparently incompatible statements of simultaneity in the special theory of relativity. To grant that there is more than one true version of reality is not to deny that some versions are false.

It may be, of course, that there *are* some truths that *any* species of rational inquirers would eventually acknowledge. (On the other hand, the set of these may be empty, or almost empty.) But to say that *by definition* these are all the truths there are is to redefine the notion in a highly restrictive way. (It also assumes that the notion of an 'ideal theory' is perfectly clear, an assumption which seems plainly false.)

Intuitionism

It is a striking fact that this entire problem does *not* arise for the standpoint of mathematical intuitionism. This would not be a surprise to Skolem: it was precisely his conclusion that 'most mathematicians want mathematics to deal, ultimately, with performable computing

---

† For a discussion of this very point, see David Wiggins (1976).

operations and not to consist of formal propositions about objects called this or that'.

In intuitionism, knowing the meaning of a sentence or predicate consists in associating the sentence or predicate with a procedure which enables one to recognize when one has a proof that the sentence is constructively true (i.e., that it is possible to carry out the constructions that the sentence asserts can be carried out) or that the predicate applies to a certain entity (i.e., that a certain full sentence of the predicate is constructively true). The most striking thing about this standpoint is that the *classical notion of truth is nowhere used* – the semantics is entirely given in terms of the notion of 'constructive proof', *including the semantics of 'constructive proof' itself*.

Of course, the intuitionists do not think that 'constructive proof' can be formalized, or that 'mental constructions' can be identified with operations in our *brains*. Generally, they assume a strongly intentionalist and *aprioristic* posture in philosophy; i.e., they assume the existence of mental entities called 'meanings' and of a special faculty of intuiting constructive relations between these entities. These are not the aspects of intuitionism I shall be concerned with. Rather I wish to look on intuitionism as an example of what Michael Dummett has called 'non-realist semantics', i.e., a semantic theory which holds that *a language is completely understood when a verification procedure is suitably mastered*, and not when truth conditions (in the classical sense) are learned.

The problem with realist semantics – truth-conditional semantics – as Dummett has emphasized, is that if we hold that the understanding of the sentences of, say, set theory consists in our knowledge of their 'truth conditions', then how can we possibly say what *that* knowledge in turn consists in? (It cannot, as we have just seen, consist in the use of language or 'mentalese' under the control of operational plus theoretical constraints, be they fixed or evolving, since such constraints are too weak to provide a determinate extension for the terms, and it is this that the realist wants.)

If, however, the understanding of the sentences of a mathematical theory consists in the mastery of verification procedures (which need not be fixed once and for all: we can allow a certain amount of 'creativity'), then a mathematical theory can be completely understood, and this understanding does not presuppose the notion of a 'model' at all, let alone an 'intended model'.

Nor does the intuitionist (or, more generally, the 'non-realist' semanticist) have to foreswear *forever* the notion of a model. He has to foreswear reference to models in his account of *understanding*; but, once he has succeeded in understanding a rich enough language to serve as a metalanguage for some theory T (which may itself be simply a sublanguage of the metalanguage, in the familiar way), he can define 'true in T' à la Tarski, he can talk about 'models' for T, etc. He can even define 'reference' (or 'satisfaction') exactly as Tarski did.

Does the whole 'Skolem paradox' arise again to plague him at this stage? The answer is that it does not. To see why it does not, one has to realize what the 'existence of a model' means in *constructive* mathematics.

'Objects' in constructive mathematics are *given through descriptions*. Those descriptions do not have to be mysteriously attached to those objects by some non-natural process (or by metaphysical glue). Rather the possibility of *proving* that a certain construction (the 'sense', so to speak, of the description of the model) has certain constructive properties is what is asserted and *all* that is asserted by saying the model 'exists'. In short, *reference is given through sense, and sense is given through verification procedures and not through truth conditions*. The 'gap' between our theory and the 'objects' simply disappears – or, rather, it never appears in the first place.

Intuitionism liberalized

It is not my aim, however, to try to convert my readers to intuitionism. Set theory may not be the 'paradise' Cantor thought it was, but it isn't such a bad neighborhood that I want to leave of my own accord, either. Can we separate the philosophical idea behind intuitionism, the idea of 'non-realist' semantics, from the restrictions and prohibitions that the historic intuitionists wished to impose upon mathematics?

The answer is that we can. First, as to set theory: the objection to *impredicativity*, which is the intuitionist ground for rejecting much of classical set theory, has little or no connection with the insistence upon verificationism itself. Indeed, intuitionist mathematics is itself 'impredicative', in as much as the intuitionist notion of constructive proof presupposes constructive proofs which refer to the totality of *all* constructive proofs.

Second, as to the propositional calculus: it is well known that the classical connectives can be reintroduced into an intuitionist theory by reinterpretation. The important thing is not whether one uses 'classical propositional calculus' or not, but how one *understands* the logic if one does use it. Using classical logic as an intuitionist would understand it, means, for example, keeping track of when a disjunction is selective (i.e., one of the disjuncts is constructively provable), and when it is non-selective; but this doesn't seem too bad an idea.

In short, while intuitionism may go with a greater interest in constructive mathematics, a liberalized version of the intuitionist standpoint need not rule out 'classical' mathematics as either illegitimate or unintelligible.

What about the language of empirical science? Here there are greater difficulties. Intuitionist logic is given in terms of a notion of *proof*, and proof is supposed to be a *permanent* feature of statements. Moreover, proof is non-holistic; there is such a thing as the proof (in either the classical or the constructive sense) of an isolated mathematical statement. But verification in empirical science is a matter of degree, not a 'yes-or-no' affair; even if we made it a 'yes-or-no' affair in some arbitrary way, verification is a property of empirical sentences that can be *lost*; and in general the 'unit of verification' in empirical science is the theory and not the isolated statement.

These difficulties show that sticking to the intuitionist standpoint, however liberalized, would be a bad idea in the context of formalizing empirical science. But they are not incompatible with 'non-realist' semantics. The crucial question is this: do we think of the *understanding* of the language as consisting in the fact that speakers possess (collectively if not individually) an evolving network of verification procedures, or as consisting in their possession of a set of 'truth conditions'? If we choose the first alternative, the alternative of 'non-realist' semantics, then the 'gap' between words and world, between our *use* of the language and its 'objects', never appears.†

Moreover, the 'non-realist' semantics is not *inconsistent* with realist semantics; it is simply prior to it, in the sense that it is the 'non-realist'

---

† To the suggestion that we identify truth with being verified, or accepted, or accepted in the long run, it may be objected that a person could reasonably, and possibly truly, make the assertion:

> A; but it could have been the case that A and our scientific development differ in such a way to make $\bar{A}$ part of the ideal theory accepted in the long run; in that circumstance, it would have been the case that A but it was not true that A.

This argument is fallacious, however, because the different 'scientific development' means here the choice of a different version; we cannot assume the *sentence* $\ulcorner A \urcorner$ has a fixed meaning independent of what version we accept.

In fact the same problem can confront a metaphysical realist. Realists also have to recognize that there are cases in which the reference of a term depends on which theory one accepts, so that A can be a true sentence if T_1 is accepted and a false one if T_2 is accepted, where T_1 and T_2 are both true theories. But then imagine someone saying,

> A; but it could have been the case that A and our scientific development differ so that T_2 was accepted; in that case it would have been the case that A but A would not have been true.

semantics that must be internalized if the language is to be understood.

Even if it is not inconsistent with realist semantics, taking the non-realist semantics as our picture of how the language is understood undoubtedly will affect the way we view questions about reality and truth. For one thing, verification in empirical science (and, to a lesser extent, in mathematics as well, perhaps) sometimes depends on what we before called 'decision' or 'convention'. Thus facts may, on this picture, depend on our interests, saliencies, and decisions. There will be many 'soft facts'. (Perhaps whether $V = L$ or not is a 'soft fact'.) I cannot, myself, regret this. If appearance and reality end up being endpoints on a continuum rather than being the two halves of a monster Dedekind Cut in all we conceive and don't conceive, it seems to me that philosophy will be much better off. The search for the 'furniture of the universe' will have ended with the discovery that the universe is not a furnished room.

Where did we go wrong? – The problem solved

What Skolem really pointed out is this: no interesting theory (in the sense of first-order theory) can, in and of itself, determine its own objects up to isomorphism. And Skolem's argument can be extended as we saw, to show that if theoretical constraints don't determine reference, then the addition of operational constraints won't do it either. It is at this point that reference itself begins to seem 'occult'; it begins to seem that one can't be any kind of a realist without being a believer in non-natural mental powers. Many moves have been made in response to this predicament, as we noted above. Some have proposed that *second-order* formalizations are the solution, at least for mathematics; but the 'intended' interpretation of the second-order formalism is not fixed by the use of the formalism (the formalism itself admits so-called 'Henkin models', i.e., models in which the second-order variables fail to range over the *full* power set of the universe of individuals), and it becomes necessary to attribute to the mind special powers of 'grasping second-order notions'. Some have proposed to accept the conclusion that mathematical language is only partly interpreted, and likewise for the language we use to speak of 'theoretical entities' in empirical science; but then are 'ordinary material objects' any better off? Are sense data better off? Both Platonism and phenomenalism have run rampant at different times and in different places in response to this predicament.

The problem, however, lies with the predicament itself. The

23

predicament only *is* a predicament because we did two things: first, we gave an account of understanding the language in terms of programs and procedures for *using* the language (what else?); and then, secondly, we asked what the possible 'models' for the language were, thinking of the models as existing 'out there' *independent of any description*. At this point, something really weird had already happened, had we stopped to notice. On any view, the understanding of the language must determine the reference of the terms, or, rather, must determine the reference given the context of use. If the use, even in a fixed context, doesn't determine reference, then use isn't understanding. The language, on the perspective we talked ourselves into, has a full program of use; but it still lacks an *interpretation*.

This is the fatal step. To adopt a theory of meaning according to which a language whose whole use is specified still lacks something – namely its 'interpretation' – is to accept a problem which *can* only have crazy solutions. To speak as if *this* were my problem, 'I know how to use my language, but, now, how shall I single out an interpretation?' is to speak nonsense. Either the use *already* fixes the 'interpretation' or *nothing* can.

Nor do 'causal theories of reference', etc., help. Basically, trying to get out of this predicament by *these* means is hoping that the *world* will pick one definite extension for each of our terms even if *we* can't. But the world doesn't pick models or interpret languages. *We* interpret our languages or nothing does.

We need, therefore, a standpoint which links use and reference in just the way that the metaphysical realist standpoint refuses to do. The standpoint of 'non-realist semantics' is precisely that standpoint. From that standpoint, it is trivial to say that a model in which, as it might be, the set of cats and the set of dogs are permuted (i.e., 'cat' is assigned the set of dogs as its extension, and 'dog' is assigned the set of cats) is 'unintended' even if corresponding adjustments in the extensions of all the other predicates make it end up that the operational and theoretical constraints of total science or total belief are all 'preserved'. Such a model would be unintended *because we don't intend the word 'cat' to refer to dogs*. From the metaphysical realist standpoint, this answer doesn't work; it just pushes the question back to the metalanguage. The axiom of the metalanguage, '"cat" refers to cats' can't rule out such an unintended interpretation of the object language, unless the metalanguage itself already has had *its* intended interpretation singled out; but we are in the same predicament with respect to the metalanguage that we are in with respect to the object language, from that standpoint, so all is in vain. However, from the viewpoint of 'non-realist' semantics, the metalanguage is completely understood, and so is the object language. So we can *say and understand*, '"cat" refers to cats'. Even though the model referred to satisfies the theory, etc., it is 'unintended'; and we recognize that it is unintended *from the description through which it is given* (as in the intuitionist case). Models are not lost noumenal waifs looking for someone to name them; they are constructions within our theory itself, and they have names from birth.

2

Equivalence

For equivalence at the level of elementary logic there is at least a complete proof procedure, even if there is no complete disproof procedure; for mathematical equivalence in general, as a consequence of the Gödel theorem, there is not even a complete proof procedure. But the notion of equivalence that is philosophically important today is not the notion of logical or mathematical equivalence, but rather the notion of *cognitive equivalence of whole theories*, and, in particular, of theoretical systems which are, taken literally, incompatible. It is to this topic – the cognitive equivalence of theories and conceptual systems, especially systems which are incompatible when taken at face value – that the present article is devoted.

'Equivalence' as a philosophical notion

For one kind of traditional realist philosopher the sort of equivalence that we are discussing does not exist at all. This is the sort of realist who believes, as Lenin did in *Materialism and Empirio-Criticism*, that theories are simply 'copies' of the world. If realism is *identified* with the view that there is 'one true theory of everything' (and exactly one), then realism is just the *denial* that there is a plurality of 'equivalent descriptions' of the world (apart from the non-controversial case of logical or mathematical equivalence). Today, however, few if any philosophers of a realist stamp would wish to be identified with *that* sort of realism. Both developments in mathematics and developments in physics have made the one true theory view look untenable, at least if one does not accompany the claim that there is 'one true theory' with the important gloss that *counting* theories is not an easy matter: what *look* as if they are different theories may be, as Quine has put it, just 'versions' of one and the same theory. But the realist who does gloss his belief in one true theory in such a way is admitting that theories which are different at the level of 'surface grammar', and even at the level of mathematical and logical equivalence – i.e., which are different, and even incompatible, in literal meaning – may be simultaneously true. If such theories are

26

'One' at some deeper level – if they are in some way equivalent descriptions – then an account of how this is possible, of how theories which are not mathematically equivalent, can be cognitively equivalent, must be provided.

Reichenbach's *Experience and Prediction*

One of the first attempts to provide a self-conscious and fully worked-out theory of equivalent descriptions was due to Hans Reichenbach, who discussed the topic in his great epistemological treatise *Experience and Prediction* (1938) and also applied it in important books in the philosophy of space and time and the philosophy of quantum mechanics. While Reichenbach's account of equivalence is not successful, in my opinion, the difficulties and tensions in Reichenbach's work admirably illustrate the problems in this area.

According to the 'positivists' (by which Reichenbach means adherents to the early views of the Vienna Circle as represented in, e.g., Ayer's famous book *Language, Truth and Logic*), *the meaning of a statement is its method of verification*. In a very early form – which Ayer did *not* subscribe to – verification was supposed to be *conclusive*; experiences could verify statements for all time and falsify them for all time. (This form sometimes survives today, especially among social scientists, under the name 'operationism'.) If this positivist meaning theory had been right, then equivalence would be easily explained: two statements are cognitively equivalent just in case the same experiences verify them and the same experiences falsify them. Reichenbach points out a decisive difficulty with this form of verificationism, however: in general an observable result, say the observation of a meter reading in physics, only verifies an empirical statement (say, 'Current is flowing in the wire') with a certain probability, not conclusively. Operationism and crude positivism distort the actual functioning of scientific concepts by misrepresenting what is actually a *probabilistic inference* (involving the confirmation of a large body of physical theory) as the simple application of a so-called 'operational definition'. The statement 'Current is flowing in the wire if and only if the voltmeter needle is deflected' is sometimes referred to as an 'operational definition'; but that does not mean that it is a meaning stipulation. Indeed, it is only approximately true; a more accurate statement would be '99 % of the time, current is flowing through the wire if and only if the voltmeter needle is deflected', or something of that kind.

Reichenbach therefore proposes the following 'probability theory of meaning':

(1) A statement is meaningful if and only if it is possible (by the procedures of inductive logic, on which Reichenbach was one of the outstanding authorities of his period) to assign it a *weight*, i.e., an assessment of probability, in some physically possible observable situation.

(2) Two statements have the *same* meaning if and only if they receive the same weight in all such situations.

If we apply these two principles not only to single statements but also to whole theories, as Reichenbach intended, then we have a criterion of cognitive equivalence, which is what we are searching for. But there are problems with this criterion, as we shall see shortly.

First, however, let us examine Reichenbach's own use of his criterion. In a fascinating discussion (the 'cubical world') he warns us against one possible misinterpretation of his theory: he does *not* intend it to turn out that any two theories with the same *testable consequences* must turn out to be equivalent descriptions.

The 'cubical world'

The case Reichenbach describes is as follows: imagine a world in which all intelligent observers live in a region which is enclosed by a large translucent cube. The material of which the cube consists allows the passage of enough light so that objects outside the cube cast shadows which are visible inside the cube; but no other causal signal of any kind passes through the cube. The physical laws of this universe are such that the cube cannot be broken; the observers inside the cube can never get out of the cube to make direct observations of what is 'out there'.

Suppose that there are birds both inside and outside the cube, and that the birds outside the cube cast shadows on the walls of the cube. These shadows have been observed for a long time by scientists in the cubical world, and an exact description in statistical terms has been formulated of the kinds of shadows, the times of the year at which they are seen, and the frequency with which each sort of shadow is seen at any given time of the year/day. The scientists, noting the similarity of the shadows to bird shadows which they are familiar with from their knowledge of birds inside the cube (and their knowledge of optics), of course infer that *there are birds outside the cube*, and that the shadows are the shadows of some of these birds.

Now a philosophical dispute breaks out among epistemologists. One group, the positivists, argues as follows: 'The statement that *there are birds outside the cube* is verified when and only when shadows (of such-and-such a shape and motion) are seen by us on the walls. Therefore, all the statement *means* is that shadows (of such-and-such a shape and motion) are seen on the walls. Talk about "birds outside the cube" is, in reality, just highly derived talk about shadows that are seen inside the cube.'

The second group, the realists, reply, 'Nonsense! A bird is one thing and a shadow is something else. Of course we mean more by the statement "There are birds outside the cube" than merely that shadows are seen *inside* the cube.'

Reichenbach allies himself with the realists in this dispute, and he defends their position on the basis of his probability theory of meaning as follows: given the observational evidence available inside the cube, the statement that there are shadows on the walls has a probability of virtually *one*. It is (neglecting the infinitesimal chance of a collective hallucination or something of that kind) *certain* that there are shadows on the walls. The statement that there are birds outside the cube does not follow *deductively* from the observation of shadows of the shape and motion in question, even if we assume the laws of optics are the same outside the cube as inside; for other objects *might* cause these shadows. But normal induction would dictate that we should assign a *high probability*, albeit a probability significantly less than *one*, to the conclusion that these shadows are cast by birds. Since the *weight* assigned to the statement 'There are shadows to be seen on the walls' is *one*, while the *weight* assigned to the statement 'There are birds outside the cube' is less than *one*, the two statements do *not* have the same meaning on the basis of the second principle of the probability theory of meaning.

What Reichenbach is saying is that verification is a matter of *degree*, and that, given our actual criteria for assessing the degree to which the statements are verified, two statements which have the same 'testable consequences' may still be verified to different degrees, and thus fail to be equivalent. Sameness of testable consequences is not a good criterion for equivalence.

The case of the cat worshippers

It is instructive to compare Reichenbach's treatment of the cubical world with his treatment of another fictitious example in the same work. Reichenbach imagines a group of cat worshippers. These people maintain the sentence *Cats are divine animals*. When asked what signs there are that this is true, or what testable consequences their belief has, they point to the fact that cats produce a state of awe (in cat worshippers).

Reichenbach deals with this example in summary fashion, just as Carnap dealt with a number of famous philosophical puzzles in his little book *Scheinprobleme in der Philosophie* (*Pseudo-problems in Philosophy*). According to Reichenbach the two sentences, 'Cats are divine animals' and 'Cats produce a state of awe (in cat worshippers)' are cognitively equivalent. The first sentence has, to be sure, a meaning element (a 'transcendental meaning') which is absent in the second; but this 'transcendental meaning' is cognitively spurious.

What is striking is that Reichenbach devotes none of the care to this example that he devoted to the cubical world case. He does not ask if the statement 'Cats are divine' is embedded in a body of theory (as it surely would be, if it were an actual religious belief), nor if that body of theory might have any degree of inductive support. In fact, he does here exactly what he warned us against doing in the cubical world case: he leaps from the fact that the two statements have *the same testable consequences* to the conclusion that they are *equivalent*.

The motive is not hard to discern. Many empiricist philosophers wish to rule out metaphysics as conceptually confused. One (especially crude) way of doing this is to contend that metaphysical utterances are *meaningless*. Some metaphysical and religious utterances have testable consequences, however; so, in such cases, these empiricists, of whom Reichenbach was one, who sought a principle which would dismiss metaphysical utterances once and for all from the camp of meaningful discourse, simply conjoined the testable consequences of the utterance in question and ruled that the utterance was, in fact, cognitively equivalent to the (usually banal) conjunction of its own testable consequences. In effect, Reichenbach is saying that 'Cats are divine animals' is 99% *meaningless*; its 1% of meaning is 'Cats produce awe (in cat worshippers)'.

Such a use of the notion of 'meaning' is today recognized as both bad semantics and bad philosophy. I shall, in this article, assume that our purpose in seeking a notion of cognitive equivalence is *not* to legislate metaphysical questions out of existence. Indeed, Reichenbach's own cubical world example shows that a sophisticated verificationist *can* (when he wants to) recognize differences in cognitive meaning between theories with the same testable consequences.

Quine's criticism of the probability theory of meaning

In his celebrated article 'Two dogmas of empiricism', published in 1951, Quine criticized a form of verificationism which is strikingly similar to Reichenbach's probability theory of meaning. Quine considers the theory that two statements have the same meaning just in case they have the same range of confirming experiences and the same range of infirming experiences. This resembles Reichenbach's theory except that (1) Quine speaks of experiences, where Reichenbach speaks of 'physically possible observations', and (2) Quine neglects the numerical *degree* to which a given confirming or infirming experience confirms or infirms a statement, whereas Reichenbach speaks of a numerical 'weight'. (In effect, the theory Quine considers only asks whether the 'weight' is *high* or *low*. If two statements have high weight (are confirmed) and have low weight (are infirmed) in the same experiential situations, then they would be counted as having the same meaning on the theory he criticizes; whereas the finer-grained theory proposed by Reichenbach would ask that the weight be *exactly the same* in all situations.) In spite of the differences between the theory Quine criticized and Reichenbach's actual theory, Quine's criticism applies also to Reichenbach's theory.

Quine's criticism, in brief, is that the mistake lies in assuming that there is such a thing as *the range of confirming (or infirming) experiences* of an isolated statement. A statement can only be confirmed or infirmed, Quine says, in the context of a large theory, at least in the general case. The whole idea that verification methods can provide a concept of the meaning of a single statement ignores the fact that our beliefs 'face the tribunal of experience' collectively and not one by one.

We can see that Quine is right by looking at the very case that Reichenbach discussed: the example of the cubical world. The assignment of a numerical weight to the statement 'There are birds outside the cube' was to proceed by *estimating the probability* that shadows of that shape and motion would be produced by birds as opposed to other sorts of opaque objects. This clearly assumes (1) that the laws of optics are the same outside the cube as inside; and (2) a large body of knowledge about birds and other sorts of objects, all of which is also assumed to hold outside the cube (or *probably* hold, although how we could assign a *number* to the probability, as required by Reichenbach's theory, is a puzzle). Thus it is only in the context of a large body of theory that we can assign a 'weight', numerical or even qualitative (e.g., 'high/low'), to the statement 'There are birds outside the cube'. If all we are given is a description of the *observable situation*, and we don't know what *theory* we are supposed to consider along with the statement 'There are birds outside the cube', then the question 'What weight does the statement have in this observable situation?' has no clear significance.

Reichenbach would, perhaps, have replied that there is such a thing as the weight a statement *would* receive in an observable situation if we made the *best* inductive inferences (where this includes *thinking up the best theories*); but such an idealized 'weight' is totally incalculable in practice. In practice, we cannot usually assign *numerical* probabilities to most statements at all, even given the theory we actually have; and to compare the weights that statements would receive if we were *ideal inductive judges* and considered *all possible theories* is surely beyond anyone's powers. Indeed, one may even doubt if the notion of the *best possible inductive inference* has any well-defined sense.

The bearing of this difficulty on the project of defining equivalence is clear. If there is no such thing as the weight of a statement in isolation from a body of containing theory, neither is there such a thing as the weight of a *theory* in isolation from a background of other beliefs of various kinds: auxiliary hypotheses, methodological beliefs, etc. The weight of the theory of evolution, for example, depends on the appraisal of various kinds of evidence from geology, paleontology, etc., and this draws on physics, geological theory, genetics, molecular biology, etc. To ask if two theories would have *the same weight in all situations* is, in general, to ask a question with no clear answer; because we have no conception of the weight even one theory would receive in *all* situations. Trying to define equivalence in terms of 'weight', or degree of confirmation, is trying to define what is unclear in terms of what is less clear.

This explains a fact about Reichenbach's criterion. Reichenbach's criterion can be convincingly used to show that two theories or statements are *not* equivalent (e.g., 'There are birds outside the cube', and 'Shadows – of such-and-such a shape and motion – are seen on the walls of the cube'), because it suffices to describe a situation (including a body of background theory) in which the two theories or statements are clearly confirmed to different degrees (receive different weights) to show *non*-equivalence. But there is no obvious way to use the criterion to show that two statements or theories *are* equivalent; and, as we saw above, when Reichenbach does claim that two statements are equivalent (e.g., 'Cats are divine animals' and 'Cats produce awe in cat worshippers'), he in fact does not use his own criterion.

The special theory of relativity

Since attempts to define the notion of equivalence (sameness of cognitive meaning) have not proved successful (or at least neo-positivist attempts, such as Reichenbach's, have not), let us turn to the use of this notion in connection with the special theory of relativity. It was, in fact, this theory which seemed to call for such a notion, and much of the attempt to apply the notion of equivalence to the philosophy of space and time derives from the various accounts philosophers of science have given of the logical structure and epistemological significance of special relativity.

Let A and B be two inertial systems. It is the very notion of an inertial system that an inertial system does not rotate or experience accelerations of any kind; so A and B must either be at rest relative to one another or else moving with a constant relative velocity. Choose A as the rest system. Then B will be described as moving with a constant velocity v (assume now that $v \neq 0$, i.e., A and B are not at rest relative to one another). Choose B as the rest system. Then A will be described as moving with a constant velocity $-v$. This much is familiar from classical physics and classical philosophical discussions of the relativity of motion.

Mathematically, the change from taking A to be the rest system to taking B to be the rest system corresponds to a transformation of the coordinate system. In classical physics, this transformation is a so-called Gallilean transformation. If one assumes the clocks in the A frame are physically identical to the clocks in the B frame, then, in classical physics, the coordinate of time in the A system, call it t, and the coordinate of time in the B system, call it t', can only differ by a constant, $t = t' + k$. In particular, then, two events which are *simultaneous* in one system are simultaneous in the other; two events which differ in time by an amount of r seconds in the one system will differ in time by r seconds in the other.

According to the special theory of relativity, change from the A system to the B system is *not* correctly accomplished by a Gallilean transformation. Instead, if one is to get the correct predictions, one must use a different mathematical transformation, a so-called *Lorentz transformation*, to determine the coordinates of an event in the B system from the coordinates in the A system or vice versa. (Geometrically this may be visualized as follows: the two systems do not agree on the spatial distance between events, if they are in relative motion, nor even on the temporal distance between events, but they are related so that they agree on the *space–time distance* between any two events, where this quantity, the space–time distance, can be defined in either system by the expression $(x^2 + y^2 + z^2 - (ct)^2)^{\frac{1}{2}}$, where c is the speed of light. The existence of this new invariant quantity, space–time distance, is the characteristic feature of the new theory.) This has a number of surprising consequences. Even if meter-sticks in the A frame are physically identical to meter-sticks in the B frame, the length of things as measured in the B frame differs from the length of the same things as measured in the A frame. In fact, the 'moving' system B seems *shorter* in the A frame than it does in the B frame. (And, symmetrically, A seems shorter in the B frame than it does in A.) Even more surprisingly, events which are *simultaneous* in one frame are not in general simultaneous in the other. And the temporal distance between two events will be described differently in the two frames. The closer the relative velocity v comes to c, the speed of light, the more significant do these phenomena become. If one system is moving at practically the speed of light relative to the other, then an event may be described as taking years to happen in the one system and as taking only days or even seconds in the other. Conversely, if the relative velocity v is small in comparison with the speed of light, then these disagreements will be experimentally insignificant, which is why the relativity of simultaneity, length, and temporal separation, was not noticed in pre-Einsteinian physics. Today when particles are constantly being accelerated to speeds close to c in the great linear accelerator in Stanford and in other accelerators in Europe and in the Soviet Union, the phenomena predicted by special relativity are constantly being observed.

Let description (A) be a description of the world in the coordinate system of A. (Imagine A is the earth, if we neglect the acceleration of the earth at a given time.) Let description (B) be the description that we obtain by transforming all the statements in description (A) according to the Lorentz transformation corresponding to the choice of B as the new rest system. (Imagine B is a rocket ship moving at one-quarter the speed of light relative to A.) Then, from the point of view of observers in the rocket ship B, description (B) is a *true* description of the world. Yet, how can this be? Description (A) says two events X and Y (say, an explosion on the moon and an explosion on Mars) happened simultaneously and description (B) says X happened *before* Y. How can two such flatly contradictory accounts *both* be true?

The idea of notational variance

The first idea that philosophers and logicians of science tried was a very natural one; they tried to account for the equivalence of the different descriptions which arise from the choice of different frames in special relativity as a case of mere notational variance. Being empiricists (almost all philosophers of science are empiricists) they did this in a way which is in keeping with the classical empiricist tradition. They took the so-called 'observation language', i.e., the terminology used to report the observations made in each frame, as itself a *neutral* language. Indeed, such statements as 'The observer in frame *A saw* his clock read 12 when he pushed the button' *are* neutral in special relativity, in the sense of being true in all frames if they are true in the frame *A* itself. (They are not neutral in the sense of *presupposing no theory at all*, of course; and this is the point at which empiricist reliance on the notion of an 'observation language' in the philosophy of science came to grief. But this does not affect the present discussion.) Having a neutral language available, they then tried to show that such terms as 'simultaneous', 'distance', and 'temporal separation' really receive *different definitions* in the different frames, i.e., *different definitions in the neutral language of observation*. Since 'simultaneous', for example, doesn't have the same *definition* (relative to the neutral language) in description (A) that it does in description (B), the incompatibility between the sentences '*X* and *Y* happened simultaneously' and '*X* and *Y* did not happen simultaneously' is only a *real* incompatibility when these sentences are uttered by an observer in the same frame; if one sentence occurs in description (A) while the other occurs in description (B), on the other hand, then the incompatibility is only apparent. Description (A) and description (B) are equivalent, then, in the sense of being *notational variants* of each other.

This idea was worked out in its classical form in Reichenbach's *The Philosophy of Space and Time*. Reichenbach analyzed the situation as follows: When I see a distant event, say, through a telescope, I can assign a time *t* to the event if I know the distance to the event (which I can measure by using meter-sticks at rest in my frame to define a coordinate grid) and I know in addition the speed light takes to travel that distance from that direction. I can measure the *round-trip speed of light* – the average speed of light over a trip to a mirror a certain distance away from the standard clock in my frame and back to the clock – using my knowledge of the distance to the mirror and my knowledge of the departure time and return time of the light ray. (This takes only the standard clock to determine.) But to determine the *one-way speed of light* – say, how fast it took the light to get *to* the mirror – I would need two clocks, one the standard clock in my frame, and another at the mirror, and *I would need to know these two clocks are synchronized*. But to know that two clocks are synchronized is just to know that, for example, they strike 12 *simultaneously*. Thus

35

it seems that I cannot determine simultaneity at a distance unless I can tell that clocks are synchronized, and I cannot tell clocks are synchronized until I can determine simultaneity at a distance!

Reichenbach's solution is to say that I need what he called a *coordinating definition* – in effect, a definition in the neutral language – and that the statement that *the one-way speed of light equals the round-trip speed* – i.e., light travels with the same velocity in every direction, relative to the frame – is such a definition. It only *appears* to be an empirical statement that the velocity of light is independent of direction; really this statement is a meaning stipulation; in fact, it defines the time coordinate *t* in the frame for events not located right at the standard clock. Similarly, given that there is a disagreement between observers in different frames over the length of meter-sticks (we on earth say that meter-sticks in the rocket frame are *shorter* than one meter long; they say that *our* meter-sticks are shorter than one meter long), the statement that the meter-sticks which are at *rest* in our frame are the ones that are really one meter long only appears to be an empirical statement; really it defines spacial distance in our frame.

Thus, on Reichenbach's analysis, when an observer in frame *A* says '*X* and *Y* happened simultaneously', what he means is that the times *t* are to be determined by using light signals and assuming that the velocity of light *in the frame A* is direction-independent. (This is the description in the neutral language of what time statements in description (A) mean.) When an observer in frame *B* says '*X* and *Y* did not happen simultaneously', what he means is that the times *t* of *X* and *Y* are not the same, where these times *t* are to be determined by using light signals and assuming that the velocity of light *in the frame B* is direction independent. (This is the description in the neutral language of what time statements in description (B) mean.) Since statements refer to different computation procedures in description (A) and description (B), the incompatibility is only apparent.

Reichenbach's analysis of the logical structure of the special theory of relativity led him to develop an entire conception of what the task of the philosophy of science should be. The special theory of relativity demonstrated, according to Reichenbach's analysis, that a statement could look like an ordinary statement of empirical fact and really be a disguised 'coordinating definition'. The statement that light travels with a direction-independent velocity (in a particular frame) is an *analytic* statement on Reichenbach's account, i.e., a definition or a statement which is true by definition. On the other hand, given the coordinating definitions, the statement that *X* and *Y* happened at the same time (in the particular frame) and the statement that the moving system is contracted in the direction of its motion are *synthetic* statements, i.e., statements which are true as a matter of fact, and *empirical* statements, i.e., experimentally testable. The task of the philosopher of science, Reichenbach held, is precisely to do the sort of work *he* did in the special case of the special theory of relativity, namely, to separate the analytic statements in scientific theory from the synthetic statements, to tell us which statements constitute the coordinating definitions in physical theory and which statements are the synthetic, empirical, consequences.

Quine's critique of the analytic–synthetic distinction

The very same paper of Quine's that we cited before, 'Two dogmas of empiricism', contained a scathing attack on this sort of program, however. Quine argued, in effect, that the statements of physical theory face experimental tests on a par; if the predictions of a theory are not confirmed, one may revise *either* the so-called 'definitions' of the theory or the so-called 'empirical consequences'. Furthermore, when one is deciding which statements to revise, it is methodologically irrelevant that some of the statements may have been considered 'definitions' at one time. Even if a statement was originally stipulated to be true by some act of conventional legislation, 'truth by convention' is not a trait of sentences which they *retain*. Some statements in physical theory may have originally been adopted as conventions, others may have originally been adopted on the basis of experiment, but once adopted they have the *same* status. *There is no such thing as analyticity in scientific theory.*

(Quine once compared the question, 'Which sentences in physical theory are definitions?' to the question, 'Which places in Ohio are starting places?' *No* place in Ohio is a 'starting place' *in itself*; it all depends on what journey you wish to take. Similarly, *no* sentence in physical theory is a 'definition' in itself; it may be convenient in one context to call one sentence a definition and a second sentence a theorem or an empirical consequence, and convenient in a different context to call the second sentence the definition and the first sentence the theorem or the empirical consequence.)

We can see the force of Quine's argument in the case of special relativity itself; why should we say that 'The velocity of light is direction independent' is the coordinating definition and 'Clocks which travel with the same velocity (in the frame) remain synchronized' is the empirical consequence, and not vice versa? Reichenbach

37

himself admits one could do either in the context of rational reconstruction. But then, Quine would ask, why should 'rational reconstruction' pretend that these sentences are not on a par when *in the
actual methodology of science* they do function on a par?

Equivalence

Attractive as it is, the idea that the different descriptions in the special
theory of relativity are equivalent by virtue of the fact that the
definitions of the terms make them mere notational variants has one
fatal weakness, which Quine's criticism of the analytic–synthetic
distinction exposes; the idea depends crucially on the idea that some
statements in physical theory are the 'definitions'. Can we formulate
a notion of equivalence which takes care of this case without assuming
the analytic–synthetic distinction, or, at least, without assuming that
that distinction applies within scientific theories? To do this, let us
turn now to technical logic.

In modern logic, a very important idea is the *relative interpretation*
of one theory in another. For example, if we wish to show that a theory
is undecidable, then a favorite method is to show that a theory which
is already known to be 'essentially undecidable' (i.e., to have no
decidable extensions) is relatively interpretable in the theory in
question. It then follows that the theory in question is also undecidable
(and, in fact, essentially so).

The definition of T_1 *as relatively interpretable in* T_2 is: there exist
possible definitions (i.e., formally possible definitions, whether these
correspond to the meanings of the terms or not) of the terms of T_1
in the language of T_2 with the property that, if we 'translate' the
sentences of T_1 into the language of T_2 by means of those definitions,
then all theorems of T_1 become theorems of T_2.

Two theories are *mutually relatively interpretable* if each is relatively
interpretable in the other, in the sense just explained. Is mutual
relative interpretability the notion of equivalence we have been
looking for?

It is easy to see that it is not. Relative interpretability is a purely
formal relation; it in no way involves the *meanings* of the terms T_1,
T_2. In fact, it applies to theories T_1 and T_2 viewed as uninterpreted
calculi. Thus mutual relative interpretability, however interesting as
a formal relation, guarantees no sort of sameness of meaning or even
subject matter between theories; it only testifies to the existence of
similar formal structures in both theories. Conceivably two theories
about wholly disparate subject matters – say, an axiomatic system of
genetics and an axiomatic system of number theory – could turn out

to be mutually relatively interpretable, but they would hardly be equivalent in cognitive meaning.

Suppose we try combining the formal requirement that the two theories in question be mutually relatively interpretable with a suitable *informal* requirement (since purely formal definitions of the concept of equivalence do not seem to be forthcoming). Can we perhaps in this way arrive at the clarification we are looking for?

It seems to me that we can. The informal notion I propose to use is the notion of *explanation*. (Granted that attempts to formalize this notion are no more successful than attempts to formalize the notion of equivalence, there is still considerable agreement in the judgments of scientists about what is and is not an explanation.)

Here is the proposal: a theory is 'complete' if every sentence of the theory is decidable in the theory, i.e., either provable or refutable in the theory. Suppose T_1 and T_2 are complete mutually relatively interpretable theories. (I confine attention to complete theories, because when we call descriptions 'equivalent' we generally have in mind a relation between ideal completions of those descriptions, and not just between the finite fragments we actually possess.) Suppose moreover that the 'translation' of each into the other preserves the relation of *explanation*, and that *the same phenomena are explained by both* (this is the informal element alluded to). Then the two theories are equivalent descriptions (we propose).

But how can we tell that *the same phenomena* are explained by two theories without already knowing that the two theories are equivalent? Look at two descriptions in special relativity, say, description (A) and description (B). If we are willing to take as the 'phenomena' to be explained such events as *collisions, coincidences of such events as a collision and the arrival of a light ray, emissions and absorptions of particles and radiation*, then it is undeniable that description (A) and description (B) offer explanations of all *these* 'phenomena', and that the explanations are translations of each other. In general, if the proposed analysis of equivalence is accepted, there will always be an element of choice in the decision to accept two theories as equivalent: the choice of a domain of events to count as the 'phenomena'.

On the account of equivalence we propose here, one can say that description (A) and description (B) in our example are *equivalent*, and speak of *translation* between description (A) and description (B), without assuming that some particular sentence is 'the definition' of the term 'simultaneous' in either description, and without assuming any distinction between 'analytic' and 'synthetic' sentences in either description.

To take a different case from modern physics, it is well known that the matrix mechanics of Heisenberg and the wave mechanics of Schrödinger were developed independently, and that physicists came to regard these two systems as equivalent in the sense we are explicating when they discovered a mathematical correspondence between the two formalisms. If we take the 'phenomena to be explained' in this case as scattering events (absorption and emission of particles), then this is in perfect agreement with the explication we are proposing. And, once again, to try to show the equivalence by seeking the 'definitions' of the crucial terms would be very difficult, indeed, impossible. Who can say which statement of physical theory is the 'definition' of the ψ-function? *After we have accepted the equivalence*, we can, of course, always construct definitions which will make the theories in question notational variants; but to say they are equivalent *because* they are notational variants is to put the cart before the horse.

But why should we even require mutual relative interpretability for equivalence of complete theories? Why should we not just require that they both explain exactly the same phenomena (and that all the predictions of both theories are empirically correct)? To do this would be to sacrifice an important distinction: the distinction between the case of *equivalence*, in which, or so it seems to us, one expects some type of translation or reduction relation to hold between the explanations provided by the different theories, and the case of radical dualism. If dualism should turn out to be true (or, more generally, pluralism), then one would expect to get theories of the world which explained the same phenomena (at least, if we take observable events as the phenomena to be explained), but which were in no way reducible to or 'translatable' into each other. This would be a great shock to our belief in empirical realism, while, it seems to us, the existence of equivalent descriptions which can be reduced to each other no longer conflicts with our belief in empirical realism. (To that extent empirical realism has gone beyond a simply 'copy' theory of knowledge.) (A similar distinction between the relation we call equivalence, and which Quine calls 'being two *versions* of the same theory', and the case of radical dualism, has been drawn by Quine (1975).)

The problem of trivial semantic conventionality

Suppose we imagine our total body of belief to have been rationally reconstructed and formalized. Call the resulting theory T_1. Now imagine that we decided to change the meaning of a term in T_1, say 'pressure'. In particular, suppose we decided to use the word 'pressure' to mean what we now refer to as 'the cube root of pressure'. This would lead to a rewriting of T_1, say as T_2. T_1 and T_2 would then be 'equivalent descriptions', by *any* criterion. The existence of *this* sort of equivalence is, of course, nothing new. All that the existence of such pairs of theories as T_1, T_2 illustrates is that the uncommitted noise 'pressure' might have been given the meaning that in the actual language is born by the expression 'the cube root of pressure' instead of the meaning it does have. More generally, it illustrates what has been called trivial semantic conventionality: the fact that the noises which we employ as meaningful words could have had different meanings assigned to them than the ones they actually have been given.

The importance of the phenomenon of the cognitive equivalence of theories which seem different or even incompatible is that it is, in actual science, *not* just a matter of trivial semantic conventionality. For example, the people in the rocket frame B in our example use the *noise* 'simultaneous' in a way which is just as much in accordance with the conventions of Italian (or English, or whatever language) usage as the people in the earth frame. Indeed, they use it in what must seem to them, if they don't know the special theory of relativity, to be 'the same way'. That there is a hidden relativity to ascriptions of simultaneity – that which events will turn out to be 'simultaneous' if we rely on, e.g., clocks which are transported to a distance to remain 'synchronized' will depend on whether the clocks are transported with the same velocity relative to the rest system – is a matter of hitherto unknown empirical *fact*. Equivalence is of philosophical importance precisely in such cases as these, cases in which it does not seem that anyone has *altered* the ordinary meaning of any expression and yet, for factual reasons, apparently incompatible bodies of theory turn out to be equivalent in the sense we have been discussing.

Neglect of the need to distinguish the trivial kind of equivalent descriptions that arise from trivial semantic conventionality from significant pairs of equivalent descriptions has led to strange doctrines in the philosophy of science. For example, it has been argued, first by Hans Reichenbach and later by Adolf Grünbaum, that the fact that we could use non-standard metrics for space and even for space–time shows that the choice of a metric is a matter of 'convention' (Reichenbach) and that space and space–time are 'intrinsically metrically amorphous' (Grünbaum). But in itself remetrizability or alternative metrizability show only the existence of trivial semantic conventionality. If the conventionality of the whole metric of general relativity is to be established, a better argument than the formal possibility of using the uncommitted noise 'space–time distance' to refer to a different magnitude than the one we do use it to refer to must be advanced. (Grünbaum has attempted to produce such arguments; but none of them are satisfactory in my opinion.)

Equivalence and realism

At first blush the existence of equivalent descriptions does not appear to pose any kind of a threat to a realist philosophy of science. In the special theory of relativity, for example, if one is bothered by the existence of apparently incompatible but equivalent descriptions of phenomena, then one can avoid terms such as 'simultaneous' and 'distance' altogether, and use the language of the *invariants*. For example, instead of talking about the 'temporal separation' and the 'spatial distance' between two events, one can give their space–time distance. This description in terms of invariant notions is certainly a complete one, since each of the frame-bound descriptions can be recovered from it when we are given the coordinate system associated with the frame. (Of course, the decision to count the invariant description as a complete description is connected with our choice to count collisions, coincidences, simultaneities-at-a-place, absorptions, and emissions as the phenomena to be explained; for the one thing the invariant description does *not* tell us is which one of the coordinate systems is 'really at rest'. In effect, deciding that the foregoing are the 'phenomena to be explained', and deciding that the invariant description is a complete description of what is going on, are two ways of expressing the same decision, i.e., the decision not to count *simultaneities-at-a-distance* as real objective phenomena.) The mathematics of invariants – the tensor calculus – was the mathematics, in fact, that Einstein used in developing the general theory of relativity.

If the realist accepts the invariant description as the true picture of what is going on, then the existence of the frame-bound descriptions is no more a puzzle to him than the fact that the surface of the world can be represented in different ways, say, the Mercator projection and Polar projection. It is *the nature of the object itself* that explains why it admits of these different representations, he will say.

But things are not in general so simple. Consider the following two stories about space–time (here I am modifying an example I used in Putnam (1976)):

Story 1. Space–time consists of objects called points (point-events). These have no extension, and extended space–time is built up out of them just as, in classical Euclidean geometry, the extended line, plane, and solid bodies are built up out of unextended spatial points.

Story 2. Space–time consists of extended space–time neighborhoods. All parts of space–time have extension. This corresponds to the theory (advanced by Whitehead), that classical Euclidean space consists of extended spatial neighborhoods. On Whitehead's view, 'points' are mere logical constructions and not real spatial objects: a point is (identified with) a convergent set of solid spheres (i.e., spheres together with their interiors).

If we take phenomena to be 'observable phenomena' or even to be the totality of all extended physical phenomena, observable and unobservable, then story 1 and story 2 are equivalent descriptions, by our criterion. For, assuming that all particles have some finite extension (that there are no true mass-points or charge-points in the real world), then the causes of any phenomenon must have extension. It can make no difference to *physical explanation* whether we treat space–time points as 'real' or as mere logical constructions.

A 'hard core' realist might claim that there is a fact of the matter as to which is true, story 1 or story 2. But a scientific realist (as opposed to a realist of the older, metaphysical kind) would hardly wish to do this for a variety of reasons. For one, this gives up the discovery that this whole article is about: the discovery that there can be incompatible but equivalent versions of the world. For another, it leads either to scepticism or to a revival of metaphysics of the kind that Kant persuaded us to abandon. It leads to the former – scepticism – if we say that there is a fact of the matter as to which story is true, but that we can never *know* that fact. (And if we *are* willing to be sceptics, then how can we be so sure there *is* a 'fact of the matter'?) It leads to metaphysics in the bad sense – the kind that claims to *a priori* knowledge about noumenal realities – if we claim that we know on extra-scientific grounds either that story 1 is true or that story 2 is. For such reasons as these, scientific realists concede that story 1 and story 2 are equivalent descriptions. In effect, they concede that extended neighborhoods are a suitable set of 'invariants': a description of the world which says what is going on in every extended neighborhood is a *complete* description.

If, once again, we are just dealing with different representations of one 'invariant' world, then it must be that it can happen that what we picture as 'incompatible' terms can be mapped onto the same real entity, though not, of course, within the same theory. Thus, if we are

43

to save the traditional realist view that theories are just representations of theory-independent entities, we must say that the real object which is labelled 'point' in one theory might be labelled 'set of convergent spheres' in another theory. And, once again, we must say that it is *the nature of the world itself* that explains why it admits of these different representations.

The problem with this claim is that in the general case there will be more than one admissible relative interpretation of one equivalent description in another. Story 1 can be interpreted in story 2 in *many* different ways. 'Points' can be sets of spheres whose radii are negative powers of 2, for example, or sets of spheres whose radii are negative powers of 3. So if such terms as 'points' and 'set of convergent spheres' are the 'images' of 'real objects' (theory-independent objects), then, once again we are faced with the alternatives of scepticism (if we say we *can't know* whether the 'correct' translation of story 1 into story 2 is the one that identifies points with set of spheres which converge and whose radii are negative powers of 2 or some other translation) or transcendental metaphysics (if we claim *a priori* knowledge of which is *the* correct translation).

Once again, the move favored by scientific realists is to deny there is a fact of the matter. *All* these translations are correct, a modern realist will say. But then, it seems, we must give up the idea of terms in our theories as 'images' of 'real objects' (noumenal objects) altogether; for how can there *not* be a fact of the matter as to which terms in two different theories are images of the same object, if terms really are images of objects? It begins to look as if Kant was right, and science only gives us *relations* between objects and not the objects themselves, if we are to keep talk of 'theory-independent objects' at all.

But talk of 'theory-independent objects' is hard to keep. The problem is that such talk may retain 'the world' but at the price of giving up any intelligible notion of *how* the world is. Any sentence that changes truth value on passing from one correct theory to another correct theory – an equivalent description – will express only a *theory-relative* property of the world. And the more such sentences there are, the more properties of the world will turn out to be theory relative. For example, if we concede that story 1 and story 2 are equivalent descriptions, then the property *being an object* (as opposed to a class or set of things) will be theory relative.

All this isn't an artifact of my simple example: actual physical theory is rife with similar examples. One can construe space–time points as objects, for example, or as events, or as properties. One can construe fields as objects or do everything with particles acting at a distance (in classical physics, at any rate). The fact is, so many properties of 'the world' – starting with just the categorical ones, such as cardinality, particulars or universals, etc. – turn out to be 'theory relative' that 'the world' ends up as a *mere* 'thing in itself'. If one cannot say *how* 'the world' is, theory-independently, then talk of theories as descriptions of 'the world' is empty.

At this point the discussion has come through a kind of Hegelian spiral. First verificationist philosophers introduced the notion of equivalent descriptions and tried to explicate it. Then scientific realists took it up (and we have offered an explication from this perspective in the present essay). But now it seems that our acceptance of the existence of equivalent descriptions, and hence of *incompatible correct versions of the world*, has undermined the metaphysics on which realism – including scientific realism – was originally based. Today the discussion of the metaphysical issue of realism versus conceptual relativism, of the distinction between empirical and metaphysical realism, and of 'realist semantics' versus 'non-realist semantics' as theories of truth are as alive as they ever were. While a final resolution of these questions is not even in sight, there is no doubt that the phenomenon of equivalent descriptions is a profoundly significant one for their discussion.

3

Possibility and necessity

The use by logicians and philosophers of the notions of possibility and necessity goes back to Aristotle. In the modern period, enormous use was made of the notion of a 'possible world' by Leibniz. Yet the epistemological and metaphysical foundations of these notions remain obscure.

Although empiricist philosophers tried to restrict necessity to linguistic necessity, or even to banish it from philosophy altogether, the notions have proved, like other perennial philosophical notions, to be extremely hardy. (Some philosophers would complain that they are hardy *weeds*.) As a result of the work described below, modal logic, possible worlds semantics (a theory due to Richard Montague which has connections with what we shall discuss here, although it falls beyond the purview of this article), the topic of 'essences', and the theory of counterfactual conditionals have all been pursued with vigor. Indeed, the concepts of necessity and possibility have enjoyed an unprecedented philosophical revival.

In this article I shall first discuss the strange subject of *quantum logic*, which well illustrates the case for abandoning the notion of necessity (in the sense of *apriority*) altogether, and then look at two representative examples of the work on the non-epistemic notion of necessity, *metaphysical necessity*, as it is grandly called. These examples are theories of Saul Kripke and David Lewis, respectively, and they have been the pace-setters for the revival of talk about possible worlds and metaphysically necessary truths.

Quantum logic and the *a priori*

The traditional idea that logic and mathematics are *a priori* disciplines, i.e., disciplines which yield *a priori* knowledge, has come under attack from an unexpected direction in the twentieth century. John von Neumann and D. Birkhoff (1936) suggested that one way of looking at quantum mechanics is to see the logic of the physical world (as described by that theory) as a *non-classical logic*. Although von

Neumann dropped work on this suggestion to work on other projects during the second world war, his biographer Ulam has reported that von Neumann himself attached great importance to it. After 1960, publications by myself, Bub, and Finkelstein led to a revival of interest in this suggestion, and today there is a great deal of research going on concerning it. At first blush, this suggestion appears to have devastating consequences for the idea that there is such a thing as necessary truth at all; if even *logic* turns out to be empirical, why should not the whole idea of 'necessity' be scrapped? Perhaps empirical knowledge is all the knowledge there is; perhaps even logic and mathematics are branches of empirical knowledge. Or so it might seem.

The mathematical details of quantum logic are too complicated to present here. (For those who know quantum mechanics: the idea is that there is a one-to-one correspondence between *propositions* about a physical system S and the subspaces of the Hilbert space used to represent that system. The logical operations of disjunction, conjunction, and complementation correspond to taking the intersection, the span, and the orthogonal subspace respectively. For logicians: a model of quantum logic is any orthocomplemented modular lattice. The models of physical interest are the lattices of subspaces of infinite-dimensional Hilbert spaces.) However the spirit of von Neumann's idea can, perhaps, be conveyed by two examples.

It is well known that in quantum mechanics the position of a particle is usually uncertain. For example, the position of an electron in orbit around a nucleus is uncertain. Moreover, this uncertainty seems to be more than a mere ignorance on our part as to where the electron is; in some respects it is as if the electron were smeared out over its possible locations. In fact, this 'smeared out' behavior is what accounts for the fact that atoms do not collapse to a mathematical point, as they should according to the laws of classical physics. One illustration of this uncertainty is the celebrated 'two-slit experiment'. In this experiment particles (photons or electrons or any other quantum mechanical particles) are released from a point source. Between the particles (say, photons, for definiteness) and the detector (say, a photographic plate) a barrier is placed in the form of a wall with two fine slits. The uncertainty in the position of the photon permits *each* photon to interact with *both* slits, so that what one gets on the photographic plate is not a simple sum of the patterns that one would obtain by just performing the experiment with the left slit open and just performing the experiment with the right slit open. Rather, it is as if *half* the photon went through the left hand slit and *half* the photon went through the right hand slit and the two halves then intermingled and interfered (in the manner of waves: in fact, this phenomenon is often referred to as the 'wave aspect' of the photon). The final result is a system of visible interference fringes in the photographic picture. Yet, in spite of all this wave-like behavior, *each individual photon strikes the emulsion at one and only one definite point.* We never succeed in *demonstrating* that the photon is physically 'smeared out' by getting it to hit the emulsion in a way that leaves a smeared out crater or other proof that something spatially extended struck; it is only that the interference fringes force us to *infer* that the photon was spatially spread out *when we were not interacting with it.* (It is like the Charles Addams cartoon of the skiier who is skiing down a hill, and whose tracks pass on opposite sides of a large tree. We do not *see* the skiier pass through a tree – we have never seen such a thing, nor will we ever – but the tracks seem to force the inference that the skiier passed through the tree before we looked.)

Let us use the sentential letters p, q, r to symbolize the three statements *The photon hit the emulsion at place R*, *The photon went through the left hand slit*, and *The photon went through the right hand slit*. In von Neumann's logic *The photon went through the left hand slit or the right hand slit* is symbolized just as in classical logic, namely, $(q \lor r)$. The statement that the *photon went through the left hand slit and hit R* and the statement that *The photon went through the right hand slit and hit R* (in classical logic, these would be $(p \And q)$, or pq for short, and $(p \And r)$ or pr for short) are *impermissible*; von Neumann's logic does not let us even *ask* which slit the photon went through, because it does not allow certain propositions, the so-called 'incompatible' propositions of quantum mechanics, to be conjoined. It is as if the propositions q, q had *no* conjunction and the propositions p, r had no conjunction. In fact, that is just what certain philosophers of quantum mechanics think is going on.

Evidently, some of the laws of classical logic have been given up. In fact, the law of *conjunction introduction* (from any two propositions p, q infer their conjunction $(p \And q)$) has to be restricted to pairs of *compatible* propositions p, q, and the distributive law

$$p \And (q \lor r) \equiv pq \lor pr$$

has to be restricted to the case in which all three propositions p, q, r are 'totally compatible' (this means there is a sublattice of the modular lattice which is itself a Boolean algebra and which contains p, q, r). The fact that there *are no such propositions* as pq and pr is the quantum logical representation of the smeared out nature of the photon in the above experiment. (See chapter 14 for details.)

Our second illustration is not an experiment (although it is a possible experiment) but a computation performed by two logicians, Kochen and Specker (1967). Kochen and Specker describe a system (an orthohelium atom in its lowest excited state in a magnetic field with rhomboidal symmetry!) with the following weird property: the property that if you measure three spin components $\mathcal{J}_x^2, \mathcal{J}_y^2, \mathcal{J}_z^2$, in any three mutually perpendicular directions you get $(1, 1, 0)$ or $(1, 0, 1)$ or $(0, 1, 1)$. What makes this result weird is that it seems to directly contradict a theorem due to Gleason: that there is *no* way to assign zeroes and ones to *all* the points of a sphere so that for *every* orthogonal triple of points of the sphere two of the points are assigned ones and one of the points is assigned zero!

Kochen and Specker found that the paradox can be stated without reference to the theorem by Gleason we mentioned. They succeeded in finding 117 directions in space (the reader may visualize these as 117 line segments of unit length meeting at a point) with the same relevant property as the whole sphere: that there is no way to assign 117 zeroes and 1s (one to each line segment) so that for every triple of orthogonal segments (segments forming a 'corner', or three right angles) contained in the 117 there are two segments in the triple which have been assigned a 1, and one segment which has been assigned a 0. (The 117 directions in question are rather rich in orthogonal triples; in fact, it is possible to form 63 different orthogonal triples from the 117 given line segments.) According to quantum mechanics, for every one of the 63 orthogonal triples that it is possible to form from the 117 directions, there are three squared spin components of which two are 1s and one is 0; yet according to classical *logic* this is impossible.

We may say 'according to *logic*' because it is possible to think of the 117 directions in space as sentential letters, $p_1, p_2, \ldots, p_{117}$. (Think of p_i as the proposition that the squared spin component in the ith direction is a 1.) Then the 63 orthogonal triples correspond to certain triples from the collection of all triples it is possible to form using just these letters; and, if (i_1, i_2, i_3) is the ith orthogonal triple, then the statement that two of the squared spin components in these directions are 1s and one of them is a 0 is just the proposition

$$(p_{i(1)}p_{i(2)}\bar{p}_{i(3)} \vee p_{i(1)}\bar{p}_{i(2)}p_{i(3)} \vee \bar{p}_{i(1)}p_{i(2)}p_{i(3)}).$$

The combinatorial impossibility of assigning two 1s and a 0 to all 63 of the orthogonal triples is the same thing as the *tautological falsity*

49

of the formula of propositional calculus that is obtained by conjoining a certain 63 formulas of the kind just illustrated.

The resolution of this paradox in quantum logic is extremely elegant (as Kochen and Specker point out). In von Neumann's logic ('quantum logic'), the formula of propositional calculus that asserts the combinatorial impossibility of assigning 117 ones and zeroes in such a way that every one of the relevant triples contains two 1s and a 0 is not valid. In other words, the conjunction of the 63 formulas $\left(p_{i(1)} p_{i(2)} \bar{p}_{i(3)} \vee p_{i(1)} \bar{p}_{i(2)} p_{i(3)} \vee \bar{p}_{i(1)} p_{i(2)} p_{i(3)}\right)$ that is tautologically false in classical propositional calculus is *consistent* in von Neumann's logic! The suggestion is that things which are *literally impossible according to classical propositional calculus* can and do happen, and that that is what we are observing in the case described by Kochen and Specker.

This paradox can also be resolved by following the ideas of the conventional interpretation of quantum mechanics (the so-called 'Copenhagen interpretation') due to Bohr and Heisenberg. According to this interpretation, quantum mechanics does not tell us what values physical parameters have when we are not measuring them; quantum mechanics only predicts the results measurements will have in well-defined experimental situations. So the formula $\mathcal{J}_x^2 + \mathcal{J}_y^2 + \mathcal{J}_z^2 = 2$ which is involved in the experiment described by Kochen and Specker, for example, does not mean that the three squared spin components sum to 2 (and hence that two of them must be 1s and one of them must be 0, since these are the two permitted values), but only means that the sum *will be found to be* 2 if we make the measurement, and that two 1s and a 0 will be found *if we make the measurement*. But if you measure one triple, then you can't measure any other triple, owing to the incompatibility relations; so there is no contradiction with classical logic, on this view: it is only a kind of miracle that the squared spin components always assume the right values *when we look*.

The view of quantum logic is not incompatible with the view of the Copenhagen interpretation (and von Neumann himself seems to have accepted both). But it seems unsatisfactory to some that quantum mechanics should draw a distinction between 'measured values' and 'unmeasured values' if the latter are *physically meaningless*. If this distinction is only forced on us by classical logic, then, to some, this has seemed a good reason to *change the logic*. Indeed, although the quantum logical point of view is only accepted by a small minority of physicists, not to say philosophers and logicians of physics, its growing appeal is perhaps due to a certain reconciliation of operationism and realism; both operationalistically minded philosophers and realistically minded ones like the elimination of the distinction between 'measured values' and 'unmeasured values'; the former because 'unmeasured values' that cannot be linked to the measured values by any theory are meaningless on even the most lenient operationalist view, and the latter because they like the idea that it is the 'real' values (whether measured or not) that physical theories describe and relate.

Writing in 1951, and referring not to von Neumann's proposal, which he was not aware of, but to a technically inferior proposal by Reichenbach to use three-valued logic in interpreting quantum mechanics, Quine asked the rhetorical question 'How would such a...[scientific revolution]...differ from the one in which Copernicus replaced Ptolemy, or Darwin Aristotle, or Einstein Newton?' And he answered his own rhetorical question by saying that it *wouldn't*, that changing one's geometry for the sake of simplifying physical theory, as we did when we adopted Einstein's theory of general relativity, and changing our logic for the sake of simplifying physical theory, as proposed by Reichenbach (of course, Quine was not commenting on whether the proposal really would simplify physical theory to a worthwhile extent), are changes of the same kind. Neither is forbidden by scientific methodology. The laws of logic, on this perspective, are as empirical as the laws of geometry, only more abstract and better protected. Logic is the *last* thing we shall ever revise, on Quine's view, but it is not *immune* from revision.

If Quine is right, 'necessary truth' is another famous subject that has no object. The discussion can stop right here. But, as always turns out to be the case, things are not so simple.

First of all, even if some of the laws of logic turn out to be empirical (or to have empirical presuppositions), it does not follow that they all are. No one has proposed revising the principle of contradiction. And what would it mean to give up the statement that 'Not every statement is both true and false?' (see chapter 7). The scope of the *a priori* is indeed shrinking; but the claim that every truth is empirical is still far from being an acceptable or even a coherent thesis.

Indeed, even the discussion that has taken place about revising the laws of classical logic has a strong *a priori* component. Our language, after all, was first used in talking about simple finite collections (the sheep in the meadow) and our logic was first formalized under idealizations which every student beginning a first logic course recognizes to be extremely severe (even if the teacher has forgotten that they are idealizations): for example, that all predicates are perfectly well defined. If we are really talking about a finite collection, and our predicates are really well defined and decidable, then the difference between, for example, a realist and an intuitionist or verificationist view of truth, can be ignored. But someone who thinks *on a priori grounds* that the classical notion of truth is wrong, and that the *law of the excluded middle* does not hold when we are dealing with undecidable predicates, will be led, as Brouwer was, to challenge classical logic. And this is, in fact, how intuitionist logic arose. Intuitionist logic is the logic one gets if one identifies truth with *constructive provability*, and not with some sort of totally non-epistemic 'correspondence with reality'.

Again, both classical logic and intuitionist logic assume that the decidability of different propositions is independent: in classical logic, it would be more correct to say, 'decidability' is not at issue, only absolute truth, and the absolute truth or absolute falsity of a meaningful proposition is a property that it has whether or not it can be decided; in intuitionist logic, it is mainly the language of pure mathematics that has been studied, so far, and in pure mathematics deciding one proposition never prevents one from deciding a different proposition. (The 'game-theoretic semantics' of Hintikka and the 'operative conception' of Lorenzen represent extension of a view-point related to intuitionism to empirical language.) But in the real world, it can happen, because of the uncertainty principle, that deciding one proposition makes it impossible to decide a certain other proposition by a measurement which would have any predictive value. There is a relation of 'incompatibility' between propositions.

Ian Hacking of Stanford University found (unpublished communication) that there is an intimate connection between classical logic, intuitionist logic, and quantum logic. In terms of one famous formalization of classical logic, the system of 'introduction rules' and 'elimination rules' due to Gentzen, the difference between classical logic and quantum logic is just that the formulas which are the premises in any application of an introduction rule or elimination rule are required to be *compatible*; it is the introduction of the new semantical relation of compatibility that accounts for the difference in the logic; there is no difference in the primitive rules, in this very natural presentation, beyond the restriction just mentioned.

Now, someone who feels that truth should be linked to *verifiability* (or at least to idealized verifiability), might well be led on *a priori* grounds to consider quantum logic once they realized that propositions might be 'incompatible' in the sense that the verification of one might *in principle* interfere with the verification of another. I don't mean that this is the *only* way in which one can be led to consider or even accept quantum logic; and it is *certainly* empirical that there *is* such a relation of incompatibility in our world. But the possibility just envisaged illustrates the fact that even if we did decide to accept quantum logic, we might be led to do so *partly for a priori reasons*, a fact which suggests once again that 'all truth is empirical' is not the appropriate conclusion from the fact that we may have to revise our logic for empirical reasons.

The point just made is one that Quine himself has long insisted on: denying that there are *a priori statements* is not the same thing as denying that there is an *a priori* factor in scientific decision making. Quine himself has suggested that '*a priori*' and '*a posteriori*' may be the names of factors present in the acceptance of all statements, rather than the names of classes of statements. And the theory of these two factors would be nothing other than *normative epistemology*: the theory of what makes statements worthy of rational acceptance.

There is, however, a very different way in which one can try to save the subject of 'necessity' from Quine's attack. Quine, following the logical positivists, assumed that if there was any such thing as 'necessity' then it was either semantical (e.g., 'analyticity') or epistemic ('*apriority*'). To Saul Kripke is due the honor of introducing into the discussion a very different kind of necessity, an objective non-epistemic kind of necessity: *metaphysical necessity*. Or so he called it.

Kripke and 'metaphysical necessity'

It used to be accepted doctrine in philosophy that the property of being *P* and the property of being *Q* cannot be one and the same unless the *concepts P* and *Q* are the same, or, at least, unless it is analytic that every *P* is a *Q* and every *Q* is a *P*. But, as I pointed out (Putnam, 1970*a*), this conflation of properties and concepts would render *inexpressible* such accepted scientific discoveries as the discovery that the magnitude *temperature* is the same magnitude as the magnitude *mean molecular translational energy*. (One could prove that temperature is not identical with any mechanical property, in fact. For one is not *contradicting oneself* when one says '*x* has temperature *T* but *x* does not have mean translational molecular energy *E*' – or whatever mechanical property one may care to substitute – even if the statement is always false as a matter of empirical fact. So, one would have to conclude, temperature is only correlated with mean molecular translational energy; the two properties cannot literally be *identical*.

Compare Moore's celebrated proof that Good cannot be identical with any 'natural' property!)

My point was that there *is* a notion of property in which the fact that two *concepts* 'are different' (say, 'temperature' and 'mean molecular translational energy') does not at all settle the question whether the corresponding *properties* are different. Not only is it the case that the identity of properties can be an empirical fact: even the *existence* of properties can be empirical. For example, when one asks how many fundamental physical magnitudes *exist* one is asking an empirical question about the existence of properties.

An idea which came into philosophy of language a few years after I introduced the 'synthetic identity of properties', and which enlarges and illuminates the point just made, is Saul Kripke's idea (1972) of 'metaphysically necessary' truths which have to be learned *empirically*, 'epistemically contingent necessary truth'. Kripke's observation, applied to the temperature/kinetic energy case, is that if someone describes a logically possible world in which people have sensations of hot and cold, in which there are objects that feel hot and cold, and in which these sensations of hot and cold are *explained by a different mechanism than mean molecular kinetic energy*, then we do *not* say that he has described a possible world in which *temperature is not mean molecular translational kinetic energy*.

A statement which is true in every possible world is traditionally called 'necessary'. A property which something has in every possible world in which that something exists is traditionally called *essential*. In this traditional terminology, Kripke is saying that 'temperature is mean translational molecular energy' is a *necessary* truth *even though we can't know it a priori*. The statement is empirical but necessary. Or, to say the same thing in different words, being mean translational molecular kinetic energy is an essential property of temperature. We have discovered the *essence* of temperature by *empirical* investigation.

To a certain extent, similar phenomena occur in pure mathematics itself. If the proof of a theorem is very long, then my confidence that the proof *is* a proof will depend on empirical assumptions of various kinds (for example, that my memory of what has been shown earlier in the proof does not deceive me, and that the lines do not change shape on the page as I read the proof). So my confidence – and the confidence I am *justified* in having – in the mathematical proposition will also depend on these empirical assumptions. Yet, as long as I accept the proof as a proof, I accept the mathematical proposition as not just true in the actual world but as true even in those worlds in which memory does deceive one, in which lines do change shape on the page, etc. In short, I accept the mathematical statement as metaphysically necessary on epistemically contingent grounds. This point is rendered more poignant by the development of the high speed computer; the only extant proof of the four color theorem, for example, was *discovered* in part by a computer search, and the proof as a whole cannot be checked by a human mathematician who eschews computer assistance.

What Kripke is suggesting, then, is that (1) the old idea that science discovers necessary truths, that science discovers the essence of things, was, in an important sense, right not wrong; (2) the necessity in question, 'metaphysical necessity', or truth in all possible worlds, is *not* the same as apriority; epistemic necessity and metaphysical necessity have been unwarrantedly conflated; (3) the problem in the philosophy of mathematics should *not* be thought of as accounting for the *unrevisability* of all proved mathematical statements. Mathematical necessity too is not, in general, epistemic. (Although Kripke does think that the truths of classical logic, and perhaps the *basic* axioms of arithmetic, *are* epistemically necessary. He has a notably conservative attitude towards such proposals as quantum logic.)

'Rigid designators'

Kripke was led to his discoveries in the philosophy of language partly by work he had done previously in a branch of mathematical logic, *modal logic*, in which he is the world's outstanding authority. Modal logic extends the classical logic by adding a symbol, the square, for the operation of *necessitation*, i.e., the operation which converts a statement p into the statement *it is necessary that p*. So-called 'normal' modal logics contain the axioms and rules (modus ponens and substitution) of classical propositional calculus, a rule of necessitation (from the theoremhood of A to infer the theoremhood of $\Box A$), and a distribution axiom: $\Box(p \Rightarrow q) \Rightarrow (\Box p \Rightarrow \Box q)$. Other common axioms are $\Box p \Rightarrow p$ (*if it is necessary that p, then p*) and $\Box p \Rightarrow \Box \Box p$ (*if it is necessary that p, then it is necessary that it is necessary that p*).

Intuitions about necessity differ, and so, not surprisingly, many different systems of modal logic exist. What Kripke did was to bring order out of this chaos by introducing a semantical notion of a *model* which enables one to study the properties of all of these systems, and to pinpoint the difference in the assumptions they make about necessity, as well as to investigate technical questions of the completeness of different systems for different notions of necessity. A model (sometimes called a 'Kripke structure', today) is a set of objects called *possible worlds* (these correspond to models in the classical sense, models for the non-modal part of the language; they determine which non-modal sentences are true and which are false) together with a relation called *relative possibility* or *accessibility*. The strongest system of modal logic, S5, is obtained by requiring the accessibility relation to be an equivalence relation (symmetric, transitive, and reflexive); the weakest, by only requiring it to be reflexive.

The difficulty (one which has led Quine to doubt the possibility of quantified modal logic) has always been how to combine modal logic with quantifiers, i.e., with the notions '(x)' (*for all x*) and '$(\exists x)$' (*there exists an x such that*). Kripke's solution is, once again, to assume a set of objects called *possible worlds* which are, in structure, just models for the non-modal part of the language; i.e., each possible world determines a universe of discourse that the quantifiers range over, and the extensions of all the predicates in the language relative to that universe of discourse. And once again there is an accessibility relation. But there is an additional relation as well: the relation of *trans-world identity*. That is, some individuals have to be *identified across possible worlds*. While the details would take us beyond both our available space and the bounds of our subject, one aspect of this technical problem is relevant to our concern here.

Consider two possible worlds which both contain the same individual, say Aristotle, but in which that individual is assigned different predicates. For example, in one of the two worlds he might be born in Stagirus and in the other in Athens. The phrase 'the great philosopher born in Stagirus' refers to Aristotle in the actual world (which we shall identify with the former of the two worlds just postulated), but not in the second of the two worlds. Indeed, it might even refer to a different individual altogether in the second world; perhaps *Plato* was born in Stagirus in the second possible world. So the same descriptive phrase, 'the great philosopher born in Stagirus' can denote different individuals in different possible worlds. In Kripke's terminology, this description is *non-rigid*.

What about the proper name 'Aristotle'? How do we customarily use this name in referring to hypothetical worlds? When we say 'Aristotle might have been born in Athens', we do not just mean that someone *named* 'Aristotle' might have been born in Athens. Indeed, when we say 'Aristotle might have been born in China', we are also likely to add 'If he had been born in China, he probably would not have been named "Aristotle"'. What we mean is that *the same individual* who was born in Stagirus, named Aristotle, and became the star pupil in Plato's Academy, etc. in the actual world, might have been born in Athens (or in China), might have been named Diogenes (or To Fu), etc. (In terms of Kripke structures, this means that there are possible worlds in which an individual who is not designated by the individual constant 'Aristotle' in those worlds, and not in the extension of 'born in Stagirus' in those worlds, stands in the relation of *trans-world identity* to the individual who is called Aristotle in the actual world.)

Since the name 'Aristotle' is customarily used to refer to the *same* individual when we talk about non-actual worlds (even if that individual is not named 'Aristotle' *in* those non-actual worlds), the proper name 'Aristotle' is a *rigid designator*, in Kripke's terminology.

Now consider a simple identity statement, such as 'Cicero is identical with Tully'. Given that this is true in the actual world, it makes no sense to say that 'there is a possible world in which Cicero and Tully are different individuals'. There are, to be sure, possible worlds in which the *names* 'Cicero' and 'Tully' are applied to different individuals, but in those worlds at least one of the two individuals is not Cicero (and hence not Tully), whatever he is called *in* that world. If the designators 'Cicero' and 'Tully' are used *rigidly*, and if 'Cicero is identical with Tully' is true in the actual world (or in *any* possible world, for that matter), then it is true in *every* possible world. On the other hand, the statement 'Cicero is identical with Tully' is an empirical statement. *Epistemically* it is 'contingent' ('synthetic', in Kant's terminology) even though it is *metaphysically* necessary. (Kripke's account of its epistemic status is in terms of his famous 'causal theory' of proper names. The intention when we use the name 'Cicero' is to refer to whomever the person who taught us to use this name in this way was referring to; in this way we get a chain of linked referring-uses, a history of referential use going back in time. The name may have even changed its pronunciation, spelling, etc., in the course of these transmissions. If we trace the chain back to the original name-giving, we find a certain individual; that this individual is the same individual that we find at the origin of another chain of linked uses, the chain ending with our present referring use of the name 'Tully', is empirical. But the name 'Cicero' is not synonymous with the *description* 'The individual dubbed at the origin of the chain which ends with my present use of "Cicero"'; rather it is that I use 'Cicero' as a *rigid designator* for a certain individual whom I am able to pick out by the – non-rigid – description.)

Formally, the principle, *if an identity statement containing rigidly used individual names, $A = B$, is true in one possible world then it is true in every possible world*, follows from an assumed formal property of the relation of trans-world identity, *transitivity*. The point is that even the investigation of the simplest identity statements in modal logic already leads to the realization that a statement which is obviously synthetic, 'Cicero is identical with Tully', must (given that it is true in the actual world) be true in every possible world, be 'metaphysically necessary'; and hence that metaphysically necessary epistemically contingent truths can exist. The temperature/mean molecular translational kinetic energy case is just an application of the same idea. (Another example, one Kripke himself gives, is 'Water is H_2O'. It is 'empirical' that water *is* H_2O; but given that water is H_2O, it must be H_2O in every possible world. When we discover the composition of water in the actual world, we also discover how a substance must be composed to *be* water, we discover the *essence* of water.)

David Lewis on counterfactual conditionals

One widely discussed application of the machinery of possible worlds, trans-world identities, etc., is the Stalnaker–Lewis theory of counterfactual conditionals. Such conditionals as 'If this light bulb were dropped, it would shatter', and 'If this light bulb were dropped, it would turn into a swan' would all be *true* if they were correctly symbolized by the logical formula '$p \Rightarrow q$'; for the truth table for the material conditional assigns the truth value *true* to all conditionals with false antecedents. Rather than accept so counterintuitive a conclusion, mathematical logicians reserve this logical form for the symbolization of ordinary indicative conditionals (e.g., 'If I drop the light bulb, it will break', uttered in a context in which I do not know whether the bulb will be dropped or not, and in which the interest in the prediction lapses once it is known that the antecedent is not true). The indicative conditional accurately expresses what we may call the *conditional assertion* of q (conditionally upon the assumption that p); calling it 'true' when p is false may be viewed as analogous to calling the number 1 the 'zeroeth power' of 2; something that at first looks arbitrary, but is actually forced by our desire to preserve certain mathematical or logical laws.

The problem is that when we talk about 'what would have happened if', we are not making a *conditional assertion that the light bulb will break* (or turn into a swan), conditional on its being dropped; an assertion that loses all interest when it is realized that the light bulb was not dropped; we *know* that the light bulb was not dropped (that is why it is a *counterfactual* conditional), and we want to know what is true in the hypothetical world in which it *was* dropped. The answer is evidently not to be determined from a knowledge of just the truth values of the antecedent and consequent; which is why the truth-functional conditional is not an adequate substitute for the subjunctive conditional in these contexts.

This problem has been discussed for over thirty years, and it is perhaps the hardest problem in the logical analysis of ordinary language. (Some logicians – e.g., Goodman and Quine – even deny that it *can* be solved; they regard the counterfactual conditional as hopelessly vague, and would rather eliminate it from scientific discourse altogether than attempt to analyze it.)

What David Lewis proposed (1973), elaborating an idea due to Robert Stalnaker (1968), is to analyze counterfactual conditionals by imposing a *metric* upon a Kripke structure. We are to think of possible worlds as more or less 'similar' or more or less 'close'. A counterfactual is true at a world just in case the consequent is true at all the *nearest* possible worlds in which the antecedent is true. If all the possible worlds in which the light bulb is dropped inside a certain neighborhood of the actual world are worlds in which it breaks, then the counterfactual 'if the light bulb had been dropped, it would have broken', is true.

The great advantage of this suggestion is that, if it is correct, then it enables one to determine for the first time which inferences involving counterfactuals are valid. For example, one can see why the inference

$$\frac{p \Rightarrow q}{\text{(therefore) } pr \Rightarrow q}$$

which is valid for the ordinary indicative conditional (*if p, then q*; therefore, *if p and r, then q*) becomes invalid if the conditional is replaced by a counterfactual one ('If Jones had jumped off the roof he would have been killed' does not imply 'If Jones had jumped off the roof and the roof had been only two meters above the ground, then he would have been killed'). When we evaluate 'If Jones had jumped off the roof he would have been killed', we look at possible worlds in which Jones jumped off the roof. If all the *most similar* worlds of this kind – all of the worlds of this kind 'less than a certain distance' from the actual world – are worlds in which Jones is killed, then the conditional is true. Assuming that the building was actually 100 meters tall, and that we regard worlds in which the building was only two meters tall as very dissimilar to the actual world, then the truth value of 'Jones is killed' in worlds in which Jones jumps off the roof *and* the roof is only 2 meters above the ground does not even enter into the calculation. But the second conditional can only be evaluated by looking at the truth value of 'Jones is killed' in the nearest worlds of precisely this kind, no matter how 'far' they may be from the actual world.

Further applications of possible worlds theory and of the Stalnaker–Lewis semantics for counterfactual conditionals have been made by Alvin Plantinga (1974), whose book is one of the best introductions to this whole area.

David Lewis himself takes an extremely metaphysical attitude towards possible worlds: he believes in their *actual existence* (almost in physical space). In David Lewis' view there is *no distinguished actual world*; 'actual' is just what people in *each* possible world call their world. (Just as 'I' is not the name of a unique distinguished individual, but is just what *each* individual calls himself.) This ontologically extravagant view is *not* shared by Kripke or other workers in the field, who regard possible worlds simply as abstract entities, hypothetical situations, not real 'parallel worlds'.

Problems with 'similarity'

The crucial notion in the Stalnaker–Lewis theory is the notion of similarity of possible worlds. This notion is not free from problems, however. Consider a simple counterfactual, say 'If the pencil were a foot to the left, the mirror image of the pencil would be displaced to the left' (i.e., to the 'right' from the point of view of my mirror image). This remark might occur in, say, a discussion of optics (imagine a pencil sitting in front of a mirror on the desk). If we imagine a world in which the same laws of nature hold as in the actual world, but in which the pencil is now a foot to the left, then different things would have had to happen in the past. Indeed, since this other world would have been different from the actual world *arbitrarily far back in time*, and since these different past events would have had consequences which would affect the present, it may be that in that world the speaker would not have been born, or, more relevantly, the mirror would not exist, or would be in a different place altogether.

What this shows, Lewis claims, is that what we consider the 'most similar worlds' for the purpose of calculating the truth value of *this* counterfactual are *not* worlds in which the same laws of nature hold (without exception) as in the actual world. What we do in our imagination is consider a world which is just like the actual world up to, say, a second ago. We imagine that at this time (one second ago) a 'small miracle' takes place, and the pencil is magically displaced one foot to the left. In short, we maximize over-all similarity to the actual world, while making the antecedent of the counterfactual true, that the pencil is one foot to the left, by 'tinkering' with the actual world at one point (one second ago), and then letting the laws of nature operate without further interference from 'miracles'.

There are problems with this 'small miracle' technique, however. For example, light takes time to travel from the pencil to the mirror. So, if the most similar world to the actual world in which the pencil is one foot to the left is the one in which the 'small miracle' just described took place, then it looks as if the counterfactual 'If the pencil were a foot to the left, then one second ago its image would have been exactly where it is' should be true (because it would still be the light rays from before the 'small miracle' that would be producing the image one second ago); but this counterfactual is intuitively false, not true.

Lewis' response this time is to say that the 'small miracle' depends on which counterfactual we are considering. (For example, it is not true that 'If the pencil had been a foot to the left, then a second ago people would have exclaimed that a small miracle has taken place: the pencil moved', because if we are considering *this* counterfactual, then we imagine a possible world in which the pencil magically changed location by one foot *and* people's memories about where the pencil had been also changed accordingly; or, perhaps, we put the 'small miracle' still further back in time.) Since the 'small miracle' is determined by the similarity metric and vice versa (the world we want is the 'most similar' to the actual world in the relevant sense), this means that *we use different similarity metrics for different counter-factuals*, even for different counterfactuals with the same antecedent.

In particular, if we are talking about where the mirror image would have been one second ago, then we put the 'small miracle' still further back in time, *assuming that we know light takes a finite time to travel*.

At this point we run into a possible objection to the significance of what Stalnaker and Lewis have done: *the vagueness objection*. The 'similarity metric' is not, obviously, an objective metric in the way that the metric of space–time is often thought to be objective. It is a subjective metric, one determined by our actual intuitions about the relative closeness of possible worlds. And these intuitions fluctuate, as Lewis admits. It is, therefore, possible to doubt whether counter-factuals really have a clear truth value, even if the theory is right; perhaps we have only explained the obscure through the obscure.

In this connection, it should be emphasized that Lewis himself is a strong metaphysical realist. (We have already referred to his realist interpretation of existence of possible worlds.) Lewis subscribes to the correspondence theory of truth; he regards statements as true or false – absolutely true or absolutely false (apart, of course, from cases of vagueness) – whether or not humans are or ever will be in a position to discover which they are. And this realism extends to counterfactuals; he sees himself as defining the truth value of a counterfactual (in this realist sense), not its assertibility or rational acceptability. But can one define a notion of the *truth value* of a counterfactual, in this strong realist sense, in terms of a similarity metric (or a collection of similarity metrics) which is admittedly subjective?

Notice that, in our examples, the need for a knowledge of the relevant laws of nature manifested itself at two points. In the case of the second counterfactual, 'If the pencil were one foot to the left, then one second ago its image would have been exactly where it is', Lewis' technique calls for a 'small miracle' a little further back than one second ago, so there will be time for the light to travel from the new position to the mirror. (Otherwise this counterfactual would come out true, not false, and clearly it is false.) But this assumes some knowledge of the speed of light. In general, we need to know the laws of physics to know when and where to put the 'small miracle'. And we need to know the laws of physics again to compute the consequences of the 'small miracle' in the hypothetical situation.

Now, it is perfectly possible that the relevant laws of physics may refer to micro-structures as far down as quarks, or even farther. Indeed, the true laws of physics may not even be intelligible to human beings. That our subjective similarity metric takes care of arbitrarily complex differences between possible worlds – differences which we may have *no* 'intuitions' about, because we can't even conceptualize them – seems unbelievable. Of course, this is just an extension of the vagueness objection.

If we are willing to give up the project of defining the truth value of a counterfactual, in the strong realist sense, and to content ourselves with defining conditions of *warranted assertibility* or *rational acceptibility*, however, then it seems to me that Lewis' ideas may be of value. As it stands, they can hardly be regarded as a solution to the problem of giving a semantics for counterfactuals; but they are certainly an important contribution.

Problems with 'essence'

Kripke's claim that, once we have discovered the composition of water in the actual world to be H_2O, we refuse to call hypothetical substances of a very different composition 'water', even if their (hypothetical) superficial properties are similar to those of water, seems correct. But the claim that the statement 'Water is H_2O' is true in all possible worlds is far too strong. Consider a possible world in which water exists only in the form of H_6O_3 molecules: Kripke may object that this example is not fair: 'Water is H_2O' is oversimplified even in the actual world (such molecules as H_4O_2, H_6O_3 actually exist), and his theory is that the composition of water in the actual world determines its composition in all possible worlds. But even if, say, $H_{20}O_{10}$ could not exist in the actual world, I think we would call a substance with similar properties which consisted of $H_{20}O_{10}$ molecules in some possible world 'water'.

Again, consider a world in which the laws of physics are slightly different, and in which hydrogen and oxygen do not exist *separately*. What we call 'oxygen atoms' and 'hydrogen atoms' are not stable bound states, but the whole 'H_2O molecule' is. It is clear that *water* exists in that world; but it is not clear that 'Water is H_2O' is true in that world (because there are no such *chemical substances* as *hydrogen* and *oxygen* in *that* world).

What Kripke wants to say that is correct is that science does more than discover mere correlations. Science discovers that certain things *can* be, that certain things *must* be, etc. And once we have discovered the chemical composition of water in the actual world to be H_2O (actually to be a quantum-mechanical superposition of H_2O, H_4O_2, H_6O_3 ... plus D_2O, D_4O_2, ...) we do not call any other actual or hypothetical substance 'water' unless it is *similar in composition* to this. But 'similar in composition' is a somewhat vague notion; saying that 'Water is H_2O', or any such sentence, is 'true in all possible worlds' seems an oversimplification.

Even the temperature/mean molecular translational kinetic energy case is over simplified. Temperature *is* mean molecular translational kinetic energy in the case of substances that consist of molecules. But the concept of temperature has been extended, for example to radiation. And who knows how much further it might be extended in application to hypothetical situations? (Speaking in terms of properties rather than 'concepts': it is doubtful that temperature *is* one single property in the case of both molecules and radiation. Even the extension from gases in which the velocity distribution of the

63

molecules is a Maxwell distribution to molecules with other distributions was a complex achievement of late nineteenth-century physics).

These examples suggest that the 'essence' that physics discovers is better thought of as a sort of *paradigm* that other applications of the concept ('water', or 'temperature') must *resemble* than as a necessary and sufficient condition good in all possible worlds. This should have been apparent already from Quine's criticism of the analytic–synthetic distinction. A notion such as temperature is controlled by many laws, notably by the Second law of thermodynamics; if we come to a possible world in which the laws are slightly different so that mean translational energy of molecules does not obey the Second law, while a slightly modified definition does, then the 'definition' of temperature may be changed in order to keep the Second law. Kripke would grant this point as far as *epistemic* necessity is concerned; but it also affects his 'metaphysical necessity', because it affects what we shall count as a relevant similarity to the paradigm case.

Kripke on 'individual essence'

The most controversial part of Kripke's theory, however, is certainly the part that deals with the notion of the essence of an *individual*.

We recall that in Kripke's modal logic individuals can be identified across possible worlds: this is how we are enabled to represent the fact that Aristotle could have been born in Athens instead of Stagirus. But there clearly have to be some bounds on this: it is clearly false that Aristotle could have been a glass bottle. Determining which individuals in other possible worlds are trans-world identical with Aristotle is precisely determining what Aristotle's *essence* is, what properties a thing must have to *be* Aristotle. And that *this* metaphysical notion too can be rehabilitated has seemed too much to take to many present-day philosophers.

Kripke's solution to the problem of individual essence is to take composition and causal continuity as the essential features. Thus a possible individual which comes from the same fertilized egg as Aristotle (i.e., from a fertilized egg with the same composition and the same identical atoms), but with a different life history from Aristotle, is a possible Aristotle: an individual with Aristotle's name, physical appearance, and character traits, who develops from a different fertilized egg is not Aristotle but only a person who resembles Aristotle. And if the boards from the original ship of Theseus are saved and a perfect copy of the original ship is constructed, identical in composition with the original ship, the copy is not the ship of Theseus because it does not have the requisite sort of causal continuity with the original ship.

To illustrate the theory with an example that Kripke has often used in lectures: one can truly say (assume there is a lectern on the desk), 'This lectern could have been painted black', but if 'this lectern' is being used 'rigidly' (i.e., if 'this lectern' really means *this very lectern*), then 'This lectern could have been made of ice' is false. This very lectern could not have been made of ice, although 'the lectern on this desk could have been made of ice' is true if understood to mean 'there could have been a lectern made of ice on this desk'. ('The lectern on this desk', in this last sentence, is what we called a 'non-rigid' description; it refers to different individuals in different possible worlds.)

To me, it does not seem that Kripke's theory is *so* very metaphysical. Rather it seems to me to be what Carnap would have called an 'explication' a *convention* which has some intuitive appeal and which enables us to systematize our pre-analytic use of such modal assertions as 'Aristotle could have been born in Athens', 'Aristotle might not have been a philosopher', 'Aristotle could not have been an inkwell', etc.

Intuitions may, however, differ very much on just these sorts of statements. Ayer has suggested (in an unpublished lecture) that there is nothing wrong with such a modal assertion as 'Aristotle could have been Chinese', although this violates Kripke's theory.

Still, if we are willing to say that natural laws tell us what can and cannot be the case, why should this not also extend to knowledge about what individuals could and could not be or do? Once we accept it that what human beings are is rivers of matter with a certain causal continuity and a certain functional organization, is this not bound to have an effect on what modal statements we shall regard as true? To a believer in the soul, there is nothing odd about 'Aristotle could have been Chinese' (that same soul could have been in a Chinese body); but if the actual Aristotle is a river of matter with a certain causal history, then he could not have been Chinese without having different *genes*. And a possible individual with different *genes* is a *different* individual from the actual Aristotle. (Also, if humans in the actual world do not have separable souls, then beings in any possible world who do have souls which can inhabit different bodies, or become disembodied, and whose personality resides in these souls and not in their brains, would not be identical with any individuals in the actual world, even if they resembled individuals in the actual world. If I do not have a separable soul in the actual world, *then I myself could not have had a separable soul.*)

Ayer would not be satisfied with this reply because Ayer does not think that natural laws tell us what objectively could or could not be the case; natural laws are, for him, only true generalizations towards which we have a certain attitude. This is, of course, just Hume's view of natural necessity; the argument against it is that it does not do justice to the *objectivity* of natural laws. For example, most scientists and most philosophers would not agree that it is only a statement about our 'attitude' that one cannot build a perpetual motion machine. But this discussion goes beyond the bounds of the present article.

It should be remarked that there are also possible alternatives to Kripke's theory within the same general framework: for example, a number of authors have suggested replacing the notion of trans-world identity with a notion of *sortal* identity (identity restricted to a predicate, for example, 'man', 'statue', 'piece of bronze'). We would say of a piece of bronze that is shaped into a statue in one possible world and not in another that it is 'the same piece of bronze' in both worlds, but not 'the same statue'. It makes no sense, in sortal identity theories, to ask if two individuals are the same, *simpliciter*; one always has to answer the question, 'the same *what?*'.

It may also be desirable to investigate giving up the assumption that trans-world identity is *transitive*.

Problems about Platonism

Some philosophers have recently gone overboard with possible worlds talk (some philosophers go overboard whenever there is a new fad or fashion in philosophy), and seen possible worlds formalization as a kind of magical way of making progress with almost every philosophical problem. This is disturbing in view of the unclarity of the foundations of the notion of a 'possible world' itself. In particular, if we assume that possible worlds are well-defined entities, abstract or even concrete (although only David Lewis seems willing to opt for the latter alternative), and that there is a well-defined totality of *all* possible worlds, then things become very murky. Is there a definite totality of *all possible objects*? A totality of *all possible predicates*? A totality of *all possible thoughts*? Not only are such 'totalities' likely to lead to antinomies (compare the Russell paradox, and the Grelling paradox of 'the least number not nameable in fewer than eighteen syllables', which we have just named in seventeen syllables!), but they pose formidable epistemological difficulties.

Some philosophers shrug these off by arguing, in effect, that if it is all right to quantify over 'all sets' in Zermelo–Frankel set theory, then it is all right to quantify over 'all possible worlds' in possible worlds theory. But set theory is mathematics, not *philosophy*. If we quantify over 'all sets' and interpret this quantification in a naive Platonist way, then there are plenty of problems from a philosophical point of view: notably, how we are supposed to have epistemic access to this Platonic heaven of sets we pretend to be describing. And, similarly, if we quantify over 'all possible worlds' and interpret this quantification in a naive Platonist way, then how are we supposed to have epistemic access to this Platonic heaven of possible worlds?

The question is: is it an advance in philosophy or rather a retreat from clarity, from analysis, from every kind of epistemological progress, to explicate such problematical notions as the modalities and the counterfactual conditional in terms of a wholly metaphysical totality of 'all possible worlds'?

While this question seems to such nominalistically minded philosophers as Nelson Goodman to be a sufficient reason for abandoning possible worlds theory entirely as philosophically irrelevant, to me the case does not seem so desperate as this. Whatever some philosophers may think about possible worlds, the work we have described (which, to be sure, is not free from problems, but then philosophical work by its very nature cannot hope to be unproblematical) does not require such Platonist assumptions. If we think of possible worlds as simply possible states of affairs relative to some fixed language (as what Carnap called 'state descriptions'), then they do not seem to be overly suspicious entities, and such language-relative possible worlds seem to be all that is required for either the Lewis theory of counterfactuals (though not, perhaps, on the very strong realist presumptions that we discussed above) or the Kripke theories that we reviewed. What makes 'possible worlds' dubious is the attempt to make them wholly independent of the linguistic frame we use to talk about possible states of affairs, or 'hypothetical situations'; but why should one make this attempt?

It is, of course, evident that one cannot explain the notion of *possibility* itself in terms of possible worlds. But that does not mean that the work we have described does nothing to clarify the notion. If we take the view that possible worlds are basically linguistic objects (say, maximal consistent sets of sentences in some language, or some subset of these), then Kripke's work reminds us that not *every* maximal consistent set of sentences can be regarded as a 'possible world'. Just as we would not call an actual liquid that we discovered tomorrow 'water' if it did not have the composition of water, so we do not describe a hypothetical liquid as 'water' if it has a different composition from the water in the actual world (beyond the limits of the 'similarity to the paradigm' we suggested as a reformulation of Kripke's requirement above). So our mechanisms of reference serve to determine not only what is actually water, but also what is possibly water. Discovering such a link between theory of reference and theory of possibility may not tell us what possibility *is* in some once-and-for-all sense, but it is surely a major contribution.

What is presupposed, rather than clarified, in all this is the notion of logical possibility and the extent to which worlds with different logics are possible. Possible worlds theory assumes the notion of logical possibility; it does not do anything for the philosophy of logic. But it is no criticism of an important philosophical idea that it does not solve all problems.

4

Reference and truth

Russell on reference and truth

According to Bertrand Russell's view in *Problems of Philosophy*, we have two kinds of knowledge: *knowledge by acquaintance* and *knowledge by description*. Knowledge by acquaintance is limited to sense data (for Russell, sense data were themselves *qualities*, and were thus universals rather than particulars; but the details of his theory are not relevant here). Sense data can be *directly* apprehended and named according to Russell; only in the case of sense data can we be certain *that* a name refers and certain of *what* it refers to. These names – names of sense data of which we have knowledge by acquaintance – Russell called 'logically proper names'.

Of other sorts of things we have knowledge by description. I can know that there was such a person as Julius Caesar, even though I do not have knowledge by acquaintance of Julius Caesar, because I can describe Julius Caesar as 'the Roman general who was named "Julius", who defeated Pompey, who crossed the Rubicon, etc.' (Of course, these clauses should be reformulated so as to contain only logically proper names: a difficult problem for Russell.)

Russell's view can be restated as a view about the reference of terms as follows.

(1) There are two sorts of terms: *basic* terms and *defined* terms.
(2) The defined terms are synonymous with *descriptions*, i.e., expressions of the form 'The one and only entity which...'. (Russell's celebrated 'theory of descriptions' showed how to translate descriptions into the notation of symbolic logic.)
(3) Basic terms refer to things to which we have some sort of epistemic access.

It can also be said that Russell held a *correspondence theory of truth*: i.e., he held that (*a*) assertions correspond to states of affairs; they are true if the corresponding state of affairs obtains, and false if it does not; (*b*) our *understanding* of an assertion consists in our knowledge of what state of affairs corresponds to it; (*c*) this grasp is made possible by the fact that the ultimate constituents of any assertion are logically proper names, and we have knowledge by acquaintance of what logically proper names refer to.

Parts of Russell's theory were problematic from the start, and were abandoned or modified even by him. The idea that all meaningful assertions can be reduced to assertions about sense data was later given up. But if we do not stipulate that the basic terms must refer to sense data, and we leave open the nature of the 'epistemic access' in (3), then many philosophers still subscribed to (1), (2), (3) until very recently (perhaps many still do). Similarly, while (c) in our statement of Russell's form of the correspondence theory of truth was later given up, most philosophers to the present day would probably accept (a) and (b).

In this account, 'term' has meant 'singular term', i.e., we have been talking about expressions such as 'Julius Caesar', 'Everest', 'The Evening Star', which purport to designate just one thing. Russell also held the view that general names such as 'horse' or 'gold' are synonymous with other expressions, namely with conjunctions of clauses expressing necessary and sufficient conditions for membership in the relevant class. For example, 'gold' was thought to be synonymous with 'heavy, incorruptible, precious, yellow metal which is soluble in *aqua regia*', or something of that kind.

Russell's theory thus said something about the kinds of terms there are (basic and defined) and how they refer, something about the nature of reference (namely, that it is a relation between terms and discourse-independent objects), and something about the nature of truth and falsity (the correspondence theory). These topics have become separated in more recent philosophical discussion; but we shall find that each of them is still hotly discussed.

The 'new theory of reference'; myself and Kripke

In a series of publications Saul Kripke and I independently proposed a number of similar and closely related views which collectively add up to a sustained assault on the 'traditional' views of Russell.

My views grew out of my work on the philosophy of mind as well as work on the philosophy of language. In 'Dreaming and "depth grammar"' (1962b), I attacked the idea that a general name is synonymous with a set of necessary and sufficient conditions for class membership. Using the example of 'multiple sclerosis', I wrote:

What we should like to say is this: there is (we presume) in the world something – say, a virus – which normally causes such-and-such symptoms. Perhaps other diseases occasionally (rarely) produce these same symptoms in a few patients. When a patient has these symptoms we say he has 'multiple sclerosis' – but, of course, we are prepared to say that we are mistaken if the etiology turns out to have been abnormal. And we are prepared to classify sicknesses as cases of multiple sclerosis, even if the symptoms are rather deviant, if it turns out that the *underlying condition* was the virus that causes multiple sclerosis, and that the deviancy in the symptoms was, say, random variation. On this view the question of interest is not, so to speak, the 'extension' of the term 'multiple sclerosis, but what, if anything, *answers* to our notion of multiple sclerosis. When we know what answers to our criteria (more or less perfectly), *that* – whatever it is – will be the 'extension' of 'multiple sclerosis'.   (310–11)

In this paragraph, one of the central ideas of what has been called 'the new theory of reference' appears: the idea that the extension of certain kinds of terms (later I was to speak of 'natural kind words', meaning names for such things as natural substances, species, and physical magnitudes) is not fixed by a set of 'criteria' laid down in advance, but is, in part, *fixed by the world*. There are *objective laws* obeyed by multiple sclerosis, by gold, by horses, by electricity; and what it is rational to include in these classes will depend on what those laws turn out to be.

It is because we do not know these laws exactly that we have to leave the extension of these classes somewhat open, rather than fixing it exactly by making the terms synonymous with sets of necessary and sufficient conditions. The extension of 'multiple sclerosis' includes whatever illnesses turn out to be *of the same nature* as the majority of the 'paradigm' cases of multiple sclerosis; we do not suppose that what that nature is (what the laws are) is completely known to us in advance. Paradigms and research programs for finding laws (or improving the accuracy of the laws we have) take the place of rigid necessary and sufficient conditions in determining extension, on this picture.

In 'Identity and necessity' (1971) and 'Naming and necessity' (1972) Saul Kripke attacked the Russell account of proper names. According to Kripke, it is *not the case* that 'Julius Caesar' is synonymous with some such description as 'the Roman general who was named "Julius", who defeated Pompey, who crossed the Rubicon, etc....'

In chapter 3 we described Kripke's theory of possibility. We recall that it makes sense to say 'Julius Caesar might not have been named "Julius"' (his parents might have named him 'Marcus' instead). Similarly, it makes sense to utter the statements (and the statements are true, both on Kripke's theory and on our pre-analytic intuitions about the matter), 'Caesar might not have defeated Pompey', 'Caesar might not have crossed the Rubicon', etc. But none of these statements could express a possibility if 'Julius Caesar' *meant* 'The one and only individual who was a Roman general, was named "Julius Caesar", defeated Pompey, crossed the Rubicon, etc...'. For, if 'Julius Caesar' is synonymous with this description, then *he would not have been Julius Caesar if he had not defeated Pompey*. But this is clearly false.

Kripke's account (summarized in chapter 3) was that an individual in any possible world who has the same parents as the actual Julius Caesar, and comes from the same fertilized egg is a possible Julius Caesar even if, in the possible world in question, he has a different life history than the actual Julius Caesar, is given a different name, etc. This explains the possibility of such statements as 'Julius Caesar might not have been named "Julius".' But it leaves us with the problem of giving an account of the meaning of the name 'Julius Caesar', since the Russell account has turned out to be false.

Kripke's theory of possibility identifies individuals across possible worlds on the basis of origin and history. These same factors – origin and history – are the factors that play the decisive role in Kripke's account of the functioning of names.

A name is originally given to a person, say by 'baptizing' that person. Later people use the name with the intention of referring to whoever was earlier known by that name (or by a variant of the name, since names change pronunciation and spelling in the course of time) by particular people in particular contexts. Given that a successful 'naming ceremony' was performed to begin with, and that the right sort of continuity in the later use of the name exists, we may treat the name 'Moses' as used today as referring to the individual to whom the original form of the name (which was something like 'Moshe') was given at the appropriate naming ceremony: the ceremony at the other end of the causal chain which terminates in our present use on the relevant occasion.

This does not mean that 'Moses' is *synonymous with the description* 'The person who was given the name "Moshe" at the naming ceremony which is connected (by the right kind of causal chain) with my present use of the name "Moses".' It means that we use that description, implicitly, to pick out the individual who will be called 'Moses' by us even when we speak of possible worlds in which he does not satisfy the description we use to pick him out in the actual world. We use descriptions to indicate who or what we are referring to, indeed; but this does not mean the names we use are synonymous with those descriptions, for the names have different logical properties (enter into different true contrary-to-fact conditionals) than the descriptions we employ to single out the bearers of the names.

In 'Is semantics possible?' (1970b) and in a more extended form in 'The meaning of "meaning"' (1975a) I made points about natural kind words which have a certain relation to these observations about proper names. The use of a word such as 'gold' depends on our possessing *paradigms*, standard examples that are agreed to be model members of the kind. (Of course, some of them may turn out upon investigation to differ in nature from most of the others; if this happens, they no longer count as paradigms.) What makes something gold is having the same nature as the paradigms; in current physical theory this is unpacked as having the same composition, since it is the atomic composition that determines the law-like behavior of a substance.

To take another example, consider the kind *lemon*. There are lemons which are green rather than yellow; and there could well be a citrus fruit which was yellow and *not* a lemon. What makes something a lemon is having the same nature (e.g., the same DNA) as paradigm lemons, and not fulfilling some set of criteria (yellow color, thick peel, tart taste,...) laid down in advance. Natural kinds do not have analytic definitions.

The relation to Kripke's account of proper names is this: in both accounts things which are given *existentially* and not by criteria help to fix reference. Actual things, whatever their description, which have played a certain causal role in our acquisition and use of terms determine what the terms refer to. A term refers to something if it stands in the right relation (causal continuity in the case of proper names; sameness of 'nature' in the case of kinds terms) to these existentially given things. In the case of proper names, the existentially given thing is the person or thing originally 'baptized' with the name; in the case of natural kind words, the existentially given things are the actual paradigms.

A second relation is that what the right sort of causal continuity is, and what sharing a nature is, is determined by our evolving theories of the objective nature of persons and of the several sorts of natural kinds, and not *a priori*.

As mentioned in chapter 3, Kripke takes the view that once we discover that *actual* water is H_2O, we refuse to call possible (hypothetical) substances of a different chemical composition *water*, even if they superficially resemble water. If we take it that it is the *local* (terrestrial) water whose nature determines the 'essence' of water (i.e., determines what it is to be water in any 'possible world'), then this account agrees totally with mine. And my point that natural kind terms cannot be analytically defined is also made by Kripke, and for similar reasons.

The philosophical significance of the new theory of reference

Part of the significance of the 'new theory of reference' (the name is due to Schwartz (1977), whose book is one of the best general references on this topic) has already been pointed out; by denying that proper names and natural kind words are synonymous with definite descriptions or conjunctions of criteria, the new theory makes possible the kind of theory of necessity described in chapter 3. This theory rehabilitates the notion that things and kinds have *essences*, i.e., that there are characteristics that something must have to be the thing (or the sort of thing) that it is, while freeing that notion from its connection with aprioristic epistemology.

But the new theory also has importance in a quite different direction, as David Wiggins (1980) has seen.

The two key ideas of the new theory are:

(1) To belong to a natural kind, something must have the same composition, or obey the same laws – indeed, what makes composition important, when it is, is its connection with laws of behavior – as model members of the class, and this composition or these laws are not usually known when the natural kind term is introduced, but require an indeterminate amount of investigation to discover.
(2) Natural kind terms and proper names are not synonymous with conjunctions of criteria and definite descriptions respectively.

The Kripke theory of necessity involves both (1) and (2), as we have seen. But (1) by itself is of philosophic interest.

What (1) says is that *the natural kinds themselves* play a role in determining the extensions of the terms that refer to them. David Wiggins has pointed out that this means that there is a great difference between natural kind terms, which involve the hypothesis of a 'nature', or set of objective laws, be they laws of behavior, or laws of 'coming to be and passing away', or laws of development of a typical member of a biological species, and what he calls 'artifactual' terms. 'Artifactual terms' are terms such as *table*, or *television set*. These refer to objects whose nature we know completely because they are invented and designed by us; we can give sets of necessary and sufficient conditions for belonging to the extension of such a term, according to Wiggins. Wiggins points out that the drawing of a sharp distinction between artifacts and members of natural kinds in this way is a kind of rehabilitation of the Aristotelian notion of a *substance*. (A living organism is Aristotle's favorite example of a substance; an artifact, e.g., an axe, is a substance only in a derivative sense, Aristotle said.) Wiggins also applies this distinction to moral philosophy: he sees an important difference between positions which treat the term 'person' as an artifactual term (i.e., *we* determine *conventionally* the conditions for personhood) and positions which treat the term as a natural kind term.

I call the feature emphasized by Wiggins the *contribution of the environment*. As I see it, 'meanings aren't in the head'; the actual nature of the paradigms enters into fixing reference, and not just the concepts in our heads. Another important feature of both Kripke's theory and mine is that reference is determined *socially*. To determine whether or not something is really gold a native speaker may have to consult an expert, who knows the nature of gold better than the average person does. The chain of historic transmissions which preserve the reference of a proper name in the Kripke theory is another form of social cooperation in the fixing of reference. The idea that the extensions of our terms are fixed by collective practices and not by concepts in our individual heads is a sharp departure from the way meaning has been viewed ever since the seventeenth century.

Tarski's theory of truth

We turn now from the topic of reference to the topic of truth. We shall start with the work of Alfred Tarski (1933) one of the greatest modern logicians. (I repeat now the account in Putnam (1976).)

Although it requires a certain amount of sophisticated logic to present Tarski's theory properly, one of the leading ideas, the idea of 'disquotation', is easy to explain. Take any sentence: say, *Snow is white*. Put quotation marks around that sentence, thus:
'Snow is white.'
Now adjoin the words 'is true', thus:
'Snow is white' is true.
The resulting sentence is itself one which is true if and only if the original sentence is true. It is, moreover, *assertible* if and only if the original sentence is assertible; it is probable to degree r if and only if the original sentence is probable to degree r; etc. According to

75

Tarski, Carnap, Quine, Ayer, and similar theorists, knowing these facts is the key to understanding the words 'is true'. In short, to understand *P is true*, where *P* is a sentence in quotes, just 'disquote' *P*: take off the quotation marks (and erase 'is true').

For example, what does

'Snow is white' is true

mean? It means

snow is white.

What does

'There is a real external world' is true

mean? It means

there is a real external world.

And so on.

The claim that 'disquotation' theorists are advancing is that an answer to the question *what does it mean to say* that something is true need not commit itself to a view about what that something in turn means or about how that something is or is not to be verified. You can have a materialist interpretation of 'Snow is white'; you can believe 'Snow is white' is verifiable, or that it is only falsifiable but not verifiable; or that it is only confirmable to a degree between zero and one; or none of the foregoing; but 'Snow is white' is still equi-assertible with '"Snow is white" is true'. On this view, 'true' is, amazingly, a *philosophically neutral* notion. 'True' is just a device for 'semantic ascent': for 'raising' assertions from the 'object language' to the 'metalanguage', and the device does not commit one epistemologically or metaphysically.

We shall now sketch the second leading idea of Tarski's theory. 'True' is a predicate of sentences in Tarski's theory; and these sentences have to be in some formalized language L, if the theory is to be made precise. (How to extend the theory to natural languages is today a great topic of concern among philosophers and linguists.) Now a 'language' in this sense has a *finite* number of undefined or 'primitive' predicates. For simplicity, let us suppose our language L has only two primitive predicates: 'is the moon' and 'is blue'. For predicates P, the locution

P refers to x

whose intimate connection with the word 'true' can be brought out by using the phrase 'is true of' instead of 'refers to', thus:

P is true of x

can also be explained by employing the idea of disquotation: if P is the predicate 'is the moon' we have:

'Is the moon' refers to x if and only if x is the moon.

And if P is the predicate 'is blue' we have:

'Is blue' refers to x if and only if x is blue.

So the 'metalinguistic' prediction:

'Is the moon' refers to x

is equivalent to the 'object-language' predication:

x is the moon.

Let us say P *primitively refers* to x if P is a primitive predicate (in the case of our language L, 'is the moon' or 'is blue') and P refers to x. Then *primitive reference* can be defined *for our particular example* L by giving a list:

Definition:

P *primitively refers to* x if and only if (1) P is the phrase 'is the moon' and x is the moon, or (2) P is the phrase 'is blue' and x is blue.

And for any *particular formalized language* a similar definition of primitive reference can be given, once we have been given a list of the primitive predicates of that language.

The rest of Tarski's idea requires logic and mathematics to explain properly. We shall be *very* sketchy now.

The non-primitive predicates of a language are built up out of primitive ones by various devices: truth functions and quantifiers. Suppose, for the sake of an example, that the only devices are disjunction and negation: forming the predicates 'P or Q', and 'not-P' from the predicate P. Then we define reference as follows:

(I) If P contains zero logical connectives, P *refers to* x if P primitively refers to x.

(II) P *or Q refers to* x if P refers to x or Q refers to x.

(III) *Not-P refers to* x if P does not refer to x.

Turning this inductive definition into an explicit definition is where much of the technical logic comes in; suffice it to say this can be done. The result is a definition of 'reference' *for a particular language*, a *definition which uses no semantical words* (no words in the same family as 'true' and 'refers').

The technique for defining the *ancestral F^** of a relation F, which was invented by Frege, is the main technique Tarski used in putting such 'inductive' definitions into the form of explicit definitions. This technique requires quantifying over arbitrary sets and relations over the universe of discourse of the language for which 'truth' is being defined; thus the explicit definition of 'true in L' is always given in a language which has a stronger set theory than L itself.

Finally, supposing that our simple language is so simple that all sentences are of the forms *For every x, Px, For some x, Px*, or truth functions of these (where *P* is a predicate), then *true* would be defined as follows (of course, Tarski actually considered much richer languages):

(I') *For every x, Px* is *true* if and only if, for every *x*, *P* refers to *x*.

(II') *For some x, Px* is *true* if and only if, for some *x*, *P* refers to *x*.

(III') If *p* and *q* are sentences, *p or q* is *true* if *p* is true or *q* is true; and *not-p* is true if *p* is not true.

While we have left out the mathematics of Tarski's work (how one turns an 'inductive definition' like the above into an 'explicit' definition of the form 'something is true if and only if...', where 'true' and 'refers' do not occur in '...') and we have ignored the immense complications which arise when the language has *relations* – two-place (or three-place, etc.) predicates – we have tried to convey three ideas:

(1) 'Truth' and 'reference' are defined *for one particular language at a time*. We are not defining the relation 'true in *L*' for *variable L*.

(2) Primitive reference is defined 'by a list'; and reference and truth in general are defined by induction on the number of logical connectives in the predicate or sentence, starting with primitive reference.

(3) The 'inductive' definition by a system of clauses such as (I), (II), (III), (I'), (II'), (III'), can be turned into a *bona fide* 'explicit definition' by technical devices from logic.

As a check on the correctness of what has been done, it is easy to derive the following theorem from the definition of 'true':

'For some *x*, *x* is the moon' is true if and only if, for some *x*, *x* is the moon.

And in fact, one can derive from the definition of true that

(T) '*P*' is true if and only if *P*

when the dummy letter '*P*' is replaced by *any* sentence of our language L.

That this should be the case – that the above schema (T) be one all of whose instances are consequences of the definition of 'true' – is Tarski's 'criterion of adequacy' (the famous 'criterion (T)') for definitions of 'is true'.

Notice that while the idea of disquotation may initially strike one as trivial, Tarski's theory is obviously very non-trivial. The reason is that the idea of disquotation only tells us that the criterion (T) is correct; but it does not tell us how to define 'true' so that the criterion (T) will be satisfied. Nor does disquotation by itself enable us to eliminate 'true' from all the contexts in which it occurs. 'Snow is white' is true is equivalent to *Snow is white*; but to what sentence *not containing the word* 'true' (or any other 'semantical' term) is the following sentence equivalent: *If the premises in an inference of the form p or q, not-p, therefore q are both true in L the conclusion is also true in L?* Tarski's method gives us an equivalent for *this* sentence, and for other sentences in which 'is true' occurs with variables and quantifiers, and that is what disquotation by itself does not do.

Davidson on truth and meaning

According to the view just described, understanding the word 'true' poses no special problem, philosophical or otherwise. In the sentence '*Snow is white*' *is true*, for example, the meaning of the word true is captured by any definition of 'true in English' which satisfies Tarski's criterion (T); i.e., which yields all equivalences of the form:

'Snow is white' is true if and only if snow is white.

'Surely you understand "Snow is white"', philosophers who follow Tarski are prone to argue (if you don't, then it isn't just 'semantical' words such as 'true' and 'refers' that are your problem), 'and if you know that "*Snow is white*" *is true* is equivalent to "Snow is white", then you know all you need to know to understand "*Snow is white*" *is true.*'

Whatever the merits of this as an answer to philosophical problems about truth may be, it is clear that the idea is to take the non-semantical terms (the descriptive words of the object language and the logical vocabulary) as *understood*, and to use these non-semantical terms (and a stronger set theory than any available in the object language) to explain the meaning of 'true'. Donald Davidson, in an influential series of papers (beginning in 1967) has proposed an interesting reversal of this procedure.

Suppose we formalize English (or a suitable part of English), and give a truth definition for the resulting language à la Tarski. This will yield as theorems all sentences of the form:

'*P*' is true if and only if *P*,

for example, once again

(*a*) 'Snow is white' is true if and only if snow is white.

This truth definition need not be given in (a set-theoretically strengthened version of) English; it could be given, for example, in

German (plus enough set theory). In this case, the truth definition will yield all sentences of the form

'P' ist wahr wenn und nur wenn P',

where P' is the German translation of the English sentence P, for example:

(b) 'Snow is white' ist wahr wenn und nur wenn Schnee weiss ist.

Now, imagine a German speaker (Karl) who knows no English but who is told (b). Understanding the notion of truth (i.e., knowing what 'wahr' means), what (b) would tell him is the *meaning* of the English sentence 'Snow is white'. If he was told the truth definition for English, he could derive from it a sentence of the form 'P' *ist wahr wenn und nur wenn P'* (a 'T-sentence') corresponding to each sentence P of English, and thus figure out what every sentence of English means. (This does not mean the German speaker has to be given the *infinite* list of all T-sentences; what he is given is the truth *definition*, and this is a finite explicit definition.)

In sum, Davidson's idea is to *invert* Tarski's argument. Instead of taking 'true' as the word whose meaning is to be explained and the object language as understood, Davidson takes the object language as what is to be explained and 'true' (or whatever the word for truth is in the language in which the explanation is to be given) as what is already understood. In this way, any truth definition for a language (in Tarski's sense) can be viewed as a *meaning theory* for that language.

Davidson goes further and argues the converse; that any meaning theory for a language, i.e., any finite description which projects meanings for the infinitely many sentences of the language, is implicitly a truth definition for the language, and that the explicit Tarski form is the ideal form for formalized meaning theories. We shall not discuss these claims here, although they are a fascinating by-product of the discussion of the topic of truth by logicians and philosophers.

The question which is of interest here is this: what is the bearing of such a notion of meaning theory, or of such a conception of the connection between theory of truth and theory of meaning, on the nature of *understanding*?

Davidson's answer to this question is unhesitating: if the theory of meaning of a language is just the truth definition for that language, then, he argues, the understanding that the native speaker has of his own language is best described as *an implicit knowledge of that truth definition*. To understand a natural language (or a formalized language, for that matter) is implicitly to know the recursive truth definition for that language, for it is that recursion that assigns truth conditions to each and every one of the infinitely many sentences of the language.

At this point it may seem as if we have been given nothing less than the correspondence theory of truth. The truth definition for English tells Karl that 'Snow is white' is true if and only if snow is white (although Karl thinks this thought in German and not in English, by thinking the sentence we wrote as (*b*)); so Karl can answer the question, what state of affairs corresponds to the English sentence 'Snow is white', by replying 'that snow is white' (or in German, 'dass Schnee weiss ist'). It does seem as though each English sentence does correspond to a state of affairs which must obtain if the English sentence is to be true (and the truth definition tells us which). And the *understanding* of the English sentence does seem to consist (if Davidson is right) in the grasp of the conditions for the sentence to be true, or, rather, in the grasp of the definition which generates a T-sentence which specifies that condition. Can it be the case that Tarski and Davidson between them have succeeded in justifying and explicating the correspondence theory of truth?

Michael Dummett's non-realist theory of truth

To this question, Michael Dummett answers a resounding 'no'. (See Dummett, 1979*a*; a much more extended version of Dummett's views will appear when his Harvard William James Lectures (1976) are published.) The heart of the correspondence theory, Dummett contends, is the idea that the world consists of mind-independent objects and facts (or discourse-independent objects and facts, if you prefer). A sentence can be true, on the correspondence theory, only if such a fact *makes* it true; and our understanding of the sentence consists in our grasp of what the corresponding mind-independent state of affairs is. Neither Tarski's theory of truth (which is plainly philosophically neutral) nor Davidson's theory of what a meaning theory is has any bearing on the truth or falsity of these metaphysical views (although some confusion is engendered by the fact that Tarski said *both* that his theory was a reconstruction of the correspondence theory of truth *and* that it was philosophically neutral).

As far as Davidson's contention that the understanding of one's language consists in a knowledge of the truth theory of that language is concerned, Dummett's reply is that one must ask in what does this 'knowledge of the truth theory' *itself* consist?

One possible reply (not Davidson's) would be to say that it consists in this: the mind thinks, consciously or unconsciously, the statements (or judgments, or propositions, depending on which of the traditional philosophical terminologies one employs) that make up that truth theory. But then one must ask: *how* does the mind think these statements? Does it think them in words, or at least in thought-signs (mental representations) of some kind? Or is the mind somehow supposed to grasp what it is for snow to be white (for example) without the aid of mental representations of any kind?

If one takes the first alternative (which is the one any naturalistically minded philosopher or cognitive psychologist would have to take), then the question arises: in what does the mind's understanding of its own mental representations, its own 'medium of representation', consist? It will do no good to say, 'in its knowledge of truth conditions for the mental representations', for this will lead us immediately either to an infinite regress or to the recognition that some signs must be understood in a way for which the correspondence theory of truth gives no account.

On the other hand, the second alternative is just the myth that we can compare a sign (e.g., the sentence 'Snow is white', or some mental representation which stands behind that sign) directly with unconceptualized reality. The notion that 'grasping truth conditions' (e.g., grasping *what it is for snow to be white*) is *prior* to understanding the corresponding signs (understanding the sentence 'Snow is white' or some representation with the same meaning) is absurd.

Davidson himself avoids this absurd view. In his view, our understanding of the truth conditions for our language is implicit knowledge, not explicit knowledge or propositional knowledge of any kind, and it consists in our using the language in such a way that the truth conditions assigned by the T-sentences which follow from the meaning theory would be good *translations* of those sentences (assuming the operational and simplicity constraints of a theory of translation). But this makes it a *tautology* (as Davidson is aware) that if you *understand* the sentence 'Snow is white', as a sentence of English, then you 'implicitly know' that the truth condition of that sentence is that snow be white (dass Schnee weiss ist).

In other words, *whatever it may be* about our use of the English sentence 'Snow is white' that makes it correct to translate it by such sentences as 'Schnee ist weiss' in German, 'La neige est blanche' in French, etc., constitutes the implicit knowledge of the fact expressed by the T-sentence (*a*) (or any one of its correct translations into another language, e.g., (*b*) in German). This says it is our *use* of the sentence 'Snow is white' that constitutes 'implicit knowledge' of the truth condition; but no theory at all of that use is provided.

In short, Dummett's claim is that 'truth' in the sense of 'correspondence to a state of affairs which obtains' cannot play any *explanatory role* in an account of understanding. You can preserve the *verbal formula* 'If you understand a sentence then you know what its truth conditions are' by making it a tautology as Davidson does; but then it *certainly* isn't playing an explanatory role.

Dummett points out that the principle that to assert that a statement is true is equivalent to asserting the statement itself (he calls this *the equivalence principle*) was already stated by Frege. What Tarski has done is to give a method for constructing definitions of 'true in *L*', where *L* is a suitably formalized language, definitions which obey the equivalence principle. This is purely *formal* work: as such, it is equally correct whether one understands truth as a mathematical intuitionist like Brouwer does, or as a subscriber to the so-called coherence theory of truth does, or as a realist does, or whatever. Tarski's work *is* philosophically neutral; that is why it does not vindicate the correspondence theory of truth.

Dummett's own view is that we need *two* notions of truth in the philosophy of language. If we employ a medium of discourse *L*, then we can extend that medium to a so-called metalanguage *ML* which contains *L* and also contains a truth predicate for *L* by following the instructions Tarski gives. It will be a feature of *ML* that (just as a fact of *logic*) '*P*' *is true* is equivalent to *P*, if *P* is any sentence of *L*. If 'Snow is white' is a sentence of *L*, then, in this sense of 'true', it will be a fact of *logic* that that sentence is equivalent to '*Snow is white*' *is true*. This (Tarskian) sense of 'true' is called *the internal sense of 'true'* by Dummett (in the William James Lectures). Understanding this internal sense gives us only the equivalences we have referred to as 'T-sentences'; it does not tell us how *either* 'Snow is white' or '"Snow is white" is true' are understood, or under what conditions it would be *correct* to assert either.

The problem is not that we don't understand 'Snow is white', to respond to the elementary Tarskian ploy we mentioned earlier; the problem is that we don't understand *what it is to understand* 'Snow is white'. *This* is the philosophical problem.

But there is a sense of 'correct' in which to understand a sentence *is* to know when that sentence is correctly asserted, Dummett claims. If this sense is equated with correspondence to mind-independent states of affairs, as it is by the correspondence theory of truth, then we are driven to either an infinite regress or else to the myth of comparing signs directly with unconceptualized reality, as we saw. Dummett contends that truth (or 'correctness') in this sense is simply the epistemic notion of justification. 'A statement is true if its assertion would be justified.' Dummett calls this the *external* notion of truth. It is a non-realist sense (statements are not 'made true', in this sense of 'true', by mind-independent states of affairs, but by states of affairs *as perceived and conceptualized*); and it is in *this* sense of 'true' that to know the meaning of a sentence is to know under what conditions it is true.

But in what does this knowledge itself consist? to repeat Dummett's question to Davidson. Dummett's answer is that it consists in the actual behavioral skill of recognizing when the justification conditions are fulfilled. Since the justification conditions are present to the mind (unlike truth conditions in the realist sense, which are in most cases external to the mind) there is no problem in principle about how the mind might have such a skill. And the skill is one that the mind can (in principle) 'grasp' (assuming that justification conditions are assigned to sentences in some recursive way). Dummett claims that his non-realist theory of truth makes truth conditions *both* behaviorally relevant and graspable.

Truth in the external sense does not obey all of the laws of classical logic, however. For conditions are not always such that either the assertion of a sentence or the assertion of its negation is justified. Thus Dummett is prepared to give up the classical law of the excluded middle and to accept something like Brouwer's intuitionist logic.

'Internal realism'

I have put forward (1976, 1981) a view with close connections to Dummett's as well as some disagreements with it. Whereas Dummett identifies truth with justification, I treat truth as an *idealization* of justification. Truth cannot simply *be* justification, I argue (1979), for any number of reasons: truth is supposed to be a property of a statement that cannot be lost, whereas justification can be lost (in fact, justification is both tensed and relative to a person), justification is a matter of degree whereas truth is not (or not in the same way), etc. A statement is true, in my view, if it would be justified under epistemically ideal conditions for many sorts of statements, and if we somewhat like 'frictionless planes' in physics; we cannot really attain epistemically ideal conditions for may sorts of statements, and if we ever can, we cannot be certain beyond the theoretical possibility of someday having to change our mind that we *have* attained them. But frictionless planes cannot really be attained either, and yet talk of frictionless planes has 'cash value' because we can approximate them to a very high degree of accuracy. Similarly, we can approximate epistemically ideal conditions for many sorts of statements to a high degree, and with a high degree of certainty, and this is what gives talk of what would be justified under such conditions 'cash value'. The simile of frictionless planes aside, the two key claims of such an idealization theory of truth are: (1) that truth is independent of justification here and now, but not independent of *all* possibility of justification. To claim that a statement is true is to claim it could be justified; (2) that truth is expected to be stable, or 'convergent'; if either a statement *or* its negation could be justified, even if conditions were as ideal as one could hope to make them, there is no sense in thinking of the statement as *having* a truth value.

Traditionally realists have claimed that truth outruns even idealized justifiability (because we might 'really' all be deceived by an evil demon, we might really be brains in a vat, etc.). I replied (1976, 1981) to these arguments by pointing out that an epistemically ideal theory would necessarily have models (for instance, by the Skolem–Löwenheim theorem: see chapter 1), and, in fact, models that satisfied all operational and theoretical constraints (and were thus 'intended' models). I concluded that metaphysical realism – the view that truth outruns even idealized justification – is incoherent. On the other hand, to identify truth with (tensed) justification, as opposed to idealized justification, is to give up the principle that some of the statements which are *now* justified may turn out not to be *true*; and this principle I regard as a central part of our empirical world view (cf. Putnam (1979) and the comment on Dummett's paper in the same volume). Thus I have revived Kant's distinction between metaphysical realism and empirical realism, and reject the former while affirming the latter ('internal' realism).

I agree with Dummett in rejecting the correspondence theory of truth. But I do not agree with Dummett's view that the justification conditions for sentences are fixed once and for all by a recursive definition. (In this respect Dummett's theory is like Davidson's: truth conditions – albeit in the 'non-realist' sense of 'truth' – are associated with sentences by a definition which involves an induction on the complexity of the sentences, and which is taken to be the meaning theory for the language as well as the truth theory.) In my view, as in Quine's (see chapter 3), the justification conditions for sentences change as our total body of knowledge changes, and cannot be taken as fixed once and for all. Not only may we find out that statements we now regard as justified are false, but we may even find out that procedures we now regard as justificatory are not, and that different justification procedures are better. Just as in the 'new theory of reference' something that passes the current tests for gold may turn out not really to be gold (and the current tests for gold may turn out to be bad tests, because they presuppose wrong theory), so a statement that is currently 'justified' may turn out not to be true, *and* the test that led us to believe the statement was justified may turn out to be a bad test. Just as the objective nature of the environment contributes to fixing the reference of terms, so it also contributes to fixing the objective truth conditions for sentences, although not in the metaphysical realist way.

Conclusion

Faced by the revival of non-realist views, a number of realists have already begun to develop rejoinders. It is clear that every one of the questions Russell discussed – the logical character of proper names and general names, the nature of reference, the nature of truth – is a perennial question. This century has been especially fertile in insights and theories which deal with these questions. The questions may never have 'final answers', but the discussion moves to ever deeper and more sophisticated levels.

5

'Two dogmas' revisited

I believe that the time has come to take another look at Quine's (1951) celebrated article 'Two dogmas of empiricism'. The analysis of this article that is usually offered in philosophy seminars is very simple: Quine was attacking the analytic–synthetic distinction. His argument was simply that all attempts to define the distinction are *circular*. I think that this is much too simple a view of what was going on. (The continuing recognition of the great importance of 'Two dogmas' shows that at some level *many* readers must be aware that something deep and momentous for philosophy was going on.)

I shall argue that what was importantly going on in Quine's paper was also more subtle and more complicated than Quine and his defenders (and not just the critics) perceived. Some of Quine's arguments were directed against one notion of analyticity, some against another. Moreover, Quine's arguments were of unequal merit. One of the several notions of analyticity that Quine attacked in 'Two dogmas of empiricism' was close to one of Kant's accounts of analyticity (namely, that an analytic judgment is one whose negation reduces to a contradiction), or, rather, to a 'linguistic' version of Kant's account: a sentence is analytic if it can be obtained from a truth of logic by putting synonyms for synonyms. Let us call this the *linguistic* notion of analyticity. Against this notion, Quine's argument is little more than that Quine cannot think how to define 'synonymy'. But Quine also considers a very different notion: the notion of an analytic truth as one that is *confirmed no matter what*. I shall contend that this is the traditional notion of apriority, or rather, *one* of the traditional notions of apriority. This notion, or variants thereof, has played a central role in all of philosophy since the ancients, and in all the different branches of philosophy. Moreover, I think that Quine's attack on this notion was correct. And Quine's argument against *this* notion was not at all concerned with circularity of definitions.

If I am right, Quine is a philosopher of historic importance. He is of historic importance because he was the first philosopher of the top rank both to reject the notion of apriority and at least to sketch an intelligible conception of methodology without apriority. Of course, if I am wrong and there is such a thing as *a priori* truth, then I am doubtless overestimating Quine's importance in the history of philosophy. There are some philosophers in the history of philosophy whose importance does not very much depend upon their being *right*. But Quine's importance does, I think, depend to a large measure upon his being right in one central claim, a claim which he expressed by saying that there is no sensible distinction between analytic and synthetic truths but which he should have expressed by saying that there is no sensible distinction between *a priori* and *a posteriori* truths.

Review of Quine's arguments

At a superficial level, what is going on in 'Two dogmas of empiricism' looks quite simple, as we remarked above. Quine is going to show us that there is no sense to be made of the notion of analyticity by showing that all of the suggested definitions lead in circles. But (as Grice and Strawson (1956) long ago pointed out) it is puzzling why this is supposed to be a good argument. Could it not, after all, just be the case that the various members of the family of linguistic notions to which the notion of analyticity belongs are not definable in terms of, or reducible to other, non-linguistic notions? If this is the case, then something more doubtless needs to be said about the status of such linguistic notions and, perhaps, about the status of linguistic theory; but a mere demonstration of definitional circularity would hardly seem to be enough to overthrow as widely accepted and used a notion as the notion of analyticity.

It is as Quine begins to carry out his program of showing that the various suggested definitions of analyticity are not satisfactory that things get more interesting. For it is not hard to see that the definitions Quine assembles for attack could not possibly be definitions of one and the same notion, however vague.

Thus, the first major notion of analyticity that Quine considered in his paper was the traditional notion of a statement that is 'true by definition'. Quine suggested that this notion might be clarified, given the notion of *synonymy*, in the following way: a statement is analytic if it can be turned into a truth of formal logic by substituting synonyms for synonyms. But, Quine argued, the notion of *synonymy* is hopelessly vague. The only evidence that Quine produced to support this remarkable claim was that he, Quine, could not clarify the notion in a few pages. Given that the even more basic linguistic notion of *grammaticality* has not been satisfactorily clarified in many pages by many authors to the present day, and that no one proposes to do linguistics without the notion, it is clear that Quine presented a bad argument against this particular notion of analyticity.†

In saying that Quine's argument was a bad argument, I am not proposing to present a theory of synonymy here, and, in any case, I do not possess a complete and satisfactory theory. But, in a paper I wrote many years ago (Putnam, 1962a) I outlined a theory that does explain the analyticity of such statements as 'All bachelors are unmarried', 'All vixens are foxes', etc. The idea, in a nutshell, is that there is an exceptionless 'law' associated with the noun 'bachelor', namely, that someone is a bachelor *if and only if* he has never been married; an exceptionless law associated with the noun 'vixen', namely, that something is a vixen *if and only if* it is a female fox; etc. Moreover, this exceptionless law has, in each case, two important characteristics: (1) that no other exceptionless 'if and only if' statement is associated with the noun by speakers; and (2) that the exceptionless 'if and only if' statement in question is a *criterion*, i.e., speakers can and do tell whether or not something is a bachelor by seeing whether or not it is an unmarried man; whether or not something is a vixen by seeing whether or not it is a female fox; etc. (An operational procedure for telling whether or not such an 'if and only if' statement is functioning as a criterion was suggested in my paper. I contended that only a few hundred words in a natural language have this 'one-criterion' character: most words are either associated with *no* exceptionless criterion, or with more than one. And I further suggested that all clear cases of analyticity involve these special few hundred words.)

In a more recent publication (Putnam, 1975a), I also present the beginnings of a theory of meaning, in terms of a 'causal' theory of reference and a theory of what I call *stereotypes*, which can, I hope, provide an account of synonymy for the natural kind words, at least. It is on the basis of this research that I feel optimistic about the

† This is probably too harsh on my part. The notion of analyticity and the notion of a 'meaning postulate' had become so overworked in philosophy (not to mention such notions as 'analysis' of a concept, 'conceptually necessary', etc.) that synonymy and analyticity had, indeed, become unclear notions *as used by philosophers*. And even if synonymy *is* a reasonably clear notion as used in *linguistics*, any *theory* of synonymy which we are likely to see will look 'Quinian' to this extent (I predict): most words will *not* be synonymous with any descriptions whatsoever, and most of the truths philosophers class as 'conceptually necessary' will not be 'analytic' in the sense discussed here. Pointing out the 'circularity' of the definitions of synonymy and analyticity offered by philosophers was Quine's way of calling attention to the alarming looseness of the *use* these philosophers were making of the notions, and to their exaggerated confidence in the clarity of the notion of *meaning*, which was Quine's real target.

legitimacy and linguistic usefulness of the notion of synonymy, whether we have a good 'definition' or not.

In the section of his paper entitled 'The verification theory and reductionism', Quine moves after a different target, and it is here that the style of his argument becomes quite different. In this section of his paper, Quine first sketches the view of the Vienna Circle. On this view (as Quine explains it), statements have a meaning by being reducible to statements about sense experience. This view went well with the view that each meaningful statement has its own individual range of confirming and disconfirming experiences. Analytical truths are simply those statements which have the universal range of confirming experiences, i.e., which are confirmed no matter what.

But why should this concept, the concept of a statement which is confirmed no matter what, be considered a concept of *analyticity*? Confirmation, in the positivist sense, has something to do with rational belief. A statement which is highly confirmed is a statement which it is rational to believe, or rational to believe to a high degree. If there are indeed statements which have the maximum degree of confirmation in all circumstances, then these are simply truths which it is *always rational to believe*, nay, more, truths which it is never rational to even begin to doubt. Many philosophers have believed that there are such truths. Perhaps this is what Aristotle thought a *first principle* was like; more likely it is what Descartes thought a *clear and distinct* idea was like. On the face of it, then, the concept of a truth which is confirmed no matter what is not a concept of *analyticity* but a concept of *apriority*. Yet both Quine and the positivists did take this to be a concept of *analyticity*. Why they did is a question to which I shall return.

Quine's argument against the notion of a truth which is *confirmed no matter what*, is not an argument from the circularity of definitions. Quine's argument is an argument from what is clearly a normative description of the history of modern science. Let me quote it in full:

Any statement can be held true come what may if we make drastic enough adjustments elsewhere in the system. Even a statement very close to the periphery can be held true in the face of recalcitrant experience by pleading hallucination or by amending certain statements of the kind called logical laws. Conversely, by the same token, no statement is immune to revision. Revision even of the logical law of the excluded middle has been proposed as a means of simplifying quantum mechanics; and what difference is there in principle between such a shift and a shift whereby Keppler superceded Ptolemy, or Einstein Newton, or Darwin Aristotle? (Quine, 1951, p. 40)

Notice what Quine is saying here. First he is saying that proposals to use non-standard logics in quantum mechanics cannot be ruled out by any legitimate principle of scientific method. He is saying that the fallibilism which Peirce recognized as contributing essentially to the success of modern science extends also to the laws of logic. He is not just making a sociological remark to the effect that some scientists and some philosophers of science are willing to consider revision of logical laws for the sake of simplifying physical theory as a whole; he clearly thinks that it is right, fitting, and proper that they should be willing to allow such a possibility. Open-mindedness even to the extent of being prepared to revise logical laws is necessary in the scientific enterprise. If this is right, then the laws of logic are not principles that a rational man is *forbidden* to revise. They are not *clear and distinct ideas*. They are not *a priori* truths.

Secondly, Quine is pointing out that previous revolutions have required us to give up principles that were once regarded as *a priori*. And thirdly, in this trenchant paragraph, he is suggesting that the proposal to use a non-standard logic in quantum mechanics is not fundamentally *different* from the proposal to use non-Euclidean geometry in the theory of space–time, which has been accepted since Einstein's general theory of relativity.

In short, Quine is saying that the history of science, properly understood, leaves no room for *this* notion of an 'analytic' statement, i.e., for the notion of an *a priori* or *unrevisable* statement.

Quine strikes the same note in other papers, although always with unfortunate brevity. In 'The scope and language of science' he writes,

We have reached the present stage in our characterization of the scientific framework not by reasoning *a priori* from the nature of science qua science, but rather by seizing upon traits of the science of our day. Special traits thus exploited include the notion of physical object, the four-dimensional concept of space–time, the classical mold of modern classical mathematics, the true–false orientation of standard logic, and indeed extensionality itself. One or another of these traits may change as science advances. Already the notion of a physical object, as an intrinsically determinate portion of the space–time continuum, squares dubiously with modern developments in quantum mechanics. Savants there are who even suggest that the findings of quantum mechanics might best be accommodated by a revision of the true–false dichotomy itself. (Quine, 1957, p. 16)

And in 'Carnap and logical truth' Quine attacks the disinterpretation of non-Euclidean geometry, writing 'the status of an interpreted non-Euclidean geometry differs in no basic way from the original status of Euclidean geometry,' (1960, p. 359). I believe that Quine's methodological argument against apriority is a correct one, and I shall try to spell it out below. But first let me deal with the question

I raised above: Why did Quine think that being confirmed no matter what is a notion of *analyticity*?

He thought so because the positivists, whom he was attacking, held that to fix a statement's range of confirming experiences is to fix it *meaning*, and that this meaning-fixing is done by *stipulation*. As a par of their view, the positivists held that *a priori* statements (statement with the universal range of confirming experiences) are *true b meaning alone*. And since truth by virtue of meaning is analyticity, it followed (for the positivists) that the aprioricity is analyticity.

Another way to put the same point is this: the positivists believed that what determines the range of confirming instances is a set of *conventions*. They believed not only that there are *a priori* truths, but that these truths are simply statements true by stipulation or convention.

In 'Two dogmas of empiricism', Quine alludes only briefly to the idea of truth by convention, but in an earlier paper, Quine (1936) dealt at length with this position of the positivists, and argued that once we refute the idea that logical truth *arises* from conventions which are explicit, or could in principle *arise* in this way, then all that is left of the claim that logical truths are true by convention is the assertion that these are statements which, as a matter of sheer behavioristic fact, we would never give up. And in 'Two dogmas of empiricism' he has advanced to the point of denying that there are (or ought to be) such statements.

Curiously enough, then, Quine *confused* analyticity and apriority because of positivist assumptions (assumptions he was attacking)! But, fortunately, this confusion does not invalidate his argument against apriority.

The 'historical' argument

I want to explain why I think Quine's very sketchy 'historical' argument against the existence of *a priori* (unrevisable) statements is correct.†

First of all, let me say a word about the esoteric subject of quantum logic (see Putnam, 1968a). What I claim is that the 'weirdness' of

---

† In recent years Quine appears to have changed his position on logic. Thus in Quine (1970) he argues *against* the possibility of revising Boolean logic without losing simplicity (however, he makes the error of considering only the simplicity of the logic in isolation, not the simplicity of the total system, which is what is relevant), and also argues that to abandon Boolean logic would be to 'change the meaning' of the logical particles. (For a reply to this argument, see Putnam (1968a).) I am ignoring this 'backsliding' on Quine's part (as I view it), because my interest is in bringing out what Quine's *best* argument was.

the quantum mechanical universe can be understood in the following way. Just perform the thought experiment of asking yourself: what experiences would we have if the world obeyed 'quantum logic' instead of Boolean logic? (Of course, a certain minimal logic, a common part of Boolean logic and the proposed quantum logic, has to be used as the metalogic.) If one allows this question as a meaningful question at all, one finds that *all* of the 'anomalies' of quantum mechanics are explained by a few simple differences in the logic, just as the apparent anomalies of general relativity are explained by the peculiarities of the space–time. Unless one has some good argument that logic *cannot* be explanatory in the way geometry can, there is, then, a *prima facie* case for considering the hypothesis that we live in a *non-Boolean world*, as, at least, an admissible hypothesis (which is all Quine would need).

Now, what do philosophers of quantum mechanics who *reject* quantum logic reply? There are those, for example van Frassen, who see *all* scientific theories strictly from an instrumentalist point of view. From their perspective, there is no need for quantum logic, of course. But what of realist philosophers of quantum mechanics? They all, without exception, seem to count on quantum mechanics being proved *false* in certain particular ways.† No doubt, quantum mechanics *will* prove false in *some* (probably unforeseen) ways. But what if future successor theories to quantum mechanics *retain* just the features that make quantum mechanics philosophically *puzzling*? I think that I can honestly claim that the quantum logic interpretation of quantum mechanics is the *only* realistic interpretation of quantum mechanics in the following sense: It is the only realist interpretation of the *present* theory. If the present theory is true, or, subjunctively, if it *were* true, or if the true theory retains certain key features of the present theory, however much it may differ from present quantum mechanics in other respects, then the interpretation I defend *is* an interpretation of the true theory, and no other realist interpretation *has ever been proposed*: only *wishes* for a different physical universe!

If I am right in the foregoing, then anyone who concedes that the present theory *could* be true should concede that there is a strong 'case' for the possibility of a quantum logical universe.

Now, back to Quine's 'historical' argument. The obvious way to try to counter Quine's oblique reference to the fact that scientific revolutions have overthrown propositions once *thought* to be *a priori*

† For example, Arthur Fine tells me that his proposed interpretation of quantum mechanics would have the consequence that one *can* simultaneously measure some non-commuting observables.

is to say that the seeming *apriority* of *those* propositions was 'merely psychological'. But the stunning case is geometry. Unless one accepts the ridiculous claim that what seemed *a priori* was only the *conditional* statement that *if* Euclid's axioms, then Euclid's theorems (I think that this is what Quine calls 'disinterpreting' geometry in 'Carnap and logical truth'), then one must admit that the key propositions of Euclidean geometry were *interpreted* propositions ('about form and void', as Quine says), and these interpreted propositions were *methodologically* immune from revision (prior to the invention of rival theory) as Boolean logic was prior to the proposal of the quantum logical interpretation of quantum mechanics. The correct moral – the one Quine draws – is that some statements can only be overthrown by rival *theory*; but there is no such thing as an absolutely unrevisable statement.

Quine's 'linguistic' definition of analyticity

The definition of analyticity that Quine proposes (but only for the purpose of knocking it down) in the section of his essay on 'truth by definition' is, let us recall, that a statement is analytic if it can be obtained from (or, equivalently, turned into) a truth of logic by substituting synonyms for synonyms. This is a *linguistic* definition, because the operative notion is *synonymy*, and this is a notion (and a legitimate notion) from the discipline of *linguistics*. Accepting the notions of 'logical truth' (in the sense of 'truth in which the only words that occur essentially are words from the restricted vocabulary of *formal* logic') and 'synonymy' only commits one to accepting this definition of analyticity as (sufficiently) *clear*. But does this notion of analyticity have any *usefulness*?

One sort of usefulness that *this* notion of analyticity does not have is this: it does not explain why such a special epistemological status was traditionally accorded to so-called logical laws. Although the truths of logic are 'analytic', on this definition of analyticity, they are, so to speak, *analytically* analytic. Any truth of logic comes from a truth of logic, namely itself, by a substitution of synonyms for synonyms (e.g., the *identity* substitution: the substitution that puts each non-logical term for itself). This makes the truths of logic analytic – by the definition of 'analytic' – but it says nothing whatsoever about how we *know* a statement is a truth of logic, or about the revisability or unrevisability of such (putative) knowledge. That logic is analytic is now an illustration of how we have decided to use the noise 'analytic', not a substantive thesis about logic.

This 'linguistic' notion of analyticity might possess a second sort of usefulness, however, but only if the notion of *logical truth* were very much restricted. It might clarify Kant's notion of a judgment whose negation reduces to a contradiction, provided we took a 'logical truth' to be a substitution instance of a theorem of *monadic* logic (i.e., logic up to but *not* including the undecidable logic of relations). The statements obtainable from the theorems of monadic logic and their substitution instances by putting synonyms for synonyms are probably more or less the class Kant had in mind. But if 'logic' is extended to mean all of set theory, then the class of 'analytic' truths, on this definition, becomes so artificial that it is hard to see why one would feel motivated to introduce a technical term to designate it.

If the special epistemological status traditionally accorded the logical laws cannot be explained by the 'analyticity' of those laws, that does not mean that we have to simply decide to accept it as inexplicable, however. I urged above that there are statements in science which can only be overthrown by a new theory – sometimes by a revolutionary new theory – and not by observation alone. Such statements *have* a sort of 'apriority' prior to the invention of the new theory which challenges or replaces them: they are *contextually a priori*. Giving up the idea that there are any absolutely *a priori* statements requires us to also give up the correlative idea (at least it was correlative for the empiricists) that *a posteriori* statements (and to empiricists this meant all revisable statements and also meant all synthetic statements, all statements 'about the world') are always and at all times 'empirical' in the sense that they have specifiable confirming experiences and specifiable disconfirming experiences. Euclidean geometry was always revisable in the sense that no justifiable canon of scientific inquiry *forbade* the construction of an alternative geometry; but it was not always 'empirical' in the sense of having an alternative that good scientists could actually conceive. The special status of logical laws is similar, in my view; they are contextually *a priori* (or were, before quantum logic).

Even if analyticity cannot explain the special status of logical laws (in so far as it is real), that special status, that contextual apriority, *and* certain very strong synonymy relations *can* explain the status of such statements as 'All bachelors are unmarried', 'All vixens are foxes', etc. And it is important to explain the special status, the contextual apriority of these in-themselves-uninteresting state-ments, because otherwise a really important thesis – the thesis that no statement is totally immune from revision – might be cast into doubt. So the notion of 'analyticity', when properly hedged (by

95

restricting the meaning of 'logical truth' as suggested above) can be of limited but real philosophical significance.

Let me close by considering one final question: can one agree with Quine's 'historical' argument and still reject Quine's 'circularity' argument? Can one hold that there are *no a priori* truths, but there *are* analytic truths (in the 'linguistic' sense)?

The answer is plainly that one can. If one accepts the distributive laws of the standard (Boolean) propositional calculus, for example, then one will accept any statement of the form†

$$p(q \lor r) \equiv pq \lor pr$$

as logically true (and *a fortiori* as analytic). But in quantum logic there are statements of the form $p(q \lor r) \equiv pq \lor pr$ which are *not* regarded as logically true ($p(q \lor r) \equiv pq \lor pr$ is not a 'tautology' in quantum logic). So if we change our minds about which logical laws are correct by going over to quantum logic, we shall change our minds about the 'analyticity' of these statements.

This does not mean that there are no analytic statements, if quantum logic is correct. Such familiar logical laws as $p \lor \sim p$, the implication of p by $p \& q$, the implication of $p \lor q$ by p alone and by q alone, all are correct according to quantum logic. But it does mean that, since the logic is revisable for empirical reasons, our decision as to *which* statements are analytic can be changed for empirical reasons. Even a statement that really is analytic is not immune from revision, for even if a statement is *in fact* a law of logic, or comes from a law of logic by synonymous substitution, we are not *prohibited* by any methodological canon from revising it; we shall just be making a mistake if we do. (Compare this case with the situation in geometry: even if we arrive at the *correct* geometry for space–time, still our geometry will not be *unrevisable*. It is just that we will – as a matter of *fact* – be making a *mistake* if we revise it. 'Fallibilism' does not become an incorrect doctrine when one reaches the truth in a scientific inquiry.)

In sum: (1) a putatively analytic statement may not really be analytic, not because we were confused about meanings, or confused about logic, but because the *logic of the world* may be different from what we suppose it to be, *as a matter of empirical fact*. (2) A really analytic statement is not *a priori*, because even when we happen to be *right* about logic, fallibilism still holds good. We never have an absolute guarantee that we are right, even when we are.

† pq is short for $p \& q$.

Notice how different the situation would be if the laws of logic *were* immune from revision. If that were the case, one could only give up an analytic statement (or the sentence which expressed an analytic statement), without an actual logical *blunder*, by altering the meaning of the words and thereby changing the language. Analytic statements would be as unrevisable as if they were true by convention. It would be as if there were truths by language alone. But on the view advanced here, there are *no* truths by language alone. There are analytic truths: truths by *logic and language*. But analytic truths are not *unrevisable* (no truth is). They are only unrevisable *unless we revise the logic or the language*, which is a very different matter.

6

There is at least one *a priori* truth

In a number of famous publications (the most famous being the celebrated article 'Two dogmas of empiricism') Quine has advanced the thesis that there is no such thing as an (absolutely) *a priori* truth. (Usually he speaks of 'analyticity' rather than apriority; but his discussion clearly includes both notions, and in his famous paper 'Carnap and logical truth' he has explicitly said that what he is rejecting is the idea that any statement is completely *a priori*. For a discussion of the different threads in Quine's arguments, see chapter 5). Apriority is identified by Quine with *unrevisability*. But there are at least two possible interpretations of unrevisability: (1) a *behavioral* interpretation, namely, an unrevisable statement is one we would never give up (as a sheer behavioral fact about us); and (2) an *epistemic* interpretation, namely, an unrevisable statement is one we would never be *rational* to give up (perhaps even a statement that it would never be rational to even *think* of giving up). On the first interpretation, the claim that we might revise even the laws of logic becomes merely the claim that certain phenomena might cause us to give up our belief in some of the laws of logic; there would be no claim being made that doing so would be rational. Rather the notion of rationality itself would have gone by the board.

I don't know if Quine actually intended to take so radical a position as this, but, in any case, I think that most of his followers understood him to be advocating a more moderate doctrine. This more moderate doctrine was put forward by me, for example, in a paper I titled 'It ain't necessarily so' (1962c). The moderate doctrine, unlike the more radical doctrine, employs the notion of rationality. The claim of the moderate doctrine is that there are no truths which it would never be rational to give up; for every truth or putative truth, there are circumstances under which it would be rational to accept its denial. This position was itself argued for, on the basis of an induction from the history of science. It was not itself supposed to be an *a priori* truth. Thus the cheap shot, which consists in arguing that the anti-apriorist position is self-refuting because if it were correct then there would still be one *a priori* truth, namely that there are no *a priori* truths, doesn't work. But the induction from the history of science was a somewhat complicated affair. It was not a simple Baconian induction; rather, a theory was put forward, a theory which was intended, among other things, to explain why certain statements *seem* to be *a priori*.

I want to emphasize this point. The moderate Quinean position tries to 'save the appearances'. It does not deny that there at least appear to be *a priori* truths, it does not deny that certain truths have a special status, it tries to explain why that is so. More precisely, it says that those truths really do have a special status, only the status has been misconceived. The key notion here was the notion I called 'contextual apriority'. The idea is that we can grant that certain truths, and even, at certain times, certain falsehoods, have a special status, but that we don't have to concede that that status is good old-fashioned apriority. The status these truths and falsehoods have, as long as they have it, is contextual apriority: apriority relative to the body of knowledge. And the thesis that there are no *a priori* truths becomes the thesis that there are no absolutely *a priori* truths. What still seems to me to be right about this is the idea that there is such a status as contextual apriority, and the idea that contextual apriority has sometimes been mistaken for absolute apriority, i.e., for the status that a statement has if indeed it could never be rational to revise it.

There is an important difference between such statements as 'the leaves always turn in October', which can be refuted by just well-confirmed observations, and such statements as the statements which comprise non-Euclidean geometry as a theory of actual space (or space–time) which can only be established when a whole new body of theory – not just geometrical theory, but physical theory and experimental interpretation – is put forward. Before the development of general relativity theory, most people, even most scientists, could not imagine any experiences that would lead them to give up, or that would make it rational to give up, Euclidean geometry as a theory of actual space; and this is what led to the illusion that Euclidean geometry was *a priori*. What I no longer think is that all cases of apparent apriority can be explained in this fashion.

Even the case of Euclidean versus non-Euclidean geometry involves features that were glossed over in my previous account. It is not the case that every mathematician regarded non-Euclidean geometry as *a priori* impossible, as a description of actual physical space, before the development of general relativity. Indeed, Lobachevskii always regarded the question of which geometry describes actual physical space as an empirical question. And it isn't just the possibility of giving an operational interpretation to non-Euclidean geometry that is important, although this was naturally stressed by empiricists such as Lobachevskii but it is also important that one can give a coherent model for a non-Euclidean world within Euclidean mathematics. Mathematicians were led by a very straightforward analogy to grant the conceivability of Euclidean spaces of four and even more dimensions. A three-dimensional non-Euclidean world – or at least a world whose intrinsic geometry, whose geometry viewed from within, is that of a three-dimensional non-Euclidean world – can be pictured as a curved hypersurface in a four-dimensional Euclidean space. (Of course, this does not explain the possibility of a non-Euclidean world which is *not* embedded in a higher-dimensional Euclidean space!)

What I want to do here is to argue that there is at least one *a priori* truth in exactly the sense that Quine and I denied; i.e., at least one truth that it would never be rational to give up. My example, not surprisingly, is going to be taken from the laws of logic. In the past I have argued that the laws of logic are revisable and that, in fact, the proper interpretation of quantum mechanics requires that we give up the distributive laws. Nothing that I say today will go against this position. It is after all perfectly possible that not all the traditional laws of logic are *a priori*, but that only some of them are. Indeed, even if, as I think, the notion of apriority has to be revived, that does not mean that we should go back to the old confident way of using it. To try to understand the epistemology of all of logic and classical mathematics in terms of a single notion of *a priori* truth would be, I think, a serious mistake. The law of logic I want to consider is a very weak version of the principle of contradiction. The principle of contradiction says that no statement is both true and false, or in the notation of propositional calculus, $\sim (p \ \& \ \sim p)$.

The example of quantum logic suggests one way in which the revision of this principle might be suggested. Namely, it might be suggested that the principle holds only for *ordinary* statements about *ordinary* macro-observable properties *of ordinary* macro-observable objects, such as 'the cat is on the mat', and it might be suggested that there is some class of recherché statements about waves and particles or whatnot for which the principle fails. Perhaps 'the electron is a particle' is both true and false, or 'the electron is a wave' is both true and false. This move might be avoided by considering what we may call the *typical* principle of contradiction, i.e., the principle that *ordinary macro-observable statements*, ordinary statements about macro-observables, *are not both true and false*, or by considering the principle that *most statements are not both true and false*, or some combination of these moves; but I shall consider the weakest possible version of the principle of contradiction, which I shall call the minimal principle of contradiction. This is simply the principle that *not every statement is both true and false*. The denial of this principle is, of course, the claim that *every statement is both true and false*. If every statement is such that under some circumstances it might be rational to revise it, then under some circumstances it might be rational to accept that *every statement is both true and false*. Is this the case? Well, it certainly doesn't seem to be the case. And if it is not the case, if, indeed, there are no circumstances under which it would be rational to give up our belief that *not every statement is both true and false*, then there is at least one *a priori truth*. And one is all we need.

My argument is in this respect like Descartes'. I believe that one of the several things that Descartes wanted to do with his *cogito* was to establish precisely that there are *a priori* truths. And for the purpose of making this point, one needs only one example. Is, then, the statement that not every proposition is both true and false not an example of an absolutely, unconditionally, truly, actually *a priori* truth?

Recall that part of the strategy of what I called the moderate Quinean position was to save the appearances by showing that what we mistake for absolute apriority is a status which some propositions truly have, a status which is truly different from ordinary, garden-variety contingency, but which is not an absolute apriority. This is the status of contextual apriority. Is it possible that the minimal principle of contradiction is then only a contextually *a priori* truth which we are tempted to mistake for an absolutely *a priori* truth?

The suggestion would be this: that there is some weird physical theory T which we have not yet thought of, but which implies the denial of the minimal principle of contradiction and that some day when some scientist – some future Einstein – invents the theory *T* and shows us what beautiful predictions it leads to, and how much it enhances our understanding and control of nature to accept the theory *T*, then we will all be converted and by a kind of 'gestalt switch' we will go over to accepting the theory *T* and to denying the minimal principle of contradiction.

But there is an obvious problem with this line. The problem is that it's quite obvious what the theory *T* will have to be. If we ever give up the minimal principle of contradiction, i.e., if we ever come to believe that every statement is both true and false, then it's perfectly obvious what the theory *T* will have to be. The theory *T* will have to be the theory which consists of every statement and its negation!

In other words the theory T will have to consist of such statements as 'the earth is round', 'the earth is not round', 'two and two are four', 'two and two are not four', 'the moon is made of green cheese', 'the moon is not made of green cheese', 'there are quarks', 'there are no quarks', etc. For once, we are in the happy position of being able to say exactly what the 'surrounding theory' will have to be if we come to revise a particular contextually *a priori* statement.

Of course, my move here might be challenged. One might, for example, suggest that we give up the minimal principle of contradiction and the law of double negation at the same time. Then we might accept *it is not the case that it is not the case that every statement is both true and false*, without accepting that every statement is both true and false. However, in that case the statement 'every statement is both true and false' would still have the status of being *a priori* false, even if the statement of which it was the negation isn't *a priori* true. And to concede the existence of such a status as *a priori* falsity is, I think, as much as to concede the existence of such a status as *a priori* truth. I assume, therefore, that I am dealing with an opponent who maintains not merely that we might accept the double negation of the statement that *every statement is both true and false*, but that we might accept that statement itself.

Again, it might be suggested that we assert 'every statement is both true and false', while at the same time giving up the principle of universal instantiation, which enables us to infer particular instances from an all-statement. Then we would say the words 'every statement is both true and false', but for no particular statement would we be committed to saying of it that *it* is both true and false. But this would clearly be playing verbal games. If I say the words 'every statement is both true and false', but I don't conclude that 'the earth is round' is both true and false, or that 'two and two equals five' is both true and false, then I simply don't mean what is normally meant, or anything what is like what is normally meant by 'every statement is both true and false'.

In the case of geometry, when we went over to non-Euclidean geometry we didn't change the meaning of the words, or at any rate we didn't *merely* change the meaning of the words. We discovered that a state of affairs which we had mistakenly regarded as inconceivable is, in fact, conceivable and quite probably actual. For example, we used to regard it as inconceivable that a three-dimensional world should be both finite and unbounded. We now think it is conceivable and quite probably the case that the whole three-dimensional universe is both finite and unbounded. The question is whether, in the same way, the state of affairs that we now regard as being inconceivable, the state of affairs that 'the earth is round' and at the same time 'the earth is not round', that 'the moon is made of green cheese', and at the same time that 'the moon is not made of green cheese', that 'two and two are five' and at the same time 'two and two are not five', and so on, is really conceivable and will perhaps someday turn out to obtain. Could it be rational to think someday that 'the moon is made of green cheese', and 'the moon is not made of green cheese', that 'two and two are five', and 'two and two are not five', that 'the earth is round', and 'the earth is not round', and so on? That is our question. And, I repeat, if that ever happens then we know exactly what the 'theory' will be that we shall be accepting. It will have to consist of every statement and its negation.

Let me refer to the statement that *Euclidean geometry is true* – the statement we gave up when we went over to non-Euclidean physics – as the *critical statement*, and to the theory of the basis of which we decided that the critical statement was false – the General Theory of Relativity – as the *embedding theory*. What I've said so far is that if we take the minimal principle of contradiction as our critical statement, then we know exactly what the embedding theory has to be. It has to consist of every statement and its negation. But it may still be argued that there is a disanalogy between accepting non-Euclidean geometry on the basis of the general theory of relativity and accepting the denial of the minimal principle of contradiction on the basis of the theory which consists of every statement together with its negation. The disanalogy is that the general theory of relativity leads to testable predictions, whereas the embedding theory which consists of every statement together with its negation leads to no testable predictions. But this is not the case either. The embedding theory in the latter case leads, for example, to the prediction that 'my hand has five fingers', and to the prediction that 'my hand has seven fingers'. It also leads to the prediction that 'my hand does not have five fingers', and to the prediction that 'my hand does not have seven fingers'. It leads to a *lot* of predictions! But, it may be objected, these are not genuine predictions for we don't know what it would be like for them all to come true. We can imagine all of the predictions of non-Euclidean physics coming true, even if we happen to be Euclidean physicists. But we don't know what it would be like for all the predictions of the theory that consists of every statement together with its negation to come true. I think this is right, but I think that this observation only poses the problem of apriority and does not solve it.

Suppose I have a box in which there is a sheet of paper. And suppose I predict that when I open the box you will see that the sheet of paper is red, and the sheet of paper is not red. Suppose I explain that I don't mean that the sheet of paper is red on one side and white on the other side, or anything like that. When I say that the sheet of paper is red, I mean that it's red on both sides: a nice normal dye which doesn't look red from one angle and some other color from a different angle, or red to some people and a different color to other people, or anything like that. And when I say that the sheet of paper is red, and the sheet of paper is not red, I mean that the statement that 'the sheet of paper is red' understood as just indicated, is both definitely true and definitely false. Now it's quite true that in a certain sense we don't know what it would be like for that prediction to be verified, and that's our reason for denying that it is a genuine prediction about what will be seen when the box is opened. But one has to be careful here.

The kind of inconceivability that is relevant is not mere unintuitability. Let me say that we can intuit a state of affairs if we can actually visualize it. (I want to stick to a notion of intuition that's close to perception.) Now, we can predict that something will happen which we cannot intuit, although we can, in a sense, conceive of it happening. For example, I might predict that when I open the box you will see that the sheet of paper is a shade of red that none of you has ever seen. I think that you would accept that as a perfectly good prediction, even though you can't intuit what it would be like for that prediction to come true. It's enough that we should be sure that that is a possible state of affairs or at least a state of affairs that we could recognize if it turned out to be actual. Similarly, if I predict that when I open the box you will see that the sheet of paper is a color – and I mean now a major color – that you've never seen before – I think that would be a perfectly good prediction. It's true that such a prediction would upset a certain amount of physical theory, namely the physical theory that says that color is determined by lambda, the wavelength of the light reflected from the paper. For if that theory is true, and it is also true that we have correctly mapped out which lambdas correspond to which colors, and which lambdas the human eye is sensitive to, then there is no room, in the sense of no room in the theory, for another major color. Nevertheless, it would be absurd to say that someone who predicted that there was another major color and who claimed to have predicted that when we opened the box and looked at the paper we would see a major color we hadn't seen before, hadn't made a prediction just because we couldn't intuit the state of affairs that would obtain if his prediction turned out to be correct.

Actually the situation is more complicated than I'm suggesting because, in fact, the physical theory that I just mentioned, although it still appears in many textbooks, is certainly false, and the work of Jerome Letvin and of Irwin Land shows that color depends in a very complicated way on many factors besides lambda, and as far as I know it would not be the case that the discovery of a new major color tomorrow would very much mess up physical theory; there just isn't a good physical theory of color to mess up. For example, standard theory doesn't really account for the color 'brown'. But even if the lambda theory were not already suspect, I think that the fact remains that the prediction of a new major color would have to be counted as a prediction, even if we knew that verification of that prediction would mess up a certain amount of well-established theory.

Now, what do we mean when we say that we don't understand what it would be like for the prediction, that when I open this box you will see that the sheet of paper that it contains is both red and not red, to turn out to be true? We mean at least that we cannot intuit what it would be like for an observational situation to obtain which would *clearly* be describable by saying that the sheet of paper is red, in the sense I explained before, and also the sheet of paper is not red; but we had better mean more than that, otherwise this counts as a perfectly good prediction. Just as the sheet of paper is a shade of red that you have seen before, and the shade of paper is a major color that you have never seen before both count as perfectly good predictions.

On the other hand, it isn't that 'the sheet of paper is red' and 'the sheet of paper is not red' is literally unintelligible in the way in which 'wa'arobi besnork gavagai' is literally unintelligible, although some philosophers have tried to assimilate the unintelligibility of contradictions to the unintelligibility of what is literally without sense in the language. 'This sheet of paper is red and this sheet of paper is not red' isn't unintelligible at all. It simply asserts what cannot possibly be the case. And the reason that *when I open the box you will see that the sheet of paper is red and the sheet of paper is not red* does not count as a prediction, is that we know – know *a priori* – that it can't possibly turn out to be the case. But this remark does not explain the phenomenon of *a priori* knowledge, it only points to its existence.

If what I've said so far is correct, then the theory that what is happening, what gives rise to the illusion of apriority, is that we mistake one status for another – mistake the status of contextual apriority for the status of absolute apriority – doesn't work in this case. That was what was going on in the case of non-Euclidean geometry. But to explain the special status of the principle of contradiction, or at least of the minimal principle of contradiction, in terms of contextual apriority, is a loser.

At this point there is a rather tough line that we might take. We might say that if every statement is both true and false, then in particular the statement 'my hand has five fingers' (or your favorite observation report) is both true and false. But I see that my hand has five fingers is true and I see that it is not false. So I *observe* that at least one statement is not both true and false, and this is enough to verify the minimal principle of contradiction. This is a tough line to take because it amounts to giving up the search for a *special status* for the minimal principle of contradiction. It amounts to saying that the minimal principle of contradiction is an *observation report* or is grounded upon a number of observation reports. But this is clearly wrong. It might turn out that there are not five fingers on my hand. For example, my hand may have been amputated and what I'm looking at may be a plastic substitute (of course we'd have to tell some story about why I don't realize that I'm not looking at my own hand, but that is not impossible, as we all know). But even if it turned out that I don't have a hand, or that my hand has only four fingers, or seven fingers, or whatever, discovering that I was wrong about the observation report would not at all shake my faith in my belief that that observation report is not both true and false. Even if I couldn't discover how many fingers there are on my right hand (imagine a drunken man looking at his hand), this would not shake my faith in my belief that it's not both true and false that the number is five. We seem to be stuck with at least one *a priori* truth: really, actually, truly *a priori*, and not just contextually *a priori*.

If we cannot successfully deny that there are *a priori* truths then it has seemed to many that we can give a conventionalist account of how *a priori* truth is possible. According to a typical such account, it is simply a *rule of language* that one must not assert both a statement and its negation or, to ascend to the metalanguage, that one must not apply both the predicates 'true' and 'false' to the same statement. Moreover, these rules are seen as constituting the meanings of negation and of falsity, or as partially constituting the meanings of negation and of falsity, respectively. Anyone who both asserts a sentence and its syntactic negation other than for special purposes, for example to call attention to an ambiguity in the situation, is going against the meaning of the negation idiom. Thus if I say 'It is raining and it is not raining', and I don't mean simply to call attention to the fact that the particular situation leaves some room for discretion in the application of the description 'it is raining', or something of that kind, then I am going against the meaning of the words. And this is *why* the principle of contradiction is correct.

This account has a very fundamental defect which seems, strangely, not to have been noticed. *It explains much too much.* The problem with this account and with a number of other attempted accounts is that if it were correct, it wouldn't merely explain the status of the principle of contradiction in our *knowledge*, it would explain the principle of contradiction itself. It wouldn't just provide a reason that we know the principle of contradiction, it would provide a reason that the principle of contradiction is true. But it is easy to see that there cannot be such a reason. The principle of contradiction is prior to anything that might be offered as an explanation for its truth. For example, suppose the principle of contradiction were not true. Suppose that even the minimal principle of contradiction were not true. Then every statement would be both true and false. Then of course it would be true that the principle of contradiction is true by convention. But it would also be true that the principle of contradiction is not true by convention. It would be true that our laying down certain linguistic stipulations does not cause the principle of contradiction to be true. To put it bluntly, we can't make the principle of contradiction true by convention unless it's *already* true. This objection, the objection of explaining too much, also applies to other historic empiricist attempts, and even non-empiricist attempts, to explain the laws of logic. For example, that they are the laws of thought, or that they arise from relations of our ideas.

Of course one might try a moderate conventionalism. That is, one might try saying that the laws of logic, or at least the principle of contradiction, or at least the typical principle of contradiction, or at least the minimal principle of contradiction, are just true, and one might agree that the truth can't sensibly be explained in terms of anything else, but one might hold that what is a matter of convention is not the truth of these laws but their necessity or the rationality of believing them. This, however, does not seem very appetizing. To take the latter proposal first, if it's simply true by convention that it's rational to believe the laws of logic and this convention is simply the convention constituting the conventional use of the tri-syllabic English word 'rational', then what we have is the somewhat notorious ordinary language solution to Hume's problem, only now proposed as the solution to the problem of deduction. With respect to the former, i.e., the appeal to ordinary language as a solution to Hume's problem, Wesley Salmon once remarked that all this amounts to is the claim that if you use induction then you have the right to apply to yourself the noise 'rational', *and isn't that nice.* Professor Strawson replied to Salmon by observing that our propensity to make inductions need not be thought of as either arbitrary on the one hand, nor as conventional on the other; it may be *natural.* I take it that by 'natural' Strawson meant something like 'innate'. Now, whatever the virtue may be of regarding our propensity to make inductions as simply an innate tendency that we have, it does seem as if in this respect deduction is different from induction. To say that our faith in the most fundamental principles of deductive logic, our faith in the principle of contradiction itself, is simply an innate propensity and that it has no need of justification just because it is an innate propensity, is to obliterate totally the distinction between reason and blind faith. Of course, I'm not accusing either Peter Strawson or David Hume of making this move; they would both restrict their nativist account to induction, and not deduction. Nor can I accept the view that the necessity of the laws of logic, i.e., the fact that they hold in all possible worlds not only in the actual world, the fact that even if we accept the laws of logic as true in the actual world, we cannot go on and say 'but of course they might not have been true', or at least we cannot say 'it might have been that every statement was both true and false', is accounted for by convention.

It is true that there are accounts of logical truth, notably Quine's, according to which such a schema as $\sim (p \,\&\, \sim p)$, if valid at all, is *ipso facto* necessary, that is to say there's no difference on Quine's account between saying that every instance of $\sim (p \,\&\, \sim p)$ is true in the actual world, and saying that it is necessary that $\sim (p \,\&\, \sim p)$; but this seems to me to be wrong. For one thing this assumes what we may call a Humean account of the modalities, i.e., it assumes that what is true in possible worlds is totally determined by what is true in the actual world plus our conventions. If this is right then there cannot be two possible worlds in which the *same* events take place, but which are such that *if* a certain experiment had been performed, which never was performed in either world, then different things would have happened in the two worlds. Now ask yourself this question: can you imagine two worlds in neither of which the experiment is performed? The experiment just requires too much energy and the government won't let the physicist use so much energy in one experiment. Exactly the same events happen in both worlds but is it the case that *if* the experiment had been performed, *if* a certain particle had been submitted to much much higher energies than were ever concentrated in a small space, then in *one* of the two worlds the particle would have split and in the other it would not have split? In other words, does the totality of facts about what events *actually* take place determine the truth value of all statements of the form 'it is *possible* that *p*'? To me, at least, it seems that the answer is 'no', and if the answer is 'no', then both Quinean accounts of logical necessity and Humean accounts of causality have to be wrong. But I don't want to discuss this here, I simply want to point out that anyone who shares my modal-realist intuitions has to reject the claim that the *necessity* of the principles of logic is any *more* a matter of convention than their truth is. If any one is tempted to hold it, the form of moderate conventionalism that consists in saying that the laws of logic are *just* true in the actual world, but that *given* that they're true in the actual world it's a matter of our convention that they're true in all *possible* worlds seems to me quite untenable.

Incidently, the claim that physical possibility statements are translatable into statements about what actually happens seems to me in no better shape than the claim that statements about material objects are translatable into statements about sense data; and if physical possibility statements are not disguised statements about what actually happens then it is hard to see how logical possibility statements can be. There is however an account which goes part of the way towards explaining the special status of at least some of the laws of logic. A version of this account was, I believe, offered by Saul Kripke in a seminar at Princeton in which he criticized my published views on quantum logic; and the root idea of the account is to be found already in Aristotle's remarks about the laws of logic.

The idea is that the laws of logic are so central to our thinking that they define what a rational argument is. This may not show that we could never change our mind about the laws of logic, i.e., that no causal process could lead us to vocalize or believe different statements; but it does show that we could not be brought to change our minds *by a rational argument.* Let me spell this out a little. Typical rational arguments either have the form of chains of deduction of the familiar 'if *a*, then *b*' form, or they have the form of inferences to the best explanation. But the latter sort of inductive arguments of the form 'if *a* then *b*'; '*b*, so probably or plausibly *a*' also rely on properties of the connective 'if then', specifically upon *modus ponens.* Both in inductive reasoning and in deductive reasoning we make use of the fact that our language contains a connective which satisfies transitivity and *modus ponens.* This does not show that these two rules of inference are separately or jointly unrevisable; but it does show that if somebody rejected both of them then we would have no way of arguing with him. And indeed, Aristotle remarks that if anyone pretends to disbelieve one of the laws of logic and undertakes to argue with us, we can easily convince him that his own argument presupposes the very laws of logic that he is objecting to.

Neither Aristotle nor Kripke make the mistake, however, of offering this account as an account of why the laws of logic are true in the first place. All this account says is that part of their very special epistemic character is explained by what Quine would call their *centrality*. That is, they're presupposed by so much of the activity of argument itself that it is no wonder that we cannot envisage their being overthrown, or all of them being overthrown, by rational argument. But we should be clear about what the centrality argument does not show. It does not show that a putative law of logic, for instance the principle of contradiction, could not be overthrown by *direct observation*. Presumably I would give up the principle of contradiction if I ever had a sense datum which was both red and not red, for example. And the centrality argument sheds no light on how we know that this could never happen.

Note

This is a first draft of a paper I never finished. I no longer agree with the conclusion for a number of reasons, but I think the arguments are still of interest. One way I would begin to meet some of the arguments in this paper is by distinguishing two senses of 'revise'. A statement may be 'revised' by *negating* it: for example, saying 'this is not white', where formerly we said 'this is white'; or it may be revised by *challenging a concept it contains*. My present position (18 February 1977) is that there are statements that cannot be revised in the *first* way (in this I think the foregoing paper is completely right), but that every statement is eligible for revision in the second way.

The question raised in the last paragraph – how do we know that a *direct observation* might not in the future contradict the principle of contradiction – assumes that *what we now say* and *what is the case* are totally independent. Even if we grant that we may in the future *say* 'this sheet of paper is white and this sheet of paper is not white', we don't have to grant that we might be *right*. It may be that under our *present* conceptual scheme it is *mandatory* to find some explanation of that *future* utterance under which it is *not literally correct*. In Quine's terminology, it may be that homophonic translation (taking the future utterances at 'face value') is inadmissible in this case. When I wrote the foregoing paper, I would have replied: 'even if we refuse to say now that the future sheet of paper might be both red and not red that does not *of itself* make it true that the future sheet of paper *won't* be both red and not red. How do we know it doesn't just make *us* stubborn?' This assumes that there is an intelligible distinction *within* our conceptual system between what it is possible to conceive of within that system and what is really (independently of all conceptual systems) the case. This is just what I criticize in the Address referred to (Putnam 1976).

On the other hand, I am not urging that we regard all logical and mathematical truth as simply the product of our translation-practices (let alone of 'convention'). I have long urged that there is an irreducible *factual* element in logic and mathematics (e.g., the *consistency* of a set of conventions is not itself a convention); which is not to deny that there is also a conventional *component* to logic and mathematics. I think it is right to say that, within our present conceptual scheme, the minimal principle of contradiction is *so* basic that it cannot significantly be 'explained' at all. But that does not make it an 'absolutely *a priori* truth', in the sense of an absolutely unrevisable truth. Mathematical intuitionism, for example, represents one proposal for revising even the minimal principle of contradiction: not by saying that it is *false*, but by denying the applicability of the classical concepts of truth and falsity at all. Of course, then there would be a *new* 'minimal principle of contradiction': for example, 'no statement is both proved and disproved' (where 'proof' is taken to be a concept which does *not* presuppose the classical notion of 'truth' by the intuitionists); but this is not the minimal principle of contradiction. Every statement is subject to revision; but not in every *way*.

Note to supersede (supplement?) the preceding note

Added 23 December 1977

As I continue to think about these matters, it now seems to me that the preceding note does not do justice to what was *right* in the original paper. Rather than simply revise it, I have chosen to supplement the original paper-plus-note-which-I-added-later with yet *another* note for a metaphilosophical reason: it seems to me, and it has also been remarked by another philosopher I respect, that we philosophers are frequently torn in just the fashion that I am torn now between opposing considerations, but we very infrequently show it in *print*. What we do is let ourselves be torn in private until we finally 'plonk' for one alternative or the other; then the published paper only shows what we plonked for, and not the being torn. For once, the present paper-plus-potentially-infinite-series-of-notes *will* show the 'being torn'.

The preceding note tried to rescue what I called the 'moderate Quinean' position by taking the line that 'every statement is revisable but not in every *way*'. Specifically, a distinction was drawn between giving up a statement by accepting its negation, and giving up a statement by giving up concepts which occur in the statement (as somehow defective).

I don't think this works. Consider the statement I used in the original paper to show that there exists *at least one a priori truth*. This was the statement: 'Not *every* statement is *both* true and false.' In the previous Note, I said we might give this up by giving up the *classical* notions of truth and falsity: for example, by going over to intuitionist logic and metatheory. But surely if we did *that* we wouldn't view it as *giving up* the concepts of truth and falsity; rather we would view it as giving up an incorrect *analysis* of those notions.

Here it seems Quine has an easy rejoinder. He can say 'See! It's just as I told you. You can't draw a non-arbitrary line between changing the meaning of the words and changing collateral beliefs. And for that very reason you can't tell if the original statement is still being expressed by the sentence "Not every statement is both true and false." Lacking any meaningful notion of synonymy, i.e., of statement identity, the question of whether some *statement* (not *sentence*!) is immune from revision lacks all sense.'

But, as I have argued in the papers cited at the beginning, Quine isn't just arguing against the notion of *synonymy*. (If he were, then if linguists were to come up with a well-motivated proposal for assigning sentences to synonymy classes, Quine's work would lose all interest.) Much of Quine's argument – specifically, his historical argument from the succession of past scientific revolutions – was *independent* of the question of whether there is a good criterion for sentence synonymy. Quine excited philosophers because he put forward a picture of epistemology in which there was no *room* for apriority (miscalled 'analyticity' by Quine *and* his positivist opponents). He excited philosophers by putting forward a view of epistemology in which 'no statement is immune from revision', a very different claim from the claim that the question 'Is every statement immune from revision?' is *meaningless*. It is this view of epistemology that I am now criticizing.

Moreover, we can finesse the question of whether adopting intuitionism would or would not be to change the meaning of 'true' and 'false'. If it is true, as I argued in the preceding Note, that we can't give up the critical statement except by changing the meaning of 'true' and 'false' (i.e., 'giving up the concepts'), then the following hypothetical must be *absolutely* unrevisable:

If the classical notions of truth and falsity do not have to be given up, then not every statement is both true and false.

(In general, as Gareth Evans once remarked to me, to say that a statement is revisable, but only in a certain way, is to say that a certain conditional is *un*revisable.)

Again, look at the situation the following way: Consider the following rule of inference (call it 'the absolutely inconsistent rule'): *from any and all premise-sets, including the null set of premises, to infer every p*. The argument of the previous paper was that, whatever might be said about everything being up for revision in the big spiderweb (or field of force, or whatever your favorite metaphor may be) of beliefs, at least one thing is sure: it can never be rational to accept the absolutely inconsistent rule. And this seems right.

Does this mean that we have to go back to the idea of fixed unchanging canons of rationality, which Quine so persuasively attacked? I don't think it does. It seems right to me that we use our scientific method to devise a better scientific method at every stage. (Reichenbach, who stressed this idea in much of his writing, compared this to all use of tools. The first crude tools were fashioned with our hands; then we used crude tools to fashion more refined tools, and so on.) We started with a 'method' which evolution has 'hard wired in' to our brains, and we used that 'method' to discover (after how many thousands of years?) some principles of deduction and induction, which, after more thousands of years, have begun to be explicitly formalized, at least in part, and to be ever more mathematically sophisticated. And these principles will undoubtedly guide us in the search for still better principles (together with the method 'hard wired in' to our brains, which we still have to fall back on more than we like to admit). But the fact that the canons of rationality are themselves evolving doesn't mean they don't exist (*pace* Feyerabend, *pace* Foucault!), nor does it mean that, in the course of the evolution, *anything whatsoever* (including acceptance of the absolutely inconsistent rule) might occur. Evolution, in the domain of *instruments*, does not imply total, protean, lack of definite structure.

But, after all, just how important is it that Quine is wrong in his *total* rejection of the *a priori*? In one way it is not very important. We do not have a good *theory* of rationality, and are unlikely to have one in the foreseeable future. Lacking the 'rigid designator' of rationality, the theoretical definition which tells us what rationality is in every possible world (as 'water is H_2O' tells us what water is in every possible world), it is virtually hopeless to show with any semblance of good argument that any specific statement is such that it would be irrational to ever give it up (apart from special examples, such as the one I constructed). Nor do we really need a proof that a statement is *a priori* in this sense (rationally unrevisable) very often. If a statement has the property that *we cannot now describe* any circumstances under which it would be rational to give it up, that will surely suffice for most purposes of philosophical argument. But, if it is always dangerous to take on the burden of trying to show that a statement is absolutely *a priori*, the foregoing reflections show that it is not just dangerous but actually wrong to make the quick leap from the fact that it is dangerous to claim that any statement is absolutely *a priori* to the absolute claim that there are no *a priori* truths.

7

Analyticity and apriority: beyond Wittgenstein and Quine

Both Wittgenstein and Quine have had important insights in connection with the nature of mathematical and logical 'necessity', and both have written things that have transformed the discussion of this topic. But it is the burden of this paper to show that the views of both are unacceptable as they stand. I hope that a short and sharp statement of why both sorts of views will not do may help take us to a new stage in the discussion.

Part 1: Why mathematical necessity is not explained by human nature, 'forms of life', etc.

Wittgensteinian views

Just *what* Wittgenstein's contention is, in connection with philosophers' opinions, theories, and arguments on the topic of 'mathematical necessity', has been a subject of considerable controversy. Clearly he thinks the whole discussion is nonsensical and confused; but *why* (in his view) it is nonsensical and confused, and whether he offers any explanation at all of why we *think* there is such a thing as mathematical necessity and of what the difference is between mathematical and empirical statements, is a subject on which there seems to be a great deal of disagreement among his interpreters.

I shall not attempt to do any textual exegesis here. I know what the (several) views of *Wittgensteinians* are, even if I do not know for sure which, if any, was Wittgenstein's; and what I shall try to show is that not even the most sophisticated of these 'Wittgensteinian' views is tenable.

Here is a first approximation to Wittgenstein's view: when we make a mathematical assertion, say '$2 + 2 = 4$', the 'necessity' of this assertion is accounted for by the fact that we would not *count* anything as a counterexample to the statement. The statement is not a 'description' of any fact, but a 'rule of description': i.e., a directive to the effect that cases in which we *seem* to add two things to two things and get five, or whatever, are to be explained away (e.g., by saying that a fifth thing must have been produced by the interaction). In a terminology employed by other philosophers, the statement is *analytic*.

The problem with such views – a problem Wittgenstein himself clearly points out, which is why the above cannot be more than a first approximation to Wittgenstein's view – is that the set of theorems of mathematics is infinite (or appears to be infinite: I shall explain the reservation shortly). Only a finite number of mathematical truths, such as '2 + 2 = 4', 'every number has a successor', can possibly be *primitive* rules of description (be what Carnap called 'meaning postulates'); most mathematical truths are not *directly* meaning stipulations, or 'rules of description', or whatever, but only *consequences* of 'rules of description'.

Now, the thesis that every theorem of mathematics is either true by convention (a meaning postulate, in Carnap's sense, or a 'rule of description' in Wittgenstein's) or else a *consequence* of statements that are true by convention has often been advanced as an *epistemologically explanatory* thesis (e.g., by Ayer in *Language, Truth, and Logic* and Carnap in the *Foundations of Logic and Mathematics*), but it cannot really explain the truth of the theorems of mathematics (*other* than the ones in the finite set that are *directly* 'true by convention') at all, for a reason pointed out by both Wittgenstein and Quine: namely, *it takes logic to derive the consequences from the conventions.* The 'exciting' thesis that logic is true by convention reduces to the unexciting claim that *logic is true by conventions plus logic.* No real advance has been made.

What then was Wittgenstein's view? Call the Wittgenstein who held (or seemed to hold) that '2 + 2 = 4' is true by convention (a 'rule of description') 'Wittgenstein$_1$'. Call the Wittgenstein who pointed out the emptiness of the Ayer–Carnap position 'Wittgenstein$_2$'. What could Wittgenstein$_2$'s position have been? (Not to mention Wittgenstein$_3$, Wittgenstein$_4$, . . .)

Michael Dummett (1959) suggested a daring possibility: namely, that Wittgenstein was a *radical conventionalist.* That is, Wittgenstein was a conventionalist who held not just that some finite set of meaning postulates is true by convention, but that whenever we accept what we call a 'proof' in logic or mathematics, an *act of decision* is involved: a decision to *accept* the proof. This decision, on Dummett's reading, is never *forced* on us by some prior thing called the 'concepts' or 'the meaning of the words'; even given these *as they have previously been specified*, it is still *up to us* whether we shall accept the proof as a valid deployment of those concepts or not. The decision to accept the proof is a *further* meaning stipulation: the 'theorems of mathematics and logic' that we actually prove and accept are not just *consequences* of conventions, but *individually* conventional. Such a 'radical' conventionalism, Dummett pointed out, would be immune to the Quine–Wittgenstein objection to the Ayer–Carnap sort of conventionalism.

In response, Barry Stroud (1965) pointed out† that the position Dummett calls 'radical conventionalism' cannot possibly be Wittgenstein's. A convention, in the literal sense, is something we can legislate either way. Wittgenstein does not anywhere say or suggest that the mathematician proving a theorem is *legislating* that it shall be a theorem (and the mathematician would get into a lot of trouble, to put it mildly, if he tried to 'legislate' it the opposite way).

Basing himself on a good deal of textual evidence, Stroud suggested that Wittgenstein's position was that it is not *convention* or *legislation* but our *forms of life* (i.e., our human nature as determined by our biology-plus-cultural-history) that cause us to accept certain proofs *as* proofs. And Stroud's reply to Dummett's interpretation appears to have been generally accepted by Wittgenstein scholars.

The consistency objection

It appears to me that Stroud's reply, while correct as a response to Dummett's interpretation, does not speak to the real philosophical point Dummett was making. The real point is that if *either* Dummett *or* Stroud is right, then Wittgenstein is claiming that mathematical truth and necessity *arise in us*, that it is human nature and forms of life that *explain* mathematical truth and necessity. If this is right, then it is the greatest philosophical discovery of all time. Even if it is wrong, it is an astounding philosophical claim. If Stroud does not dispute that Wittgenstein advanced this claim – and he does not seem to dispute it – then *his* interpretation of Wittgenstein is a revision of Dummett's rather than a total rejection of it.

Unfortunately, there seems to be a devastating objection to Wittgenstein's position (i.e., to 'Wittgenstein$_2$') if Stroud has really got him right: consider number theory (Peano arithmetic) in any of its standard formalizations. Even if our acceptance of the Peano axioms is just the acceptance of a bunch of *meaning determinations* (whether these be *stipulations*, i.e., acts of legislation, as on the 'conventionalist' interpretation, or fixed by our 'forms of life', as

† For a related discussion see Canfield (1975).

on Stroud's interpretation), still they are not *logically arbitrary* determinations, for they are, after all, required to be *consistent*. Our nature, our forms of life, etc., may explain why we *accept* the Peano axioms *as opposed to some other consistent set*; but our nature cannot possibly make an *inconsistent* set of axioms *true*. And consistency is an *objective mathematical fact*, not an *empirical* fact. Thus, there is at least *one* mathematical fact – namely the consistency of the meaning determinations themselves, *whatever* these be produced by – which is *not* explained by our nature or 'forms of life' in any intelligible sense.

Sometimes the reply to this is merely the textual point that Wittgenstein pooh-poohed consistency ('Why this *one* bug-a-boo?'), pointed out that an inconsistent system could still be usable (if one avoids drawing the contradiction), etc. But these remarks do not speak to the objection. Wittgenstein had better have something *better* than this to say in response to the objection or he is done for (as a philosopher of logic and mathematics).

And he does have something better than this to say. His *real* response to the consistency objection goes to the very depths of his philosophy, and without drawing it out, one cannot begin to do justice to his thought.

Wittgenstein on 'following a rule'

Suppose I have a certain concept in my mind. Whatever introspectible *signs* there may be that I have the concept, whatever mental presentations I am able to call up in connection with the concept, cannot specify the *content* of the concept, as Wittgenstein argued in the famous sections of *Philosophical Investigations* which concern 'following a rule': say the rule 'add one'. For, if two species in two possible worlds (I state the argument in *most* un-Wittgensteinian terminology!) have the same mental signs in connection with the expression 'add one', it is still possible that their *practice* might diverge; and it is the practice, as Wittgenstein shows, that fixes the *interpretation*; signs do not interpret themselves – not even mental signs (or, one might add for the benefit of physicalists like Hartry Field or David Lewis, signs in the brain). To take a simple example – a variant of Wittgenstein's own 'add one' example – even if someone *pictures* the relation 'C is the ponential of A and B' (i.e., C follows from A and B by *modus ponens*) in his mind just as we do and has agreed with us on finitely many cases, (e.g., that q is the potential of $(p \lor r) \supset q$ and $(p \lor r)$), still he may have a divergent interpretation of 'ponential of' which will only reveal itself in some future cases (even if he agrees with us in his 'theory'; i.e., what he *says* about 'ponential of'; for he may have a divergent interpretation of the whole theory, as the Skolem–Löwenheim theorem shows).

The relevance of this to philosophy of mathematics is immediate. First of all, there is the question of *finitism*: human practice, actual and potential, only extends finitely far. We cannot 'go on counting forever', even if we say we can, not really. If there are possible *divergent extensions of our practice*, then there are possible *divergent interpretations of even the natural number sequence*: our practice, our mental representations, etc., do not (in set-theoretic terminology) single out a unique 'standard model' of even the natural number sequence. We are tempted to think they do because we easily shift from 'we could go on counting' to 'an *ideal machine* could go on counting' (or 'an *ideal mind* could go on counting'); but talk of ideal machines (or minds) is very different, Wittgenstein reminds us, from talk of *actual* machines and persons. Talk of what an ideal machine could do is talk *within* mathematics; it cannot fix the interpretation *of* mathematics.

Second, if Wittgenstein is right (and I am presently inclined to think that he is), then the statement 'there are seven consecutive sevens in the decimal expansion of π' may have *no* truth value: speaking set-theoretically, it may be true in some models that fit our practice and false in others. And similarly, and for the same reason, 'Peano arithmetic is consistent' may have *no* truth value: for this statement too talks about an infinite sequence (the sequence of *all* theorems of Peano arithmetic), and the sequence may not really be determinate.

Still, assuming some number – say 10^{20} – is small enough so that we could collectively and over time (perhaps several generations) examine all proofs with fewer than that number of symbols, the question 'Is Peano arithmetic 10^{20}-consistent?' should have a determinate answer even on Wittgenstein's view.

Why Wittgenstein's view does not work

To see why Wittgenstein's view does not work, it is necessary to resolve an ambiguity in the view. It is true (and, as we have conceded, it is also a profound observation) that even so simple an operation as *modus ponens* is not 'fixed' once and for all by our mental representation of the operation; it is our actual 'unpacking' of the mental representation in action, our *de facto* dispositions which determine what we *mean* by 'ponential of'. But there are two 'scenarios' as to *how* our dispositions might determine the extension of 'ponential of'. *Scenario* 1: Given a putative proof (with less than 10^{20} symbols) one checks it by going down by line, verifying that each line with *ax* next to it is an axiom, and that each line with two numbers (n) (m) next to it is the ponential of the lines numbered (n), (m) respectively. If the last line is '$1 = 0$', one announces 'Peano arithmetic has turned out to be inconsistent'. *Scenario* 2: Given a putative proof (with less than 10^{20} symbols) one proceeds as in scenario 1 *except that if any* line is '$1 = 0$' (or anything verifiably false by just elementary calculation and truth-functional logic), then one *modifies what counts as ponential* so that the line in question is said *not* to be the ponential of the relevant lines (n), (m).

Both scenarios are logically possible. And if our actual dispositions *were* as described in scenario 2, then Peano arithmetic would certainly be consistent in the absolute sense, and this consistency would *arise from us*, be explained by our nature (our dispositions) in a clear sense. But the actual scenario, the scenario that describes the dispositions we actually *have*, is scenario 1. And *that* scenario does not 'build in' absolute consistency. Perhaps 'ponential of' is only defined 'finitistically' in the way we described in the preceding section; perhaps the extension of 'ponential of' is not *fixed* in the case of proofs and formulas that are beyond human and machine reach; certainly, in the cases where it *is* fixed, it is fixed only by our dispositions and not just by the thought-signs in our minds or the representations in our brains; *but the 10^{20}-consistency of Peano arithmetic is still not an artifact of this dispositionally fixed interpretation.*

Note that I am *not* denying that mathematical truth is 'perspectival' in the sense of depending for its very *content* on our actual existential natures and dispositions (think of how many different things could be *meant* by the words, thought-signs, etc., that we use to represent Peano arithmetic to ourselves and each other; imagine different possible worlds in which the words, thought-signs, etc., are the same but the *practice* diverges from ours at various points). *All* truth is perspectival in this sense, and I agree with Wittgenstein that this makes nonsense of metaphysical talk of our representations 'copying' reality. But perspectival facts are still facts. The content of the judgment that there is a large Mountain Ash on my property depends on our 'forms of life', *granted*; the fact that there is a Mountain Ash on my property is in that sense, perspectival, *granted*; but it is *not an artifact of the way we use the words* that there is a large Mountain Ash on my property. And no more is it an *artifact of the way we use the words* that Peano arithmetic is 10^{20}-consistent. The truth of the judgment that there is a Mountain Ash on my property depends on our nature, but also on more than our nature; it is not a truth that is *explained* by facts about human nature; it does not *arise from us*. And similarly, the fact that Peano arithmetic is 10^{20}-consistent depends on our nature, but also on more than our nature; it similarly is not a truth that is *explained* by facts about human nature; it too does not *arise from us*. Only if our dispositions were described in scenario 2 would they *explain* the truth of the consistency statement.

Another Wittgensteinian move

There is a move that may also have been in Wittgenstein's mind which we shall briefly consider here. One might hold that it is a presupposition of, say, '$2 + 2 = 4$', that we shall never *meet* a situation we would count as a counterexample (this is an *empirical* fact); and one might claim that the appearance of a 'factual' element in the statement '$2 + 2 = 4$' arises from *confusing* the mathematical assertion (which has *no* factual content, it is claimed) with the empirical assertion first mentioned.

This move, however, depends heavily on overlooking or denying the circumstance that an empirical fact can have a partly mathematical *explanation*. Thus, let T be an actual (physically instantiated) Turing machine so programmed that if it is started scanning the input '111', it never halts. Suppose we start T scanning the input '111', let T run for two weeks, and then turn T off. In the course of the two-week run, T did not halt. Is it not the case that the *explanation* of the fact that T did not halt is simply the *mathematical* fact that a Turing machine with that program never halts on the input, *together with* the empirical fact that T instantiates that program (and continued to do so throughout the two weeks)?

Similarly, if human beings spend millions of years searching through all the proofs with less than 10^{20} symbols in Peano arithmetic and they never find a proof of '$1 = 0$', is not the *explanation* of this fact simply that, as a matter of *mathematical* fact, Peano arithmetic is 10^{20}-consistent, *and* the human beings took sufficient care so that the putative proofs they examined during the long search really *were* proofs in Peano arithmetic?

As for the case of the statement '$2 + 2 = 4$': suppose that on five thousand occasions two things are added to two other things (using some physical operation of combination) and the resulting group is counted. Suppose that 4,800 times the result of the count is '4'; that 198 times the result is '5'; and that 2 times the result is '3'. Suppose a careful investigation is made, and it is found that in the 198 cases in which the result was '5', some interaction (e.g., sexual reproduction) added an individual to the group, and that in the two cases in which the result was '3', some interaction destroyed a member of the group. Is not the explanation of the fact that in the remaining 4,800 cases the result of the count was '4' just the fact that in *those* cases no individual involved in the combining process was destroyed or otherwise removed from the group counted at the end; that no individuals were added to the final group by any interactions; and that, as a matter of simple arithmetic fact, $2 + 2 = 4$?

If this is merely something we *say* then, *granted* that that explains what we say about these 4,800 cases, how is it that we actually *found* (as opposed to just *posited*) an explanation of what went wrong in the deviant 200 cases? If one says that it is just a *surd* empirical fact that one *does* find such explanations in such cases, then is one not abandoning the whole world view of science since Newton for a very strange metaphysics? On the scientific view, *many* facts have partly mathematical explanations (and much of the business of science consists in giving them); on the alternative metaphysical picture, there are just all these surd empirical facts *and* a way we *talk* about them. We do not often come up with apparent counterexamples to '$2 + 2 = 4$', but it is not *because* two and two *do* make four that we do not. Rather, on the picture just suggested, it is *because* we do not often come up with apparent counterexamples that we say '$2 + 2 = 4$'. Why should anyone believe this?

Perhaps if the world were such that we regularly came up with apparent counterexamples to '$2 + 2 = 4$' in some context (say, counting bosons), then the best language-cum-theory might be one that said that in some cases two and two make five. If such a case could be coherently described, this would be reason to think that *arithmetic is empirical*; but it still would not be reason to think that arithmetic is not *factual*.

The conceivability of the mathematically impossible

What I have argued is that 'Peano arithmetic is 10^{20}-consistent' and 'Turing machine T will not halt if run for so-and-so many operations on input "111"' are *mathematical facts*, and that these facts are not explained by our 'natures' or 'forms of life'. It is not that these statements are true because we have a disposition to *protect* them from what would otherwise be falsifiers; we have no such disposition. What I want to consider in the present section is the nature of such mathematical facts.

Unlike '$2+2=4$', which certainly seems *a priori*, the two facts just mentioned have a quasi-empirical character. We can conceive of their being false, whereas we doubt we can conceive of '$2+2=4$' being false; it may be, in the case of the second fact, that there is no *proof* that Turing machine T won't halt on the given input in so-and-so many steps which does not amount to *running* the machine, or a calculation which exactly simulates the operations of the machine, *through* so-and-so many steps (some combinatorial facts seem 'brute'); both statements can be overthrown by a well-attested *calculation*.

But is there *really* a sense of 'conceivable' (of any philosophical importance) in which the *falsity* of these *mathematically true* statements is *conceivable*? How can the *mathematically impossible* be conceivable?

The answer is that there is no part of our language in which it is more wrong to think of our understanding of the sentences as consisting in a sort of Cartesian 'clear and distinct idea' of the *conditions under which they are true* than mathematics. We do not understand Fermat's last theorem by having a 'clear and distinct idea' of the conditions under which it is true: how could we? Our mastery of mathematical language resides, at least in part, in our knowledge of *proof conditions* as opposed to *truth conditions*, in our knowledge of the *conditions of verification* holistically associated with the sentences by mathematical practice. But part of the notion of a *verification condition* in both mathematical science and empirical science is this: verification conditions are conditions that correspond to a certain *skill*: the skill of being able to tell when a sentence has been proved (or, in empirical science, confirmed). It is part of the notion of such a skill that one can have it without knowing in advance whether the sentence in question *will* be proved or disproved (confirmed or disconfirmed).

Understanding Fermat's last theorem, for example, consists at least in part of being able to recognize a proof or at least a counter-example; the weird view is the view of Ayer and Carnap according to which *all* true mathematical assertions have 'the same meaning' and it requires a *psychological* explanation (allegedly) to say why we do not *recognize* that Fermat's last theorem has the same meaning (assuming it is true) as '$2+2=4$'. *Only* the supposition that the meaning is the *truth conditions* could have led to such a view (and then only on a view according to which grasp of the truth conditions is something like an eidetic image of all the worlds in which they obtain).

In short, we can understand 'T will halt', although, in fact, it may be *mathematically impossible* for T to halt, because we are not mathematically omniscient, because our *understanding* of most mathematical sentences has to consist (in part) in a skill of recognizing whether they are proved or disproved, and because *this* kind of understanding *never* involves *knowing in advance* whether the statement *will be proved or disproved*. In this respect, '$2+2 = 4$' may be different; knowing that '$2+2 = 4$' may be involved in knowing the arithmetical language; but knowing whether Peano arithmetic is 10^{20}-consistent or not is *not* presupposed by knowing the arithmetical language. I *understand* the statement 'Peano arithmetic is *not* 10^{20}-consistent', even though it is in fact *mathematically false*, because I have a skill (or participate in a society that has that skill!). I (we) could *tell* if we found a proof that Peano arithmetic is inconsistent. The fact that the *specification* of that ability is possible *independently* of whether the proposition to be understood *can* be proved or not should not surprise us; if it were *not* the case we could *understand* only those mathematical statements that are already decided!

The 'revisability' of mathematics

The remarks I have been making have a connection with a curious fact which I now wish to point out: although *all* mathematical truths are 'metaphysically necessary', i.e., true in all possible worlds, simply because nothing that violates a truth of mathematics *counts* as a *description* of a 'possible world', *some* mathematical truths are 'epistemically contingent'. What I have in mind is the following: there may be no way in which we can *know* that a certain abstract structure is consistent other than by seeing it instantiated either in mental images or in some physical representation. For example, the only way to convince myself that it is possible to make n triangles using m rigid bars of equal length (for certain values of n and m) may be to actually produce the figure; the only way to show that a certain Turing machine halts may be to run it (or simulate its running on paper) until it halts; the only way to know that a certain formal system is inconsistent may be to *derive* the contradiction in it. Now the statement that *these m* matches (or whatever) are arranged so as to form n triangles is certainly an *a posteriori* statement. It is even an *empirical* statement. Yet my rational confidence in the mathematically necessary statement 'it is possible to form n triangles with m rigid bars' is *no greater* than my confidence in the empirical statement. If I come to doubt the empirical statement, then, unless I have some *other* example that establishes the truth of the mathematical statement, I will come to doubt the mathematical statement too. Nor need there be any way in which I could 'in principle' *know* the truth of the mathematical statement without depending on some such empirical statement about mental or physical objects, diagrams, calculations, etc.

If this point has not been very much appreciated in the past (although Descartes was clearly aware of this problem) it is because of the tendency, we remarked, to think that a fully rational ('ideally rational') being should be mathematically omniscient: should be able to 'just know' all mathematical truths *without proof*. (Perhaps by surveying all the integers, all the real numbers, etc., in his head.) This is just forgetting, once again, that we *understand* mathematical language *through* being able to recognize *proofs* (plus, of course, certain empirical applications, e.g., *counting*). It is not irrational to need a *proof* before one believes, for example, Fermat's last theorem – quite the contrary.

Of course, the status of '$2 + 2 = 4$' is quite different. We do not need a *proof* for this statement (barring epistemological catastrophe, e.g. coming to doubt *all* our past *counting*: but it is not clear what becomes of the concept of rationality itself when there is an epistemological catastrophe). Perhaps '$2 + 2 = 4$' is rationally unrevisable (or, at least, rationally unrevisable as long as 'universal hallucination', 'all my past memories are a delusion', and the like are not in the field). But, if we consider that '$2 + 2 = 4$' can sometimes be part of an *explanation*, is the fact (if it is a fact) that a rational being could not believe the denial of '$2 + 2 = 4$' (barring epistemological catastrophe) an explanation of the *truth* of '$2 + 2 = 4$'? Or is it rather just a fact about *rationality*?

Putting this question aside, like the hot potato it is, let us briefly consider the status of such mathematical truths as 'Peano arithmetic is consistent' and the principle of mathematical induction. These are not like the singular or purely existential combinatorial statements lately considered ('This formal system is inconsistent', 'There exists a way of forming m triangles with n matches', 'This Turing machine halts in less than N steps'). Certainly our beliefs in the consistency of Peano arithmetic and in induction are not epistemically contingent in the way that my belief that one can form m triangles using n matches (imagine I have just convinced myself by finding the arrangement) is epistemically contingent. I believe that arithmetic is consistent because I believe the axioms are true, and I believe that from true premises one cannot derive a contradiction; I have also studied and taught the Gentzen consistency proof; and these are *a priori* reasons. Yet there are still circumstances under which I would abandon my belief that Peano arithmetic is consistent; I would abandon that belief *if I discovered a contradiction.*

Many philosophers will feel that this remark is 'cheating'. They would say 'But you *could not* discover a contradiction.' True, it is mathematically impossible (and even 'metaphysically impossible', in the recently fashionable jargon) that there should be a contradiction in Peano arithmetic. But, as I remarked above, it *is not epistemically impossible.* We can conceive of finding a contradiction in Peano arithmetic, and we can make sense of the question 'What would you do if you came across a contradiction in Peano arithmetic?' ('Restrict the induction schema', would be my answer.)

As a matter of fact, there are circumstances in which it would be rational to believe that Peano arithmetic was inconsistent *even though it was not.*

Thus suppose I am caused to hallucinate by some marvelous process (say, by making me a 'brain in a vat' without my knowing it, and controlling all my sensory inputs superscientifically), and the content of the hallucination is that the whole logical community learns of a contradiction in Peano arithmetic (Saul Kripke discovers it). The proof is checked by famous logicians and even by machine, and it holds up. Perhaps I do not have time to check the proof myself; but I would believe, and rationally so, I contend, that Peano arithmetic *is* inconsistent on such evidence. And this shows that even 'Peano arithmetic is consistent' is not a fully rationally unrevisable statement. (Neither is full first-order induction, since an inconsistency in Peano arithmetic would make it rational to suppose that unrestricted induction was contradictory.)

This is messy. Clearly, philosophy of mathematics is *hard*. But the Wittgensteinian views that (1) mathematical statements do not express objective facts; and (2) their truth and necessity (or appearance of necessity) arise from and are explained by *our* nature, cannot be right.

If *our* nature explains why we shall never come across a contradiction in Peano arithmetic then, in exactly the same sense and to the same degree, it explains why there is a Mountain Ash in my yard. Both facts are dependent on my conceptual lenses; but neither fact is an artifact of these lenses. I do not create the properties of individual proofs in Peano arithmetic any more than I create the berries on the Mountain Ash.

Part 2: Re Quine

Introduction

These criticisms of Wittgenstein are grist for Quine's mill. Quine, at least as early as Wittgenstein, criticized the moderate conventionalist position for emptiness. But, whereas Wittgenstein departed from moderate conventionalism in the direction of radical conventionalism (which holds that the truth of the theorems as well as that of the axioms arises from us), Quine departed from moderate conventionalism in the direction of *empiricism*. In Quine's view, the unrevisability of mathematical statements is greater in degree than that of, say, the three-dimensionality of space or the conservation of energy, but not absolute. Truths of mathematics are partly empirical and partly 'conventional' like *all* truths; mathematics is as factual as physics, only better 'protected'.

Everything I said against Wittgenstein's view is consonant with these views of Quine. But Quine's views, like Wittgenstein's, will not do as they stand.

The problem with Wittgenstein's views is that they exaggerate the unrevisability of mathematics and logic. The problem with Quine's views is that they underestimate it. The view I wish to defend is not that classical logic or mathematics are *a priori*; I myself have argued elsewhere that logic is revisable, and that a form of modular logic ('quantum logic') should be adopted for the purpose of formalizing physical theory, and not classical logic. What I think (I blush to confess) is that what *is a priori* is that *most* statements obey certain logical laws. This will very likely offend both Platonistically minded and constructively minded philosophers (and both Wittgensteinians and Quinians); nevertheless, I shall try to make it plausible.

Quine and the *a priori*

Are there *a priori* truths? In other words, are there true statements which (1) it is rational to accept (at least if the right arguments occur to me), and (2) which it would never subsequently be rational to reject no matter how the world turns out (epistemically) to be? More simply, are there statements whose truth we would not be justified in denying in any *epistemically* possible world? Or is it rather the case that for *every* statement s there is an epistemically possible world in which it is fully rational to believe that not-s?

It is easy to see that this question depends crucially on the notion of a *statement*. *Statement* and not *sentence*: since for any *sentence* φ we can imagine a circumstance in which it would be rational to deny φ by just imagining a world in which it is rational to *change the meanings* of the words in φ in some suitable way (as those meanings are given by a standard translation manual connecting the language to which φ belongs at the two different times to some neutral language). So no one can possibly hold that there are unrevisable *sentences*. Accordingly, one response to the question for a philosopher who denies, as Quine does, that *synonymy* makes any sense – i.e., a philosopher who denies that there is any clear sense to the question 'does φ express the same statement at the two different times?' – is simply to say that apriority is a meaningless notion. The notion of apriority presupposes the notion of synonymy as much as the notion of analyticity does, and is meaningless for the same reason that the notion of synonymy is meaningless.

There is one trouble with this argument, and that is that it has not the slightest persuasive force for someone who is unconvinced, as I am unconvinced, that no sense can be made of the notion of *synonymy*. To my way of thinking, any philosophical claim that rests on the contention that no reasonable standard of synonymy exists at all, not even an interest-relative one, founders in absurdity. It may well be, of course, that Quine would not wish to deny the existence of an *interest-relative* standard of synonymy; however, if there is such a standard, then it makes sense to ask whether there are any sentences φ such that (1) *given the way we presently interpret them*, no fully rational being could deny them; and/or (2) if the world turns out to be such that a fully rational being *does* subsequently deny φ, then that will be because the *meaning* of φ, as specified by the way *we* translate φ into our present language, given *our* interests, will have changed. In short, if there is something – something useful and important, even if, in a sense, 'relative' – to the notion of synonymy, then why should there not be *as much* to the notion of apriority?

As I have pointed out elsewhere, however, Quine has another argument against apriority, one that does not depend at all upon his attacks on synonymy and on a 'linguistic' notion of analyticity. As Quine puts the argument, in the form of a rhetorical question,

Any statement can be held true come what may if we make drastic enough adjustments elsewhere in the system. Even a statement very close to the periphery can be held true in the face of recalcitrant experience by pleading hallucination or by amending certain statements of the kind called logical laws. Conversely, by the same token, no statement is immune to revision. Revision even of the logical law of the excluded middle has been proposed as a means of simplifying quantum mechanics; and what difference is there in principle between such a shift and a shift whereby Keppler superceded Ptolemy, or Einstein Newton, or Darwin Aristotle? (Quine, 1951, p. 43)

The revisions from which statements are not immune in the cases Quine describes are not changes of reference but of belief. To say, 'Einstein changed the meaning of "straight line"' would not explain away the appearance of a revision of belief; for how can we now say which paths were straight 'in the old sense' if the space-like geodesics of our space–time aren't? Something we thought to be *a priori* impossible turned out to be true.

In 'Carnap and logical truth', where he employs a similar argument, Quine draws the moral explicitly: 'We had been trying to make sense of the role of convention in *a priori* knowledge. Now the very distinction between *a priori* and empirical begins to waver and dissolve, at least as a distinction between sentences. (It could of course still hold as a distinction between factors in one's adoption of a sentence, but both factors might be operative everywhere.)' (Quine, 1966, p. 115)

It is this *argument from the history of science* that I challenge.

Here is a simple counterexample:

Could a fully rational being deny that *not every statement is both true and false*? To fix our ideas, let us specify that by a statement we mean simply a *belief or possible belief*, either one's own or someone else's, and that the term 'statement' is not intended to presuppose that beliefs are or are not 'propositions' as distinct from 'sentences' or even 'inscriptions'. Could someone, then, think all his own beliefs (and everyone else's) were both true and false? Let us also stipulate that we do not presuppose any particular account of 'truth' (e.g., that truth is or is not distinct from maximum warranted assertibility). If you do not like 'true', could someone believe that all his own beliefs (and everyone else's), and all possible beliefs, for that matter, are both fully warrantedly assertible and that their negations are fully warrantedly assertible as well?

At first blush, the answer is clearly 'no'. By *our* lights, to believe that all one's beliefs are both true and false (or whatever) is to give up *both* the notions of *belief* and *truth* (or warranted assertibility). In short, to believe *all* statements are correct (which is what we are talking about) would be to have no notion of rationality. At least *one* statement is *a priori*, because to deny that statement would be to forfeit rationality itself.

One a priori truth. It is, of course, possible to be skeptical about the existence of rationality itself. What I have in mind is not the possibility of total skepticism or relativism; what I am rather thinking of is the possibility that 'rational' or 'rationally acceptable' or 'warrantedly assertible' may not be the right notions for epistemology/methodology. Perhaps one should not say that statements are warrantedly assertible, but that they have a certain numerical 'degree of confirmation', as Carnap urged, or perhaps one should use some notion that is not thought of yet. But then the question, whether some statements (and some rules of inference) are such that it is always rational to accept (deny) them, will have an analog in terms of the new notion of degree of confirmation, or whatever. The question '*Are there any a priori truths?*' is a question *within* the theory of rationality; as long as we accept the theory, or the prospect of such a theory, we cannot justify rejecting or accepting any particular answer by the consideration that the theory of rationality itself may need recasting. What we are trying to answer by our lights (and by who else's lights should we try to answer it? – a question Quine is fond of asking) is whether an ideal theory of rationality would have certain features: we can speculate about this just as physicists speculate about whether an ideal physical theory would have certain features, while recognizing, just as they do, that our answer itself is a provisional one and that the true shape of future theory will be different in many unforeseen ways, from what we now envisage.

This being said, it does seem, as we remarked, that there is at least one *a priori* truth: that not every statement is both true (or fully correct to assert) and at the same time false (or fully correct to deny). But, of course, this statement itself admits of more than one interpretation. To bring out more clearly the interpretation I have in mind, let me speak of the rule: *infer every statement from every premise and from every set of premises, including the empty set* as the absolutely inconsistent rule (AIR). It is clear from the notion of rationality itself that to accept the AIR would be to abandon rationality. And the interpretation of 'Not every statement is both true and false' (or, more simply, 'Not every statement is true') that I have in mind is simply the interpretation under which to affirm this statement is simply to *reject* the AIR. In particular, acceptance of this statement, like rejection of the AIR, does not commit one to any particular view of what truth and falsity are (or what correctness is, or what inference is). It assumes what we may call the *generic* notions of truth (or correctness) and falsity (or incorrectness), and not the particular philosophical notions (e.g., the realist notion of truth, or the notion of warranted assertibility) which arise when one *refines* or *philosophically* analyzes the generic notions. I take it that there is a clear enough sense to the notions of rejecting the AIR, and of denying that every statement is both true and false. What I suggest is that it cannot seriously be maintained that there is an epistemically possible world in which acceptance of the AIR would be fully rational and warranted; and, further, I maintain that the point that acceptance of the AIR would involve abandonment of rationality itself is one that a fully rational mind should be able to see in any world. In short, the AIR is *a priori* rejectable.

The reader may wonder why I stated the principle of contradiction in such a weak form. Why did I not take 'not both p and not-p' as my example of an *a priori* truth? The answer is that our intuitions about what is true of *every* statement are much hazier than our intuitions about typical or normal statements. Consider the Russell antinomy: 'There is a set Z such that Z has as members all and only those sets that do not have themselves as members.' Suppose some future logical genius discovers a very elegant way of avoiding the antinomy without paying the usual price of stratifying the universe into types by admitting that some statements – in particular the 'paradoxical' ones, such as the Russell antinomy – are *both true and false*. Is this *really* ruled out *a priori*?

The reader may reply that this would not work because it is well known that from even one instance of 'p & $\sim p$' one can derive every statement. But this assumes that certain rules of propositional calculus are retained; perhaps the new scheme would depend on relevance logic (in which *it is not* true that 'every statement follows from a contradiction'). It seems to be that this is not something we can rule out *a priori*. Rather, this is just the sort of case in which we want to look at the complete proposal in the whole theoretical context before deciding. Perhaps there are epistemically possible worlds in which it is rational to believe that the Russell antinomy is both true and false. But this does not affect our argument that it would be an abandonment of rationality to believe that *every* statement was both true and false (or to believe that *typically* statements are both true and false).

Again, it may be objected that 'Normally statements are not both true and false' contains the vague term 'normally'. And also, even the statement 'Not every statement is both true and false' involves rather vague (I called them 'generic') notions of 'statement', 'truth', and 'falsity'. If *all a priori* truths contain such vague notions, then it may be that apriority is a phenomenon that affects only our ordinary language; that in the canonical, regimented, totally precise notation that Quine refers to in *Word and Object* as 'our first class conceptual system', there are indeed no *a priori* truths.

But the fact is that most of science and metascience cannot even be expressed in a perfectly precise notation (and all the more so if one includes philosophy under the rubric 'metascience' as Quine does). Words such as 'normally', 'typically', etc., are indispensable in biology and economics, not to mention law, history, sociology, etc.; while 'broad spectrum' notions such as 'cause' and 'factor' are indispensable for the introduction of new theoretical notions, even if they do not appear in 'finished science', if there is such a thing. Philosophy cannot be limited to commentary upon a supposed 'first-class conceptual system' which scarcely exists and whose expressive resources cover only a tiny fragment of what we care about.

So far the picture that is emerging from our discussion looks like this: there are some *a priori* truths, truths certified by the theory of rationality itself; but they have the character of *maxims* – general principles that are not, or at least may not be, exceptionless, and they involve 'generic', or somewhat pretheoretical, notions rather than the (supposedly) perfectly precise notions of an ideal theory in the exact sciences. That, barring a new treatment of very exceptional cases such as the Russell antinomy, a statement is not both true and false (in the ordinary pretheoretic sense of 'true' and 'false') is an example.

Apriority and analyticity

The argument I have given for the apriority of 'not every statement is true' and 'not every statement is both true and false' suggests another argument, and argument based on meaning theory rather than theory of rationality. This argument goes as follows: if someone accepts 'All statements are true', then, by the principle of universal instantiation (which we may take to be involved in the *meaning* of the universal quantifier), he is committed to '*Snow is white*' *is true*, to '*Snow is not white*' *is true*, to '*My hand has five fingers*' *is true*, to '*My hand does not have five fingers*' *is true*, etc. In short, given the rule of universal instantiation, acceptance of 'Every statement is true' (and of one's various beliefs and candidate beliefs and their negations as 'statements', in the relevant sense) commits one to acceptance of the AIR. And this is why the statement must be rejected.

Even if this argument is correct, it does not wholly avoid the theory of rationality, for the argument depends on the fact that one cannot accept the AIR, and this is based on considerations about rationality rather than upon considerations about meaning. It might be suggested, however, that if we agree that the *meaning* of the universal quantifier requires us to accept universal instantiation, then we can *immediately* give an example of an *a priori* (in fact, of an *analytic*) truth, namely, any suitable instance of ' If for every *x*, *Fx*, then *Fv*'; we already committed ourselves to *a priori* truth (it might be contended) when we rejected Quine's contention that the theory of meaning is an unsalvageable wreck.

One answer to this contention might be Quine's answer, already alluded to in my discussion of Wittgenstein: to derive the individual statements ' If for every *x*, *Fx*, then *Fv*' (where '*v*' is a name for some member of the domain the quantifier ranges over) from the principle of universal instantiation (and the fact that implication is validity of the conditional) one needs *logic*; the argument does not show that the 'UI-conditionals' just mentioned (the conditionals corresponding to individual applications of the rule of universal instantiation) are true by meaning theory *alone*. This answer does not affect the argument I gave for rejecting 'Every statement is both true and false'; for that argument did not purport to explain the *origin* of logical truth (whatever that might mean); we were concerned to determine something about the notion of rationality, assuming reasonable constraints and reasoning in a reasonable way (which, of course, means using logic). We were not showing *why* logic is true (whatever that might mean), but rather showing that if there is such a thing as rationality at all, then it seems that it could never be rational to reject one very weak logical principle. That we had to assume logical principles to argue this is not any kind of vicious circle.

Even if the meaning-theoretic argument is advanced in the same spirit as ours, as a defense of the claim that certain statements are unrevisable but not as an explanation of their truth, its conclusion cannot be as strong as the conclusion we reached above. For even if 'for every *x*, *Fx*' implies '*Fv*' by virtue (in part) of the *meaning* of the quantifier itself, this only shows that the inference $(x)Fx \supset Fv$ must be a good one *in every language that contains the universal quantifier*. Whether an adequate language *must* have or can have quantifiers with such properties as this one is certainly not a question about *meaning*. Just as there are adequate languages that lack the *Euclidean* notion of a straight line, so, it might be claimed, there could be adequate languages that lack the classical quantifiers.

Our argument was that (1) the AIR cannot be accepted by any rational being; (2) it seems reasonable that a fully rational being should see and be able to express the fact that the AIR is incorrect;

133

(3) any clear statement to the effect that the AIR is incorrect can be translated into *our* language here and now by the words 'Not every statement is true.' Only (3) depends at all on meaning theory; (1) and (2) are premises from the theory of rationality. In particular, I only require that the *whole thought* 'Not every statement is true' should somehow be expressible by a rational being; not that it be expressible in those words. In particular, some rational being might express that thought by a sentence no part of which corresponds to our universal quantifier.

Finally, I am not claiming that it is *analytic* that 'A rational being cannot believe that every statement is true.' Nothing said here commits me to the view that we can develop the theory of rationality by just reflecting on the meaning of the word 'rational'. And this is good, since the whole history of philosophy, methodology, and logic is strong evidence to the contrary.

Revision of logic

Intuitionists propose to revise classical logic by giving up the *law of the excluded middle*, $p \lor \sim p$, among others. Such a proposal is instructively different from the proposal to give up $p \ \& \sim p$, which no one has advanced, or to give up the even weaker principles of contradiction discussed above.

I have alluded a number of times to the existence of a family of truth notions: being verified (proved, warrantedly assertible, justified, etc.) and being true in the full 'realist' sense (which builds in bivalence and the notion that what is true is *made* true by a mind-independent reality, according to Michael Dummett) being the best-known members of the family. There are other members of the family as well; there are notions of truth like Peirce's which identify truth with some *idealization* of warranted assertibility rather than with (tensed) warranted assertibility itself; and there are notions of truth which I would consider 'realist', but which are not realist in the very strong metaphysical sense Dummett has in mind. I agree with Sellars that the primitive notion of a correct statement does not yet distinguish between these 'realist' and 'non-realist' conceptions of truth; that it represents a generic conception from which the others arise by a process of philosophical reflection.

The law of the excluded middle is not evident on the *generic* notion of truth, however, at least not for *undecidable* statements. If truth is given a 'verificationist' interpretation, and disjunction is given the standard intuitionist semantics (to verify a disjunction one must verify one of the disjuncts, and also verify *that* a *particular* one of the disjuncts has been verified), then undecidable statements will give rise to instances of $p \vee \sim p$ which fail to be true (although their negations are not true either). My argument for the apriority of the law of contradiction (or of a suitably 'hedged' version of the law of contradiction) did not depend on *choosing between* realist and non-realist views of truth; if a decision between these views of truth cannot be made on *a priori* grounds (or if it can, but it goes *against* the classical view, as Dummett thinks), then not all of classical propositional calculus will be included in the part of logic that is *a priori* correct. The debate about whether there is *a priori* truth is somewhat separate from the debate over 'deviant logics', even if some logical principles are *a priori* (or '*a priori* in normal cases': itself a significant weakening of classical claims).

The issues raised by proposals to use modular logic ('quantum logic') in the interpretation of quantum mechanics are still more complex. Quantum logic has been advocated under *both* 'realist' and 'verificationist' construals. The issues posed by the suggestion to adopt quantum logic plus a 'verificationist' semantics are similar to those posed by the suggestion to adopt intuitionist logic; on the other hand, the suggestion to adopt quantum logic plus a 'realist' semantics cannot be properly worked out and evaluated until one has further clarified the notion of 'realism'. If 'realism' is simply the commitment to the empirical model of the cognitive subject as a system which constructs a representation of its environment, for example, then it would seem that realism, in that sense, is compatible with a 'verificationist' account of how the cognitive subject *understands* his representation. Such issues, however, are far beyond the present paper.

Fallibilism

I do not see any reason to believe that the nature of rationality can be figured out *a priori*. Not only would it be utopian to expect rationality itself to become theoretically transparent to us in the foreseeable future, but even the partial descriptions of rationality we are able to give have had to be revised again and again as our experience with the world, our experience in cooperating with and understanding each other, and our experience with theory construction and explanation have all increased. Even if we restrict ourselves to scientific rationality, the fact is that we construct, test, and evaluate theories today that are of *kinds* undreamed of in earlier centuries. Neither the objects we call 'theories' today (e.g., quantum mechanics and relativity) nor the sorts of considerations involved in the testing and acceptance of these objects are of sorts an ancient Greek could have envisaged.

But is it consistent to say, on the one hand, that some things are *a priori*, i.e., rational to believe in all epistemically possible worlds, but on the other hand, that the metatheory of rationality on which we base this claim (or the considerations which I have advanced as to what such a theory should say if there really were one worthy of the name) is itself in the process of endless change and revision? In other words is it consistent to say that any sketch of a theory of rationality or of parts of a theory of rationality that we ever give are to be accepted in the open-minded and tentative spirit that Peirce called 'fallibilism'? The answer is that it *is* consistent; but perhaps it does not seem so, and this may be the deep reason that Quine's appeal to fallibilism tends to convince some scientifically minded philosophers that there are no *a priori* truths at all.

Of course, if fallibilism requires us to be *sure* that for every statement *s* we accept *there is* an epistemically possible world in which it is rational to deny *s*, then fallibilism is *identical* with the rejection of *a priori* truth; but surely this is an unreasonable conception of fallibilism. If what fallibilism requires, on the other hand, is that we never be totally sure that *s* is true (even if we believe *s* is *a priori*), or, even more weakly, that we never be totally sure that the *reasons* we give for holding *s* true are final and contain no element of error or conceptual vagueness or confusion (even when *s* is 'Not every statement is true'), then there is nothing in such a modest and sane fallibilism to prejudge the question we have been discussing.

Quine and Wittgenstein

The present discussion of Quine's view may not seem to connect directly with the problems discussed by Wittgenstein, but the relevance is, in fact, immediate. If there were *nothing* to the idea that logic and mathematics are *a priori*, then we would resolve the difficulties with Wittgenstein's view by concluding that all of mathematics and logic is empirical. To Kripke's (unpublished) objection that this is incoherent, because the notion of *testing* a statement makes no sense unless *something* is fixed (*Why should we accept the view that quantum mechanics requires us to change our logic?*, Kripke asks. *If nothing is a priori, why do we not instead conclude that we should revise the statement that quantum mechanics requires us to change our logic?*), we could answer, with Quine, that we are not denying the existence of an *a priori* factor in *all* judgment: we are simply denying that it is as *simple* as a rule that some statements are never to be revised. Answering Wittgenstein in his way would in no way require us to reject the insight contained in 'use' accounts of meaning, or Wittgenstein's insights about the way our practice unfolds the very meaning of our terms. But if, in fact, some logical and/or mathematical truths (the principle of contradiction, 'every number has a successor') *are a priori*, then this is blocked.

On the other hand, if large parts of logic and mathematics are revisable (and many of the parts that are not, as far as we know, revisable for *empirical* reasons are *a posteriori* in the way that I argued the statement that a proof exists of a certain theorem or that a particular Turing machine halts may be known *a posteriori*), then any philosophy that takes the *problem* to be: '*given* that logic and mathematics consist of *a priori* knowledge, how do we account for it?' is also blocked.

Actually, things are even worse. Even with respect to the part of logic and mathematics that is *a priori*, it seems to me that the apriority tells us something about the nature of *rationality*, not something about the nature of *logic*. There is a temptation to say, 'the truth of the minimal principle of contradiction (*Not every statement is true*) is explained by the fact that (in so far as we are rational) we hold it immune from revision'. But I find this unintelligible.

The analogy people use is to a game such as chess: if we assume 'chess' is a rigid designator for a game with certain rules, 'in chess the rook moves in straight lines' is a necessary truth. Moreover, it was known *a priori* by the people who invented the game of chess. (Compare Kripke's famous discussion of 'the meter stick in Paris is one meter long'.) In the same way it is suggested, 'Not every statement is true' can be known *a priori* because it is *we* who have made up the 'language game' to which 'statement', 'not', and 'true' belong.

The trouble is that if we are puzzled about whether there is a *possible* (consistent) game with certain rules, we appeal *not* to our stipulations but to an appropriate theorem of mathematics (which may be quite elementary if the game is simple). But if we are puzzled about why it is *possible* to have a language in which not every statement is true, this is (on the view I am criticizing) supposed to be answered *just* by a appeal to our stipulations or, alternatively, our 'forms of life'. I frankly do not see the analogy. I do not see any explanation. If one gets *comfort* by saying 'The principles of logic (some of them) are true *because* we hold them immune from revision', that is fine (some people enjoy chanting 'Hare Krishna', too), but the 'because' escapes me. Why should one not just as well say, 'We are *able* to stipulate that *some* but not *all* statements should be true (or assertible) *because* the minimal principle of contradiction is true'? My own guess is that the truths of logic we are speaking of are *so* basic that the notion of *explanation* collapses when we try to 'explain' why they are true. I do not mean that there is something 'unexplainable' here; there is simply no room for an explanation of what is presupposed by every explanatory activity, and that goes for philosophical as well as scientific explanations, including explanations that purport to be therapy.

So where does all of this leave us? Let us return for a moment to our earlier example: the statement that Peano arithmetic is consistent (or 10^{20}-consistent). This is hardly *a priori* in the strong sense: conceivable mathematical findings would lead us to change our minds. (It may, of course, be '*a priori*' in weaker senses than I have considered.) There is clearly a *factual* element – an element of *objective combinatorial fact* – in the consistency of Peano arithmetic. But nothing argued here goes against the view that *if* Peano arithmetic *is* consistent as far as human beings can tell (and has no *mathematical* consequences that would lead us to modify it, e.g., provable ω inconsistency), *then* it counts as *true* partly by convention, or something analogous to convention (though not, of course, in the sense of *arbitrary* convention). Quine's view that there may be an *element* of convention, or apriority, or whatever, in mathematical knowledge, as in all knowledge, even where there is some revisability, is unshaken. On the other hand, our notion of rationality cannot be quite as flexible as Quine suggests.

8

Computational psychology and interpretation theory

I once got into an argument after dinner with my friend Zenon Pylyshyn. The argument concerned the following assertion which Pylyshyn made: 'cognitive psychology is impossible if there is not a well-defined notion of *sameness of content* for mental representations'. It occurred to me later that the reasons I have for rejecting this assertion tie in closely with Donald Davidson's well-known interests in both meaning theory and the philosophy of mind. Accordingly, with Zenon's permission and (I hope) forgiveness, I have decided to make my arguments against his assertion the subject of this paper.

Mental representation

Let us consider what goes on in the mind when we think 'there is a tree over there', or any other common thought about ordinary physical things. On one model, the computer model of the mind, the mind has a 'program', or set of rules, analogous to the rules governing a computing machine, and thought involves the manipulation of words and other signs (not all of this manipulation 'conscious', in the sense of being able to be verbalized by the computer). This model, however, is almost vacuous as it stands (in spite of the heat it generates among those who do not like to think that a mere device, such as a computing machine, could possibly serve as a model for something as special as the human mind). It is vacuous because the program, or system of rules for mental functioning, has not been specified; and it is this program that constitutes the psychological theory. Merely saying that the correct psychological theory, whatever it may be, can be represented as a program (or something analogous to a program) for a computer (or something analogous to a computer) is almost empty; for virtually any system that can be described by a set of *laws* can at least be *simulated* by a computer. Anything from Freudian depth psychology to Skinnerian behaviorism can be represented as a kind of computer program.

Today, however, computer scientists working in 'artificial intelligence', and cognitive psychologists thinking about reference, semantic representation, language use, and so on, have a little more specific hypothesis in mind than the almost empty hypothesis that the mind can be modelled by a digital computer. (Even that hypothesis is not wholly empty because it does imply *something*: the causal structure of mental processes; it implies that they take place according to deterministic or probabilistic rules of sequencing according to a finite program.) The further hypothesis to which workers on computing machines and cognitive psychologists have been converging is this: that the mind thinks with the aid of *representations*. There seem to be two different ideas, actually, which are both involved in talk of 'representations' today.

The first idea, based on experience with trying to program computers to simulate intelligent behavior is that thinking involves not just the manipulation of arbitrary objects or symbols, but requires the manipulation of symbols that have a very specific structure, the structure of a *formalized language*. The experience of computer people was that the most interesting and successful programs in 'artificial intelligence' *typically* turned out to involve giving the computing machine something like a formalized language and a set of rules for manipulating that formalized language ('reasoning' in the language, so to speak).

The second idea associated with the term 'representation' is that the human mind thinks (in part) by constructing some kind of a 'model' of its environment: a 'model of the world'. This 'model' need not, of course, literally *resemble* the world. It is enough that there should be some kind of *systematic relation* between items in the representational system and items 'out there', so that what is going on 'out there' can be read off from its representational system by the mind.

Once a reference definition has been given for a formalized language, a set of sentences in that language can serve as a 'representational system' or 'model of the world'.

Suppose, for example, we wish to represent the fact that the city of Paris is bigger than the city of Vienna. If we have a predicate, say, F, which represents the relation *bigger than* (i.e., if the open sentence which we write in the formal notation as 'Fxy' is correlated to the relation which holds between any two things if and only if they are both cities and the first is larger – in, say, population – than the second), and if we have 'individual constants' or proper names, say, a and b, which represent the cities of Paris and Vienna (i.e., 'a' is correlated to Paris and 'b' is correlated to Vienna by the reference definition for the language), then we can represent the fact that Paris is a bigger city than Vienna by just including in our list of accepted sentences (our 'theory of the world') the sentence '*Fab*'. In a similar way, any state of affairs, however complex, that can be expressed using the predicates, proper names, and logical devices of the formal language can be asserted to obtain by including in the 'theory of the world' the formula that represents that state of affairs.

When our 'representational system' is itself a *theory*, and when our method of employing our representational system involves *making formal deductions*, we see that *one and the same object* – the formalized language, including the rules for deduction – can be the formalized language that computer scientists have been led to postulate as the brain or mind's (the difference does not appear particularly significant, from this perspective) medium of computation, and, simultaneously, the medium of representation. *The mind uses a formalized language* (or something significantly like a formalized language) *both as medium of computation and medium of representation*. This may be called the working hypothesis of cognitive psychology today.

Part of this working hypothesis seems to me certainly correct. I believe that we cannot account at all for the functioning of thought and language without regarding at least some mental items as representations. When I think (correctly) 'there is a tree in front of me', the occurrence of the word 'tree' in the sentence I speak in my mind is a *meaningful* occurrence and one of the items in the *extension* of that occurrence of the word 'tree' is the very tree in front of me. Moreover, the open sentence 'x is in front of me' is correlated (in the correct semantics for my language) with the relational property of being in front of me, and the entire sentence 'there is a tree in front of me' is, by virtue of these and similar facts, one which is *true* if and only if there is a tree in front of me.

Where there is room for psychologists to differ is over *how many* mental items are representations, how useful it is to postulate a large and complex *unconscious* system of representations in order to explain conscious thought and intelligent action, etc.

The verificationist semantics of 'mentalese'

So far what I have said is in line with the thinking of Pylyshyn and other 'propositionalist' cognitive psychologists. For the sake of the argument, we shall assume all this is right. Of course, the actual story may be much more complicated. The mind may employ more than *one* formalized language (or, rather, formalized-language-analog). Different parts of the brain may compute in different 'media'. And both sentence-analogs and image-analogs may be used in the actual computational procedures, along with things that are neither. But let us assume the best case for Pylyshyn's view: a mind which does *all* its computing in *one* formalized language.

In what does the mind's *understanding* of its *own* medium of computation consist? It will do no good to say, as Fodor (1975) has, that we should not apply the word 'understand' to 'mentalese' itself. ('Mentalese' is a name for the hypothetical formalized-language-analog in the brain.) For 'mentalese' and 'formalized-language-in-the-brain' are *metaphors*. They may be scientifically useful and rich metaphors; but *as* metaphors they are inseparable from the notion of *understanding*. Something cannot literally be a language unless it can be *understood*; and something cannot be a language-*analog* unless there is a suitable *understanding-analog*. If some representations in the brain are sentence-analogs and predicate-analogs, then what is the corresponding *understanding-analog*?

The answer, I suggest, is this: the brain's 'understanding' of its own 'medium of computation and representation' consists in its possession of a *verificationist semantics* for the medium, i.e. of a computable predicate† which can represent acceptability, or warranted assertibility, or credibility. Idealizing, we treat the language as interpreted (in part) *via* a set of rules which assign *degrees of confirmation* (i.e., subjective probabilities) to the sentence-analogs relative to experiential inputs and relative also to other sentence-analogs. Such rules must be computable; and their 'possession' by the mind/brain/machine consists in its being 'wired' to follow them, or having come to follow them as a result of learning. (I do *not* assume that mentalese must be *innate*, or that it must be disjoint from the natural language the speaker has acquired.)

But why a verificationist semantics? Why not a meaning theory in Davidson's sense?

Obviously, if we interpret mentalese as a 'system of representation' we do ascribe extensions to predicate-analogs and truth conditions to sentence-analogs. But the 'meaning theory' which represents a particular interpretation of mentalese is not *psychology*. In fact, if we formulate it as Davidson might, its only primitive notion is 'true',

---

† Strictly speaking a *semi-computable* (*partial* recursive) predicate: in *psychology*, as opposed to idealized inductive logic, we cannot require that degrees of belief be always *defined*. Let me emphasize also that in a psychological model not all learning is a matter of *induction* even in the wide sense in which inductive logicians use that term. We learn many things just by being *told* them or *shown* them: believing things that other people tell us or show us (to some extent) must be incorporated into the 'degree of confirmation' function whether or not one thinks this is good 'inductive logic'.

and 'true' is not psychological notion. To spell this out: the meaning theory yields such theorems ('T-sentences') as (pretend that mentalese is English): '"Snow is white" is true in mentalese if and only if snow is white'. This contains no psychological vocabulary at all.

We might try to say 'well, the understanding consists in the brain's *knowing* the T-sentences of the meaning theory'. But the notion of *knowing* cannot be a *primitive* notion in sub-personal cognitive psychology.†

Suppose we try to say: the mind understands *without using representations* what it is for snow to be white, and it knows the representation 'snow is white' is true if and only if that state of affairs holds. Not only does this treat the mind as something that 'knows' things, instead of *analyzing knowing into more elementary and less intentional processes*, but it violates the fundamental assumption of cognitive psychology, that understanding what states of affairs are, thinking about them, etc., *cannot be done without representations*. At bottom, we would be stuck with the myth of comparing representations directly with unconceptualized reality.

On the other hand, if we say, 'the brain's/mind's *use* of the sentence "Snow is white" (or the corresponding sentence-analog) is such as to warrant the interpretation that "Snow is white" is true in mentalese if and only if snow is white, *and this is what it means to say that the brain (implicitly) "knows" the T-sentence*', then we do not give any theory of what that 'use' consists in. This is what a *verificationist* semantics gives (and, as far as I can see, what *only* a verificationist semantics gives). I suggest, then, that verificationist semantics is the natural semantics for functionalist (or 'cognitive') psychology. Such a semantics has a notion of 'belief' (or 'degree of belief') which is what makes it *cognitive*; at the same time it is a *computable* semantics, which is what makes it functionalist.

Of course, we want the semantics to connect with *action*, and this means that the model must incorporate a *utility function* as well as a degree of confirmation function. This function, too, must be computable (or, strictly speaking, semi-computable). This idealization is, of course, severe: we are assuming that the belief-analog (represented by the degree-of-confirmation function) and the

---

† The reason is that, as both Fodor and Dennett have emphasized, cognitive psychology is *computational* psychology. It is alright to have 'homunculi' who make inferences, etc., as part of one's explanations provided the homunculi are eventually 'discharged' (as Dennett puts it), i.e. explained away as computer algorithms. But this means 'knowing' must eventually be 'discharged'.

preference-analog (represented by the utility function) are both *fully consistent*. The actual (neurologically realized) analogs of both belief *and* preference (or belief-representations and preference-representations) may well be *inconsistent*, as long as there are procedures for resolving the inconsistencies when practical decisions have to be made. In a terminology used by Reichenbach in another context, consistency may be '*de faciendo* and not *de facto*'. What significance this has for philosophy of mind, I shall discuss briefly at the end of this paper.

For now, the problem is this: if the *brain*'s semantics for its medium of representation is verificationist and not truth-conditional, then what happens to the notion of the 'content' of a mental representation?

Two Ruritanian children

Imagine that there is a country somewhere on earth called Ruritania. In this country let us imagine that there are small differences between the dialects which are spoken in the north and in the south. One of these differences is that the word 'grug' means silver in the northern dialect and aluminum in the southern dialect. Imagine two children, Oscar and Elmer, who grow up in Ruritania. They are as alike in genetic constitution and environment as you please, except that Oscar grows up in the south of Ruritania and Elmer grows up in the north of Ruritania. Imagine that in the north of Ruritania, for some reason, pots and pans are normally made of silver, whereas in the south of Ruritania pots and pans are normally made of aluminum. So northern children grow up knowing that pots and pans are normally made of 'grug', and southern children grow up knowing that pots and pans are normally made of 'grug'.

We may suppose that Oscar and Elmer have the same 'mental representation' of 'grug', that they have the same *beliefs* in connection with grug, etc. Of course some of these beliefs will differ in meaning even if they are identical in verbal and mental representation. For example, when Oscar believes 'my mother has grug pots and pans' and when Elmer believes 'my mother has grug pots and pans' the indexical word 'my' refers to different persons, and hence the term 'my mother' refers to different mothers. But unless such small differences in collateral information are already enough to constitute a difference in the *content* of the mental representation (in which case it would seem that the ordinary distinction between the meaning of a sign and collateral information that we have in connection with the sign has been wholly abandoned),† then it would seem that we should say that the content of the mental representation of 'grug' is exactly the same for Oscar and for Elmer at this stage in their lives.

I do not mean to suggest that the *word* 'grug' has the same meaning in Oscar's idiolect as it does in Elmer's idiolect at this stage; I've argued elsewhere (Putnam, 1975*a*) that the difference in reference in the two communities should be regarded as infecting the speech of the individual speakers. To spell this out: when Oscar tries to determine what *is* grug he will ultimately have to rely on 'experts'. These experts need not necessarily be scientists, he may simply ask his parents (who may in turn consult store owners or even scientists). But the point is that since the extension of 'grug' is in fact different in the two communities, and since, on the theory of meaning that I have defended in other places, difference in extension constitutes difference of meaning, and since extension is fixed collectively and not individually, it ends up that the *meaning* of the word 'grug' in the idiolects of Oscar and Elmer is not the same even though there is nothing 'psychological', nothing 'in their heads', which constitutes the difference in meaning. *Meanings aren't in the head.* There is a difference in the meaning of the word 'grug' in this case; but it is in the *reference* of the word, as objectively fixed by the practices of the community, and not in the conceptions of grug entertained by Oscar and Elmer.

But the concept of content that Pylyshyn is interested in and that Chomsky‡ has expressed an interest in is one that would factor out such objective differences in extension. What Pylyshyn is looking for is a notion of the content of a mental representation in which 'water' on earth and 'water' on Twin Earth would be said to have the same content for speakers who had identical conceptions of 'water' even though it might be the case that 'water' on earth referred to H_2O and 'water' on Twin Earth referred to XYZ. And what I have said

† The reason that we cannot count every difference in the collateral information we have as difference in the meaning of a *word*, is that to do so abandons the distinction between our 'concepts' and what beliefs we have that contain those concepts, and just this distinction is the *basis* of the intuitive notions of meaning, synonymy, analyticity, etc. To give up the meaning/belief distinction amounts to agreeing with Quine that we may as well give up the notion of *meaning* altogether. The same goes for the distinction between the 'content' of our mental representations and our beliefs involving them; this is nothing but a *picture*, a picture of 'words in the head'. Pictures are not always a *mistake*; they can be useful models. But if the picture of 'mental representations' and their 'content' is to have any use, then 'content' must remain stable under *some* changes of *belief*.

‡ Chomsky wrote me a long letter after the appearance of 'The meaning of "meaning"' defending this way out. Fodor (1979) defends the same program.

so far is that *on any such notion of content it would seem that 'grug' in Oscar's mind would have the same content as 'grug' in Elmer's mind.*

Not only would the words have the same content; any mental signs or predicate-analogs that the brain might use in its computations and that corresponded to the verbal item 'grug' would have the same content at this stage. But if the word 'grug', and the mental representations that stand behind the word 'grug' on a theory of the kind Pylyshyn advocates, have the same content at this stage, then *when do they come to differ in content?* By the time Oscar and Elmer have become adults, have learned foreign languages, and so on, they certainly will not have the same conception of grug. Oscar will know that *grug* is the metal called 'aluminum' in English (I assume that everybody in Ruritania learns English as a second language in High School), and Elmer will know that the metal called *grug* in his part of Ruritania is the metal called 'silver' in English. Each of them will know many facts which serve to distinguish silver from aluminum, and 'grug' in the south Ruritanian sense from 'grug' in the north Ruritanian sense.

However, on a verificationist model of the kind described in the first section of this paper there is no stage at which the word 'grug' or the corresponding mental representation in the mind of Oscar (or in the mind of Elmer) is ever treated as changing its reference. *Internally* to treat a sign as changing its reference is to treat it as, in effect, a different sign. This never happens; in the internal point of view all that happens is that Oscar acquires more information about grug. At one time he knew only that pots and pans are made of grug; that grug is a metal; and that grug has a certain color. Later he learned additional facts about grug (e.g., what it is called in English). When the use of a word is modified by the continual acquisition of collateral information, without it being supposed that at any stage the word is being committed to a new extension, all that happens (in the verificationist model) is that the degree of confirmation of various sentences containing the word changes. Moreover this change in the degree of confirmation of various sentences containing the word is a *continuous* change; it is continuous because it is brought about merely by the conditionalization of prior probabilities to added information. What this simple example shows is that there is nothing in a functionalist model of the use of a language (or even of a system of internal representations) which automatically gives us a decision as to when we should say that a representation has changed its 'content'. We can have a complete description of the use of mental signs without thereby having a criterion which distinguishes changes in the content of mental signs from changes in collateral information. So we have a problem with synonomy *for mental signs*.

Possible solutions

In 'The meaning of "meaning"' I proposed to decide whether or not words of a certain kind (natural kind words) are synonymous by looking at two things: the extension and the correlated *stereotype*. By the *stereotype* I meant a certain set of beliefs, or idealized beliefs, which all speakers are expected to have in connection with the word. For example, if all speakers are expected to believe that a tiger is striped (or that idealized tigers are striped) then stripes are part of the 'stereotype' of a tiger. Can the idea of a stereotype be extended to mental representations, and can *sameness of stereotype* provide us with a criterion for the synonymy of mental representations? To explore this, let me again imagine an Oscar, only this time let me imagine that Oscar lives in an experimental research station very near the north pole. Perhaps this is a community of scientists and engineers experimenting with finding oil in extreme arctic conditions. I shall imagine that in this community, for some reason, there are no green plants, but that there are artificial plants and even artificial grass which people have introduced in order to make the place look more hospitable.

Now consider the word 'grass' in the idiolect of Oscar and in the idiolect of an ordinary American child, whom we shall call Elmer. If we take the stereotype of grass to be simply the perceptual prototype, then the stereotype of grass may be exactly the same in Oscar's mind as in Elmer's mind; but Oscar does not know that grass is in any sense a living or growing thing. I think we would regard it as wrong in such a case to suppose that the mental representation, or *the word* 'grass', had the same content in Oscar's mind as in Elmer's mind.

Perhaps we should require that in addition to having the same perceptual prototype for 'grass', Oscar and Elmer should have the same 'markers': for example, they should both believe that 'grass is a plant'. But this simply raises what I shall call the *infection problem*. If they do believe that grass is a plant, how similar do their notions of a *plant* have to be in order for their belief that *grass is a plant* to be relevantly the same belief? I think that in actual *interpretation* our policy is not to let infection go very far; i.e., for the purposes of deciding that an Oscar and an Elmer have the same notion of grass we may require that they both believe that grass is a plant *without* requiring that their notion of a plant be exactly the same. But this is already to accept the stance that interpretation is an essentially informal and interest-relative matter.

If we try for a notion of *exact sameness of content of mental representations*, which is what Pylyshyn is arguing for, then the infection problem becomes an infinite regress problem. Suppose, for example, that Oscar and Elmer are two children who both live in the United States; who both know that grass is a plant; but that Elmer knows that plants can be microscopic, whereas Oscar's notion of a plant involves being of visible size, being green, etc. Then the problem of distinguishing what is a difference in the content of the representations and what is a difference in collateral information re-arises again at the level of the marker 'plant'.

The point is that while discovering whether or not stereotypes are the same is good methodology for translation, it is nothing like an *algorithm*. Stereotypes themselves are beliefs expressed in *words*. Once we have accepted translations, however tentative, for some words or representations, then stereotype theory may give us a handle on how to translate other words or representations; but it cannot serve to *define* a notion of sameness of content for words or mental representations.

Nor can *sameness of perceptual prototype*, another notion that we have mentioned. We have seen that even if two words are associated with the same perceptual prototypes they may differ in meaning; for the meaning of the word is not just a function of associated perceptual prototypes, but also of various more or less abstract beliefs that one has in connection with the word ('grass is a plant'). Not only would it be wrong to say that two words (or two mental representations) have the same content when they are associated with the same perceptual prototypes; it would be wrong to take sameness of perceptual prototype as even a *necessary* condition for sameness of content of mental representations. For two speakers may have exactly the same meaning for the word 'bachelor', i.e., male adult human of marriageable age who has never been married, and have quite different perceptual prototypes associated with the word. On any intuitive notion of semantic content, to count every difference in perceptual prototype as a difference in semantic content would be just as unnatural as to count every difference in collateral information as a difference in semantic content.

Chomsky's response to my 'The meaning of "meaning"' was to suggest that one might be able to save the Fregean notion of an 'intension' by giving up the principle that 'intension determines extension'. On Chomsky's proposal, as applied to my Twin Earth example, we should say that the word 'water' has the same *intension* on earth and on Twin Earth even though it has a different *extension* on earth than on Twin Earth. In terms of what has just been said, however, it would seem that this is the wrong way to go. For if we go the way I went in 'The meaning of "meaning"', and take the extension of a term as one of the components of its 'meaning vector', then we have a clear reason for saying that 'grug' has a different meaning in north Ruritanian and in south Ruritanian. Since the word 'grug' clearly has a different reference in the two dialects of Ruritanian, it also has a different meaning. Once we decide to put the reference (or rather the difference in reference) aside, and to ask whether 'grug' has the same 'content' in the minds of Oscar and Elmer, we have embarked upon an impossible task. Far from making it easier for ourselves to decide whether the representations are synonymous, we have made it impossible. In fact, the first approximation we have to a principle for deciding whether words have the same meaning or not in actual translation practice is to look at the extensions. 'Factoring out' differences in extension will only make a principled decision on when there has been a change in meaning totally impossible.

On the other hand, if we do decide to take extension as a factor in determining synonymy, either of words or of mental representations, then we still will not arrive at anything like an algorithm. For, just as determining the stereotype involves determining the meanings of other words, so determining the extension of a term always involves determining the extension of other terms. That words should not be regarded as the same in content if they have different extensions is a useful principle in translation after we already have the enterprise of interpretation underway. But until we have started interpreting a language we don't have any idea what the extension of a term is.

How then do we ever get started in interpretation? The answer that I would defend is one which has been vigorously urged by Donald Davidson and by Quine. (David Wiggins has pointed out that the germ of this view can already be found in Vico.) This is the view that *interpretation is essentially a holistic enterprise*. To interpret a language (and it makes no difference whether the language be a public language or 'mentalese', assuming the existence of 'mentalese') involves finding a translation scheme, an 'analytical hypothesis', which is capable of being learned, capable of yielding ready equivalents in our home language to the expressions being translated, and, most important, which is such that when we interpret the speakers of the alien language as meaning what the translation scheme says they mean we are able to 'understand' their purposes, beliefs, and behavior. As Vico put it, in interpretation we seek to maximize the *humanity* of the beings being translated. If this is right then the only criteria that we actually have for the 'content' of any signs, or sign-analogs, are our intuitive criteria of successful interpretation; and to *formalize* these would involve formalizing our entire conception of what it is to be human, of what it is to be intelligible in human terms (see Putnam, 1976).

This discussion is not meant to suggest that interpretation theory is something incapable of study. Interpretation is something that can be studied in many ways and from many perspectives. But it is meant to suggest that, contrary to Pylyshyn's suggestion, the theory of interpretation and cognitive psychology deal with quite different projects and that to a large extent success in one of these projects is independent of success in the other. What the example I have developed shows is that it may be possible to give a complete functionalist psychology, including a complete verificationist semantics for mentalese, without in any way solving the problem of interpretation, or even the problem of reference-preserving translation (assignment of extensions). To have a description of how a system of representations works in functionalist terms is one thing; to have an *interpretation* of that system of representations is quite another thing.

The difference between functionalist psychology and interpretation theory is in part due to this: functionalist psychology treats the human mind as a computer. It seeks to state the rules of computation. The rules of computation have the property that although their interactions may be complicated and global, their action at any particular time is local. The machine, as it might be, moves a digit from one address to another address in obedience to a particular instruction, or to finitely many instructions, and on the basis of a finite amount of data. Interpretation is never local in this sense. A translation scheme, however well it works on a finite amount of corpus, may always have to be modified on the basis of additional text.

Let me illustrate this point by means of what may seem to be a digression. Some years ago Hartry Field (1972) advocated the view that *reference* is a physicalistic relation between sign-uses and things (including properties). When he commented on my paper 'Language and reality' (Putnam, 1975*b*) at Chapel Hill some years ago, Field spelled this out a little further with some examples. Considering the case of a Newtonian scientist who used the term 'gravitation', Field suggested that the decision we should make as to which objects or properties this term refers to should be based on .finding which objects the scientist had better be referring to as a matter of objective fact, if his theory as a whole is to be a rationally acceptable approximation to the truth. The reason I mention this is that, although the notion of interpretation involved here is as different from Pylyshyn's notion of finding 'content' as could possibly be imagined, the same considerations turn up. It turns out that the 'physicalistic relation' that Field is looking for is one whose very definition will involve *interpreting the language as a whole*, and not just individual signs (since what constitutes an interpretation of a theory that makes the theory rationally acceptable depends on looking at the *whole* theory), and is a relation whose very definition involves an analysis of rationality in its normative sense. Whether any relation whose definition involves these elements is properly called 'physicalistic' I shall not inquire; but the point is that *every* project for analyzing the notion of *interpretation* sooner or later involves recognizing that the analysis of the notion of interpretation is inseparable from the analysis of either the normative notion of rationality, or from some such notion as Vico's 'humanity'.

To expect anything like complete success at stating in a completely rigorous and formal way what the correct procedures are in inter-pretation would obviously be utopian. This may not, in itself, seem like a terribly important point. After all, complete success at stating the laws of physics may well be a utopian project; certainly complete success at describing the functional organization of a human brain is a utopian project. But physics is possible, even though complete success eludes us, because the laws of physics can be successively approximated; and functional psychology is possible because (we hope) the functional organization of the human brain can be partly described and approximated. Similarly one might hope that one could obtain partial success in describing the practices and procedures of interpretation.

I have no doubt that this is true; indeed I have no doubt that each of these subjects can be studied at more than one level (physics, after all, is not just elementary particle theory; it is also magneto-hydrodynamics, solid state physics, and many things besides) and in connection with many different projects requiring many different notions of precision and many different vocabularies. The important point is that the kind of partial success that is realistically foreseeable in cognitive psychology and the kind of partial successes that is realistically foreseeable in interpretation theory are quite different.

In one sense, I hope the present paper is a contribution to

interpretation theory. The interesting successes that we are likely to have in interpretation theory are more likely to be philosophical discussions than technical 'results'. But even if we confine attention to the sorts of contributions to interpretation theory that are likely to come from computer science and related areas, then, as Marvin Minsky (1975) has pointed out, these successes are likely to be by their very nature partial. When we mechanize interpretation, Minsky points out, what we typically do is *restrict* it to a definite set of texts which are on a specific subject matter and which share a common vocabulary, a common set of projects, and a common set of empirical or other assumptions. The reason that partial successes in interpretation theory are always so limited is that any global success, any program for interpretation of sentences in a variable language, a variable theory, on variable topics and with variable presuppositions, would involve an analysis of the notion of humanity, or of the notion (which in my view is closely related) of rationality. The function of limiting interpretation to a specific frame is to avoid having to tackle the totally utopian project of algorithmic analysis of these notions.

The kind of partial success we are likely to have in cognitive psychology, however, is quite different. Here what we might hope for are the identification of the kinds of physical states that realize various functional roles. If the hypothesis that the brain computes in something analogous to a formalized language is correct then we might hope to identify such things as predicate-analogs and sentence-analogs in the brain, or to say something about the computation rules for manipulating these. I think that anyone who has a clear idea of what these two kinds of partial success amount to, and who does not allow himself to be carried away by utterly utopian dreams of a complete mathematical analysis of what it is to be human (or what it is to be rational), will see at once that they are independent projects and neither really presupposes the other at all.

Nelson Goodman (1978) has advocated 'pluralism' as opposed to 'monism'. In this terminology, the view that we should aim for a single science of cognitive psychology which solves the problems of syntax and semantics together and at one stroke (and which solves the problems of semantics both in the sense of verificationist semantics and in the sense of interpretation) is a species of monism. In opposition to it I suggest that we should let a hundred flowers blossom, that we should let them blossom in their separate ways, in their separate seasons, and even in their separate gardens.

Relevance to Davidson's philosophy of mind

I think that the points that I have made have a certain 'Davidsonian' quality. It may be appropriate in this place to bring out more explicitly how this is so. In 'Mental events', Davidson (1970) put forward the thesis of 'anomalous monism'. This is the thesis that there are token–token identities between physical events and mental events (i.e., events described in the vocabulary of belief and desire), but no type–type identities. The argument that he gives for the non-existence of type–type identities has been widely misunderstood. To many it has seemed like a 'howler'; Davidson has been charged with arguing for the non-existence of type–type identities from the mere fact that mental concepts and physical concepts owe allegiance to different criteria. (Such an argument would be fallacious since it would block all type–type identities, even the identity 'water is H_2O', or 'light is electromagnetic radiation'. For certainly, before the reduction, 'water' and 'H_2O' owed allegiance to different criteria, as did 'light' and 'electromagnetic radiation'.) This is simply a misreading, however; Davidson does have an argument, and it is both a subtle and an interesting one.

Davidson is very familiar with the work of Amos Tversky (see Tversky & Kahneman, 1975, 1982). Thus he is extremely aware that *preferences* cannot be read off from even *sincere verbal reports*. As Tversky's very careful empirical research shows, people's sincere verbal reports of their own preferences are totally incoherent. If we acted on the maxim of ascribing to people all of the preferences they say (sincerely) they have then we would be unable to interpret their behavior at all, for *expressed* preferences are totally contradictory (e.g., they violate the logical property of the transitivity of preference very badly). Now, and perhaps this is the step that Davidson should have spelled out a little more explicitly, there is no reason to think that the availability of a 'cerebroscope' which enabled us to directly read off the subject's 'mentalese' could make things any better. Sincere verbal reports presumably correspond to mental representations that are present in the subject's brain. There is no reason to believe that the patient's 'mentalese' representations are any more consistent than his sincere verbal reports. If we could *read* the 'mentalese' we would undoubtedly find coded in the brain itself such reports as 'I prefer A to B', 'I prefer B to C', 'I prefer C to A', on certain occasions. What we do when we discover such reports in a discourse is look at the subject's total behavior and try to decide on the basis of his total behavior, and also on the basis of further linguistic material, further 'corpus', what is the most reasonable *reconstruction* of the patient's behavior and talk. A reasonable reconstruction accounts for the subject's behavior, or for most of his behavior, in terms of preferences which may be a subset of those he avows or which may even be slightly different from any that he avows, and accounts for those expressed preferences which we decide the patient does not really have as being confusions of various kinds. We may decide that some of the patient's expressed preferences were the product of suggestion in the particular context, for example.

Of course, someone may say that at a deeper level than even the patient's mentalese there must be a level of what we might call Platonic mentalese which records in the form of neurologically salient representations in a hidden code what the subject's *true* preferences are. But there is absolutely no reason to believe this. People may just be computers which are wired so that most of the time what they end up doing admits of some rational explanation or other; it need not be the case that the rational explanation which is the best *rational reconstruction* of the behavior is itself actually physically coded in their brains somewhere.

In short, Davidson's point is that what is true of public language is almost certainly going to be true of any 'mental representations' or salient neurological states which stand causally *behind* public language. Just as we have to say that a person's true preferences are not exactly the same as the preferences he *avows*, so we will have to say that a person's 'true preferences' (i.e., the ones it would be best to ascribe to him in rationally reconstructing his behavior) are not the same as the one's coded in his brain representations. Belief-desire explanation belongs to the level of what I've been calling *interpretation theory*. It is as holistic and interest relative as all interpretation. Psychologists often speak as though there were *concepts* in the *brain*. The point of my argument (and, I think, of Davidson's) is that there may be *sentence-analogs* and *predicate-analogs* in the brain, but not concepts. 'Mental representations' require interpretation just as much as any other signs do.

9

Reflections on Goodman's *Ways of Worldmaking*

Is there a privileged basis?

One of the most important themes in Goodman's (1978) *Ways of Worldmaking* (*WoW*) is that there is no privileged basis. Reducing sense data to physical objects or events is an admissible research program for Goodman; it is no *more* (and no less) reasonable than reducing physical objects to sense data. As research programs, there is nothing wrong with either physicalism or phenomenalism; as dogmatic monisms there is everything wrong with both of them.

This is decidedly not the fashionable opinion today. Physicalism and 'realism' are at the high tide of fashion; phenomenalism has sunk out of sight in a slough of philosophical disesteem and neglect. Goodman's assumption that physicalism and phenomenalism are *analogous* would be disputed by many philosophers.

It is this assumption that I wish to explain and defend before considering other aspects of *WoW*. Because it runs so counter to the fashion, it is of great importance to see that it is correct. At the same time, the analogy leads directly to the heart of Goodman's book, which is its defense of pluralism.

In *WoW*, Goodman points out that the phenomenal itself has many equally valid descriptions. In his view, this arises from two causes. First of all, perception is itself notoriously influenced by interpretations provided by habit, culture, and theory. (Goodman's long and close acquaintance with actual psychological research shines through many sections of *WoW*.) We see toothbrushes and vacuum tubes *as* toothbrushes and vacuum tubes, not as arrangements of color patches. Secondly, there is, for Goodman as for Wittgenstein, no sharp line to be drawn between the character of the experience and the description given by the subject. Thus, after reporting a finding by Kolers that a disproportionate number of engineers and physicians are unable to see apparent motion at all, Goodman comments:

Yet if an observer reports that he sees two distinct flashes, even at distances and intervals so short that most observers see one moving spot, perhaps he means that he sees the two as we might say we see a swarm of molecules when we look at a chair, or as we do when we say we see a round table top even when we look at it from an oblique angle. Since an observer can become adept at distinguishing apparent from real motion, he may take the appearance of motion as a sign that there are two flashes, as we take the oval appearance of the table top as a sign that it is round; and in both cases the signs may be or become so transparent that we look through them to physical events and objects. When the observer visually determines that what is before him is what we agree is before him, we can hardly charge him with an error in visual perception. Shall we say, rather, that he misunderstands the instruction, which is presumably just to tell what he sees? Then how, without prejudicing the outcome, can we so reframe the instruction as to prevent such a 'misunderstanding'? Asking him to make no use of prior experience and to avoid all conceptualization will obviously leave him speechless; for to talk at all he must use words.   (*WoW*, p. 92)

In the same way, there are different possible ways of reporting physical events and motions. And here too there is no sharp line to be drawn between the character of the object or motion and the description we give of it. As Goodman puts it:

Did the sun set a while ago, or did the earth rise? Does the sun go around the earth or the earth go around the sun? Nowadays, we nonchalantly deal with what was once a life-and-death issue by saying that the answer depends on the framework. But here again, if we say that the geocentric and heliocentric systems are different versions of 'the same facts', we must ask not what these facts are but rather how such phrases as 'version of the same facts' or 'descriptions of the same world' are to be understood. This varies from case to case; here, the geocentric and the heliocentric versions, while speaking of the same particular objects – the sun, moon, and planets – attribute very different motions to these objects. Still, we may say the two versions deal with the same facts if we mean by this that they not only speak of the same objects but are also routinely intertranslatable each into the other. As meanings vanish in favor of certain relationships among terms, so facts vanish in favor of certain relationships among versions. In the present case the relationship is comparatively obvious; sometimes it is much more elusive. For instance, the physical and perceptual versions of motion we were talking about do not evidently deal with the same objects, and the relationship if any that constitutes license for saying that the two versions describe the same facts or the same world is no ready intertranslatability.   (*WoW*, p. 93)

In the case of the subject who is being asked to describe apparent motion, Goodman says:

The best we can do is to specify the sort of terms, the vocabulary, he is to use, telling him to describe what he sees in perceptual or phenomenal rather than physical terms. Whether or not this yields different responses, it casts an entirely different light on what is happening. That the instrument to be used in fashioning the facts must be specified makes pointless any identification of the physical with the real and of the perceptual with the merely apparent. The perceptual is no more a rather distorted version of the physical facts than the physical is a highly artificial version of the perceptual facts.   (*WoW*, pp. 92–3)

The examples are well selected, but they would not convince a die-hard physicalist. In the rest of this section I intend, therefore, to examine some standard physicalist rejoinders to the line Goodman takes.

The 'We're not looking for translations' response

'Phenomenalists were trying to find meaning-preserving translations from thing language into sense datum language. Physicalists who hope that future science will vindicate them by finding a neural event or a functional state of the nervous system, or whatever, which can be identified with any given mental event are looking for empirical identities, not analytic ones. Thus Goodman's analogy between phenomenalism and physicalism fails.'

Goodman, however, has never accepted the analytic–synthetic distinction, nor (as far back as *The Structure of Appearance*) has he ever required that reductions must be meaning preserving. If one could find what Goodman (in *Structure of Appearance*) called an 'extensional isomorphism' between thing language and (a part of) sense datum language which enabled one to preserve truth value in 'translating' from thing language into sense datum language, then, even if the translation did not preserve 'meaning', it could still be of great interest. If the physicalist is allowed to look for 'reductions' in more than one sense, so is the phenomenalist. Indeed, one of Goodman's points is precisely that there are many senses of 'reduction'.

At this point the physicalist is likely to respond that physicalistic 'translations' (of psychological talk into brain-state or functional-state talk) *will* eventually be found by neurology, or by cognitive psychology, while translations of thing talk into sense datum talk will never be found for the simple reason that they don't exist. When one looks at an article such as 'Mental representation' by Hartry Field (1978), however, it turns out that the translation will not be of psychological talk as it is but of a specially constructed substitute, and that even the translation of this substitute will depend on the successful carrying out of the program for translating 'refers' (i.e., the two-place predicate 'x refers to v', or, more generally, the relation of *satisfaction* in the sense of formal semantics) into physicalist language that Field proposed some years ago (1972). How to do this, Field gives no hint, and his discussion suggests that carrying out his program would require defining a physicalistic relation between signs (or sign-uses) and things (or properties) which analyzes such things as the application of the principle of charity: i.e., analyzing exhaustively scientific and interpretative rationality itself.†

At this point the analogy between physicalism and phenomenalism begins to emerge. Just as the phenomenalist runs into trouble when he tries to specify in phenomenal terms *all* of the circumstances under which it would be true, or even warrantedly assertible, to say that there is a chair in a certain place, so the physicalist will run into trouble when he tries to specify in physical terms *all* of the circumstances under which it would be true, or even warrantedly assertible, to say that some utterance-part refers to some thing or property. And the reasons are not unrelated. Just as an indefinite amount of theory (including theories which are not yet thought of) can intervene between the phenomenal data and the physical interpretation, so likewise an indefinite amount of theory can intervene between the physicalist data and the intentional interpretation. Both the physicalist and the phenomenalist leave their increasingly dubious clients with mere promissory notes for future translations, or else they say that the existence 'in principle' of possibly infinite (and not effectively specifiable) translations is good enough.

The 'nobody here but us ontologists' response

Some sophisticated physicalists have begun to suggest that physicalism should never have been stated as a thesis concerning relations between languages, or a thesis concerning *syntactic* facts, at all. Donald Davidson (1970) and Richard Boyd (1980) both defend the idea that one can say that mental events *are* physical events (Davidson), or even that mental properties are somehow physical properties or aspects (Boyd), without being committed to the existence of a finite open sentence in physicalist language with the same extension as a given term in 'psychological' language. 'We are talking about what mental events *are*, not about relations between open sentences' is the position of these ontologists.

There is something here with which I sympathize, and to which Goodman may not do full justice. Talk of 'reduction' or 'translation'

---

† For a detailed criticism of Field's program and of the idea that reference is a 'physicalistic' relation, see Putnam, 1978. That his 'physicalistic definition' of reference would incorporate such principles of interpretation as charity was stated by Field in a discussion of my 'Reference and understanding' (1978, part 3) at a Chapel Hill conference some years ago.

invites the rejoinder 'put up or shut up'. But certainly one can sometimes know that an object or system of objects has a certain kind of description on the basis of a well-confirmed *theory*; and in such cases actually exhibiting the description may be beyond human powers, even beyond human powers *in principle*, and yet we do not doubt the existence of the sort of description in question.

For example, I may ask a physicist to explain why the engine fell off the DC10 that crashed in Chicago. The physicist will assume that the DC10 has a description as a system of molecules (he may have to go to an even deeper level if metallurgy enters), and he will approximate that description by estimating the relevant parameters. Now, if a philosopher should object that we cannot actually write down a necessary and sufficient condition for a system of molecules to be a DC10 wing-cum-engine-cum-pylon, and that such a description, if it exists at all, may be practically infinite and not actually able to be written down by human beings, we would say that he was missing the point.

The point is that we know that a DC10 wing consists of molecules in a certain arrangement; knowing this is not the same thing as actually being able to *say* which molecules in what arrangement. And the suggestion is that, in the same way, we might know that any given psychological event *consists* of neurological events without actually being able to say which events.

But none of this actually goes against what Goodman maintains. Combining versions and objects from versions so as to get a version which speaks of 'airplane wings and molecules' (or 'objects ranging from elementary particles through cells, trees, mountains, planets, stars, and whole galaxies', to give the sort of list one sometimes sees in a physics text) is one way of worldmaking, as is extending such relations as 'part/whole', so that we can speak of the 'molecules which are part of the wing' (see *WoW*, chapter 1, especially section 4). Composition, decomposition, and supplementation are all among the standard devices for making worlds. And that one could not speak of the airplane wing as consisting of molecules if one did not first have the notions of a wing and a molecule is also grist for Goodman's mill; for as he says, 'facts are small theories, and true theories are big facts. This does not mean, I repeat, that right versions can be arrived at casually, or that worlds are built from scratch. We start, on any occasion, with some old version or world that we have on hand and that we are stuck with until we have the determination and skill to remake it into a new one. Some of the felt stubbornness of fact is the grip of habit: our firm foundation is indeed stolid. World making begins with one version and ends in another.' (p. 97) There is nothing in this, as far as I can see, that would preclude a version in which mental events consist of physical ones, as airplane wings consist of molecules.

But there is one important difference between the two cases that the *monistic* physicalist often fails to note. That airplane wings consist of molecules is uncontroversial; that the property of *being an airplane wing* can be identified with any property definable in physicalistic language is much more controversial. (Even if the number of structures that represent physically possible airplane wings is finite, if they are not graspable by human minds, there may not be a possible well-defined cut that we could actually make between the ones which are airplane wings and the ones which are not.) However, we do not feel that we need a general criterion for being an airplane wing to say that any particular wing consists of molecules, or even to say something significant about *which* molecules it contains. In the mind/body case one could not decide that a particular mental event (say, a visual sensation of blue) 'consisted of' particular neural events on a particular occasion without having some idea of a *general* necessary and sufficient condition. (This is what is wrong with Davidson's 'anomalous monism'.) For what it means to say that a particular mental event 'consists of' certain neural events, or is 'identical' with their union, is that this union has the 'causal powers' of the mental event, or, in other words, that the neural event can adequately *explain* the actions (described in *human action language*; otherwise every question is begged!) that the mental event explains. But one can say nothing about the 'causal powers' of particulars apart from a *relevant theoretical description* of those particulars. The whole idea of saying that a *particular* brain event is a *sensation* without *any* 'type–type' theory is a chimera.

To illustrate this point with an example, suppose that whenever I have a blue sense datum a particular event E takes place in the visual cortex. Was the event of my having a blue sense datum just now *identical* with the event E in my visual cortex just now? Or was it rather identical with the *larger* event of E *plus* signals to the speech center? If you say the *latter*, then very likely you will deny that patients with a split corpus collosum have blue sense data when blue is presented to the right lobe only; if you say the former, then very likely you will say they *do* (i.e., that there are two 'loci' of consciousness in the split brain). In this way, even the decision about 'token identity' in a particular case is inextricably bound up with what one wants to say about general issues, as fact is always bound up with theory.

The *special* trouble about the mind/body case is that it will never make an empirical difference whether we say the right lobe is conscious in the split brain case or not. That the right lobe is only, so to speak, simulating consciousness and that it is 'really' conscious are observationally indistinguishable theories as far as observers with unsplit brains are concerned. My own view is that there is an element of legislation or posit that enters here; the idea of a firm fact of the matter, not at all made by us, in the area of mind/brain relations is illusory.

If I am right, then this is another illustration of a theme to which Goodman constantly returns; that even where reduction is possible it is typically non-unique. Ontological identification is just another form of reduction and shares the non-uniqueness and the dependence upon legislation and posit characteristic of all reduction.

I wish now to make a different point about the physicalism–phenomenalism analogy. Those physicalists who say that such predicates as 'is an airplane wing' refer to physical properties whose definition in the language of physics might be infinite – practically infinite for sure – often explain this in terms of what an 'ideal theory' would say. I don't wish to say that talk of ideal theories is a bad thing (if we don't pretend 'ideal' is better defined than it is); regulative ideals and research programs are important in science as in everything else, and speculation about what the specification of an airplane wing or a mental state might look like in some ideal limit could be important in focussing thinking and research in a particular area. But if the physicalist avails himself of 'ideal limit' talk, he cannot consistently deny it to the phenomenalist. The phenomenalist can come back and tell the following sort of story about *his* 'ideal limit':

'An ideally intelligent being could divide all the state descriptions in an ideal sense datum language – i.e., all the descriptions of possible total sets of experiences that observers might have (or of experiences that they *would* have if they did various things, if you are more tolerant than Nelson Goodman towards counterfactuals) – into three classes: those in which "There is ivy growing on Emerson Hall on 9 June 1979" is true (or, not to beg questions, warrantedly assertible on the totality of all experiential evidence); those in which this sentence's negation is warrantedly assertible on total experiential evidence; and those in which it is undecided in the limit of total experiential evidence.

'Let S_1 be the infinite disjunction of all the state descriptions of the first kind. These are themselves denumerably infinite sentences, so this is an infinite disjunction of infinite conjunctions. Let S_2 be the infinite disjunction of all the state descriptions of the second kind.

Then I maintain that "There is ivy growing on Emerson Hall on 9 June 1979" *does* have a *translation* into phenomenalist language: for the ordered pair (S_1, S_2) is such a translation. The first member gives the cases in which the sentence is true; the second member gives the cases in which the sentence is false; and the remaining state descriptions are the truth-value gaps.'

Of course, the physicalist can reject the translation as *really* (metaphysically) wrong. But the point is that if the technique the phenomenalist envisages is applied to the sentences of the physicalist's own 'ideal scientific theory', then the result is a 'translation' of that theory into phenomenalistic language which preserves truth value as far as we shall ever be able to tell. 'Real metaphysical truth or falsity' is just what, in so far as it differs from ultimate warranted assertibility, we can never know.

What I have been saying is that whether we talk of reduction or of ontological identification, Goodman's two major points still hold: all species of reduction and ontological identification involve posits, legislation, non-uniqueness; and there are both different kinds of reduction and different directions of reduction. If all versions can be reduced in one way to a physicalist version (in principle, in the ideal limit, as a regulative ideal), then they can all be reduced to a phenomenalist version in another way (in principle, in the ideal limit, as a regulative ideal).

One world or many?

In his writings Goodman has consistently reminded us that there is no such thing as *comparing* any version with an 'unconceptualized reality'. We do check scientific theories against experiential data; but experiential data, as Goodman points out in his discussion of apparent motion, are themselves doubly the result of construction and interpretation: construction by the brain itself, and construal through the need of the subject to use language and public concepts to report and even grasp what he 'sees'. Comparison of theory with experience is *not* comparison with unconceptualized reality, even if some positivists once thought it was. It is comparison of one or another version with the version we take to be 'experience' in the given context.

On the other hand, we can invert the comparison: we can take some physicalistic description of the environment as 'the world' and analyze perceptual data (as construed) for salient correspondence or lack of salient correspondence to 'the world' (as construed). This is not like comparing two versions of the morning newspaper, but more like comparing *Newsweek* with *US News and World Report*. Such a comparison is legitimate and important; in his insistence on this Goodman is as much of an *empirical* realist as I am; but comparison of experience with physical theory is not comparison with unconceptualized reality, even if some of my friends in such places as Princeton and Australia think it is. All we have is comparison of versions with versions.

If reduction to one version were possible, were unique, and were always in the preferred direction, then the philosophers I refer to would have an easy rejoinder to Goodman. 'We don't *need* to suppose we can compare any version with an *unconceptualized* reality', they could say. 'Since (to the extent that it is more than folk theory)† any version is embeddable in the physicalist version, we have, appearances to the contrary (in the ideal limit, some of them would add), *one* version. There is, as Goodman says, no point in talking about "the world" apart from all versions, when there are incompatible true versions. But there *aren't* incompatible true versions; there is only one true version.'

The problem of the non-uniqueness of reduction is the key difficulty with this stance. But Hartry Field (1972*b*; 1974) has suggested an ingenious way for the metaphysical realist to meet it. The idea (which is closely related to Carnap's idea of 'partial interpretation') is to regard some terms as *partly referring* to one property or magnitude or whatever and partly referring to another. The terms so treated do not have *both* of the properties in question in their extension; rather, in one admissible interpretation such a term has the one, and in another admissible interpretation it has the other in its extension. (I am speaking of singular terms denoting properties, but the idea may be extended to any kind of term.) The various multiply-referring terms are *linked* so that the choice of one admissible interpretation of one can force or restrict the choice of the admissible interpretation of another.

Thus, in the case of the split brain problem I described above, a philosopher who agrees with me that there is no fact of the matter as to whether the occurrence of the neural event E in the right lobe of the split brain constitutes an occurrence of a visual sensation of blue

---

† The use of the notion of 'folk theory' by *scientistic* philosophers turns on a confusion that should be noted: a confusion between *false* theories (e.g., astrology) and theories whose terms are not 'scientifically precise' by the standards of physics and other *exact* sciences. 'Brown' and 'angry' might be said to belong to 'folk color theory' and 'folk psychology' respectively; but it doesn't follow (*pace* 'eliminative materialism') that there aren't brown objects or angry people.

could say that 'event of the occurrence of the visual sensation of blue' *partly refers* to the occurrence of neural events of kind E and partly refers to, say, the occurrence of E plus further processing in the speech center (which does not take place when the association paths between the right lobe and the speech center are cut). The element of posit that I described is just the choice of an admissible interpretation. All versions *still* reduce to one – the physicalist version – but the ontological reducing function is a many-valued function and not a single-valued one.

The trouble with this move is that the version chosen as basic – the physicalist version – has *incompatible reductions to itself*. Goodman illustrates this problem with geometrical examples. For example, *points* can be identified with sets of concentric spheres or, alternatively, with intersections of three planes. Even if we were to bite the bullet and say, 'Well, *point* partly refers to sets of of concentric spheres and partly refers to triples of planes', we would have the problem that one of the things planes and spheres can be identified with is sets of points. When there are incompatible relative interpretations of a theory in itself, the Hartry Field idea of 'partial reference' will not restore the kind of determinateness that the realist desires.

One can give similar examples from physics. In Newtonian physics, fields can be reduced to particles acting at a distance, and particles exerting forces at a distance can be replaced by particles interacting locally with fields. Even general relativity, long thought to be inseparable from curved space–time, has an equivalent version due to Steven Weinberg which dispenses with warped space. Nor will it help to hope for an ideal limit in which uniqueness will finally appear: if there were an ideal limit, and some cognitive extensions of ourselves actually reached it, then they would have nothing left to do but construct equivalent incompatible versions of the ideal limit – and, given ingenuity, I am sure they would succeed!

Another move that has been made to avoid Goodmanian pluralism, but one opposite in spirit to the Hartry Field move, is due to Quine. Quine holds that the failure of mentalistic psychology to reduce uniquely to physics shows that the sentences of mentalistic psychology and of all the discourses which employ mentalistic locutions have no truth value. These discourses are indispensable for daily life, but not truly cognitively significant. In *Word and Object*, Quine calls them 'second class'. Physical facts are all the facts there are, and to be underdetermined by all the facts there are is to lack truth value, so says Quine.

On the other hand, the existence of equivalent versions of physics which differ in ontology is now handled by Quine (1975) by saying that such versions are mere notational variants. There is *one* Newtonian physics and *one* general relativity, notwithstanding the existence of the notational variants. The true physics, whatever it may be, is Quine's candidate for the true and ultimate description of the world. The world does have a true and ultimate description, on Quine's view, *even if it doesn't have a true and ultimate ontology*.

The deep differences between Quine and Goodman, notwith-standing certain commonalities, have burst out in the *New York Review of Books*.† In his review of *WoW* in that journal, Quine reaffirms that only *physical* versions describe worlds, and justifies this by saying 'full coverage in this sense is the business of physics and only of physics'. But all Quine has to say about *what* sense of 'full coverage' physics aims at is that nothing happens without some redistribution of micro-physical states. There are clearly missing premises between 'nothing happens without some redistribution of micro-physical states' and 'full coverage'.

What the missing premises are, I can only guess. The 'full coverage' is only 'the business' of physics, so once again we have physicalism defended on the basis of the achievements of the program *in the ideal limit*. Even assuming this ideal limit were at hand, in what does its 'full coverage' *consist*?

If the 'full coverage' consists in explaining all *physical* facts, then the argument is circular. A theory may predict all of the motions of John's body without predicting that *John is angry*; and in what sense is such a theory 'complete'? It may be true that 'Nothing happens without some *gravitational* change', but that would not justify calling a theory that predicted all gravitational fields and nothing else 'complete'.

But there is a still more important objection. Imagine we belong to a community of art experts (it could be the entire species, if we all became art experts) for whom 'This painting has the characteristic Rembrandt paint quality' is an observation sentence, in Quine's sense (which requires that members of the language community have sufficiently high inter-subjective agreement on when they assent and when they dissent). Even if the ideal physics explained the sensations we would have on viewing *The Polish Rider*, it would certainly not explain them *under this description*. And Goodman's point is that

---

† Quine's review of *WoW* appeared in *New York Review* on 25 November 1978 (p. 25). Exchanges of letters by Quine, and Goodman and others appeared in *New York Review* on 25 January and 17 May 1979.

there is no reason to regard an explanation of which of our neurons fired as an explanation of our experience of the characteristic Rembrandt paint quality. From Goodman's perspective (as well as my own: see Putnam, 1975c), Quine's insistence that the physicalist description provides 'full coverage' is a mere prejudice.

Goodman's attitudes are deeply connected with his attitudes towards an appreciation of the arts. In chapter 4 ('When is art'), Goodman makes points which are extremely relevant to what we have been discussing. Consider the experience of reading a novel such as *Don Quixote*. One thing that happens to us is that our conceptual and perceptual repertoire becomes enlarged; we become able to 'see' Don Quixote, not only in the book but in ourselves and in other people. This enlargement of our stock of predicates and of metaphors is *cognitive*; we now possess descriptive resources we did not have before. And these are immensely valuable for their own sake, and not only for the sake of the stimulations of nerve endings they allow us to anticipate.

Similarly, even an abstract work of art *exemplifies* patterns and formal properties which we have to learn to perceive *in* and *through* the work; and this too is an enlargement of perceptual and conceptual skills. Fundamentally, Quine sees cognition as having just two aims: guiding the anticipation of sensation, and, beyond that, satisfying methodological canons of simplicity, conservativism, etc. Goodman is a pluralist about the *purposes* as well as about the content of cognition; and these two pluralisms are intimately connected.

Goodman on truth

It seems to me that Goodman's view is closely related to points made by Michael Dummett and by myself,† notably the point that the metaphysical realist notion of truth cannot play any role in a theory of how we *understand* our various versions and languages. This is clear, on Goodman's view, since no actual psychological mechanism can play the required role of comparing our statements with unconceptualized reality. Donald Davidson has proposed to retain the verbal formula that to know the meaning of, say, 'Snow is white', is to know under what conditions that sentence is true; one can say that *whatever it takes to understand a sentence* is to be called implicit knowledge of the conditions under which the sentence is true. But

† Dummett's views were most completely stated in his still unpublished William James Lectures at Harvard in the spring of 1976; mine are stated in 'Realism and reason' (Putnam, 1976). See also Putnam (1981) and chapter 1 of this volume.

if one plays the game *that* way, then it is a *tautology* that 'If *X* understands the sentence *Snow is white*, then *X* knows (implicitly) the truth conditions of the sentence *Snow is white*'. If we make this a tautology, then we can't also claim it to be an *explanatory account of understanding*. But if the notion that truth is correspondence to reality cannot do any work for us, how are we to explain the notion of truth? The formal semantics of 'true' (especially the equivalence principle: that to say of any sentence that it is true is equivalent to asserting the sentence) enables us to decide as many sentences of the form *S is true* as there are sentences *S* we are willing to assert or deny. But how are we to account for what we are doing when we assert and deny statements? We can say, 'when we assert statements we hope and intend that they should be true'; but this is almost empty, since there are not and cannot be independent tests for truth and for present warranted assertibility. In the first chapter of *WoW* Goodman writes, 'A version is taken to be true when it offends no unyielding beliefs and none of its own precepts'; but evidently this is not meant as a *definition* of 'true'.

Goodman tells us that truth itself is only one aspect of a more general virtue he calls *rightness*, just as statement-making and referential use of language represent only one sort of symbolic functioning (*expression* and *exemplification* being cited as others). Truth and rightness may sometimes conflict, even in science, as when what we want is a perspicuous but only approximately true general law rather than a strictly true statement which is overburdened with unnecessary information. Truth applies only to versions that consist of statements; and in chapter 7 we are told that it depends on credibility and coherence, as well as being given some details about deductive and inductive rightness.

All this, however, occupies only a few pages in *WoW*. Perhaps Goodman has not yet worked out exactly what he wishes to say on this central issue. But the direction is clear.

The direction in which Goodman's thought takes him is the direction of verificationist or 'non-realist' semantics. That is, Goodman is saying, I think, that we understand our languages in terms of a grasp of conditions of warranted assertibility and 'rightness'; not a grasp of 'truth conditions' in the old realist sense. Truth is an idealization of warranted assertibility.

Perhaps I am reading too much in here; if so, the author will set us right. But my reading is supported, I think, by two passages in the book. The first is surely the most unfortunate sentence in the book for anyone to quote out of context, 'Truth, like intelligence, is perhaps just what the tests test.' (p. 122) The meaning is not that Bridgemanian operationism is right (Goodman embraces coherence as a 'test' on pp. 124–5), but rather that we understand truth is a 'verificationist' way. The second passage is the open question on p. 124, 'Shall we, then, identify unattainable total and permanent credibility with total truth?': which, in the context, seems to say that 'total truth' is an idealization of 'credibility'.

The discussion of truth, and of tests for truth, in *WoW* bothers me, however, by its descriptive stance.

Consider, for example, the position of a man who thinks that one must commit himself to versions, precepts and unyielding beliefs, and who has so committed himself, all the while believing that there is nothing to be said in favor of his choice except that it is his existential choice. The position of such a man might be logically analyzed thus: it is as if he had decided that 'true' and 'right' are *indexical* words. 'True' (or rather, 'warrantedly assertible') means 'true for me' – i.e., in keeping with *my* precepts and unyielding beliefs – and 'right' means 'right for me' – i.e., in keeping with my standards and seat-of-the-pants feelings of rightness. I am sure Goodman would be horrified at such a position. But it could be the position of a culture (the young in California *do* say 'true for me'), and the whole story Goodman tells about how we build versions from versions, about not starting *ex nihilo*, about precepts and unyielding beliefs, could be told about 'true for me'. Goodman says that not all versions are true; but imagine a voice saying 'Not all versions are true for you, Professor Goodman, but so what?'

Goodman would, no doubt, reply that any superiority of our versions over other versions must be judged and claimed from *within* our collection of versions; there is no neutral place to stand. I heartily agree. But what I hope Goodman will say something about in the future is what makes our versions superior to others *by our lights*, not by some inconceivable neutral standard. 'Our versions are true, or closer to the truth' is purely formal; even the relativist can say his versions are 'truer for me': truer for *him*.

For Quine, as we saw, there is no such problem. Quine does say from within his versions – the scientific versions he likes – what makes those versions better than non-scientific versions: it is simply that they better predict stimulations of nerve-endings. But Goodman does not agree that the be-all and end-all of versions is just to predict stimulations of nerve-endings (or to do so economically and in a way that accords with tradition). Goodman recognizes that we wish to build worlds because doing so enriches us in many ways. And this, it seems to me, requires him to recognize that the notions of truth and rightness subserve a vision of the good.

Consider, for example, the often-mentioned desiderata of simplicity and generality in scientific theory. The search for these is part of the search for what Goodman calls 'rightness'; and if we refuse to accept versions which wilfully depart from this sort of rightness it is because having scientific versions which are simple and universal and exhibit internal coherence of a high order, as well as being technologically and predictively useful, is an end in itself for us; because it is part of our notion of human flourishing to have our scientific worlds be like that.

And if, as Goodman reminds us, art also serves cognitive functions, the reason for valuing the enlarged perception and conception that art provides is again the place of such perception and conception in our notion of human flourishing, of eudaemonia. The very term that Goodman chooses for the characteristic of the versions that meet our desiderata – *rightness* – is a term that bears its normative character on its face.

Goodman himself toys with the idea of extending what he has to say to the moral domain in a footnote on the first page of his concluding chapter. He writes, 'Any treatment of rightness may, of course, give rise to speculation concerning an application to moral rightness; but I willingly leave that to others. One point might be pondered, though: in the present context at least, relativity of rightness and the admissibility of conflicting right renderings in no way precludes rigorous standards for distinguishing right from wrong.' The direction that this footnote points out, however hesitantly, is the direction I think philosophers sympathetic to the general story Goodman tells should pursue.

Convention: a theme in philosophy

When one reads Quine, or Carnap, or Wittgenstein one encounters virtually no references to literature, or, indeed, to the arts. Yet certain themes in literature have a striking resemblance to themes in analytical philosophy. Thus Carnap celebrates the conventional, the artificial, the *planned*; Wittgenstein the natural, the organic, the traditional (although Wittgenstein's celebration of the traditional has a distinctively modern quality; it is the traditional without any of the traditional premises that he wishes us to retain). A deep examination of the notion of convention is one of the great contributions of analytical philosophy. In this essay, I want to review that contribution. At the end, I shall return to the remark that themes in the discussion have echoed themes in literature, and permit myself to speculate on what that shows about philosophy itself.

The conventional versus the natural

The nature of logical and mathematical truth has been a problem for empiricism from the beginning. Hume's explanation of logical necessity, that it has to do with one idea 'containing' another, presupposed the atomistic and sensationalistic psychology which he helped to found. 'All bachelors are unmarried' is analytic (true in virtue of the relations among our ideas) because the idea of being unmarried is contained in the idea of a bachelor; but does this mean simply that my mental picture of a bachelor happens to be a picture of an unmarried person? Kant retained some of the flavor of Hume's verbal formulation while giving up the identification of ideas with mental pictures or anything like mental pictures. More consequentially, Kant rejected this entire explanation as an explanation of the necessity of arithmetical or geometrical truth.

The necessity of 'all bachelors are unmarried' was still explained by saying that the 'conception' of the predicate *being unmarried* is contained in the idea or conception of the subject *bachelor*; but the truth and necessity of arithmetical judgments was said to be *synthetic a priori*. To philosophers working in the 1890s and at the beginning of the twentieth century, this talk of 'ideas' or 'conceptions' seemed horribly obscure. Philosophers representing as different tendencies as Peirce (pragmatism), Mach (positivism), Husserl (phenomenology), and Meinong (realism) all came to feel that many ideas cannot even be formed by the mind without the use of language, and that an investigation of the way in which the human mind understands and uses language is necessary before one can given an account of logical or mathematical truth.

For empiricism this 'linguistic turn' meant a shift from psychologism to conventionalism. The necessity of logical truths, and, in the case of the positivists, of mathematical truths as well, was accounted for by simply saying that all of this was 'truth by convention'. We stipulate or legislate that 'bachelor' is to be interchangeable with 'male adult human who has never been married'. That is what accounts for the necessity of the statement 'all bachelors are unmarried'.

Of course, the interchangeability of 'bachelor' and 'male adult human who has never been married', even if explained by the notion of linguistic convention, only explains why 'all bachelors are unmarried' may be regarded as synonymous with 'all male adult humans who have never been married are unmarried'. It does not really explain the truth of the *latter* statement, which is, rather, being presupposed.

But, in their enthusiasm for the notion of convention, the logical positivists argued that not only are *substitution relations*, like the inter-substitutibility of 'bachelor' and 'male adult human who has never been married', explained by convention, but that the correctness of the fundamental logical laws, the fundamental mathematical laws, and the fundamental rules of derivation in logic and mathematics, is likewise a matter of legislation or stipulation or had best be viewed as such.

So far, the notion of convention plays a role which is clear. Talk of words and sentences is clearer than talk of 'ideas', and talk of 'linguistic rules' seemed likewise to be clearer than talk of mysterious relations of 'containment' between ideas, or talk of a mysterious 'synthetic *a priori*'. The doctrine that mathematics consists of truth by convention permitted one to explain away the embarrassing fact that a major exact science seemed to proceed in a wholly non-empirical way, founding itself upon intuitions and not observations and carrying on by means of proofs and not by means of experiments. If mathematics is really the contentless transformation of linguistic expressions, then one could say with Einstein that 'in so far as mathematics is certain, it says nothing about the world'.

Thinking of language as if it were formal language, i.e., as if it were a system of signs governed by explicit rules, is thinking of language as it *ought* to be (at least from Carnap's point of view). In the autobiographical chapter in *The Philosophy of Rudolf Carnap* (Schilpp, 1963), Carnap makes no bones about the fact that he regards planned language and planned society as clearly superior to unplanned language and unplanned society just because they are *planned*. The formal systems that he talks about are seen by Carnap not as mere rational reconstructions of the language that scientists use, but as forerunners of a future symbolic language that scientists will eventually employ *instead of* unformalized language. Logical empiricism, at least in Carnap's hands, turns into a sort of futurist intellectual architecture.

In 1936, Quine, who was then just five years into his career, found himself compelled to break decisively with this whole conventionalist theory. The break was not without pain for him. Quine is an empiricist; he liked the idea of explaining mathematical necessity in an empiricist way; just three months before writing 'Truth by convention' (Quine, 1936) he had given a lecture at Harvard (which was never published) giving the best and most careful statement of the theory that mathematics is true by convention that has perhaps ever been written. It was not initial hostility to the doctrine of truth by convention, but deep reflection upon the consequences of that doctrine that led Quine to see that the theory is unworkable.

The argument is too intricate even to sketch here, but it turns on one of the themes that I had in mind when I spoke of themes which echo one another in philosophy and in literature. This is the theme of the opposition between the conventional and the natural.

Quine's argument (here I *will* permit myself to summarize one small bit) is that the very activity of laying down conventions, making stipulations, formulating rules, presupposes *language*. And language, Quine argues (this is the part I shall *not* summarize) presupposes logic. There is no possibility of a language (certainly not of a language rich enough to state generalizations and formulate conventions in) without logical words (*all, some, not, and, or, if-then*) and without logic enough for their employment. In short, the level at which logic lies is too *deep* (relative to the level at which convention lies) for convention to be prior to logic.

Quine is not merely making the obvious point that the axioms and inference procedures which constitute logic and mathematics did not (as a matter of contingent historical fact) arise through a process of explicit legislation. No one supposes that some ancient pre-Babylonian monarch bestowed logic upon a world which had previously been devoid of it by means of a Codex. What the empiricists recommended was that we give up thinking about natural language in philosophy, and consider a rational reconstruction. Conventionalism was a form of 'as-ifism'. Carnap said, in effect, that our language is *as if* logic and mathematics had come into existence through the adoption of a set of conventions. Quine's point is that this story is incoherent even as make-believe. Logic and mathematics *could not have* come into existence as the result of the adoption of conventions.

Quine's argument turns on the identification of conventions with *explicitly formulated rules*; but Quine has an answer to those who would object to this identification. If we widen the notion of convention, so that something counts as convention which was not explicitly formulated, even though it could not have been explicitly formulated (unless something of the same kind was already present), then have we not drained the notion of all its content? What of philosophical interest does there remain in the thesis that logic and mathematics are true by convention, Quine closes his essay by asking, beyond the 'still barer behavioristic statement' that we do accept the rules and procedures of logic and mathematics?

The very same strategy that we have seen operative in Quine's argument, the strategy of contrasting what we do *naturally* (either by virtue of our constitutions or by virtue of the particular cultural traditions that have become a part of our make-up) with what we do *conventionally* (i.e., by memorizing rules, reading signs, following instructions) may be observed at work in the later Wittgenstein. In one of the most celebrated parts of the *Philosophical Investigations*, Wittgenstein subjects the whole picture of a language as something that we understand and employ by grasping *rules* to a devastating critique. Like Quine, he comes to the conclusion that the fact that in certain contexts we just 'go on' the way we do – perhaps as the result of having a certain number of examples or of having watched members of our community or interacted with them in 'language games' – is more fundamental and in every way prior to such activities as giving and interpreting explicit directions.

When I am taught to obey a simple instruction, such as the instruction to *add one* over and over starting with a given number, the directions themselves cannot be understood by following explicit directions on pain of an infinite regress. Nor can the solution be the discovery of directions which are self-interpreting, directions such that there is only one way of understanding them (only one way of 'going on' given the verbal formula); for there are no such directions.

Ways of 'going on' that are natural to us, given the 'forms of life' that we have inherited, are prior to and presupposed by everything that could be called 'convention'.

Two great analytic philosophers have reached the conclusion that convention is a relatively superficial thing. It rests upon facts about us that are natural and not conventional.

Once one has taken the step of seeing the natural as in every way prior to the conventional, it is not far to the next step: to see the natural as that from the standpoint of which we may criticize the conventional. This step is taken, for example, by Stanley Cavell (1979, in a chapter titled 'Natural and conventional'):

> If the topic is that of continuing a series, it may be learning enough to find that I *just do*; to rest upon myself as my foundation. But if the child, little or big, asks me: Why do we eat animals? or Why are some people poor and others rich? or Why do I have to go to school? or Do you love black people as much as white people? or Who owns the land? or Why is there anything at all? or How did God get here?, I may find my answers thin, I may feel run out of reasons without being willing to say 'This is what I do' (What I say, what I sense, what I know), and honor that.
>
> Then I may feel my foregone conclusions were never conclusions *I* had arrived at, but were merely imbibed by me, merely conventional. I may blunt that realization through hypocrisy or cynicism or bullying. But I may take the occasion to throw myself back upon my culture, and ask why we do what we do, why we judge as we judge, how we have arrived at these crossroads. What is the natural ground of our conventions, to what are they in service? It is inconvenient to question a convention; that makes it unserviceable, it no longer allows me to proceed as a matter of course; the paths of action, the paths of words, are blocked. 'To imagine a language means to imagine a form of life.' In philosophizing, I have to bring my own language and life into imagination. What I require is a convening of my culture's criteria, in order to confront them with my words and life as I pursue them and as I may imagine them; and at the same time to confront my words and life as I pursue them with the life my culture's words may imagine for me: to confront the culture with itself along the lines in which it meets in me.   (p. 125)

Some of the conceptual unclarity surrounding the notion of convention itself was alleviated by the publication of *Convention* by David Lewis in 1969. Lewis, a young philosopher who had studied with Quine, proposed to clarify the idea of convention with the aid of notions from game theory, drawing upon the work of Thomas Schelling. It is certainly not arbitrary that cars should drive on the same side of the road: that they should all drive upon the right or all drive upon the left. What is arbitrary is that the agreed-upon-side should be the right side rather than the left side. In Schelling's terminology, the problem of getting all the cars to drive on the *same* side so as to prevent accidents is a 'coordination problem', and getting them to all drive on the right side (respectively the left side) is a 'solution to a coordination problem'. Lewis proposed to take precisely this feature, of being a solution to a coordination problem, as the *defining* characteristic of conventions. On the Lewis definition, something can *only* be a convention if it is *arbitrary*. More importantly from our present point of view, what is natural, inevitable, in every way not up for questioning, given our constitutions and forms of life, cannot intelligibly be described as 'conventional'. The opposition between the natural and the conventional pointed out by Quine and Wittgenstein has been taken to be the very defining feature of the conventional by Lewis. That our mathematics and logic are true by convention is itself *logically false*, given Lewis' definition.

The conventional and the objective

For empiricism, knowledge based upon intuition and proof rather than experiment was something that had to be explained away and not simply tolerated. Mathematical objects also had to be explained away. Mathematical objects – numbers, functions, sets – are neither sensible, nor are they causally connected with the sensible. To accept them as entities that really exist appears to threaten the naturalism which is at the heart of empiricism. To explain them away as a mere *façon de parler*, to show that the language of science can be reformulated so as to avoid the appearance of referring to abstract entities, is an idea which has attracted many empiricists; but careful logical investigation by the empiricists themselves led them to the conclusion that this idea is unworkable. To strip scientific language of all reference to abstract entities† would leave it so impoverished that we would not be able to formulate our powerful theories in physics, chemistry, molecular biology, and so on.

The positivists generally took the meaning of a sentence to be a function of the conditions under which the sentence is confirmed or infirmed. The larger the number of situations in which a sentence is infirmed, or the larger the number of situations which the sentence deductively or inductively *excludes*, the greater is the information

† Hartry Field (1980) has claimed that one can do physics without reference to abstract entities. But his construction requires that we accept *absolute space–time points* and arbitrary sets of space–time points as 'concrete'; most philosophers (including myself) would regard this as 'cheating'.

content of the sentence. On such a theory, a sentence of logic or mathematics which is counted as true in all experiential situations, a sentence which is never infirmed because the rule which constitutes the meaning of the sentence *says* that that sentence is never to count as being infirmed, a sentence which excludes *no* experiential state of affairs, is absolutely vacuous. Such sentences may still be useful in discourse, the positivists explained, because they enable us to transform the content of other sentences which do have non-vacuous meaning.

In effect, the positivists held that a sentence could both be meaningful (have a place in the language, a use in discourse, even a role in science itself) and meaningless (contain no information). On this view, sentences asserting the existence of mathematical objects may be true, but their truth is an empty sort of truth, for they convey no 'information'. To put it in another way, the existence of mathematical objects is an empty sort of existence.

This view too collapsed under the Quine–Wittgenstein critique of conventionalism (although Wittgenstein seems to have wanted to retain some of this view in his writing on the philosophy of mathematics). Behind the view are motives which guide philosophers of many kinds, and not just empiricist philosophers. Ordinary language is not a single 'conceptual scheme', but a motley of conceptual schemes, of 'versions', of 'worlds'.† A few philosophers – Dewey, Wittgenstein, Goodman – have been willing to opt for pluralism, i.e., the doctrine that many or most of these 'worlds' are legitimate, or legitimate in certain contexts, and that we should not ask which version 'copies' the world, which version represents 'the way the world is'. (There are *many* ways the world is, say the pluralists – and, of course, even more ways it *isn't*.) Most philosophers – even most analytic philosophers – continue to seek 'the furniture of the world', however. Such philosophers continue to distinguish between entities which are 'really', metaphysically, *there*, and entities which are somehow fictitious, somehow the product of our invention. To say that physical objects really exist (or that the statement that they do has 'empirical content') and that mathematical objects have only a conventional or linguistic existence (or that the statement that they exist is 'vacuous') is one expression of the desire to distinguish between what is *objectively*, mind independently, *there*, and what is 'made up' or fictitious. A philosopher who is a conventionalist (or who employs conventionalist ideas) for this reason, sees the conventional as opposed to the objective, not to the natural.

† 'Versions' and 'world' and the perplexing problem of their identity or non-identity are brilliantly discussed in Nelson Goodman's *Ways of Worldmaking* (1978).

It is not always and not only the mathematical objects that are seen as belonging to the conventional part of our ontology. At certain times and in certain places sense data have been regarded as the objective ground floor, and material objects have been thought of as a sort of make-believe that we introduce in order to facilitate predicting sensations on the basis of other sensations. Quine regards the Intentional – meanings, desires, beliefs – as part of that whose exist-ence is not 'factual' (in spite of his repudiation of conventionalism!). The Oxford philosopher John Mackie (1977) argues that *values* are 'ontologically queer', i.e., not part of the furniture of the world. What is so strange about all this is that Kant already taught us that the whole idea of comparing our conceptual system with a world of things-in-themselves (which Kant did accept, as a sort of postulate of reason) to see if the conceptual system 'copies' the unconcep-tualized reality is incoherent. The idea of comparing our conceptual system with a conceptual system which is 'built in' to the world, a unique 'right way' in which the world can be seen, is also incoherent. The pluralists are surely right: there are many right ways of representing the world, and even more wrong ways, as every artist knows.

I shall not review the arguments that led philosophers to give up the idea that sense data are the furniture of the world. The corrigibility of sensation reports, the very small part that such reports play in the actual construction of public knowledge, and the failure of the program of conceptual reduction (i.e., the program of showing that talk about material objects is highly derived talk about sensations) all played a role in this. The modern scientifically minded philosopher does not want to take ordinary material objects – the trees and grass, the tables and chairs – as exhausting the furniture of the world, because his science tells him that these are built up out of more fundamental parts. For this reason, a modern physicalist is likely to say that the furniture of the world is the space–time points, or the elementary particles, or something of that sort. *These* objects are so surrounded with mathematical devices, with alternative notations, even with whole alternative-but-somehow-equivalent theories, that no physicist would regard the question 'What of all this is convention and where in all this are the objects?' as making the slightest sense. (A physics book I once read contained the wonderful sentence, 'The electron that we observe is not the bare electron of the theory but the bare electron surrounded by a cloud of virtual particles.' In other words, the electron that we 'observe' is not the mathematical fiction of the theory, but the mathematical fiction surrounded by a cloud of other mathematical fictions!) Not only has modern physics failed to reveal to us any ready-made objects, any objects with a built-in and unique description, but the objects it does postulate are intimately connected with the observer and his way of observing them. The realism of modern physics is the realism of a Pirandello.

The factual and the conventional

The attempt to sort out the roles of 'fact' and 'convention' in our knowledge can lead even the soberest of analytical philosophers to employ poetic language. Quine ends a famous paper (1960) criticizing the idea that some sentences are true by convention by describing the 'lore of our fathers' as a grey fabric – 'black with fact and white with convention'. And he adds, 'but I have not found any quite black threads nor any wholly white ones'. Goodman (1978), writing on convention and content remarks,

In practice, of course, we draw the line wherever we like, and change it as often as suits our purposes. On the level of theory, we flit back and forth between extremes as blithely as a physicist between particle and field theories. When the verbiage view threatens to dissolve everything into nothing, we insist that all true versions describe worlds. When the right-to-life sentiment threatens an overpopulation of worlds, we call it all talk. Or to put it another way, the philosopher like the philanderer is always finding himself stuck with none or too many.

The problem is this: we don't wish to suggest that knowledge is merely made up by the human mind; that would be an idealism beyond all idealisms. So we say that there is a 'factual component' to knowledge. We don't, or at least we shouldn't, want to say that knowledge is simply a 'copy' of mind-independent reality or an approximation to the 'one true theory'. So we say that knowledge has a 'conventional component'. But this talk of 'components' lands us in the soup. For to speak of two components is to suggest that we should be able, in principle at least, to factor our knowledge into parts; that we should be able to say which part is factual and which part is conventional. But to do this would precisely be to recover the idea that there is a 'world in itself'; for that is what a statable 'factual component', freed of all 'conventional components', would amount to.

A better way to describe the situation would be to say that our knowledge, or any piece of it, is conventional relative to certain alternatives and factual relative to certain others. Saying that there is an electrical field in a certain place *as opposed to saying that* there are particles interacting by exchanging other particles, may be a matter of convention. Saying that there is an electrical field in that place as opposed to no electrical field in that place, is a matter of fact (at least in a fixed reference frame). To use a more familiar example, it is a matter of fact that my car is moving at sixty miles an hour relative to the ground, and not at twenty miles an hour; but it is conventional (at least from a physicist's point of view) that I describe the speed of my car relative to the ground and not relative to a moving airplane. *Everything* we say is conventional in the sense that we might have said something else, perhaps something verbally incompatible; and *everything* we say is factual in the sense that we could not have said just anything else. The fact that we say X rather than Y may be conventional, wholly or in part, while the fact that we say X rather than Z is not at all conventional.

Such a formulation may unpack Quine's metaphor. It may explain how there can be conventionality and factuality (the colors white and black) without there being a conventional component and a factual component (white threads and black threads).

Goodman's remark is more challenging. If there are many right versions of the world (Goodman includes artistic as well as scientific versions), and no specifiable set of invariants to which they can all be reduced, what becomes of the notion of a *world*? Goodman would say that it doesn't matter; that one can either say that there is one world, or no worlds, or as many worlds as there are versions; and it is best to say all three of these to keep us on our toes. I am more staid than Goodman; I would say that any version we accept as right can be regarded as a description of the world; and I would finesse Goodman's point by conceding that if one chooses to speak in this way, one must add that identity goes soft. In many cases there will be no hard and fast answer to the question which object in one version is 'identical' with an object in another version (if any). Field theory can be translated into particle theory; but in many right ways (right but *incompatible* ways!). Such traditional philosophical questions as whether material objects are bundles of actual and possible sensations, and whether sensations are brain states, have no unique right answers. They have many right answers or none.

Themes and philosophy

It is now time to say a little about what all this means. In this essay I have not been trying to 'do' analytical philosophy. I have alluded to arguments rather than really given them, and such history of analytical philosophy as I have given is a selection, a selection designed to help us see analytical philosophy once again as a humanistic discipline, and its problems and themes as common problems and themes in the humanities. Such a selection is a necessity because the self-image and self-definition of analytical philosophy have too long been accepted uncritically. According to its self-definition, analytical philosophy has three characteristics.

(1) Analytical philosophy is non-ideological: which means above all that it is non-political and non-moralizing.

(2) Analytical philosophy consists of piece-meal problem solving. Analytical philosophers need not have integrated positions; they write articles proposing and discussing arguments on specific philosophical problem and topics.

(3) Although this has begun to change as the result of the publication of John Rawls' *A Theory of Justice* in 1970 analytical philosophy for a long time regarded value theory as second-class philosophy, and a concern with literature, the arts, culture, and the history of culture, as at best optional for an analytical philosopher.

Each of these three self-characterizations contains a substantial element of truth, but also a substantial element of self-deception. The fact is that Carnap and the logical positivists were intensely ideological philosophers, even if their ideology did not take the form of *overt* politics or moralizing. The arguments that analytical philosophers discussed were sometimes piece-meal arguments, but very often they were produced by philosophers who were highly ideological in the sense that Carnap was. Without the motor of a certain amount of ideology which kept producing arguments that divided analytical philosophers into sides, analytical philosophy could hardly have kept going; it has already begun to lose shape as a tendency, with the demise of logical positivism. The fact that analytical philosophers were not interested in cultural history does not mean that they escaped being a part of it.

I think that the phenomenon called 'analytical philosophy' is best understood as a part of the larger phenomenon of modernism. What it had in common with the modernism of the 1930s was an extreme form of the rejection of the tradition that was characteristic of modernism in the beginning. (Some analytical philosophers still speak of an enemy called 'traditional philosophy' even now.) But modernism itself was not a unified movement; and the strains and conflicts in analytical philosophy reflect the strains and conflicts in modernism generally. One side of modernism is perhaps best represented by modern architecture. This is the side of modernism that is also represented by Carnap and the Vienna Circle (which is why I earlier referred to Carnap's work as futurist architecture). Ada

Louise Huxtable (1981) has described the systems of belief that formed modern architecture: she stresses a 'devout' belief in social justice ('The Bauhaus taught that the machine would put beauty and utility within the reach of everyone. Le Corbusier's "machine to live in" and "radiant cities" would reform human habitation.'), a belief that 'what was useful was beautiful and good' and that 'what was good was good for all of us'. 'Walter Gropius's "teamwork" and Mies's modular simplicity were meant to alleviate the inequities and inadequacies of the man-made environment. The architect was to be central to these aesthetic and social solutions – inextricably linked – of age-old problems, and the gratification of new expectations.'

Carnap's belief in Esperanto, socialism, and ideal languages that would actually be used in scientific work, was of a piece with Le Corbusier's 'radiant cities'. Carnap too was trying to build a 'machine to live in'.

Huxtable goes on to write,

In retrospect, the hopes and beliefs of this century have been both admirable and naive, but they have also been humanitarian to an extraordinary degree. Perhaps we in the advanced Western countries have come as close to genuine civilization as we ever will, if we define civilization as the unselfish preoccupation with the betterment of the human condition at the highest level of shared experience and universal concern. The eighteenth-century Age of Reason was followed by the nineteenth-century Age of Scientific Inquiry, which exploded, in the twentieth century, into the Age of Perfectability through science and art. It was, of course, an impossible dream.

Huxtable's description may be a fair description of the ideas that animated modern architecture; but as a description of modernism *as a whole* it is simply wrong. There was always a utopian wing to modernism; but there was always a pessimistic wing (perhaps both can be traced back to Rousseau). Marx was a modernist, but so was Nietzsche. As Huxtable rightly points out, the optimistic wing of modernism sought to deconstruct the tradition in order to make room for the New Man and the perfect society; the pessimistic wing sought to deconstruct the tradition *and* the idea of the New Man.

In his play 'Die Schwärmer', Musil plays the two wings of modernism against each other. In the third act, Thomas, a Privatdozent who is on the verge of renouncing his academic career (as Musil himself did), has the following exchange with Josef, his former Professor:

THOMAS: You desire ideals; but also that no one should go to extremes because of them. You allow the widow to remarry, but you declare that love is forever, that's why remarriage only succeeds *after* death. You believe in the struggle of life, but you soften it with the commandment: Love Thy Neighbor. You believe in loving your neighbor, but you soften it with the struggle of life. You teach that there are *unconditionally* valid laws, but one must be merciful. You are for property *and* welfare. You declare that one must die for the supreme good, because you already assume that no one lives for *you* so long as a single hour –

JOSEF (*interrupts*): You could say in a single word that I am too demanding, too rigorous. Or the reverse: that my nature is that of an ordinary compromiser?

THOMAS: I only want to say, what nobody will deny, that you are an able man who needs to build a solid foundation for himself. I will not say anything else. You are walking on an extended network of girders; but there are people who are compelled to look down through the holes between the girders.

The 'people who are compelled to look down through the holes between the girders' are the modernists in the tradition of Nietzche.

Even if Quine and Wittgenstein deployed similar *arguments* against Carnapian conventionalism, they did not represent the same *kind* of modernism. Quine is not a socialist, an Esperantist, or a believer in formal languages as languages for actual scientific use; but in a more moderate way he shares Carnap's scientism. Wittgenstein was deeply hostile to scientism and saw philosophy as an independent (virtually presuppositionless) activity of 'untying knots'. Towards the end of 'Die Schwärmer', Regine reproaches Thomas for not having given her any idea what to *do* with her life. Thomas replies: 'Man wandert einfach so umher. Feindlich sind dir alle, die ihren bestimmten Weg gehn, während du auf der unbestimmten Bettlerfahrt des Geistes durch die Welt bist. Trotzdem gehörst du ihnen irgendwie zu.' (One simply wanders around so. All those people who go their determinate ways are hostile to you, while you are on your indeterminate beggar's journey through the world. Nevertheless you belong to them somehow.) There is an echo of the same outside-of-the-show mood in Wittgenstein's remark (*Zettel*, 455) 'Der Philosoph ist nicht Bürger einer Denkgemeinde. Das ist, was ihn zum Philosophen macht.' (The philosopher is not a citizen of any community of ideas. That is what makes him a philosopher.)

More concretely, for Quine the failure of conventionalism means that we have to *find something else*. If the existence of mathematical objects is not conventional, vacuous, unrevisable ('Revision can strike anywhere', Quine writes) then, even if we would prefer to be nominalists if we could, we must face up to the situation and become 'robust realists' with respect to the existence of abstract entities. For

Wittgenstein, it is enough to point out the failure of conventionalism. Once one has explained how we talk in mathematics and how we talk in other language games, it is futile to ask whether the existence of mathematical objects is 'like' or 'unlike' the existence of electrons. (Wittgenstein is not a 'debunker': the philosophical *search* fascinates him; it is answers that he rejects.)

Since the reduction of philosophy to a kind of pure logic of language has failed (because, on Quine's view, logic itself can only be justified by regarding it as the most abstract part of physics), Quine proposes to reduce logic, mathematics, and philosophy itself to physics. The price he pays for his futurism is an enormous implausibility: virtually no one has followed Quine into the belief that the axioms of number theory, for example, are justified by their (indiect) utility in physics and natural science. Quine's claim that his own philosophical arguments (which are, at their best, marvels of intricacy and depth) are similar to propositions of natural science is likewise false on the face of it. (Yet the analogy to modern architecture holds here too: the same phenomenon, the issuing of crazy manifestos, has been a feature of many modernist movements – especially of the 'futurist' ones.) The price Wittgenstein pays for his quietism is a constant teetering on the edge of a cultural relativism that would turn everything he says into a monstrous irrationalism (the threat of nihilism).

I am not a fan of any sort of historicism. Every discipline must be understood in its own terms. But recognizing that there *are* broad currents in the culture is not being simplistic (nor, necessarily, 'structuralist'). Modernism is such a current, and we can recognize its forms and tensions in the development of analytical philosophy without deluding ourselves that that is all there is to analytical philosophy.

The fact that specific themes: a search for a kind of 'objectivity' that always runs through our fingers like quicksilver, and a struggle between the celebration of the artificial and the celebration of the natural, should appear in philosophy *and* in the arts, will then seem less astonishing. More important, just as we look forward to a post-modernism in the arts, we can look forward to a post-modernism in philosophy. I do not think it will have the shape of either scientism or Wittgensteinian quietism, though both scientism and quietism remain dangers for philosophy as they do for the life of the spirit in general.

Philosophers and human understanding

I find myself in the position that Jerome Bruner (1976) found himself in a few years before me. I agreed to give a Herbert Spencer lecture; I planned to give a lecture on the topic of scientific explanation; I intended to discuss a particular controversy in that field, the controversy about whether scientific theories are 'incommensurable', about whether there is any 'convergence' in scientific knowledge; but I felt increasing dissatisfaction with this entire idea as the day approached. Bruner's dissatisfaction led him to some reflections about the history and present state of psychology. I intend to follow his example and ruminate on the activity itself, the activity of philosophy of science, in my own case, and on certain dissatisfactions I feel with the way that activity has been pursued, rather than discuss a particular issue within it. However, the particular issue I mentioned will come up in the course of these ruminations.

Logical positivism is self-refuting

In the late 1920s, about 1928, the Vienna Circle announced the first of what were to be a series of formulations of an empiricist meaning criterion: *the meaning of a sentence is its method of verification.* A. J. Ayer's *Language, Truth and Logic* spread the new message to the English-speaking philosophical world: *untestable statements are cognitively meaningless.* A statement must either be (*a*) analytic (logically true, or logically false to be more precise) or (*b*) empirically testable, or (*c*) *nonsense*, i.e., not a real statement at all, but only a pseudo-statement. Notice that this was already a change from the first formulation.

An obvious rejoinder was to say that the logical positivist criterion of significance was *self-refuting*: for the criterion itself is neither (*a*) analytic (unless, perhaps, it is analytically *false*!), nor (*b*) empirically testable. Strangely enough this criticism had very little impact on the logical positivists and did little to impede the growth of their movement. I want to suggest that the neglect of this particular philosophical gambit was a great mistake; that the gambit is not only correct, but contains a deep lesson, and not just a lesson about logical positivism.

The point I am going to develop will depend on the following observation: the forms of 'verification' allowed by the logical positivists are forms which have been *institutionalized* by modern society. What can be 'verified' in the positivist sense can be verified to be correct (in a non-philosophical or pre-philosophical sense of 'correct'), or to be probably correct, or to be highly successful science, as the case may be; and the public recognition of the correctness, or the probable correctness, or the 'highly successful scientific theory' status, exemplifies, celebrates, and reinforces images of knowledge and norms of reasonableness maintained by the culture.

The *original* positivist paradigm of verification was not this publicly institutionalized one, it is true. In Carnap's *Logische Aufbau der Welt* (*The Logical Construction of the World*) verification was ultimately private, based on sensations whose subjective quality or 'content' was said to be 'incommunicable'. But, under the urgings of Neurath, Carnap soon shifted to a more public, more 'inter-subjective', conception of verification.

Popper has stressed the idea that scientific predictions are confronted with 'basic sentences', sentences such as 'the right pan of the balance is down' which are publicly accepted even if they cannot be 'proved' to the satisfaction of a skeptic. He has been criticized for using 'conventionalist' language here, for speaking as if it were a convention or social decision to accept a basic sentence; but I think that what some take to be the conventionalist element in Popper's thought is simply a recognition of the *institutionalized* nature of the implicit norms to which we appeal in ordinary perceptual judgments. The nature of our response to a skeptic who challenges us to 'prove' such statements as 'I am standing on the floor' testifies to the existence of social norms *requiring* agreement to such statements in the appropriate circumstances.

Wittgenstein argued that without such public norms, norms shared by a group and constituting a 'form of life', language and even thought itself would be impossible. For Wittgenstein it is absurd to ask if the institutionalized verification I have been speaking of is 'really' justificatory. In *On Certainty* Wittgenstein remarks that philosophers can provide one with a hundred epistemological 'justifications' of the statement 'cats don't grow on trees', but *none* of them starts with anything which is more sure (in just this institutionalized sense of 'sure') than the fact that cats don't grow on trees.

Skeptics have doubted not only perceptual judgments but ordinary inductions. Hume, whose distinction between what is *rational* and what is *reasonable* I am not observing, would have said there is no *rational* proof that it will snow (or even that it will probably snow) in the United States this winter (although he would have added that it would be most unreasonable to doubt that it will). Yet our response to a skeptic who challenges us to 'prove' that it will snow in the United States this winter testifies that there are social norms requiring agreement to such 'inductions' just as much as to ordinary perceptual judgments about people standing on floors and about equal arm balances (indeed, 'cats don't grow on trees' is an 'induction' in this sense.)

When we come to high-level theories in the exact sciences, people's reactions are somewhat different. Ordinary people cannot 'verify' the special theory of relativity. Indeed, ordinary people do not at the present time even *learn* the special theory, or the (relatively elementary) mathematics needed to understand it, although it is beginning to be taught in first-year physics courses in some universities. Ordinary people defer to scientists for an informed (and socially accepted) appraisal of a theory of this type. And because of the instability of scientific theories, a scientist is not likely to refer to even so successful a theory as special relativity as 'true' *tout court*. But the judgment of the scientific community is that special relativity is a 'successful' – in fact, like quantum electrodynamics, an unprecedentedly successful – scientific theory, which yields 'successful predictions' and which is 'supported by a vast number of experiments'. And these judgments are, in fact, deferred to by other members of the society. The difference between this case and the cases of institutionalized norms of verification previously referred to (apart from the hedging of the adjective 'true') is the special role of experts and the institutionalized deference to experts that such a case involves; but this is no more than an instance of the division of intellectual labor (not to mention intellectual authority relations) in the society. The judgment that special relativity and quantum electrodynamics are 'the most successful physical theories we have' is one which is made by authorities which the society has appointed and whose authority is recognized by a host of practices and ceremonies, and in that sense institutionalized.

Recently it occurred to me that Wittgenstein may well have thought that *only* statements that can be verified in some such 'institutionalized' way can be true (or right, or correct, or justified) at all. I don't mean to suggest that any philosopher ever held the view that *all* things which count in our society as 'justifications' really are such. Philosophers generally distinguish between institutions which are constitutive of our concepts themselves and those which have some other status, although there is much controversy about how to make such a distinction. I mean to suggest that Wittgenstein thought that it was some subset of our institutionalized verification norms that determines what it is right to say in the various 'language games' we play and what is wrong, and that there is no objective rightness or wrongness beyond this. Although such an interpretation does fit much that Wittgenstein says – for instance, the stress on the need for 'agreement in our judgments' in order to have concepts at all – I do not feel sure that it is right. It is just too vague who the 'we' is in Wittgenstein's talk of 'our' judgments; and I don't know whether his 'forms of life' correspond to the institutionalized norms I have mentioned. But this interpretation occurred to me upon reading Wittgenstein's *Lectures and Conversations*. In this Wittgenstein rejects both psychoanalysis and Darwin's theory of evolution (although unlike the positivists he does not regard such language as *meaningless*, and he has admiration for Freud's cleverness). Wittgenstein's view about psychoanalysis (which he calls a 'myth') does not signify much, although the reasons given are interesting, since so many people have the view – mistakenly in my opinion – that psychoanalysis is total nonsense. Indeed, Wittgenstein is, as I mentioned, considerably more charitable than this. But his rejection of *evolution* is quite striking.† Wittgenstein contrasts Darwin's theory unfavorably with theories in physics ('One of the most important things about an explanation is that it should work, that it should enable us to predict something. Physics is connected with Engineering. The bridge must not fall down.' ('Lectures on aesthetics', in

---

† Concerning evolution what Wittgenstein said was 'People were certain on grounds which were extremely thin. Couldn't there have been an attitude which said: "I don't know. It is an interesting hypothesis which may eventually be well confirmed."': 'Lectures on aesthetics', p. 26, in Burret (1967). What it would be like for evolution to be 'well confirmed' Wittgenstein does not say, but the paragraph suggests that actually *seeing* speciation occur is what he has in mind ('Did anyone see this process happening? No. Has anyone seen it happening now? No. The evidence of breeding is just a drop in the bucket.')

It is instructive to contrast Wittgenstein's attitude with Monod's (1975): '...the selective theory of evolution, as Darwin himself had stated it, required the discovery of Mendelian genetics, which of course was made. This is an example, and a most important one, of what is meant by the content of a theory, the content of an idea....[A] good theory or a good idea will be much wider and much richer than even the inventor of the idea may know at his time. The theory may be judged precisely on this type of development, when more and more falls into its lap, even though it was not predictable that so much would come of it.'

Burret, 1967, p. 25)). And he says people were persuaded 'on grounds which were extremely thin'. 'In the end you forget entirely every question of verification, you are just sure it must have been like that.'

Again, the great discussions about 'analyticity' that went on in the 1950s seem to me to be connected with the desire of philosophers to find an objective *uncontroversial* foundation for their arguments. 'Analyticity', i.e., the doctrine of truth by virtue of meaning alone, came under attack because it had been *overused* by philosophers. But why had philosophers been tempted to announce that so many things which are in *no* intelligible sense 'rules of language', or consequences of rules of language, were analytic or 'conceptually necessary', or whatever? The answer, I think, is that the idea that there is a definite set of *rules of language* and that *these* can settle what is and is not rational, had two advantages, as philosophers thought: (1) the 'rules of language' (or the 'depth grammar', or whatever) are constitutive institutionalized practices (or norms which underlie such practices), and as such have the 'public' status I have described; (2) at the same time, it was claimed that only philosophers (and not linguists) could discover these mysterious things. It was a nice idea while it lasted, but it was bound to be exploded, and it was.

I shall call any conception according to which there are institutionalized norms which define what is and is not rationally acceptable a *criterial* conception of rationality. The logical positivists, Wittgenstein (at least on the admittedly uncertain interpretation I have essayed) and some though not all† of the 'ordinary language'

† One might develop an 'ordinary language' philosophy which was not committed to the public and 'criterial' verification of philosophical theses if one could develop and support a conception in which the norms which govern linguistic practices are not themselves discoverable by ordinary empirical investigation. In *Must We Mean What We Say*, Stanley Cavell took a significant step in this direction, arguing that such norms can be known by a species of 'self-knowledge' which he compared to the insight achieved through therapy and also to the transcendental knowledge sought by phenomenology. While I agree with Cavell that my knowledge as a native speaker that certain uses are deviant or non-deviant is not 'external' inductive knowledge – I can know without evidence that in my dialect of English one says 'mice' and not 'mouses' – I am inclined to think this fact of speaker's privileged access does not extend to *generalizations* about correctness and incorrectness. If I say (as Cavell does) that it is part of the rule for the correct use of locutions of the form *X is voluntary* that there should be something 'fishy' about *X*, then I am advancing a *theory* to explain my intuitions about specific cases, not just reporting those intuitions. It is true that something of this sort also goes on in pyschotherapy; but I am not inclined to grant self-knowledge any kind of immunity from criticism by others, including criticisms which depend on offering rival *explanations*, in either case. And if one allows the legitimacy of such criticism, then the activity of discovering such norms begins to look like social science or history: areas in which, I have argued, traditional accounts of 'the scientific method' shed little light (see Putnam, 1978).

In any case, whatever their status, I see no reason to believe that the norms for the use of *language* are what decide the extension of 'rationally acceptable', 'justified', 'well confirmed', and the like.

philosophers at Oxford shared a criterial conception of rationality even if they differed on other issues, such as whether to call unverifiable statements 'meaningless', and over whether or not some ethical propositions could be 'conceptually necessary'.

The gambit I referred to at the outset, the gambit that refutes the logical positivists' verification principle, is *deep* precisely because it refutes every attempt to argue for a criterial conception of rationality, i.e., because it refutes the thesis that nothing is rationally verifiable unless it is criterially verifiable.

The point is that although the philosophers I mentioned often spoke as if their arguments had the same kind of *finality* as a mathematical proof or a demonstration experiment in physics; that although the logical positivists called their work *logic* of science; although the Wittgensteinians displayed unbelievable arrogance towards philosophers who could not 'see' that all philosophical activity of a pre-Wittgensteinian or non-Wittgensteinian kind is nonsensical; and although ordinary language philosophers referred to each others arguments and those of non-ordinary language philosophers as 'howlers' (as if philosophical errors were like mistakes on an arithmetic test); no philosophical position of any importance can be verified in the conclusive and culturally recognized way I have described. In short, if it is true that only statements that can be criterially verified can be rationally acceptable, that statement itself cannot be criterially verified, and hence cannot be rationally acceptable. If there is such a thing as rationality at all – and we commit ourselves to believing in *some* notion of rationality by engaging in the activities of *speaking* and *arguing* – then it is self-refuting to *argue* for the position that it is identical with or properly contained in what the institutionalized norms of the culture determine to be instances of it. For no such argument can be certified to be correct, or even probably correct, by those norms alone.

I don't at all think that rational argumentation and rational justification are impossible in philosophy, but rather I have been driven to recognize something which is probably evident to laymen if not to philosophers, namely that we cannot appeal to public norms to decide what is and is not rationally argued and justified in philosophy. The claim which is still often heard that philosophy is 'conceptual analysis', that the *concepts themselves* determine which philosophical arguments are right, is, when combined with the doctrine that concepts are norms or rules underlying public linguistic practices, just a covert form of the claim that all rational justification in philosophy is criterial, and that philosophical truth is (barring 'howlers') as publicly demonstrable as scientific truth. Such a view seems to me to be simply unreasonable in the light of the whole history of the subject, including the recent history.

Let me emphasize again that I *do* think that there are rationally justified and rationally unjustified views in philosophy. I have argued at length in a whole series of publications that mind–body dualism is an unreasonable view; and I stand by that argument. My argument appealed to the great explanatory attractiveness of a 'monist' view, i.e., a view which does not require substance dualism, and tried at the same time to concede what was *right* in dualism (e.g., that belief-desire explanation is not simply 'reducible' to mechanistic explanation). In general I tried to account for dualist intuitions. But a dualist can, of course, point out counter-intuitive consequences of my view; and, just as I say it is more *reasonable* to believe that we are material objects in a physical world, he can say it is more *reasonable* to believe that mental events are non-identical with physical events. There is no neutral place, no neutral conception of rationality, from which to decide who is right. Even if one is a neutral *on this issue* – i.e., one thinks *neither* of us has a more reasonable position than the other – *that* isn't a neutral position either. One can't *criterially* verify that neither of us has reason on his side by appeal to the cultural norms. In fact, both of us are trying to *shape* the *future* cultural norms; so even if there *were* a culturally indoctrinated conception supporting one of us, that wouldn't convince the other.

What goes for philosophical argument goes for arguments about religion and about secular ideology as well. An argument between an intelligent liberal and an intelligent Marxist will have the same character as a philosophic dispute at the end, even if more empirical facts are relevant. And we all do have views in religion, or politics, or philosophy, and we all argue them and criticize the arguments of others. Indeed, even in 'science', outside of the exact sciences, we have arguments in history, in sociology, in clinical psychology of exactly this character. It is true that the logical positivists broadened their description of the 'scientific method' to include these subjects; but so broadened it cannot be shown to clearly *exclude* anything whatsoever.

The positivists, I will be reminded, *conceded* that the verification principle was 'cognitively meaningless'.† They said it was a *proposal*,

† The weakest argument offered in defense of the verification principle construed as a proposal was that it 'explicated' the 'pre-analytic' notion of meaningfulness. (For a discussion of this claim, see Putnam (1965).) Reichenbach (1938) defended a form of the verification principle as *preserving all differences in meaning relevant to behavior*. Against an obvious objection (that the non-empirical belief in a divinity – Reichenbach used the example of Egyptian cat worshippers – could alter behavior) Reichenbach replied by

and as such not true or false. But they *argued* for their proposal, and the arguments were (and had to be) non-starters. So the point stands.

In sum, what the logical positivists and Wittgenstein (and perhaps Quine as well) did was to *produce philosophies which leave no room for a rational activity of philosophy*. This is why these views are self-refuting; and what the little gambit I have been discussing rests upon is really a very significant argument of the kind philosophers call a 'transcendental argument': arguing about the nature of rationality is an activity that *presupposes* a notion of rational justification wider than the positivist notion, indeed wider than institutionalized criterial rationality.

Anarchism is self-refuting

Let me now discuss a very different philosophical tendency. Thomas Kuhn's (1962) *The Structure of Scientific Revolutions* (*SSR*) enthralled vast numbers of readers, and appalled most philosophers of science because of its emphasis on what seemed to be *irrational* determinants of scientific theory acceptance and by its use of such terms as 'conversion' and 'Gestalt switch'. In fact, Kuhn made a number of important points about how scientific theories and scientific activity should be viewed. I have expressed a belief in the importance of the notions of *paradigm*, *normal science*, and *scientific revolution* elsewhere; here I want to focus on what I do *not* find sympathetic in Kuhn's book, what I have described elsewhere as 'Kuhn's extreme relativism'.

The reading that enthralled Kuhn's more sophomoric readers was one on which he is saying there is no such thing as rational justification in science, it's *just* Gestalt switches and conversions.

---

proposing to translate 'Cats are divine animals' as 'Cats inspire feelings of awe in cat worshippers'. Clearly the acceptance of this substitute would *not* leave behavior unchanged in the case of a cat worshipper!

The most interesting view was that of Carnap. According to Carnap, *all* rational reconstructions are proposals. The only factual questions concern the logical and empirical consequences of accepting this or that rational reconstruction. (Carnap compared the 'choice' of a rational reconstruction to the choice of an engine for an airplane.) The conclusion he drew was that in philosophy one should be tolerant of divergent rational reconstructions. However, this principle of tolerance, as Carnap called it, *presupposes* the verification principle. For the doctrine that no rational reconstruction is uniquely *correct* or corresponds to the way things 'really are', the doctrine that all 'external questions' are without cognitive sense, *is* just the verification principle. To apply the principle of tolerance to the verification principle itself would be circular.

Kuhn has rejected this interpretation of *SSR*, and has since introduced a notion of 'non-paradigmatic rationality' which may be closely related to if not the same as what I have just called 'non-criterial rationality'.

The tendency that most readers thought they detected in Kuhn's *SSR* certainly manifested itself in Paul Feyerabend's *Against Method* (1975). Feyerabend, like Kuhn, stressed the manner in which different cultures and historic epochs produce different paradigms of rationality. He suggests that the determinants of *our* conception of scientific rationality are largely what *we* would call irrational. In effect, although he does not put it this way, he suggests that the modern scientific-technological conception of rationality is fraudulent by its own standards. (I think I detect a similar strain in Michel Foucault.) And he goes far beyond Kuhn or Foucault in suggesting that even the vaunted instrumental superiority of our science may be somewhat of a hoax. Faith healers can do more to relieve our pain than doctors, Feyerabend claims.

It is not these terrifyingly radical claims that I want to talk about, although they are the reason Feyerabend calls his position 'anarchism'. I wish to discuss a claim Kuhn does make in both *SSR* and subsequent papers, and that Feyerabend made both in *Against Method* and in technical papers. This is the thesis of *incommensurability* (the very thesis I originally intended to devote this lecture to). I want to say that this thesis, like the logical positivist thesis about meaning and verification, is a self-refuting thesis. In short, I want to claim that *both* of the two most influential philosophies of science of the twentieth century, certainly the two that have interested scientists and non-philosophers generally, the only two the educated general reader is likely to have even heard of, are self-refuting. Of course, as a philosopher of science I find it a bit troublesome that this should be the case. We shall shortly come to the question of what to make of this situation.

The incommensurability thesis is the thesis that terms used in another culture, say, the term 'temperature' as used by a seventeenth-century scientist, cannot be equated in meaning or reference with any terms or expressions *we* possess. As Kuhn puts it, scientists with different paradigms inhabit 'different worlds'. 'Electron' as used around 1900 referred to objects in one 'world'; as used today it refers to objects in quite a different 'world'. This thesis is supposed to apply to observational language as well as to so-called 'theoretical language'; indeed, according to Feyerabend, ordinary language *is* simply a false theory.

The rejoinder this time is that if this thesis were really true then we could not translate other languages – or even past stages of our own language – at all. And if we cannot interpret organisms' noises at all; then we have no grounds for regarding them as *thinkers*, *speakers*, or even *persons*. In short, if Feyerabend (and Kuhn at his most incommensurable) were right, then members of other cultures, including seventeenth-century scientists, would be conceptualizable by us only as animals producing responses to stimuli (including noises that curiously resemble English or Italian). To tell us that Galileo had 'incommensurable' notions *and then go on to describe them at length* is totally incoherent.

This problem is posed in a sympathetic essay on Feyerabend's views by Smart (1965):

Surely it is a neutral fact that in order to see Mercury we have to point the telescope over the top of that tree, say, and not, as predicted by Newtonian theory, over the top of that chimney pot. And surely one can talk of trees, chimney pots, and telescopes in a way which is independent of the choice between Newtonian and Einsteinian theory. However Feyerabend could well concede that we use Euclidean geometry and non-relativistic optics for the theory of our telescope. He would say that this is not the real truth about our telescope, the tree, and the chimney pot, but nevertheless it is legitimate to think in this way in order to discuss the observational tests of general relativity, since we know on theoretical grounds that our predictions will be unaffected (up to the limits of observational error) if we avail ourselves of this computational convenience.

But the trouble with Smart's rescue move is that I must understand *some* of the Euclidean non-relativists' language to even say the 'predictions' are the same. If *every word has a different significance*, in what sense can any prediction be 'unaffected'? How can I even translate the logical particles (the words for 'if-then', 'not', and so on) in seventeenth-century Italian, or whatever, if I cannot find a translation manual connecting seventeenth-century Italian and modern English that makes some kind of systematic sense of the seventeenth-century corpus, both in itself and in its extra-linguistic setting? Even if I am the speaker who employs both theories (as Smart envisages) how can I be justified in equating any word in my Newtonian theory with any word in my general relativistic theory?

The point I am making comes into even sharper focus when we apply to it some of Quine's and Davidson's observations about meaning and translation practice. Once it is conceded that we can find a translation scheme which 'works' in the case of a seventeenth-century text, at least in the context fixed by our interests and the use to which the translation will be put, what sense does it have *in that context* to say that the translation does not 'really' capture the sense or reference of the original? It is not, after all, as if we had or were likely to have criteria for sameness of sense or reference apart from our translation schemes and our explicit or implicit requirements for their empirical adequacy. One can understand the assertion that a translation fails to capture exactly the sense or reference of the original as an admission that a better translation scheme might be found; but it makes only an illusion of sense to say that all possible translation schemes fail to capture the 'real' sense or reference. Synonymy exists only as a relation, or better, as a family of relations, each of them somewhat vague, which we employ to equate different expressions for the purposes of interpretation. The idea that there is some such thing as 'real' synonymy apart from all workable practices of mutual interpretation, has been discarded as a myth.

Suppose someone tells us that, in certain contexts, the German word 'Rad' can be translated as 'wheel'. If he goes on to say his translation is not perfect, we naturally expect him to indicate how it might be improved, supplemented by a gloss, or whatever. But if he goes on to say that 'Rad' can be translated as 'wheel', but it doesn't actually refer to wheels, or indeed to any objects recognized in your conceptual system, what do we get from this? To say that a word A can be translated as 'wheel', or whatever, is to say that, to the extent that the translation can be relied upon, A *refers* to wheels.

Perhaps the reason that the incommensurability thesis intrigues people so much, apart from the appeal which all incoherent ideas seem to have, is the tendency to confuse or conflate concept and conception. To the extent that the analytic–synthetic distinction is fuzzy, this distinction too is fuzzy; but all interpretation involves such a distinction, even if it is relative to the interpretation itself. When we translate a word as, say, *temperature* we equate the reference and, to the extent that we stick to our translation, the sense of the translated expression with that of our own term 'temperature', at least as we use it in that context. (Of course, there are various devices we can use, such as special glosses, to delimit or delineate the way we are employing 'temperature', or whatever the word may be, in the context.) In this sense we equate the 'concept' in question with our own 'concept' of temperature. But so doing is compatible with the fact that the seventeenth-century scientists, or whoever, may have had a different *conception* of temperature, i.e., a different set of beliefs about it and its nature than we do, different 'images of knowledge', and different ultimate beliefs about many other matters as well. That conceptions differ does not prove the impossibility of ever translating anyone 'really correctly' as is sometimes supposed; on the contrary, we could not say that conceptions differ or how they differ if we couldn't translate.

But, it may be asked, how do we ever know that a translation scheme 'works' if conceptions always turn out to be different? The answer to this question, as given by various thinkers from Vico down to the present day, is that interpretative success does not require that the translated beliefs come out the *same* as our own, but it does require that they come out *intelligible* to us. This is the basis of all the various maxims of interpretative charity or 'benefit of the doubt', such as 'interpret them so they come out believers of truths and lovers of the good', or 'interpret them so that their beliefs come out reasonable in the light of what they have been taught and have experienced', or Vico's own directive to maximize the *humanity* of the person being interpreted. It is a constitutive fact about human experience in one world of different cultures interacting in history while individually undergoing slower or more rapid change that we are, as a matter of universal human experience, able to *do* this; able to interpret one another's beliefs, desires, and utterances so that it all makes some kind of *sense*.

Kuhn and Feyerabend, not surprisingly, reject any idea of *convergence* in scientific knowledge. Since we are not talking about the same things as previous scientists, we are not getting more and more knowledge about the same microscopic or macroscopic objects. Kuhn argues that science 'progresses' only instrumentally; we get better and better able to transport people from one place to another, and so on. But this too is incoherent. Unless such locutions as 'transport people from one place to another' retain some degree of fixity of reference, how can we understand the notion of instrumental success in any stable way?

The argument I have just employed is essentially related to Kant's celebrated argument about preconditions for empirical knowledge. Replying to the contention that the future might be wholly lawless, might defeat every 'induction' we have made, Kant pointed out that if there is any future at all – any future *for us*, at any rate, any future we can grasp as thinkers and conceptualize to see if our predictions were true or false – then, in fact, many regularities must *not* have been violated. Otherwise why call it a *future*? For example, when we imagine balls coming from an urn in some 'irregular' order, we forget that we *couldn't even tell they were balls*, or tell *what order they came out in*, without depending on many regularities. *Comparison* presupposes that there are some commensurabilities.

There is a move Kuhn and Feyerabend could make in reply to all these criticisms, but it is not one they would feel happy making, and that would be to introduce some kind of observational/theoretical dichotomy. They could concede commensurability, translatability, and even convergence with respect to observational facts, and restrict the incommensurability thesis to the theoretical vocabulary. Even then there would be problems (why shouldn't we describe the meanings of the theoretical terms *via* their relations to the observational vocabulary à la Ramsey?). But Kuhn and Feyerabend reject this alternative, and with reason, for in fact the need for principles of interpretative charity is just as pervasive in 'observational language' as in 'theoretical language'. Consider, for example, the common word 'grass'. Different speakers, depending on where and when they live have different perceptual prototypes of grass (grass has different colors and different shapes in different places) and different conceptions of grass. Even if all speakers must know that grass is a plant, on pain of being said to have a different concept altogether, the conception of a *plant* today involves photosynthesis, and the conception of a plant two hundred years ago did not. Without interpretative charity which directs us to equate 'plant' 200 years ago with 'plant' today (at least in ordinary contexts) and 'grass' 200 years ago with 'grass' today, no statement about the reference of this word 200 years ago could be made. Nor is it only natural kind words that are so dependent for interpretation on principles of charity; the artifact word 'bread' would pose exactly the same problems. Indeed, without interpretative charity we could not equate a simple color term such as 'red' across different speakers. We interpret discourse always as a whole; and the interpretation of 'observation' terms is as dependent on the interpretation of 'theoretical' terms as is the interpretation of the latter on the former.

What I have given is, once again, a transcendental argument. We are committed by our fundamental conceptions to treating not just our present time-slices, but also our past selves, our ancestors, and members of other cultures past and present, as *persons*; and that means, I have argued, attributing to them shared references and shared concepts, however different the *conceptions* that we also attribute. Not only do we share objects and concepts with others, to the extent that the interpretative exercise succeeds, but also conceptions of the reasonable, of the natural, and so on. For the whole justification of an interpretative scheme, remember, is that it renders the behavior of others at least minimally reasonable by *our* lights. However different our images of knowledge and conceptions of rationality, we share a huge fund of assumptions and beliefs about what is reasonable with even the most bizarre culture that we can succeed in interpreting.

What to make of this?

The two arguments I have just set out convinced me that the two most widely known philosophies of science produced in this century are both incoherent. (Of course, neither of them is *just* a 'philosophy of science'.) This naturally led me to reflect on the meaning of this situation. How did such views arise?

Logical positivism, I recalled, was both continuous with and different from the Machian positivism which preceded it. Mach's positivism, or 'empirio-criticism', was, in fact, largely a restatement of Humean empiricism in a different jargon. Mach's brilliance, his dogmatic and enthusiastic style, and his scientific eminence made his positivism a large cultural issue (Lenin, afraid that the Bolsheviks would be converted to 'empirio-criticism', wrote a polemic against it). Einstein, whose interpretation of special relativity was operationalist in spirit (in marked contrast to the interpretation he gave to general relativity), acknowledged that his criticism of the notion of simultaneity owed much to Hume and to Mach, although, to his disappointment, Mach totally rejected special relativity.

But the most striking event that led up to the appearance of logical positivism was the revolution in deductive logic. By 1879 Frege had discovered an algorithm, a mechanical proof procedure, that embraces what is today standard 'second-order logic'. The procedure is *complete* for the elementary theory of deduction ('first-order logic'). The fact that one can write down an algorithm for proving *all* of the valid formulas of first-order logic – an algorithm which requires no significant analysis and simulation of full human psychology – is a remarkable fact. It inspired the hope that one might do the same for so-called 'inductive logic': that the 'scientific method' might turn out to be an algorithm, and that these two algorithms – the algorithm for deductive logic (which, of course, turned out to be *incomplete* when extended to higher logic) and the algorithm-to-be-discovered for inductive logic – might exhaustively describe or 'rationally reconstruct' not just *scientific* rationality, but all rationality worthy of the name.

When I was just starting my teaching career at Princeton University I got to know Rudolf Carnap, who was spending two years at the Institute for Advanced Studies. One memorable afternoon, Carnap described to me how he had come to be a philosopher. Carnap explained to me that he had been a graduate student in physics, studying logic in Frege's seminar. The text was *Principia Mathematica* (imagine studying Russell & Whitehead's *Principia* with Frege!). Carnap was fascinated with symbolic logic and equally fascinated with the special theory of relativity. So he decided to make his thesis a formalization of special relativity in the notation of *Principia*. It was because the Physics Department at Jena would not accept this that Carnap became a philosopher, he told me.

Today, a host of negative results, including some powerful considerations due to Nelson Goodman, have indicated that there *cannot* be a completely *formal* inductive logic. Some important aspects of inductive logic can be formalized (although the adequacy of the formalization is controversial), but there is always a need for judgments of 'reasonableness', whether these are built in via the choice of vocabulary (or, more precisely, the *division* of the vocabulary into 'projectible' predicates and 'non-projectible' predicates) or however. Today, virtually no one believes that there is a formalizable scientific method, one that can be completely formalized without formalizing complete human psychology (and possibly not even then).

The story Carnap told me supports the idea that it was the success of formalization in the special case of deductive logic that played a crucial role. If that success inspired the rise of logical positivism, could it not have been the failure to formalize inductive logic, the discovery that there is no *algorithm* for empirical science, that inspired the rise of 'anarchism'? I am not a historian, so I won't press this suggestion. In any case, additional factors are at work. While Kuhn has increasingly moderated his view, both Feyerabend and Michel Foucault have tended to push it to extremes. Moreover there is something political in their minds: both Feyerabend and Foucault link our present institutionalized criteria of rationality with capitalism, exploitation, and even with sexual repression. Clearly there are many divergent reasons why people are attracted to extreme relativism today, the idea that all existing institutions and traditions are bad being one of them.

Another reason is a certain *scientism*. The scientistic character of logical positivism is quite overt and unashamed; but I think there is also a scientism hidden behind relativism. The theory that all there is to 'rationality' is what our local culture says there is is never quite embraced by any of the 'anarchist' thinkers, but it is the natural limit of their tendency: and this is a reductionist theory. That rationality is defined by an ideal computer program is a scientistic theory inspired by the exact sciences; that it is simply defined by the local cultural norms is a scientistic theory inspired by anthropology.

I will not discuss here the expectation aroused in some by Chomskian linguistics that cognitive psychology will discover *innate* algorithms which define rationality. I myself think that this is an intellectual fashion which will be disappointed as the logical positivist hope for a symbolic inductive logic was disappointed.

All this suggests that part of the problem with present-day philosophy is scientism inherited from the nineteenth century: a problem that affects more than one intellectual field. I do not deny that logic is important, or that formal studies in confirmation theory, in semantics of natural language, and so on, are important. I do tend to think that they are rather peripheral to philosophy, and that as long as we are too much in the grip of formalization we can expect this kind of swinging back and forth between the two sorts of scientism I described. Both sorts of scientism are attempts to evade the issue of giving a sane and human description of the scope of human reason. Let me soften the rather portentous tone of this last remark by suggesting a good title for a philosophy book: 'An essay concerning human understanding'. Seriously, human understanding *is* the problem, and philosophers *should* try to produce essays and not scientific theories.

Non-criterial rationality

If we agree that rationality (in the wide sense, including Hume's 'reasonableness') is neither a matter of following a computer program nor something defined by the norms of the culture, or some subset of them, then what account *can* we give of it?

The problem is not without analogues in other areas. Some years ago I studied the behavior of natural kind words, for example, *gold*, and I came to the conclusion that here too the extension of the term is not simply determined by a 'battery of semantical rules', or other institutionalized norms. The norms may determine that certain objects are *paradigmatic examples* of gold; but they do not determine the full extension of the term, nor is it impossible that even a paradigmatic example should turn out not to really be gold, as it would be if the norms simply *defined* what it is to be gold.

We are prepared to count something as belonging to a kind, even if our *present* tests do not suffice to show that it is a member of the kind, if it ever turns out that it has the same essential nature as (or, more vaguely, is 'sufficiently similar' to) the paradigmatic examples (or the great majority of them). What the essential nature is, or what counts as sufficient similarity, depends both on the natural kind and on the context (iced tea may be 'water' in one context but not in another); but for gold what counts is ultimate composition, since this has been thought since the ancient Greeks to determine the lawful behavior of the substance. Doubtless Locke had something like this in mind when he said we could see the 'real essences' of things if we were only able to 'see with a microscopical eye'. And, unless we say that what the ancient Greeks meant by *chrysos* was *whatever had the same essential nature* as the paradigmatic examples, then neither their search for new methods of detecting counterfeit gold (which led Archimedes to the density test) nor their physical speculations will make sense.

It is tempting to take the same line with rationality itself, and to say that what determines whether a belief is rational is not the norms of rationality of this or that culture, but an *ideal theory* of rationality, a theory which would give necessary and sufficient conditions for a belief to be rational in the relevant circumstances in any possible world. (Such a theory would tell us what property rationality 'rigidly designates', in Kripke's sense.) Such a theory would have to *account for* the paradigmatic examples, as an ideal theory of gold accounts for the paradigmatic examples of gold; but it could go beyond them, and provide criteria which would enable us to understand cases we cannot at present see to the bottom of, just as our present theory of gold enables us to understand cases which the most brilliant ancient Greek could not have understood.

One suggestion has already been advanced as to the content such a theory might have. Basing himself on the model of causal theories of knowledge, Alvin Goldman (1978) has suggested that, in essence, what makes a method of arriving at beliefs *justificatory* is just that the method tends to produce *true* beliefs. But this suggestion, I think, cannot be right.

Part of the reason I think Goldman's idea cannot be right is that truth itself, on my view, is an idealization of rational acceptability. The idea that we have some notion of truth which is totally independent of our idea of rational acceptability just seems untenable to me. But I do not wish to defend or even presuppose the claim that it is untenable today.

Independently of considerations about the correct conception of truth, it seems quite clear that a belief can be rational (or 'justified') even though the method by which it was arrived at will not in fact lead to true beliefs in the future, and even though it turns out it did not really lead to true beliefs in the past. Goldman himself concedes that when we discuss counterfactual cases (other 'possible worlds') we sometimes say people had justified beliefs even though the methods by which they arrived at them are not reliable *in those worlds*. It seems to me that Goldman has confused a genetic explanation of the origin of the notion with an elucidation of the concept of justification. It may be that we would not have the concept of justification that we do have if certain methods were not reliable; but this does not mean that *given* the concept we have, there is a necessary connection between being justified and being arrived at by a method which is reliable. It is not impossible to have a fully justified belief even though the method by which that belief was arrived at is in fact highly unreliable; there might not be any *reason* to think the method was anything but reliable. In addition, explicating 'method' will, I suspect, pose exactly the same problems as explicating 'projectibility'; and this is the rock on which inductive logic foundered.

Goldman's suggestion aside, a general difficulty with the proposal to treat 'rational', 'reasonable', 'justified', etc., as natural kind terms is that the prospects for actually *finding* powerful generalizations about all rationally acceptable beliefs seem so poor. There are powerful universal laws obeyed by all instances of gold, which is what makes it possible to describe gold as the stuff that will turn out to obey these laws when we know them; but what are the chances that we can find powerful universal generalizations obeyed by all instances of rationally justified belief? The very same considerations that defeated the program of inductive logic, the need for a criterion of 'projectability' or a 'prior probability metric' which is 'reasonable' by a standard of reasonableness which seems both topic-dependent and interest-relative, suggests that (1) the theory of rationality is not separable from our ultimate theories about the nature of the various things which make up both ourselves and the domains being investigated; and (2) even in a restricted domain, for example physics, nothing like precise laws which will decide what is and is not a reasonable inference or a justified belief are to be hoped for.

This does not at all mean that there are *no* analogies between scientific inquiry into the nature of gold, and moral inquiry or philosophical inquiry. In ethics we start with judgments that individual acts are right or wrong, and we gradually formulate maxims (*not* exceptionless generalizations) based on those judgments, often accompanied by reasons or illustrative examples, as for instance 'Be kind to the stranger among you, because you know what it was like to be a stranger in Egypt'. These maxims in turn affect and alter our judgments about individual cases, so that new maxims supplementing or modifying the earlier ones may appear. After thousands of years of this dialectic between maxims and judgments about individual cases, a philosopher may come along and propose a moral conception, which may alter both maxims and singular judgments and so on.

The very same procedure may be found in all of philosophy (which is almost coextensive with theory of rationality). In Putnam (1978) I described the desiderata for a moral system, following Grice and Baker, and I included (1) the desire that one's basic assumptions, at least, should have *wide appeal*; (2) the desire that one's system should be able to withstand rational criticism; (3) the desire that the morality recommended should be *livable*. It is striking that these same desiderata, unchanged, could be listed as the desiderata for a methodology or a system of rational procedure in *any* major area of human concern.

But an analogy is not an identity. We should and must proceed in a way analogous to the way we proceed in science (thinking of 'judgments about individual cases' as analogous to 'basic sentences', 'maxims' as analogous to 'low-level generalizations', and 'conceptions' as analogous to 'theories'); but we cannot reasonably expect that *all* determined researchers are destined to converge to one moral theory or one conception of rationality.

But, as David Wiggins (1976) has reminded us, this isn't such a bad position to be in. For, indeed, how much is there ultimately that 'all determined researchers' are destined to converge upon? We cannot expect total convergence on political conceptions, on interpretations of history or even of specific historical events, on sociological conceptions or descriptions of specific institutions, any more than we can on moral conceptions or philosophical conceptions generally. Even such notions as 'earthquake' or 'person' may be discarded by or not easily translatable into the language of some cultures.

To one philosophical temperament this is sure proof that there is 'no fact of the matter' about any of these subjects; about what is right or wrong, about philosophical conceptions themselves, about liberal versus Marxist interpretation of social phenomena, or even, according to Quine, about any intentional phenomena at all: i.e., no fact of the matter about any statement involving *belief*, *desire*, or *meaning*. But I have already pointed out the self-refuting character of such a view.

To me, it seems rather that the problem, if it is a problem, has no solution – and that *is* the solution. The correct moral to draw is not that nothing is right or wrong, rational or irrational, true or false, and so on, but, as I said before, that there is no neutral place to stand, no external vantage point from which to judge what is right or wrong, rational or irrational, true or false. But is this not relativism after all? Or am I saying that each of us is a prisoner of his private conception of rationality, that for each of us there is no difference between 'justified' and 'justified by *my* lights' (a species of solipsism).

Let me speak to the question of solipsism first. I have already rejected the thesis of incommensurability. But not only are we mutually intelligible beings; we are as mutually dependent cognitively as we are materially. Whatever our differences, we all depend on others for data and (since they cannot be separated from the data) interpretations. Examples of the vast extent of this dependence could easily be given in every area. Not only do we depend on persons with whom we have a variety of disagreements for data and interpretations, but we also rely on others for corroboration. The claim that something is *true* typically involves the one who makes it in the further claim that that something could be corroborated by other rational persons; this is not empty in practice, because there are generally independent tests for the requisite sort of competence. Psychologists have pointed out that even in the simplest cases of perceptual judgment, we will change our minds if others fail to corroborate the judgment: and this is as it should be. Far from showing a distressing spinelessness in our culture, it shows a healthy respect for the good sense of others.

Even where I will stand fast against others – for example, in thinking that torture is totally wrong – the *application* of the principle in question is dependent upon data and interpretations from others. I would not let others convince me that torture is sometimes right, but I would listen to and be influenced by the opinions and perceptions of others in deciding whether there was torture in a given case, and what the degree of moral guilt was.

As for relativism, that comes in two forms. There is the old relativist view that since there is a plurality of cultures and conceptions, they are therefore all equally good. This is really a disguised absolutist view, for 'equally good' can only be said from some external vantage point, and I have denied that there *is* a possible external vantage point. And there is the newer relativism that seeks to show that *our* conception of rationality is fraudulent by its own lights, a mere rationalization of transient and repressive institutions. I have already said that I do not agree with this. We can differ on fundamental questions, even on questions of methodology, and still listen to arguments, consider each other's assumptions and inferences, and so on. It is true that some judgments of 'reasonableness' must be made simply on the basis of ultimate intuition; not everything can be proved. And it is true that here responsible and careful thinkers may disagree, and may even consider that the other accepts illegitimate arguments. But this is very far from saying that our attempts to be rational are a fraud.

Let me close with a picture. My picture of our situation is not the famous Neurath picture of science as the enterprise of reconstructing a boat while the boat floats on the open ocean, but it is a modification of it. I would change Neurath's picture in two ways. First, I would put ethics, philosophy, in fact the whole culture, in the boat, and not just 'science', for I believe all the parts of the culture are interdependent. And, second, my image is not of a single boat but of a *fleet* of boats. The people in each boat are trying to reconstruct their own boat without modifying it so much at any one time that the boat sinks, as in the Neurath image. In addition, people are passing supplies and tools from one boat to another and shouting advice and encouragement (or discouragement) to each other. Finally, people sometimes decide they don't like the boat they're in and move to a different boat altogether. (And sometimes a boat sinks or is abandoned.) It's all a bit chaotic; but since it is a fleet, no one is ever totally out of signalling distance from all the other boats. There is, in short, both collectivity and individual responsibility. If we hanker for more, is that not our old and unsatisfiable yearning for Absolutes?

Why there isn't a ready-made world*

Two ideas that have become a part of our philosophical culture stand in a certain amount of conflict. One idea, which was revived by Moore and Russell after having been definitely sunk by Kant and Hegel (or so people thought) is metaphysical realism, and the other is that there are no such things as intrinsic or 'essential' properties. Let me begin by saying a word about each.

What the metaphysical realist holds is that we can think and talk about things as they are, independently of our minds, and that we can do this by virtue of a 'correspondence' relation between the terms in our language and some sorts of mind-independent entities. Moore and Russell held the strange view that *sensibilia* (sense data) are such *mind-independent* entities: a view so dotty, on the face of it, that few analytic philosophers like to be reminded that this is how analytic philosophy started. Today material objects are taken to be paradigm mind-independent entities, and the 'correspondence' is taken to be some sort of causal relation. For example, it is said that what makes it the case that I refer to chairs is that I have causally interacted with them, and that I would not utter the utterances containing the word 'chair' that I do if I did not have causal transactions 'of the appropriate type' with chairs. This complex relationship – being connected with x by a causal chain of the appropriate type – between my word (or way of using the word) and x constitutes the relevant *correspondence* between my word and x. On this view, it is no puzzle that we can refer to physical things, but reference to numbers, sets, moral values, or anything not 'physical' is widely held to be problematical if not actually impossible.

The second doctrine, the doctrine that there are no essential properties, is presaged by Locke's famous rejection of 'substantial forms'. Locke rejected the idea that the terms we use to classify things (e.g., 'man' or 'water') connote properties which are in any sense the 'real essences' of those things. Whereas the medievals thought

* This was a lecture delivered at the University of California, Berkeley, on 27 April 1981. It was the first of two Howison Lectures on 'The transcendence of reason'.

that the real essence of water was a so-called substantial form, which exists both in the thing and (*minus* the matter) in our minds, Locke argued that what we have in our minds is a number of conventional marks (e.g., being liquid) which we have put together into a descriptive idea because of certain interests we have, and that any assumption that these marks are the 'real essence' of anything we classify under the idea is unwarranted.

Later empiricists went further and denied there was any place for the notion of an essence at all. Here is a typical way of arguing this case: 'Suppose a piece of clay has been formed into a statue. We are sure the piece of clay would not be what it is (a piece of clay) if it were dissolved, or separated into its chemical elements, or cut into five pieces. We can also say the *statue* would not be what it is (*that* statue) if the clay were squeezed into a ball (or formed into a different statue). But the piece of clay and the statue are *one* thing, not two. What this shows is that it only makes sense to speak of an "essential property" of something *relative to a description*. Relative to the description "that statue", a certain shape is an essential property of the object; relative to the description "that piece of clay", the shape is *not* an essential property (but being clay is). The question "what are the essential properties of the thing *in itself*" is a nonsensical one.'

The denial of essences is also a denial of intrinsic structure: an electron in my body has a certain electrical charge, but on the view just described it is a mistake to think that having that charge is an 'intrinsic' property of the object (except *relative to the description* 'electron') in a way in which the property of being a part of my body is not. In short, it is (or was until recently) commonly thought that

> A thing is not related to any one of its properties (or relations) any more 'intrinsically' than it is to any of its other properties or relations.

The problem that the believer in metaphysical realism (or 'transcendental realism' as Kant called it) has always faced involves the notion of 'correspondence'. There are many different ways of putting the signs of a language and the things in a set S in correspondence with one another, in fact infinitely many if the set S is infinite (and a very large finite number if S is a large finite set). Even if the 'correspondence' has to be a reference relation and we specify which *sentences* are to correspond to *states of affairs which actually obtain*, it follows from theorems of model theory that there

are still infinitely many ways of *specifying* such a correspondence.†
How can we pick out any *one* correspondence between our words (or
thoughts) and the supposed mind-independent things *if we have no
direct access to the mind-independent things*? (German philosophy
almost always began with a particular answer to this question – the
answer 'we can't' – after Kant.)

One thing is clear: an act of will (or intention) won't work. I can't
simply *pick* one particular correspondence C and *will* (or stipulate) that
C *is to be* the designated correspondence relation, because in order
to do that I would need *already* to be able to *think about* the
correspondence C – and C, being a relation to things which are
external and mind-independent, is itself something outside the mind,
something 'external'! In short, if the mind does not have the ability
to grasp external things or forms directly, then no *mental* act can give
it the ability to single out a correspondence (or anything else external,
for that matter).

But if the denial of intrinsic properties is correct, then no external
thing or event is connected to any one relation it may have to other
things (including our thoughts) in a way which is special or essential
or intrinsic. If the denial of intrinsic properties is right, then it is not
more essential to a mental event that it stand in a relation C_1 to any
object x than it is that it stands in any other relation C_2 to any other
object y. Nor is it any more essential to a non-mental object that it
stand in a relation C to any one of my thoughts than it is that it stand
in any one of a myriad other relations to any one of my other thoughts.
On such a view, no relation C is metaphysically singled out as *the*
relation between thoughts and things; reference becomes an 'occult'
phenomenon.

The tension or incompatibility between metaphysical realism and
the denial of intrinsic properties has not gone unnoticed by modern
materialists. And for this reason we now find many materialists
employing a metaphysical vocabulary that smacks of the fourteenth
century: materialists who talk of 'causal powers', of 'built-in'
similarities and dissimilarities between things in nature, even
materialists who speak unabashedly of *essences*. In this lecture I want
to ask if this modern mixture of materialism and essentialism *is
consistent*; and I shall argue that it *isn't*.

---

† See chapter 1; in Putnam (1981) this result is extended to intensional logic; it is shown
that even if we specify which sentences are to be true in each possible world, and not just
in the actual world, the extensions of the extra-logical predicates are almost totally
undetermined in almost all worlds.

Why I focus on materialism

The reason I am going to focus my attack on materialism is that materialism is the only *metaphysical* picture that has contemporary 'clout'. Metaphysics, or the enterprise of describing the 'furniture of the world', the 'things in themselves' apart from our conceptual imposition, has been rejected by many analytic philosophers (though *not*, as I remarked, by Russell), and by all the leading brands of continental philosophy. Today, apart from relics, it is virtually only materialists (or 'physicalists', as they like to call themselves) who continue the traditional enterprise.

It was not always thus. Between the tenth and twelfth centuries the metaphysical community which included the Arabic Averroes and Avicenna, the Jewish Maimonides, and the Angelic Doctor in Paris disagreed on many questions, creation in particular. It was regarded as a hard issue whether the world always existed obeying the same laws (the doctrine ascribed to Aristotle), or was created from pre-existing matter (the doctrine ascribed to Plato) or was created *ex nihilo* (the Scriptural doctrine). But the existence of a supersensible Cause of the contingent and moving sensible things was taken to be *demonstrable*. Speculative reason could *know* there was an Uncaused Cause.

When I was seven years old the question 'if God made the world, then who made God?' struck me one evening with vivid force. I remember pacing in circles around a little well for hours while the awful regress played itself out in my mind. If a medieval theologian had been handy, he would have told me that God was self-caused. He might have said God was the *ens necessarium*. I don't know if it would have helped; today philosophers would say that the doctrine of God's 'necessary' existence invokes a notion of 'necessity' which is incoherent or unintelligible.

The issue does, in a covert way, still trouble us. Wallace Matson (1967) ended a philosophic defense of atheism with the words, 'Still, why *is* there something rather than nothing?'. The doctrine that 'you take the universe you get' (a remark Steven Weinberg once made in a discussion) sounds close to saying it's some sort of metaphysical *chance* (we might just as well have *anything*). The idea of a super-sensible Cause outside of the universe leads at once to the question that troubled me when I was seven. We don't even have the comfort of thinking of the universe as a kind of *ens necessarium*: *it* only came into existence a few billion years ago!

This situation was summed up by Kant: Kant held that the whole enterprise of trying to *demonstrate* the existence and nature of a supersensible world by speculation leads only to antinomies. (The universe *must* have a cause; but *that* cause would have to have a cause; but an infinite regress is no explanation and self-causation is impossible...) Today, as I remarked, only a few relics would challenge this conclusion, which put an end to rationalism as well as to the medieval synthesis of Greek philosophy with revealed religion.

This decline of medieval philosophy was a long process which overlapped the decline of medieval science (with its substantial forms). Here too Kant summed up the issue for our culture: the medievals (and the rationalists) thought the mind had an intellectual intuition (*intellektuelle Anschauung*), a sort of perception that would enable it to perceive essences, substantial forms, or whatever. But there is no such faculty. 'Nothing is in the mind that was not first in the senses *except the mind itself*', as Kant put it, quoting Leibnitz.

Again, no one but a few relics challenge *this* conclusion. But Kant drew a bold corollary, and this corollary is hotly disputed to the present day.

The corollary depends upon a claim that Kant made. The claim can be illustrated by a famous observation of Wittgenstein's. Referring to the 'duck–rabbit' illusion (the figure that can be seen as either a duck or a rabbit), Wittgenstein remarked that while the physical image is capable of being seen either way, no 'mental image' is capable of being seen either way: the 'mental image' is always unambiguously a duck image or a rabbit image (*Philosophical Investigations* II, xi, 194–6). It follows that 'mental images' are really very different from physical images such as line drawings and photographs. We might express this difference by saying the interpretation is *built in* to the 'mental image'; the mental image is a *construction*.

Kant made the same point with respect to *memory*. When I have a memory of an experience this is not, contrary to Hume, *just* an image which 'resembles' the earlier experience. To be a memory the interpretation has to be 'built in': the interpretation that this is a *past* experience of *mine*. Kant (1933, Transcendental Deduction) argues that the notion of the *past* involves causality and that causality involves laws and objects (so, according to Kant, does the assignment of all these experiences to *myself*). Past experiences are not directly available; saying we 'remember' them is saying we have succeeded in constructing a version with causal relations and a continuing self in which they are located.

The corollary Kant drew from all this is that even experiences are in part constructions of the mind: I know what experiences I have and have had partly because I know what *objects* I am seeing and touching and have seen and touched, and partly because I know what *laws* these objects obey. Kant may have been overambitious in thinking he could specify the *a priori* constraints on the construction process; but the idea that all experience involves mental construction, and the idea that the dependence of physical object concepts and experience concepts goes *both* ways, continue to be of great importance in contemporary philosophy (of many varieties).

Since sense data and physical objects are interdependent constructions, in Kant's view, the idea that 'all we know is sense data' is as silly as the idea that we can have knowledge of objects that goes beyond experience. Although Kant does not put it this way, I have suggested elsewhere (Putnam, 1981, ch. 3) that we can view him as rejecting the idea of truth as correspondence (to a mind-independent reality) and as saying that the only sort of truth we can have an idea of, or use for, is *assertibility* (by creatures with our rational natures) *under optimal conditions* (as determined by our sensible natures). Truth becomes a radically epistemic notion.

However, Kant remarks that the *desire* for speculative metaphysics, the desire for a theory of the furniture of the world, is deep in our nature. He thought we should abandon the enterprise of trying to have speculative knowledge of the 'things in themselves' and sublimate the metaphysical impulse in the moral project of trying to make a more perfect world; but he was surely right about the strength of the metaphysical urge.

Contemporary materialism and scientism are a reflection of this urge in two ways. On the one hand, the materialist claims that physics is an approximation to a sketch of the one true theory, the true and complete description of the furniture of the world. (Since he often leaves out quantum mechanics, his picture differs remarkably little from Democritus': it's all atoms swerving in the void.) On the other hand, he meets the epistemological argument against metaphysics by claiming that we don't *need* an intellectual intuition to do *his* sort of metaphysics: his metaphysics, he says, is as open ended, as infinitely revisable and fallible, as science itself. In fact, it *is* science itself! (interpreted as claiming absolute truth, or, rather, claiming *convergence* to absolute truth). The appeal of materialism lies precisely in this, in its claim to be *natural* metaphysics, metaphysics within the bounds of science. That a doctrine which promises to gratify both our ambition (to know the noumena) and our caution (not to be unscientific) should have great appeal is hardly something to be wondered at.

This wide appeal would be reason enough to justify a critique of metaphysical materialism. But a second reason is this: metaphysical materialism has replaced positivism and pragmatism as the dominant contemporary form of scientism. Since scientism is, in my opinion, one of the most dangerous contemporary intellectual tendencies, a critique of its most influential contemporary form is a duty for a philosopher who views his enterprise as more than a purely technical discipline.

Causation

What makes the metaphysical realist a *metaphysical* realist is his belief that there is somewhere 'one true theory' (two theories which are true and complete descriptions of the world would be mere notational variants of each other). In company with a correspondence theory of truth, this belief in one true theory requires a *ready-made* world (an expression suggested in this connection by Nelson Goodman): the world itself has to have a 'built-in' structure since otherwise theories with different structures might correctly 'copy' the world (from different perspectives) and truth would lose its absolute (non-perspectival) character. Moreover, as I already remarked, 'correspondence' between our symbols and something which has no determinate structure is hardly a well-defined notion.

The materialist metaphysician often takes *causal relations* as an example of built-in structure. Events have causes; objects have 'causal powers'. And he proudly proclaims his realism about these, his faith that they are 'in' the world itself, in the metaphysical realist sense. Well, let us grant him that this is so, for the sake of argument: my question for the moment is not whether this sort of realism is justified, but whether it is really compatible with materialism. Is *causation* a physical relation?

In this discussion, I shall follow the materialist in ignoring quantum mechanics since it has *no* generally acceptable interpretation of the kind the realist advocates:† the standard (Copenhagen) interpretation makes essential reference to *observers*, and the materialist wants to imagine a physics in which the observer is simply another part of the system, as seen from a God's eye view. Physics is then a theory whose fundamental magnitudes are defined at all points in

---

† I ignore here my *own* past attempts at a realist interpretation of quantum mechanics (using non-standard logic) for two reasons: they have never found much acceptance, and (more importantly) I no longer think quantum logic enables one to reconcile quantum mechanics with realism. (See chapter 14.)

space and time; a property or relation is physically definable if it is definable in terms of these.†

I shall also assume that the fundamental magnitudes are basically the usual ones: if no restraint at all is placed on what counts as a possible 'fundamental magnitude' in future physics, then *reference* or *soul* or *Good* could even be 'fundamental magnitudes' in future physics! I shall not allow the naturalist the escape hatch of letting 'future physics' mean we-know-not-what. Physicalism is only intelligible if 'future physics' is supposed to resemble what *we* call 'physics'. The possibility of natural metaphysics (metaphysics within the bounds of science) is, indeed, not conclusively refuted by showing that present-day materialism cannot be a correct sketch of the one true (metaphysical) theory: but present-day materialism is, as already remarked, the view with clout.

Now if '*A* causes *B*' simply meant 'whenever an *A*-type event happens, then a *B*-type event follows in time', 'causes' would be physically definable. Many attempts have been made to give such a definition of causation – one which would apply to genuine causal laws while not applying to sequences we would regard as coincidental or otherwise non-causal. Few philosophers believe today that this is possible.

But let us assume that 'causes' (in this sense) *is* somehow physically definable. A cause, in the sense this definition tries to capture, is a *sufficient* condition for its effect; whenever the cause occurs, the effect *must* follow (at least in a deterministic world). Following Mill, let us call such a cause a *total cause*. An example of a total cause at time t_0 of a physical event e occurring at a later time t_1 and a point x would be the entire distribution of values of the dynamical variables at time t_0 (inside a sphere S whose center is x and whose radius is sufficiently large so that events outside the sphere S could not influence events at x occurring at t_1 without having to send a signal to x faster than light, which I assume, on the basis of relativity, to be impossible).

Mill pointed out that in ordinary language 'cause' rarely (if ever) means 'total cause'. When I say 'failure to put out the campfire caused the forest fire', I do *not* mean that the campfire's remaining lit during a certain interval was the *total cause* of the forest fire. Many

† Strictly speaking, 'if it is definable in terms of these, using, if necessary, constants for all real numbers and functions, infinite conjunctions and disjunctions, etc.': there is no philosophical significance to the question of whether a physical magnitude can be defined by a formula of finite length (or one containing a constant for some undefinable real number) from a metaphysical materialist's point of view.

other things – the dryness of the leaves, their proximity to the campfire, the temperature of the day, even the presence of oxygen in the atmosphere – are part of the *total* cause of the forest fire. Mill's point is that we regard certain parts of the total cause as 'background', and refer only to the part of interest as 'the' cause.

Suppose a professor is found stark-naked in a girl's dormitory room at midnight. His being naked in the room at midnight $- \varepsilon$, where ε is so small that he could neither get out of the room or put on his clothes between midnight $- \varepsilon$ and midnight without moving faster than light, would be a 'total cause' of his being naked in the girl's room at midnight; but no one would refer to this as the 'cause' of his presence in the room in that state. On the other hand, when it is said that the presence of certain bodies of H_2O in our environment 'causes' us to use the word 'water' as we do, it is certainly *not* meant that the presence of H_2O is the 'total cause'. In its ordinary sense, 'cause' can often be paraphrased by a locution involving *explain*; the presence of H_2O in our environment, our dependence on H_2O for life, etc., are 'part of' the *explanation* of our having a word which we use as we use the word 'water'. The forest fire is *explained* (given background knowledge) by the campfire's not having been extinguished; but the professor's state at midnight $- \varepsilon$ is not what we consider an *explanation* of the state of affairs at midnight.

When it is said that a word refers to x just in case the (use of the) word is connected to x by a 'causal chain of the appropriate type', the notion of 'causal chain' involved is that of an *explanatory* chain. Even if the notion of 'total cause' *were* physically definable, it would not be possible to *use* it either in daily life or in philosophy; the notion the materialist really uses when he employs 'causal chain', etc., in his philosophical explications is the intuitive notion of an *explanation*.

But this notion is certainly not physically definable. To see that it isn't, observe, first, that 'explains' (and 'caused', when it has the force of 'explains why x happened') are abstract notions. Even when we imagine a possible world in which there are non-physical things or properties, we can conceive of these things and properties *causing* things to happen. A disembodied spirit would not have *mass* or *charge*, but (this is a conceptual question of course; I don't mean to suggest there *are* disembodied spirits) it could *cause* something (say, an emotional reaction in another spirit with which it communicated telepathically).

A definition of 'caused' (in this 'explanatory' sense) which was too 'first order', too tied to the particular magnitudes which are the 'fundamental magnitudes' of physics in *our* world, would make it *conceptually impossible* that a disembodied spirit (or an event involving magnitudes which are not 'physical' in *our* world) could be a cause. This is why the suggested Humean definition of *total* cause – *A* is the (total) cause of *B* if and only if an *A*-type event is always followed in time by a *B*-type event – contained no *specific* physical term (except 'time'): this definition *is* abstract enough to apply to possible worlds different from our own. (Although it fails even so.) Could there be an equally abstract (and more successful) definition of 'cause' in the explanatory sense?

Imagine that Venusians land on Earth and observe a forest fire. One of them says, '*I* know what caused that – the atmosphere of the darned planet is saturated with oxygen.'

What this vignette illustrates is that one man's (or extra-terrestrial's) 'background condition' can easily be another man's 'cause'. What is and what is not a 'cause' or an 'explanation' depends on background knowledge and our reason for asking the question.

No purely *formal* relation between events will be sensitive to this relativity of explanatory arguments to background knowledge and interests.

Nelson Goodman has shown that no purely formal criterion can distinguish arguments which are intuitively sound inductive arguments from unsound arguments: for every sound inductive argument there is an unsound one of the very same form. The actual predicates occurring in the argument make the difference, and the distinction between 'projectible' and 'non-projectible' predicates is not a formal one. It is not difficult to show that the same thing is true of *explanations*. If we think of explanation as relation in 'the world', then to define it one would need a predicate which could sort projectible from non-projectible properties; such a predicate could not be purely formal for then it would run afoul of Goodman's result, but it could not involve the particular fundamental magnitudes in *our* world in an essential way for then it would be open to counterexamples in other possible worlds.

'Non-Humean' causation

Richard Boyd (1980) has suggested that the whole enterprise of *defining* causation was a mistake: physicalists should simply take the notion as a primitive one. He may only mean that to insist on a definition of 'causes' (or anything else) in the standard formalism for mathematics and physics (which contains *names* for only countably many real numbers, etc.) is unreasonable: if so, this would not be an argument against expecting every *physical* property and relation to be definable in an *infinitary extension* of physics, a language which allows *infinitely long* names and sentences. (Indeed, if a property or relation is *not* physically definable even in this liberal sense, what is meant by calling it 'physical'?) But he may have meant that one should literally take 'causes' as an irreducible notion, one whose failure to be physically definable is not due to syntactic accidents, such as the limit on the length of formulas. But can a philosopher who accepts the existence of an irreducible phenomenon of *causation* call himself a materialist?

'Causes', we have just seen, is often paraphrasable as 'explains'. It rarely or never means 'is the total cause of'. When Boyd, for example, says that a certain micro-structure is a 'causal power' (the micro-structure of sugar is a 'causal power' in Boyd's sense, because it *causally explains* why sugar dissolves in water) he does not mean that the micro-structure in question is the *total cause* of the explained events (sugar will not dissolve in water if the water is *frozen*, for example, or if the water is already saturated with sugar, or if the water-cum-sugar is in an exotic quantum mechanical state). 'Causal powers' are properties that *explain* something, given background conditions and given standards of salience and relevance.

A metaphysical view in which 'causation' and 'causal explanation' are built into the world itself is one in which explanation is wrenched out of what Professor Frederick Will (1974) has called 'the knowledge institution', the inherited tradition which defines for us what is a background condition and what a salient variable parameter, and projected into the structure of reality. Boyd would probably reply that the 'causal structure' of reality *explains* the success of the knowledge institution: our successful explanations simply copy the built-in causal structure.

Be that as it may, salience and relevance are attributes of thought and reasoning, not of nature. To project them into the realist's 'real world', into what Kant called the *noumenal* world, is to mix objective idealism (or, perhaps, medieval Aristoteleanism) and materialism in a totally incoherent way. To say 'materialism is *almost* true: the world is completely describable in the language of physics *plus* the one little added notion that some events intrinsically *explain* other events' would be ridiculous. This would not be a 'near miss' for materialism, but a total failure. If events *intrinsically* explain other events, if there are saliencies, relevancies, standards of what are 'normal' conditions, and so on, built into the world itself independently of minds, then the world is in many ways *like* a mind, or infused with something very much like reason. And if *that* is true, then materialism *cannot* be true. One can try to revive the project of speculative metaphysics, if one wishes: but one should not pass *this* sort of metaphysics off as (future) *physics*.

Counterfactuals and 'similarity'

Suppose I take a match from a new box of matches (in perfect condition), break it, and throw the pieces in the river. After all this, I remark, 'If I had struck that match (instead of breaking it, etc.) it would have lit'. Most of us would say, 'true', or 'probably true'. But what does the statement actually assert?

A first stab at an explication might go as follows: the statement is true if it follows from physical laws (assume these to be given by a list – otherwise there are further problems about 'laws') that if the match is struck (at an average (for me?) angle, with an average amount of force) against that striking surface, then, it ignites. But this doesn't work: even if we describe the match down to the atomic level, and ditto for the striking surface and the angle and force involved, there are still many other relevant variables unmentioned. (Notice the similarity to the problem of 'cause' as 'total cause': the statement '*A* caused *B*', and the statement 'If *X* had happened, *Y* would have happened' have simple truth conditions when *all* the 'background conditions' – and all the 'laws' – are specified; but typically they *aren't* specified, and the speaker can't even conceive of *all* of them.) If no oxygen molecules happen to be near the top of the match, or if the entire match-cum-striking-surface-cum-atmosphere system is in a sufficiently strange quantum mechanical state, etc., then the match *won't* ignite (even if struck with that force, at that angle, etc.)

One is tempted to try: 'It follows from the physical laws that if the match is struck against that surface (at the specified force and angle) and everything is *normal* then the match ignites', but this brings the very strange predicate 'normal' into the story. Besides, maybe conditions *weren't* 'normal' (in the sense of 'average') at the time. (In infinitely many respects, conditions are *always* 'abnormal': a truism from statistical theory). Or one is tempted to say: 'It follows from the laws that if the match is struck against that surface (with the specified force and at the specified angle), and *everything else is as it actually was at the time*, then the match must ignite.' But, as Nelson Goodman (1947) pointed out in a celebrated paper on this logical question, *everything* else *couldn't* be as it was at the time if the match were struck. The gravitational fields, the quantum mechanical state, the places where there were oxygen molecules in the air, and infinitely many other things *couldn't have been* 'as they actually were at the time' if the match had been struck.

The reason I mention this is that David Lewis (in 'Causation', *Journal of Philosophy* LXX, 1973) proposed to analyze 'causes' using precisely this sort of contrary-to-fact conditional. The idea is that '*A* caused *B*' can be analyzed as 'if *A* had *not* happened, *B* would *not* have happened'.

Actually, this doesn't seem right. (Even if *A* caused *B*, there are situations in which it just isn't true that if *A* hadn't happened, *B* wouldn't have happened.)† But suppose it were right, or that, if it isn't right, contrary-to-fact conditionals can at any rate be used to explicate the notions that we wanted to use the notion of causality to explicate. How are the truth conditions for contrary-to-fact conditionals *themselves* to be explicated?

One famous materialist, John Mackie (1974), thinks contrary-to-fact conditionals aren't true or false. He regards them as ways of indicating what inferences are allowable in one's knowledge situation, rather than as asserting something true or false in the realist sense, independently of one's knowledge situation. 'If I had struck that match it would have lit' indicates that my *knowledge situation* is such that (if I delete the information about what actually happened to the match) an inference from 'the match was struck' to 'the match ignited' would be *warranted*. The contrary-to-fact conditional signals the presence of what Wilfred Sellars calls a 'material rule of inference'. It has *assertibility conditions*, rather than truth conditions in the sense of absolute truth semantics.

Mackie, who follows Lewis in using counterfactuals to analyze 'causes', concludes that *causation* (in the ordinary sense) is something *epistemic*, and not something in the world at all. But he believes there is another notion of causation, 'mechanical causation', which is in the world. (It has to do with energy flow; as Mackie describes it, it is hard to see either what it is, or that it could be spelled out without

---

† These are situations in which *B* would have been produced by some other cause if *A* hadn't caused it. Another kind of counterexample: John and George are identical twins and have black hair. Is the following counterfactual true?
    'If John hadn't had black hair, George wouldn't have had black hair either.'
Everyone I've asked assures me it is. But then, on Lewis' theory it follows that
    'John's having black hair *caused* George to have black hair too'
which is absurd.

using counterfactuals,† which would be fatal to Mackie's project of having a non-epistemic notion of causation.)

But Lewis, following Professor Robert Stalnaker, chooses to give *truth conditions* for contrary-to-fact conditionals. He postulates that there actually exist 'other possible worlds' (as in science fiction), and that there is a 'similarity metric' which determines how 'near' or how 'similar' any two possible worlds are (Lewis, 1973). A contrary-to-fact conditional, 'If X had happened, then Y would have happened', is true just in case Y is *actually* true in all the *nearest* 'parallel worlds' to the actual world in which X is actually true.

To me this smacks more of science fiction than of philosophy. But one thing is clear: a theory which requires an ontology of parallel worlds and a built-in 'similarity metric' certainly does not have a *materialist* ontology. More important, it does not have a *coherent* ontology: not only is the actual existence of parallel worlds a dotty idea, but the idea of an *intrinsic* similarity metric, a metric highly sensitive to what we regard as relevant conditions, or normal conditions, one which gives weight to what sorts of features *we* count as similarities and dissimilarities between states of affairs, is one which once again implies that the world is like a mind, or imbued with something very much like reason. And if *this* is true, then it must have a (suitably metaphysical) *explanation*. Objective idealism can hardly be a *little bit* true. ('It's all physics, except that there's this similarity metric' just doesn't make *sense*.)

Essences and objects

In this philosophical culture, the denial of intrinsic or 'essential' properties began with examples like the example of the thing whose shape is an 'essential' property under *one* description ('that statue') but not under a different description ('that piece of clay'). One philosopher who thinks a wholly wrong moral was drawn from this example is Saul Kripke.

According to Kripke, the statue and the piece of clay are two objects, not one. The fact that the piece of clay has a model property, namely the property 'being a thing which *could have been* spherical

---

† If 'mechanical causation' is simply momentum transfer, for example, then my flicking a virtually frictionless switch is *not* the 'mechanical cause' of the light going on. Similarly, my putting my hand in front of a light is not the 'mechanical cause' of the shadow. Such a narrow notion might be physical, but would be of no use in explicating *reference*. If, on the other hand, the switching case *is* a case of 'mechanical causation', how does one characterize it without using the clause 'the current *would not have* travelled to the light if the switch *had not been* moved', or some such subjunctive clause?

in shape', which the statue lacks (I assume this is not one of those contemporary statues) already proves the two objects cannot be identical, in Kripke's view.

Now, this sounds very strange at first hearing. If I put the statue on the scale, have I put *two objects* on the scale? If the piece of clay weighs 20 pounds and the statue weighs 20 pounds, why doesn't the scale read 40 and not 20 if both objects are on it right now? But what Kripke has in mind is not silly at all.

First of all, it also sounds strange to be told that a human being is not identical with the aggregation of the molecules in his body. Yet on a moment's reflection each of us is aware that he was not *that* aggregate of molecules a day ago. Seven years ago, precious few of those molecules were in my body. If after my death that exact set of molecules is assembled and placed in a chemical flask, it will be the same aggregation of molecules, but it won't be *me*. David Lewis (1976) has suggested that I and the aggregation of molecules are 'identical for a period of time' in somewhat the way that Highway 2 and Highway 16 can be 'identical for a stretch'; as he points out, 'identity for a time' is not strict logical identity. If A and B are identical in the strict sense, every property of A is a property of B; but it is not the case that every property of the aggregation of molecules is a property of *me*.

Just as we can recognize that I am not the same object as the aggregation of molecules in my body without denying that I *consist* of those molecules right now (the difference between the objects lies in the different statements that are true of them, not in their physical distinctness), so, one can agree with Kripke that the statue is not the same object as the piece of clay without denying that the piece of clay is the matter of the statue; once again the difference between the objects lies in the different statements that are true of them, not in their physical distinctness.

But now it begins to look as if objects, properly individuated, *do* have essences, do have *some* properties in a special way. Can Kripke's doctrine be of aid to materialism? (Kripke himself is quite averse to materialism, as is well known.)

A materialist whose ontology includes 'possible worlds' might introduce suitable intensional objects by identifying them with functions taking possible worlds as arguments and space–time regions in those worlds as values. Thus, the statue would be the function defined on each possible world Y in which the statue exists, whose value on Y is the space–time region occupied by the statue in Y. This would, indeed, make the 'statue' and the 'piece of clay' different 'objects' (different logical constructions) even if they occupy the same space–time region in the actual world, since there are other possible worlds in which they do not occupy the same space–time region.

But functions of this kind are standardly used in modern semantics to represent *concepts*. No one doubts that the *concept* 'that statue' is a different *concept* from the *concept* 'that piece of clay'; the question is whether there is some *individual* in the actual world to which one of these concepts *essentially* applies while the other only accidentally applies. The space–time region itself is *not* such an individual; and it is hard to see how a materialist is going to find one in *his* ontology.

Moreover, clever logical constructions are no answer to the philosophical difficulty. Doubtless one can come up with as many 'objects' as one wants given 'possible worlds' plus the resources of modern set theory; (the difficulty, indeed, is that one can come up with *too many*). Consider the metaphysical claim that my thoughts have some sort of intrinsic connection with external objects. If the events that take place in my brain are in a space–time region that has a set-theoretic connection with some abstract entity that involves certain external objects, then that same space–time region will have similar set-theoretic connections with some other abstract entities that involve some other external objects. To be sure, the materialist can say that my 'thoughts' *intrinsically* involve certain external objects by *identifying them* (the thoughts) with one abstract entity and not with another; but if this identification is supposed to be a feature of reality itself, then there must really *be* essences in the world in a sense which pure set theory can't hope to explicate.

The difficulty is that Kripke individuates objects *by their modal properties*, by what they (essentially) *could* and *could not* be. Kripke's ontology *presupposes* essentialism; it can not be used to ground it. And modal properties are not, on the face of it, part of the materialist's furniture of the world.

But, I will be reminded, I have myself spoken of 'essential properties' elsewhere (see Putnam, 1975a). I have said that there are possible worlds (possible *states* of the world, that is, not parallel worlds à la Lewis) in which some liquid other than H_2O has the taste of water (we might have different taste buds, for example), fills the lakes and rivers, etc., but no possible world in which *water* isn't H_2O. Once we have discovered what water is in the actual world, we have discovered its *nature*: is this not essentialism?

It *is* a sort of essentialism, but not a sort which can help the materialist. For what I have said is that it has long been our *intention* that a liquid should *count* as 'water' only if it has the same composition as the paradigm examples of water (or as the majority of them). I claim that this was our intention even before we *knew* the ultimate composition of water. If I am right then, *given those referential intentions*, it was always impossible for a liquid other than H_2O to be water, even if it took empirical investigation to find it out. But the 'essence' of water in *this* sense is the product of our use of the word, the kinds of referential intentions we have: this sort of essence is not 'built into the world' in the way required by an *essentialist theory of reference itself* to get off the ground.

Similarly, Kripke has defended *his* essentialist theories by arguments which turn on speakers' referential intentions and practices; to date he has carefully refrained from trying to provide a metaphysical theory of reference (although he does seem to believe in mind-independent modal properties). I conclude that however one takes Kripke's theories (or mine); whether one takes them metaphysically, as theories of objective 'essences' which are somehow 'out there', or one takes them as theories of our referential practices and intentions, they are of no help to the materialist. On the metaphysical reading they are realist enough, but their realism is not of a materialist sort; on the purely semantical reading they *presuppose* the notion of reference, and cannot be used to support the metaphysical explanation of reference as intrinsic correspondence between thought and thing.

Reference

Some metaphysical materialists might respond to what has been said by agreeing tht '*A* causes *B*' does *not* describe a simple 'relation' between *A* and *B*. 'All you're saying is that causal statements *rest on* a distinction between background conditions and differentiating factors, and I agree that this distinction isn't built into the things themselves, but is a reflection of the way we think about the things', such a philosopher might say. But here he has used the words 'think about', i.e., he has appealed to the notion of *reference*.

The contemporary metaphysical materialist thinks about reference in the following way: the brain is a computer. Its computations involve *representations*. Some of these (perhaps all) are 'propositional': they resemble sentences in an internal *lingua mentis*. (They have been called 'sentence-analogs'.) Some of them could be sentences in a public language, as when we engage in interior monolog. A person refers to something when, for example, the person thinks 'the cat is on the mat' (the sentence-analog is 'subvocalized') and the entire organism-cum-environment situation is such that the words 'the cat' in the particular sentence-analog stand in a physical relation R (the relation of *reference*) to some cat and the words 'the mat' stand in the relation R to some mat.

. But what is this relation R? And what on earth could make anyone think it is a *physical* relation?

Well, there is *one* way in which *no one*, to my knowledge, would try to define R, and that is by giving a list of all possible reference situations. It is useful, however, to consider why not. Suppose someone proposed to define reference (for some set of languages, including '*lingua mentis*') thus:

X refers to Y if and only if X is a (token) word or word-analog and Y is an object or event and the entire situation (including the organism that produced X and the environment that contains Y) is S_1 or S_2 or S_3 or... (infinite – possibly non-denumerably infinite – list of situations, described at the level of physics).

There are (at least) three things wrong with this.

First, besides the fact that the list would have to be infinite, such a list would not tell us what the situations S_1, S_2, ... *had in common*. To define a physical property or relation by *listing* the situations in which it is found is not to say what it *is*. In fact, the materialists themselves object to *Tarski*'s definition of reference on just this ground: that Tarski defines primitive reference (for a fixed language), by a list of cases, and, as Hartry Field (1972 a, p. 363) writes,

Now, it would have been easy for a chemist, late in the last century, to have given a 'valence definition' of the following form:

(3) (E) (n) (E has valence $n \equiv E$ is potassium and n is $+1$, or ... or E is sulphur and n is -2)

where in the blanks go a list of similar clauses, one for each element. But, though this is an extensionally correct definition of valence, it would not have been an acceptable reduction; and had it turned out that nothing else was possible – had all efforts to explain valence in terms of the structural properties of atoms proved futile – scientists would have eventually had to decide either (a) to give up valence theory, or else (b) to replace the hypothesis of physicalism by another hypothesis (chemicalism?). It is part of scientific methodology to resist doing (b); and I also think it is part of scientific methodology to resist doing (a) as long as the notion of valence is serving the purposes for which it was designed (i.e., as long as it is proving useful in helping us characterize chemical compounds in terms of their valences). But the methodology is not to resist (a) and (b) by giving lists like (3); the methodology is to look for a real reduction. This is a methodology that has proved extremely fruitful in science, and I think we'd be crazy to give it up in linguistics. And I think we are giving up this fruitful methodology, unless we realize that we need to add theories of primitive reference to T1 or T2 if we are to establish the notion of truth as a physicalistically acceptable notion.

Secondly, it would be philosophically naive to think that such a list could answer any *philosophical* question about reference. For example, one could hold Quine's view, that there are definite *true* and *false* sentences† in science, but *no* determinate reference relation (the true sentences have infinitely many models, and there is no such thing as *the* model, in Quine's view), and still accept the list. Quine would simply say that the terms used to describe the situations S_1, S_2, ... etc. refer to different events in different models; thus the list, while correct in *each* admissible model, does not define a *determinate* reference relation (only a determinate reference relation *for each model*). Now Quine's view may be right, wrong, or meaningless; the question of the truth or falsity of metaphysical realism may be meaningful or meaningless (and if meaningful, may have a realist or a non-realist answer), but a list of cases (either this list or the one involved in the Tarskian truth definition referred to by Field), cannot speak to *this* issue. To think that it can is analogous to thinking (as G. E. Moore did) that one can refute Berkeley by holding up one's hand and saying 'This is a material object. Therefore matter exists.' This is, as Myles Burnyeat has put it, 'to philosophize as if Kant had never existed'. For better or worse, philosophy has gone second order.

Thirdly, the list is *too specific*. Reference is as 'abstract' as causation. In possible worlds which contain individual things or properties which are not physical (in the sense of 'physical₂':‡ not definable in terms of the fundamental magnitudes of the physics of the actual world), we could still *refer*: we could refer to disembodied minds, or to an emergent non-material property of Goodness, or to all sorts of things, in the appropriate worlds. But the relevant situations could not, by hypothesis, be completely described in terms of the fundamental magnitudes of the physics of *our* world. A definition of reference from which it followed that we could not refer to a non-physical magnitude if there were one is just *wrong*.

---

† For Quine, this means true and false relative to our evolving doctrine; Quine rejects metaphysical realism and the idea of a unique 'correspondence' between our terms and things in themselves. Quine's views are discussed in chapter 13.

‡ Paul Meehl and Wilfred Sellars (1956) introduced the terms 'physical₁' and 'physical₂'. 'Physical₁' properties are simply properties connected with space–time and with causal laws: thus a dualist could subscribe to the thesis 'all properties are physical₁'. 'Physical₂' properties are physical in the sense used here.

I know of only one realist who has sketched a way of defining reference which meets these difficulties, and that is David Lewis (1974). Lewis proposes to treat reference as a *functional* property of the organism-cum-environment-situation.

Typical examples of functional properties come from the world of computers. Having a particular program, for example, is a functional (or in computer jargon a 'software' property) as opposed to an ordinary first-order physical property (a 'hardware' property). Functional properties are typically defined in batches; the properties or 'states' in a typical batch (say, the properties that are involved in a given computer program) are characterized by a certain *pattern*. Each property has specified cause and effect relations to the other properties in the pattern and to certain non-functional properties (the 'inputs' and 'outputs' of the programs).

Lewis' suggestion is that *reference* is a member of such a batch of properties: not functional properties of the organism, but functional properties of the organism–environment system. If this could be shown, it would answer the question of what all the various situations in which something refers to something else 'have in common': what they would have in common is something as abstract as a program, a scheme or formal pattern of cause–effect relationships. And if this could be shown, it would characterize reference in a way that makes it sufficiently abstract; the definition would not require any particular set of magnitudes to be the fundamental ones any more than the abstract description of a computer program does. Whether the second difficulty I noted would be met, I shall not attempt to judge.

The crucial point is that functional properties are defined *using the notions of cause and effect*. This is no problem for Lewis; Lewis believes he can define cause and effect using counterfactuals, and, as already mentioned, he gives truth conditions for counterfactuals in terms of a primitive notion of 'similarity of possible worlds'. Since he has a non-physical primitive in his system, he does not have to show that any of the notions he uses is physically definable. But the notion of 'similarity of possible worlds' is not one to which the materialist is entitled; and neither is he entitled to counterfactuals or to the notion of 'functional organization'.

As Charles Fried remarked in his Tanner Lectures,† it is easy to *mistake* causality for a physical relation. *Act, smash, move*, etc. are causal verbs and describe events which are clearly physical ('Smashed', for example, conveys two kinds of information: the

---

† 'Is liberty possible?' *The Tanner Lectures on Human Values*, vol. 3, Cambridge 1982 pp. 89–135.

information that *momentum* was transferred from one thing to another, which is purely physical information, and the information that the *breaking* of the second thing was *caused* by the momentum transfer.) As Fried points out, the causal judgment may be quite complicated in cases when both objects were in motion before the collision. Once one has made the error of taking causality to be a physical relation, it is easy to think that functional properties are simply higher-order physical properties (an error I myself once committed), and then to think that reference (and just about anything else) may be a functional property and hence physical. But once one sees this is an error, there is no vestige of a reason that I know of to think reference is a physical relation.

If the materialist cannot *define* reference, he can, of course, just take it as *primitive*. But reference, like causality, is a flexible, interest-relative notion: what we count as *referring* to something depends on background knowledge and our willingness to be charitable in interpretation. To read a relation so deeply human and so pervasively intentional into the world and to call the resulting metaphysical picture satisfactory (never mind whether or not it is 'materialist') is absurd.

The failure of natural metaphysics

As I've already pointed out, there are two traditional ways of attempting to overcome the obvious difficulties with a correspondence theory of truth. One way was to postulate a special mental power, an *intellektuelle Anschauung*, which gives the mind access to 'forms'. If the mind has direct access to the things in themselves, then there is no problem about how it can put them in correspondence with its 'signs'. The other way was to postulate a built-in structure of the world, a set of essences, and to say (what is certainly a dark saying) that this structure itself singles out *one* correspondence between signs and their objects. The two strategies were quite naturally related; if a philosopher believes in essences, he usually wants us to have epistemic access to them, and so he generally postulates an *intellektuelle Anschauung* to give us this access.

If all this is a failure, as Kant saw, where do we go from there? One direction, the only direction I myself see as making sense, might be a species of pragmatism (although the word 'pragmatism' has always been so ill-understood that one despairs of rescuing the term), 'internal' realism: a realism which recognizes a difference between '*p*' and 'I think that *p*', between being *right*, and merely thinking one is right without locating that objectivity in either transcendental correspondence or mere consensus. Nelson Goodman has done a wonderful job of 'selling' this point of view in *Ways of Worldmaking* (a book short enough to be read in an evening, and deep enough to be pondered for many). The other main direction – the one that does not make sense to me – is natural metaphysics, the tendency I have criticized here.

Goodman urges, shockingly, that we give up the notion of '*the* world'. Although he speaks of us as making *many* worlds, he does not mean that there are many worlds in the David Lewis (or science fiction) sense, but that rightness is relative to medium and message. We make many versions; the standards of rightness that determine what is right and what is wrong are corrigible, relative to task and technique, but not *subjective*. The question this tendency raises is whether a narrow path can indeed be found between the swamps of metaphysics and the quicksands of cultural relativism and historicism; I shall say more about this in the next chapter.

The approach to which I have devoted this paper is an approach which claims that there *is* a 'transcendental' reality in Kant's sense, one absolutely independent of our minds, that the regulative ideal of knowledge *is* to copy it or put our thoughts in 'correspondence' with it, *but* (and this is what makes it 'natural' metaphysics) we need no *intellektuelle Anschauung* to do this: the 'scientific method' will do the job for us. 'Metaphysics within the bounds of science alone' might be its slogan.

I can sympathize with the urge behind this view (I would not criticize it if I did not feel its attraction). I am not inclined to scoff at the idea of a noumenal ground behind the dualities of experience, even if all attempts to talk about it lead to antinomies. Analytic philosophers have always tried to dismiss the transcendental as nonsense, but it does have an eerie way of reappearing. (For one thing, almost every philosopher makes statements which contradict his own explicit account of what can be justified or known; this even arises in formal logic, when one makes statements about 'all languages' which are barred by the prohibitions on self-reference. For another, almost everyone regards the statement that there is *no* mind-independent reality, that there are *just* the 'versions', or there is just the 'discourse', or whatever, as itself intensely paradoxical.) Because one cannot talk about the transcendent or even deny its existence without paradox, one's attitude to it must, perhaps, be the concern of religion rather than of rational philosophy.

The idea of a coherent theory of the noumena; consistent, systematic, and arrived at by 'the scientific method' seems to me to be chimerical. True, a metaphysician could say 'You have, perhaps, shown that *materialist* metaphysics is incoherent. If so, let us assume some primitive notions of an "intentional" kind, say "thinks about", or "explains", and construct a scientific theory of *these* relations.' But what reason is there to regard this as a reasonable program?

The whole history of science seems to accord badly with such dreams. Science as we know it has been anti-metaphysical from the seventeenth century on; and not just because of 'positivistic interpretations'. Newton was certainly no positivist; but he strongly rejected the idea that his theory of universal gravitation could or should be read as a description of metaphysically ultimate fact. ('*Hypotheses non fingo*' was a rejection of metaphysical 'hypotheses', not of scientific ones.)

And Newton was certainly right. Suppose we lived in a Newtonian world, and suppose we could say with confidence that Newton's theory of gravity and Maxwell's theory of electromagnetism (referred to a privileged 'ether frame') were perfectly accurate. Even then, these theories admit of a bewildering variety of empirically equivalent formulations; formulations which agree on the equations while disagreeing precisely on their metaphysical interpretation. There are action-at-a-distance versions of *both* electromagnetism and gravity; there are versions of both in which an extended physical agent, the field, mediates the interactions between distant bodies; there are even *space–time* versions of *Newtonian* gravitational theory. Philosophers today argue about which of these would be 'right' in such a case; but I know of not a single first-rate physicist who takes an interest in such speculations.

The physics that has replaced Newton's has the same property. A theorist will say he is doing 'field theory' while his fingers are drawing Feynman diagrams, diagrams in which field interactions are depicted as exchanges of *particles* (calling the particles 'virtual' is, perhaps, a ghost of empiricist metaphysics). Even the statement that 'the electron we measure is not the bare electron of the theory, but the bare electron surrounded by a cloud of virtual *particles*' counts as a statement of *field* theory, if you please! What used to be the metaphysical question of atom or vortex has become a question of the choice of a notation!

Worse still, from the metaphysician's point of view, the most successful and most accurate physical theory of all time, quantum mechanics, has *no* 'realistic interpretation' that is acceptable to physicists. It is understood as a description of the world as *experienced by observers*; it does not even pretend to the kind of 'absoluteness' the metaphysician aims at (which is not to say that, given time and ingenuity, one could not come up with any number of empirical equivalents which *did* pretend to be observer independent; it is just that physicists refuse to take such efforts seriously).

There is, then, nothing in the history of science to suggest that it either aims at or should aim at one single *absolute* version of 'the world'. On the contrary, such an aim, which would require science itself to decide which of the empirically equivalent successful theories in any given context was 'really true', is contrary to the whole spirit of an enterprise whose strategy from the first has been to confine itself to claims with clear *empirical* significance. If metaphysics *is* ever revived as a culturally and humanly significant enterprise, it is far more likely to be along the lines of a Kurt Gödel or, perhaps, Saul Kripke – i.e., along the lines of those who *do* think, in spite of the history I cited, that we *do* have an *intellektuelle Anschauung* – than along the lines of natural metaphysics. But a successful revival along either line seems to be overwhelmingly unlikely.

13

Why reason can't be naturalized*

The preceding chapter described the failure of contemporary attempts to 'naturalize' metaphysics; in the present chapter I shall examine attempts to naturalize the fundamental notions of the theory of knowledge, for example the notion of a belief's being *justified* or *rationally acceptable*.

While the two sorts of attempts are alike in that they both seek to reduce 'intentional' or mentalistic notions to materialistic ones, and thus are both manifestations of what Peter Strawson (1979) has described as a permanent tension in philosophy, in other ways they are quite different. The materialist metaphysician often uses such traditional metaphysical notions as *causal power*, and *nature* quite uncritically. (I have even read papers in which one finds the locution 'realist truth', as if everyone understood this notion except a few fuzzy anti-realists.) The 'physicalist' generally doesn't seek to *clarify* these traditional metaphysical notions, but just to show that science is progressively verifying the *true* metaphysics. That is why it seems just to describe *his* enterprise as 'natural metaphysics', in strict analogy to the 'natural theology' of the eighteenth and nineteenth centuries. Those who raise the slogan 'epistemology naturalized', on the other hand, generally *disparage* the traditional enterprises of epistemology. In this respect, moreover, they do not differ from philosophers of a less reductionist kind; the criticism they voice of traditional epistemology – that it was in the grip of a 'quest for certainty', that it was unrealistic in seeking a 'foundation' for knowledge as a whole, that the 'foundation' it claimed to provide was by no means indubitable in the way it claimed, that the whole 'Cartesian enterprise' was a mistake, etc., – are precisely the criticisms one hears from philosophers of all countries and types. Hegel already denounced the idea of an 'Archimedean point' from which epistemology could judge all of our scientific, legal, moral, religious, etc. beliefs (and set up standards for all of the special subjects). It is true that Russell and Moore ignored these strictures

* This was delivered as the second Howison Lecture at the University of California on 30 April 1981.

of Hegel (as they ignored Kant), and revived 'foundationalist epistemology'; but today that enterprise has few defenders. The fact that the naturalized epistemologist is trying to reconstruct what he can of an enterprise that few philosophers of any persuasion regard as unflawed is perhaps the explanation of the fact that the naturalistic tendency in epistemology expresses itself in so many incompatible and mutually divergent ways, while the naturalistic tendency in metaphysics appears to be, and regards itself as, a unified movement.

Evolutionary epistemology

The simplest approach to the problem of giving a naturalistic account of reason is to appeal to Darwinian evolution. In its crudest form, the story is familiar: reason is a capacity we have for discovering truths. Such a capacity has survival value; it evolved in just the way that any of our physical organs or capacities evolved. A belief is rational if it is arrived at by the exercise of this capacity.

This approach assumes, at bottom, a metaphysically 'realist' notion of truth: truth as 'correspondence to the facts' or something of that kind. And this notion, as I have argued in the papers in this volume, is incoherent. We don't have notions of the 'existence' of things or of the 'truth' of statements that are independent of the versions we construct and of the procedures and practices that give sense to talk of 'existence' and 'truth' within those versions. Do *fields* 'exist' as physically real things? Yes, fields really exist: relative to one scheme for describing and explaining physical phenomena; relative to another there are particles, plus 'virtual' particles, plus 'ghost' particles, plus...Is it true that *brown* objects exist? Yes, relative to a common-sense version of the world: although one cannot give a necessary and sufficient condition for an object to be brown,†

---

† I chose brown because brown is not a spectral color. But the point also applies to spectral colors: if being a color were purely a matter of reflecting light of a certain wavelength, then the objects we see would change color a number of times a day (and would all be black in total darkness). Color depends on background conditions, edge effects, reflectancy, relations to amount of light etc. Giving a description of all of these would only define *perceived* color; to define the 'real' color of an object one also needs a notion of 'standard conditions': traditional philosophers would have said that the color of a red object is a power (a disposition) to look red to normal observers under normal conditions. This, however, requires a counterfactual conditional (whenever the object is *not* in normal conditions) and we saw in the previous chapter that the attempt to define counterfactuals in 'physical' terms has failed. What makes color terms physically undefinable is not that color is subjective but that it is *subjunctive*. The common idea that there is some one molecular structure (or whatever) common to all objects which look red 'under normal conditions' has no foundation: consider the difference between the physical structure of a red star and a red book (and the difference in what we count as 'normal conditions' in the two cases).

(one that applies to all objects, under all conditions) in the form of a finite closed formula in the language of physics. Do *dispositions* exist? Yes, in our ordinary way of talking (although disposition talk is just as recalcitrant to translation into physicalistic language as counterfactual talk, and for similar reasons). We have many irreducibly different but legitimate ways of talking, and true 'existence' statements in all of them.

To postulate a set of 'ultimate' objects, the furniture of the world, or what you will, whose 'existence' is *absolute*, not relative to our discourse at all, and a notion of truth as 'correspondence' to these ultimate objects is simply to revive the whole failed enterprise of traditional metaphysics. We saw *how* unsuccessful attempts to revive *that* enterprise have been in the last chapter.

Truth, in the only sense in which we have a vital and working notion of it, is rational acceptability (or, rather, rational acceptability under sufficiently good epistemic conditions; and which conditions are epistemically better or worse is relative to the type of discourse in just the way rational acceptability itself is). But to substitute this characterization of truth into the formula 'reason is a capacity for discovering truths' is to see the emptiness of that formula at once: 'reason is a capacity for discovering what is (or would be) rationally acceptable' is *not* the most informative statement a philosopher might utter. The evolutionary epistemologist must either presuppose a 'realist' (i.e., a metaphysical) notion of truth or see his formula collapse into vacuity.

Roderick Firth† has argued that, in fact, it collapses into a kind of epistemic vacuity on *any* theory of rational acceptibility (*or* truth). For, he points out, whatever we take the correct epistemology (or the correct theory of truth) to be, we have no way of *identifying* truths except to posit that the statements that are currently rationally acceptable (by our lights) are true. Even if these beliefs are false, even if our rational beliefs contribute to our survival for some reason *other* than truth, the way 'truths' are identified *guarantees* that reason will seem to be a 'capacity for discovering truths'. This characterization of reason has thus no real empirical content.

The evolutionary epistemologist could, I suppose, try using some notion *other* than the notion of 'discovering truths'. For example, he might try saying that 'reason is a capacity for arriving at beliefs

---

† This argument appears in Firth's Presidential Address to the Eastern Division of the American Philosophical Association (29 December 1981), titled 'Epistemic merit, intrinsic and instrumental'. Firth does not specifically refer to evolutionary epistemology, but rather to 'epistemic utilitarianism'; however, his argument applies as well to evolutionary epistemology of the kind I describe.

which *promote our survival* (or our 'inclusive genetic fitness'). But this would be a loser! Science itself, and the methodology which we have developed since the seventeenth century for constructing and evaluating theories, has *mixed* effects on inclusive genetic fitness and all too uncertain effects on survival. If the human race perishes in a nuclear war, it may well be (although there will be no one alive to say it) that scientific beliefs did *not*, in a sufficiently long time scale, promote 'survival'. Yet that will not have been because the scientific theories were not rationally acceptable, but because our *use* of them was irrational. In fact, if rationality were measured by survival value, then the proto-beliefs of the cockroach, who has been around for tens of millions of years longer than we, would have a far higher claim to rationality than the sum total of human knowledge. But such a measure would be cockeyed; there is no contradiction in imagining a world in which people have utterly irrational beliefs which for some reason enable them to survive, or a world in which the most rational beliefs quickly lead to extinction.

If the notion of 'truth' in the characterization of rationality as a 'capacity for discovering truths' is problematic, so, almost equally, is the notion of a 'capacity'. In one sense of the term, *learning* is a 'capacity' (even, a 'capacity for discovering truths'), and *all* our beliefs are the product of *that* capacity. Yet, for better or worse, not all our beliefs are rational.

The problem here is that there are no sharp lines in the brain between one 'capacity' and another (Chomskians to the contrary). Even seeing includes not just the visual organs, the eyes, but the whole brain; and what is true of seeing is certainly true of *thinking* and *inferring*. *We* draw lines between one 'capacity' and another (or build them into the various versions we construct); but a sharp line at one level does not usually correspond to a sharp line at a lower level. The table at which I write, for example, is a natural unit at the level of everyday talk; I am aware that the little particle of food sticking to its surface (I must do something about that!) is not a 'part' of the table; but at the physicist's level, the decision to consider that bit of food to be outside the boundary of the table is not natural at all. Similarly, 'believing' and 'seeing' are quite different at the level of ordinary language psychology (and usefully so); but the corresponding brain-processes interpenetrate in complex ways which can only be separated by looking outside the brain, at the environment and at the output behavior *as structured by our interests and saliencies*. 'Reason is a capacity' is what Wittgenstein called a 'grammatical remark'; by which he meant (I think) not an analytic truth, but simply the sort of remark that philosophers often *take* to be informative when in fact it tells us nothing useful.

None of this is intended to deny the obvious scientific facts: that we would not be able to reason if we did not have brains, and that those *brains* are the product of evolution by natural selection. What is wrong with evolutionary epistemology is not that the scientific facts are wrong, but that they don't answer any of the philosophical questions.

The reliability theory of rationality

A more sophisticated recent approach to these matters, proposed by Professor Alvin Goldman (1978), runs as follows: let us call a *method* (as opposed to a single belief) *reliable* if the method leads to a high frequency (say, 95%) of *true* beliefs in a long run series of representative applications (or *would* lead to such a high truth-frequency in such a series of applications). Then (the proposal goes) we can define a *rational* belief to be one which is *arrived at by using a reliable method*.

This proposal does not avoid the first objection we raised against evolutionary epistemology: it too presupposes a metaphysical notion of truth. Forgetting that rational acceptability does the lion's share of the work in fixing the notion of 'truth', the reliability theorist only pretends to be giving an analysis of rationality in terms that do not presuppose it. The second objection we raised against evolutionary epistemology, namely that the notion of a 'capacity' is hopelessly vague and general, is met, however, by replacing that notion with the notion of an arbitrary method for generating true or false statements, and then restricting the class to those methods (in this sense) whose reliability (as defined) is high. 'Learning' may be a method for generating statements, but its *reliability* is not high enough for every statement we 'learn' to count as rationally acceptable, on this theory. Finally, *no* hypothesis is made as to whether the reliable methods we employ are the result of biological evolution, cultural evolution, or what: this is regarded as no part of the theory of what rationality *is*, in this account.

This account is vulnerable to many counterexamples, however. *One* is the following: suppose that Tibetan Buddhism is, in fact, *true*, and that the Dalai Lama is, in fact, *infallible* on matters of faith and morals. Anyone who believes in the Dalai Lama, and who invariably believes any statement the Dalai Lama makes on a matter of faith or morals, follows a method which is 100% reliable; thus, if the reliability theory of rationality were correct, such a person's beliefs on faith and morals would all be rational *even if his argument for his belief that the Dalai Lama is never wrong is 'the Dalai Lama says so'*.

Cultural relativism

I have already said that, in my view, truth and rational acceptability – a claim's being right and someone's being in a position to make it – are relative to the sort of language we are using and the sort of context we are in. 'That weighs one pound' may be true in a butcher shop, but the same sentence would be understood very differently (as demanding four decimal places of precision, perhaps) if the same object were being weighed in a laboratory. This does not mean that a claim is right *whenever* those who employ the language in question would accept it as right in its context, however. There are two points that must be *balanced*, both points that have been made by philosophers of many different kinds: (1) talk of what is 'right' and 'wrong' in any area only makes sense against the background of an *inherited tradition*; but (2) traditions themselves can be *criticized*. As Austin (1961) says, remarking on a special case of this, 'superstition and error and fantasy of all kinds do become incorporated in ordinary language and even sometimes stand up to the survival test (only, when they do, why should we not detect it?)'.

What I am saying is that the 'standards' accepted by a culture or a subculture, either explicitly or implicitly, cannot *define* what reason is, even in context, because they *presuppose* reason (reasonableness) for their interpretation. On the one hand, there is no notion of reasonableness at all *without* cultures, practices, procedures; on the other hand, the cultures, practices, procedures we inherit are not an algorithm to be slavishly followed. As Mill said, commenting on his own inductive logic, there is no rule book which will not lead to terrible results 'if supposed to be conjoined with universal idiocy'. Reason is, in this sense, both immanent (not to be found outside of concrete language games and institutions) and transcendent (a regulative idea that we use to criticize the conduct of *all* activities and institutions).

Philosophers who lose sight of the immanence of reason, of the fact that reason is always relative to context and institution, become lost in characteristic philosophical fantasies. 'The ideal language', 'inductive logic', 'the empiricist criterion of significance' – these are the fantasies of the positivist, who would replace the vast complexity of human reason with a kind of intellectual Walden II.

WHY REASON CAN'T BE NATURALIZED

'The absolute idea': this is the fantasy of Hegel, who, without ignoring that complexity, would have us (or, rather, 'spirit') reach an endstage at which we (it) could comprehend it all. Philosophers who lose sight of the transcendence of reason become cultural (or historical) relativists.

I want to talk about cultural relativism, because it is one of the most influential – perhaps the most influential – forms of naturalized epistemology extant, although not usually recognized as such.

The situation is complicated, because cultural relativists usually *deny* that they are cultural relativists. I shall count a philospher as a cultural relativist for our purposes if I have not been able to find anyone who can explain to me why he *isn't* a cultural relativist. Thus I count Richard Rorty as a cultural relativist, because his explicit formulations are relativist ones (he identifies truth with right assertibility by the standards of one's cultural peers, for example), and because his entire attack on traditional philosophy is mounted on the basis that the nature of reason and representation are non-problems, because the only kind of truth it makes sense to seek is to convince one's cultural peers. Yet he himself *tells* us that relativism is self-refuting (Rorty, 1980b). And I count Michel Foucault as a relativist because his insistence on the determination of beliefs by language is so overwhelming that it is an incoherence on his part not to apply his doctrine to his *own* language and thought. Whether Heidegger ultimately escaped something very much like cultural, or rather historical, relativism is an interesting question.

Cultural relativists are not, in their own eyes, scientistic or 'physicalistic'. They are likely to view materialism and scientism as just the hang-ups of one particular cultural epoch. If I count them as 'naturalized epistemologists' it is because their doctrine is, none the less, a product of the same deference to the claims of nature, the same desire for harmony with the world version of some science, as physicalism. The difference in style and tone is thus explained: the physicalist's paradigm of science is a *hard* science, *physics* (as the term 'physicalism' suggests); the cultural relativist's paradigm is a *soft* science: anthropology, or linguistics, or psychology, or history, as the case may be. That reason is whatever the norms of the local culture determine it to be is a naturalist view inspired by the *social* sciences, including history.

There is something which makes cultural relativism a far more dangerous cultural tendency than materialism. At bottom, there is a deep irrationalism to cultural relativism, a denial of the possibility of *thinking* (as opposed to making noises in counterpoint or in chorus).

An aspect of this which is of special concern to philosophy is the suggestion, already mentioned, that the deep questions of philosophy are not deep at all. A corollary to this suggestion is that philosophy, as traditionally understood, is a *silly* enterprise. But the questions *are* deep, and it is the easy answers that are silly. Even seeing that relativism is inconsistent is, if the knowledge is taken seriously, seeing something important about a deep question. Philosophers *are* beginning to talk about the great issues again, and to feel that something can be *said* about them, even if there are no grand or ultimate solutions. There is an excitement in the air. And if I react to Professor Rorty's book (1980*a*) with a certain sharpness, it is because one more 'deflationary' book, one more book telling us that the deep questions aren't deep and the whole enterprise was a mistake, is just what we *don't* need right now. Yet I am grateful to Rorty all the same, for his work has the merit of addressing profound questions head-on.

So, although we all know that cultural relativism is inconsistent (or say we do) I want to take the time to say again that it is inconsistent. I want to point out one reason that it is: not one of the quick, logic-chopping refutations (although every refutation of relativism teaches us something about reason) but a somewhat messy, somewhat 'intuitive', reason.

I shall develop my argument in analogy with a well-known argument against 'methodological solipsism'. The 'methodological solipsist' – one thinks of Carnap's *Logische Aufbau* or of Mach's *Analyse der Empfindungen* – holds that *all* our talk can be reduced to talk about experiences and logical constructions out of experiences. More precisely, he holds that everything he can conceive of is identical (in the ultimate logical analyses of his language) with one or another complex of his *own* experiences. What makes him a *methodological* solipsist as opposed to a real solipsist is that he kindly adds that *you*, dear reader, are the 'I' of this construction when *you* perform it: he says *everybody* is a (methodological) solipsist.

The trouble, which should be obvious, is that his two stances are ludicrously incompatible. His solipsist stance implies an enormous asymmetry between persons: my body is a construction out of my experiences, in the system, but *your* body isn't a construction out of *your* experiences. It's a construction out of *my* experiences. And your experiences – viewed from within the system – are a construction out of your bodily behavior, which, as just said, is a construction out of *my* experiences. My experiences are different from everyone else's (within the system) in that they are what *everything* is constructed from. But his transcendental stance is that it's all symmetrical: the 'you' he addresses his higher-order remark to cannot be the *empirical* 'you' of the system. But if it's really true that the 'you' of the system is the only 'you' he can *understand*, then the transcendental remark is *unintelligible*. Moral: don't be a methodological solipsist unless you are a *real* solipsist!

Consider now the position of the cultural relativist who says, 'When I say something is *true*, I mean that it is correct according to the norms of *my* culture.' If he adds, 'When a member of a different culture says that something is true, what he means (whether he knows it or not) is that it is in conformity with the norms of *his* culture', then he is in exactly the same plight as the methodological solipsist.

To spell this out, suppose R.R., a cultural relativist, says

> When Karl says 'Schnee ist weiss', what Karl means (whether he knows it or not) is that snow is white *as determined by* the norms of Karl's culture

(which we take to be German culture).

Now the sentence 'Snow is white as determined by the norms of German culture' is itself one which R.R. has to *use*, not just mention, to say what Karl says. On his own account, what R.R. means by *this* sentence is

> 'Snow is white as determined by the norms of German culture' is true by the norms of R.R.'s culture

(which we take to be American culture).

Substituting this back into the first displayed utterance, (and changing to indirect quotation) yields:

> When Karl says 'Schnee ist weiss', what he means (whether he knows it or not) is that it is true as determined by the norms of American culture that it is true as determined by the norms of German culture that snow is white.

In general, if R.R. understands *every* utterance p that *he* uses as meaning 'it is true by the norms of American culture that p', then he must understand his own hemeneutical utterances, the utterances he uses to interpret others, the same way, no matter how many qualifiers of the 'according to the norms of German culture' type or however many footnotes, glosses, commentaries on the cultural differences, or whatever, he accompanies them by. Other cultures become, so to speak, logical constructions out of the procedures and practices of American culture. If he now attempts to add 'the situation is reversed from the point of view of the *other* culture' he lands in the predicament the methodological solipsist found himself in: the transcendental claim of a *symmetrical* situation cannot be *understood* if the relativist doctrine is right. And to say, as relativists often do, that the other culture has 'incommensurable' concepts is no better. This is just the transcendental claim in a special jargon.

Stanley Cavell (1979, part IV) has written that skepticism about other minds can be a significant problem because we don't, in fact, always fully acknowledge the reality of others, their equal *validity* so to speak. One might say that the methodological solipsist is led to his transcendental observation that everyone is equally the 'I' of the construction by his praiseworthy desire to *acknowledge* others in this sense. But you *can't* acknowledge others in this sense, which involves recognizing that the situation *really is* symmetrical, if you think they are really constructions out of *your* sense data. Nor can you acknowledge others in this sense if you think that the *only* notion of truth there is for *you* to understand is 'truth-as-determined-by-the-norms-of-*this*-culture'.

For simplicity, I have discussed relativism with respect to truth, but the same discussion applies to relativism about rational acceptability, justification, etc; indeed, a relativist is unlikely to be a relativist about one of these notions and not about the others.

Cultural imperialism

Just as the methodological solipsist can become a *real* solipsist, the cultural relativist can become a cultural imperialist. He can say, 'Well then, truth – the only notion of truth I understand – is defined by the norms of *my* culture.' ('After all', he can add, 'which norms should I rely on? The norms of *somebody else's* culture?') Such a view is no longer relativist at all. It postulates an *objective* notion of truth, although one that is said to be a product of our culture, and to be defined by our culture's criteria (I assume the culture imperialist is one of *us*). In this sense, just as consistent solipsism becomes indistinguishable from realism (as Wittgenstein said in the *Tractatus*), consistent cultural relativism also becomes indistinguishable from realism. But cultural imperialist realism is a special *kind* of realism.

It is realist in that it accepts an objective difference between what is true and what is merely thought to be true. (Whether it can consistently *account for* this difference is another question.)

It is not a *metaphysical* or transcendental realism, in that truth cannot go beyond right assertibility, as it does in metaphysical realism. But the notion of right assertibility is fixed by 'criteria', in a positivistic sense: something is rightly assertible only if the norms of the culture specify that it is; these norms are, as it were, an *operational definition* of right assertibility, in this view.

I don't know if any philosopher holds such a view, although several philosophers have let themselves fall into talking at certain times as if they did. (A philosopher in this mood is likely to say, '*X* is *our* notion', with a certain petulance, where *X* may be *reason, truth, justification, evidence*, or what have you.)

This view is, however, self-refuting, at least in our culture. I have discussed this elsewhere (Putnam, 1981); the argument turns on the fact that our culture, unlike totalitarian or theocratic cultures, does not have 'norms' which decide *philosophical* questions. (Some philosophers have thought it does;but they had to postulate a 'depth grammar' accessible only to *them*, and not describable by ordinary linguistic or anthropological investigation.) Thus the philosophical statement:

> A statement is true (rightly assertible) only if it is assertible according to the norms of modern European and American culture

is itself neither assertible nor refutable in a way that requires assent by everyone who does not deviate from the norms of modern European and American culture. So, if this statement is true, it follows that it is not true (not rightly assertible). Hence it is not true QED. (I believe that *all* theories which identify truth or right assertibility with what people agree with, or with what they would agree with in the long run, or with what educated and intelligent people agree with, or with what educated and intelligent people would agree with in the long run, are contingently self-refuting in this same way.)

Cultural imperialism would not be contingently self-refuting in this way if, as a matter of contingent fact, our culture were a totalitarian culture which erected its own cultural imperialism into a required dogma, a culturally normative belief. But it would still be wrong. For every culture has norms which are vague, norms which are unreasonable, norms which dictate inconsistent beliefs. We have all become aware how many inconsistent beliefs about *women* were culturally normative until recently, and are still strongly operative, not only in subcultures, but in all of us to some extent; and examples of inconsistent but culturally normative beliefs could easily be multiplied. Our task is not to mechanically *apply* cultural norms, as if they were a computer program and we were the computer, but to interpret them, to criticize them, to bring them and the ideals which inform them into reflective equilibrium. Cavell has aptly described this as 'confronting the culture with itself, along the lines in which it meets in me'. And he adds (Cavell, 1979, p. 125), 'This seems to me a task that warrants the name of Philosophy.' In this sense, we are all called to be philosophers, to a greater or lesser extent.

The culturalist, relativist or imperialist, like the historicist, has been caught up in the fascination of something really fascinating; but caught up in a sophomorish way. Traditions, cultures, history, deserve to be emphasized, as they are not by those who seek Archimedian points in metaphysics or epistemology. It is true that we speak a public language, that we inherit versions, that talk of truth and falsity only make sense against the background of an 'inherited tradition', as Wittgenstein says. But it is also true that we constantly remake our language, that we make new versions out of old ones, and that we have to use reason to do all this, and, for that matter, even to understand and apply the norms we do not alter or criticize. Consensus definitions of reason do not work, because consensus among grown-ups *presupposes* reason rather than defining it.

Quinian positivism

The slogan 'epistemology naturalized' is the title of a famous paper by Quine (1969). If I have not discussed that paper up to now, it is because Quine's views are much more subtle and much more elaborate than the disastrously simple views we have just reviewed, and it seemed desirable to get the simpler views out of the way first.

Quine's philosophy is a large continent, with mountain ranges, deserts, and even a few Okefenokee Swamps. I do not know how all of the pieces of it can be reconciled, if they can be; what I shall do is discuss two different strains that are to be discerned in Quine's epistemology. In the present section I discuss the positivistic strain; the next section will discuss 'epistemology naturalized'.

The positivist strain, which occurs early and late, turns on the notion of an *observation sentence*. In his earliest writings, Quine gave this a phenomenalistic interpretation but, since the 1950s at least, he has preferred a definition in neurological and cultural terms. First, a preliminary notion: The *stimulus meaning* of a sentence is defined to be the set of stimulations (of 'surface neurons') that would 'prompt assent' to the sentence. It is thus supposed to be a *neurological* correlate of the sentence. A sentence may be called 'stimulus-true' for a speaker if the speaker is actually experiencing a pattern of stimulation of his surface neurons that lie in its stimulus meaning; but one should be careful to remember that a stimulus-true sentence is not necessarily true *simpliciter*. If you show me a life-like replica of a duck, the sentence, 'That's a duck', may be stimulus-true for me, but it isn't true. A sentence is defined to be an *observation* sentence for a community if it is an occasioned sentence (one whose truth value is regarded as varying with time and place, although this is not the Quinian definition) and it has the *same* stimulus meaning for all speakers. Thus 'He is a bachelor' is not an observation sentence, since different stimulations will prompt you to assent to it than will prompt me (we know different people); but 'That's a duck' is (nearly enough) an observation sentence. Observe that the criterion is supposed to be entirely physicalistic. The key idea is that observation sentences are distinguished among occasioned sentences by being keyed to the same stimulations *intersubjectively*.

Mach held that talk of unobservables, including (for him) material objects, is justified only for reasons of 'economy of thought'. The business of science is *predicting regularities in our sensations*; we introduce 'objects' other than sensations only as needed to get theories which neatly predict such regularities.

Quine (1975) comes close to a 'physicalized' version of Mach's view. Discussing the question, whether there is more than one correct 'system of the world', he gives his criteria for such a system: (1) it must predict a certain number of stimulus-true observation sentences;† (2) it must be finitely axiomatized; (3) it must contain nothing unnecessary to the purpose of predicting stimulus-true observation sentences and conditionals. In the terminology Quine introduces in this paper, the theory formulation must be a 'tight fit'‡ over the relevant set of stimulus-true observation conditionals. (This is a formalized version of Mach's 'economy of thought'.)

If this were all of Quine's doctrine, there would be no problem.

---

† Quine actually requires that a 'system of the world' predict that certain 'pegged observation sentences' be true. I have oversimplified in the text by writing 'observation sentence' for 'pegged observation sentence'. Also the 'stimulus meaning' of an observation sentence includes a specification of conditions under which the speaker *dissents*, as well as the conditions under which he assents. The details are in Quine (1975).

‡ A theory is a 'tight fit' if it is interpretable in *every* axiomatizable theory which implies the observation conditionals (conditionals whose antecedent and consequent are pegged observation sentences) in question in a way that holds the pegged observation sentences fixed. To my knowledge, no proof exists that a 'tight fit' even exists, apart from the trivial case in which the observation conditionals can be axiomatized *without* going outside of the observation vocabulary.

It is reconciling what Quine says here with what Quine says elsewhere that is difficult and confusing. I am *not* claiming that it is impossible however; a lot, if not all, of what Quine says *can* be reconciled. What I claim is that Quine's position is much more complicated than is generally realized.

For example, what is the *status* of Quine's ideal 'systems of the world'? It is tempting to characterize the sentences in one of Quine's ideal 'theory formulations' as *truths* (relative to that language and that choice of a formulation from among the equivalent-but-incompatible-at-face-value formulations of what Quine would regard as the *same* theory) and as *all* the truths (relative to the same choice of language and formulation), but this would conflict with *bivalence*, the principle that *every* sentence, in the ideal scientific language Quine envisages, is true or false.

To spell this out: Quine's ideal systems of the world are *finitely axiomatizable theories*, and contain standard mathematics. Thus Gödel's celebrated result applies to them: there are sentences in them which are neither provable nor refutable on the basis of the system. If being *true* were just being a theorem in the system, such sentences would be neither true nor false, since neither they nor their negations are theorems. But Quine (1981) holds to bivalence.

If Quine were a metaphysical realist there would again be no problem: the ideal system would contain everything that could be *justified* (from a very idealized point of view, assuming knowledge of all observations that *could* be made, and logical omniscience); but, Quine could say, the undecidable sentences are still determinately true or false – only we can't tell which. But the rejection of meta-physical realism, of the whole picture of a determinate 'copying' relation between words and a noumenal world, is at the heart of Quine's philosophy. And, as we shall see in the next section, 'justification' is a notion Quine is leery of. So what *is* he up to?†

I hazard the following interpretation: bivalence has *two* meanings for Quine: a 'first-order' meaning, a meaning as viewed *within* the system of science (including its Tarskian metalanguage) and a 'second-order' meaning, a meaning as viewed by the philosopher. In effect, I am claiming that Quine too allows himself a 'transcendental' standpoint which is different from the 'naive' standpoint that we get by just taking the system at face value. (I am not claiming that this is *inconsistent* however; some philosophers feel that such a move

† Quine *rejected* the interpretation I offer below (discussion at Heidelberg in 1981), and opted for saying that our situation is 'asymmetrical': he is a 'realist' with respect to his *own* language but not with respect to other languages. See pp. xii–xiii above and pp. 278–9 below for my rejoinder.

is *always* an inconsistency, but taking this line would preclude using *any* notion in science which one would explain away as a useful fiction in one's commentary on one's first-order practice. There was an inconsistency in the case of the methodological solipsist, because he claimed his first-order system reconstructed the *only* way he could understand the notion of another mind; if he withdraws that claim, then his position becomes perfectly consistent; it merely loses all philosophical interest.)

From *within* the first-order system, '*p* is true or *p* is false' is simply true; a derivable consequence of the Tarskian truth definition, given standard propositional calculus. From *outside*, from the meta-metalinguistic point of view Quine occupies, there is no unique 'world', no unique 'intended model'. Only *structure* matters; every model of the ideal system (I assume there is just one ideal theory, and we have fixed a formulation) is an intended model. Statements that are provable are true in *all* intended models; undecidable statements are true or false in each intended model, but not *stably* true or false. Their truth value varies from model to model.

If *this* is Quine's view, however, then there is still a problem. For Quine, what the philosopher says from the 'transcendental' standpoint is subject to the same methodological rules that govern ordinary first-order scientific work. Even mathematics is subject to the same rules. Mathematical truths, too, are to be certified as such by showing they are theorems in a system which we need to predict sensations (or rather, stimulus-true observation conditionals), given the physics which we are constructing as we construct the mathematics. More precisely, the *whole system of knowledge* is justified *as a whole* by its utility in predicting observations. Quine emphasizes that there is no room in this view for a special status for philosophical utterances. There is no 'first philosophy' above or apart from science, as he puts it.

Consider, now, the statement:

> A statement is *rightly assertible* (true in all models) just in case it is a theorem of the relevant 'finite formulation', and that formulation is a 'tight fit' over the appropriate set of stimulus-true observation conditionals.

This statement, like most philosophical statements, does not imply *any* observation conditionals, either by itself or in conjunction with physics, chemistry, biology, etc. Whether we say that some statements which are undecidable in the system are really rightly assertible or deny it does not have any effects (that one can foresee) on prediction.

Thus, *this* statement *cannot* itself be rightly assertible. In short, *this* reconstruction of Quine's positivism makes it *self-refuting*.

The difficulty, which is faced by all versions of positivism, is that positivist exclusion principles are always self-referentially inconsistent. In short, *positivism produced a conception of rationality so narrow as to exclude the very activity of producing that conception.* (Of course, it also excluded a great many other kinds of rational activity.) The problem is especially sharp for Quine, because of his explicit rejection of the analytic/synthetic distinction, his rejection of a special status for philosophy, etc.

It may be, also, that I have just got Quine wrong. Quine would perhaps reject the notions of 'right assertibility', 'intended model', and so on. But then I just don't know *what* to make of this strain in Quine's thought.

'Epistemology naturalized'

Quine's paper 'Epistemology naturalized' takes a very different tack. 'Justification' has failed. (Quine considers the notion only in its strong 'Cartesian' setting, which is one of the things that makes his paper puzzling.) Hume taught us that we *can't* justify our knowledge claims (in a foundational way). Conceptual reduction has also failed (Quine reviews the failure of phenomenalism as represented by Carnap's attempt in the *Logische Aufbau*.) So, Quine urges, let us give up epistemology and 'settle for psychology'.

Taken at face value, Quine's position is sheer epistemological eliminationism: we should just *abandon* the notions of justification, good reason, warranted assertion, etc., and *reconstrue* the notion of 'evidence' (so that the 'evidence' becomes the sensory stimulations that *cause us* to have the scientific beliefs we have). In conversation, however, Quine has repeatedly said that he didn't mean to 'rule out the normative'; and this is consistent with his recent interest in such notions as the notion of a 'tight fit' (an economical finitely axiomatized system for predicting observations).

Moreover, the expression 'naturalized epistemology' is being used today by a number of philosophers who explicitly consider themselves to *be* doing normative epistemology, or at least methodology. But the paper 'Epistemology naturalized' really does rule all that out. So it's all *extremely* puzzling.

One way to reconcile the conflicting impulses that one sees at work here might be to replace justification theory by reliability theory in the sense of Goldman; instead of saying that a belief is justified if it is arrived at by a reliable method, one might say that the notion of justification should be *replaced* by the notion of a verdict's being the product of a reliable method. This is an *eliminationist* line in that it does not try to reconstruct or analyze the traditional notion; that was an intuitive notion that we now perceive to have been defective from the start, such a philosopher might say. Instead, he proposes a *better* notion (by his lights).

While some philosophers would, perhaps, move in this direction, Quine would not for a reason already given: Quine rejects metaphysical realism, and the notion of reliability presupposes the notion of *truth*. Truth is, to be sure, an acceptable notion for Quine, if defined à la Tarski, but so defined, it cannot serve as the primitive notion of epistemology or of methodology. For Tarski simply defines 'true' so that '*p* is true' will come out equivalent to '*p*'; so that, to cite the famous example, '*Snow is white*' *is true* will come out equivalent to 'Snow is white'. What the procedure does is to define 'true' so that saying that a statement is true is equivalent to *assenting* to the statement; truth, as defined by Tarski, is not a *property* of statements at all, but a syncategoramatic notion which enables us to 'ascend semantically', i.e., to talk about sentences instead of about objects.†

I will assent to '*p* is true' whenever I assent to *p*; therefore, I will accept a method as reliable whenever it *yields verdicts I would accept*. I believe that, in fact, this is what the 'normative' becomes for Quine: the search for methods that yield verdicts that one oneself would accept.

Why we can't eliminate the normative

I shall have to leave Quine's views with these unsatisfactory remarks. But why not take a full blown eliminationist line? Why *not* eliminate the normative from our conceptual vocabulary? Could it be a superstition that there is such a thing as reason?

If one abandons the notions of justification, rational acceptability, warranted assertibility, right assertibility, and the like, completely, then 'true' goes as well, except as a mere device for 'semantic ascent', that is, a mere mechanism for switching from one level of language to another. The mere introduction of a Tarskian truth predicate cannot define for a language any notion of *rightness* that was not already defined. To reject the notions of justification and right assertibility while *keeping* a *metaphysical realist notion of truth* would, on the other hand, not only be peculiar (what ground could there be

---

† Quine himself puts this succinctly. 'Whatever we affirm, after all, we affirm as a statement within our aggregate theory of nature as we now see it; and to call a statement true is just to reaffirm it.' (Quine, 1975, p. 327)

for regarding truth, in the 'correspondence' sense, as *clearer* than right assertibility?), but incoherent; for the notions the naturalistic metaphysician uses to explain truth and reference, for example the notion of causality (explanation), and the notion of the *appropriate type* of causal chain depend on notions which presuppose the notion of reasonableness.

But if *all* notions of rightness, both epistemic and (metaphysically) realist are eliminated, then what are our statements but noise-makings? What are our thoughts but *mere* subvocalizations? The elimination of the normative is attempted mental suicide.

The notions, 'verdict I accept' and 'method that leads to verdicts I accept' are of little help. If the *only* kind of rightness any statement has that I can understand is 'being arrived at by a method which yields verdicts *I* accept', then I am committed to a solipsism of the present moment. To solipsism, because this *is* a methodologically solipsist substitute for assertibility ('verdicts *I* accept'), and we saw before that the methodological solipsist is only consistent if he is a real solipsist. And to solipsism of the present moment because this is a *tensed* notion (a substitute for warranted assertibility at *a time*, not for assertibility in the best conditions); and if the *only* kind of rightness my present 'subvocalizations' have is *present* assertibility (however defined); if there is no notion of a *limit* verdict, however fuzzy; then there is no sense in which my 'subvocalizations' are *about* anything that goes beyond the present moment. (Even the thought 'there is a future' is 'right' only in the sense of being *assertible at the present moment*, in such a view.)

One could try to overcome this last defect by introducing the notion of 'a verdict I would accept *in the long run*', but this would at once involve one with the use of counterfactuals, and with such notions as 'similarity of possible worlds'. But it is pointless to make further efforts in this direction. Why should we expend our mental energy in convincing ourselves that we aren't thinkers, that our thoughts aren't really *about* anything, noumenal *or* phenomenal, that there is *no* sense in which any thought is *right* or *wrong* (including the thought that no thought is right or wrong) beyond being the verdict of the moment, and so on? This is a self-refuting enterprise if there ever was one! Let us recognize that one of our fundamental self-conceptualizations, one of our fundamental 'self-descriptions', in Rorty's phrase, is that we are *thinkers*, and that *as* thinkers we are committed to there being *some* kind of truth, some kind of correctness which is substantial and not merely 'disquotational'. That means that there is no eliminating the normative.

If there is no eliminating the normative, and no possibility of reducing the normative to our favorite science, be it biology, anthropology, neurology, physics, or whatever, then where are we? We might try for a grand theory of the normative in its *own* terms, a formal epistemology, but that project seems decidedly overambitious. In the meantime, there is a great deal of philosophical work to be done, and it will be done with fewer errors if we free ourselves of the reductionist and historicist hang-ups that have marred so much recent philosophy. If reason is both transcendent and immanent, then philosophy, as culture-bound reflection and argument about eternal questions, is both in time and eternity. We don't have an Archimedean point; we always speak the language of a time and place; but the rightness and wrongness of what we say is not *just* for a time and a place.

14

Quantum mechanics and the observer

The thing that strikes everyone who looks at quantum mechanics is 'superposition of states'. For example, one can have a hydrogen atom in such a condition that the probability that it is at one energy level is 25 % and the probability that it is at the next higher energy level is 75 %. Now, the problem is that one should not think of this as meaning that the atom is either at the first energy level or the second but we don't know which. *What then does it mean?* That is the question! That is what 'interpretations' of quantum mechanics are all about.

I shall not review the argument to show that one cannot think of it in a classical way, that one cannot think of it as meaning that the energy level is one or the other (nor can one think of it as meaning that the hydrogen atom is at an in-between energy level). Physicists gave up that way of viewing it (which is, unfortunately, the only way of viewing it that one can 'explain to a barmaid', in Rutherford's phrase) long before there were more-or-less formal proofs that one cannot view it that way.

Formal proofs that there are no hidden variables are not, I think, what has played a role in the thinking of physicists; what physicists are more impressed by is the fact that if one tries to think of it that way then it doesn't square with any intelligible physical picture at all. Somehow the way of thinking that works is to think of the superpositions as a new kind of state, a new condition. Sometimes people try to picture it as the atom fluctuating between the two energy levels, but that doesn't seem to work either. It is, of course, the case that if one makes the appropriate measurement, which in this case would be a measurement of energy, then in 25 % of the cases one will find the lower energy level and in 75 % of the cases one will find the next higher energy level. But one shouldn't think of this as meaning that it is already at one or the other before one looks.

I am not necessarily saying what I believe, by the way. So far I am just repeating the conventional wisdom of physicists. Later on we can discuss whether any of this needs to be revised. Of course, every philosopher of quantum mechanics does challenge the conventional wisdom at one point or another. But let's start with the conventional wisdom.

The famous two-slit experiment (see page 47) also involves super-position. Indeed, so does the orbiting of an electron around a nucleus. For the position of an electron in orbit is uncertain. Moreover, this uncertainty is, again, more than a mere ignorance on our part as to where the electron is; in some respects it is as if the electron were smeared out over its possible locations. In fact, this 'smeared out' behavior, the fact that the electron is in a superposition of its various possible position states and not in any one of them, is what accounts for the fact that atoms do not collapse to a mathematical point, as they should according to the laws of classical physics.

Physicists have concluded that the two-slit experiment is not a case in which we are dealing with a classical 'statistical mixture', i.e., the particle goes through slit A or it goes through slit B but we don't know which. The correct formula for the state of the particles is:

$$\Psi(x, y, z, t) = \frac{1}{\sqrt{2}} \Psi_A(x, y, z, t) + \frac{1}{\sqrt{2}} \Psi_B(x, y, z, t).$$

In this formula, Ψ_A and Ψ_B represents *states* or *conditions* of the particle; they are (mathematically represented by) vectors in Hilbert space. Ψ_A is the state of a particle which definitely goes through slit A (i.e., the state of a particle which hits the screen when slit B is closed). Ψ_B is the state of a particle which definitely goes through slit B. Notice that the formula does not give the probability that the particle hits any region R, it rather gives a mathematical representation of the state of the particle after the interaction with the slits. From that we get the probability by an integration, i.e., the probability that it hits the region R on the photographic emulsion is the squared absolute value of Ψ integrated over the region R. So the probability calculation is not performed by considering two cases: 'either the true state is Ψ_A or the true state is Ψ_B', as we would if we were dealing with a merely *unknown* event (whether the particle went through A or B), but is rather performed by *superimposing* the two cases (mathematically: forming an appropriate vector sum of the two state-vectors).

The dynamics is roughly as follows (I follow von Neumann (1955)). A closed system is thought of as starting out in either a pure state or a classical mixture. Since a classical mixture can be thought of as a situation in which there is some pure state but we don't know which, it is as if closed systems always started out in pure states. Then the state evolves according to the completely deterministic Schrödinger equation. This is the first model for change of state, and I shall refer to it as *time evolution*.

If, on the other hand, one disturbs the system by coming in from outside with a measuring device and measuring the value of an observable O, then the system 'jumps', and it jumps into a so-called eigenstate of the observable measured, i.e., a state in which the observable has a definite value. For example, when I make an energy measurement upon an atom which is in a superposition of different energy states, the atom jumps into a definite energy level. The mathematical postulate which says what the probabilities are with which the system jumps into each one of the available eigenstates is called the projection postulate.

To summarize, there are two forms of change of state: there is the deterministic change of state in a closed system which we called *time evolution*, and there is the indeterministic, discontinuous (in general), jump which takes place upon measurement. Now the problem is obvious, isn't it?

If a system M comes along and performs a measurement upon a system S out in deep space, it looks as if I can view it in two ways: I can say S was a closed system undergoing time evolution until M came along and caused an intrinsically unpredictable quantum jump, or I can say, 'No, there was just one system all along, $M + S$, and the entire interaction between M and S was just a physical interaction in a single closed system', in which case there should have been deterministic change of state. In the one interpretation (the one in which M performed a 'measurement' upon S) one will get a jump into *one* of the eigenstates of the observable measured; in the other (time evolution in the single closed system $M + S$) one will get a superposition of *all* the possible results of the measurement.

What von Neumann (1955) says about this – and his ideas will be at the center of my discussion – is that the two ways of looking at this can be reconciled. Consider, to be specific, a system consisting of a geiger counter, a tape recorder, and some radioactive material. The tape recorder records whether or not the geiger counter (which is at such a distance from the radioactive material that the clicks are not too frequent) does or does not click at a pre-set time. Von Neumann's view is that we can think of the system as just being the radioactive material, and in that case the geiger counter causes that system to jump into one of two states: 'beta particle or whatever emitted' or 'beta particle not emitted' at the pre-set time; or one can think of the system as being the geiger counter plus the radioactive material, in which case the system would go into a superposition of the states 'beta particle emitted and geiger counter clicking' and 'no particle emitted (in the relevant direction) and geiger counter not clicking', if it weren't for the tape recorder; or one can think of the system as the radioactive material plus the geiger counter plus the tape recorder, and say that when I play back the tape the system jumps out of the superposition of geiger counter clicking and geiger counter not clicking at the pre-set time. So there is a certain relativity here; in fact, it seems reasonable to call quantum mechanics (in von Neumann's presentation of it, anyway), a 'theory of relativity' (a term Einstein never liked for *his* theory). On von Neumann's view there is a dependence of the truth upon one's perspective; there is no master truth.

In fact, one can push the 'relativity' farther. Von Neumann says one can put the cut between the observer and the system *inside the brain*. One can view the lateral geniculate nucleus as measuring the eyes and causing them to make 'quantum jumps'; or one can view the cortex as measuring the lateral geniculate nucleus and causing it to jump into one of a number of states; or...(Perhaps the ultimate observer on von Neumann's view is the Kantian transcendental ego.)

I want to examine this thing more closely. Let me take a case that Schrödinger raised for the purpose of criticizing the orthodox interpretation of quantum mechanics; this is the famous case of 'Schrödinger's cat'. The idea is that one has a system, think of it as a satellite out in deep space, which contains a cat to which electrodes are attached (a repulsive idea, by the way!). The system includes an emitter that is pre-set to emit a photon at noon. When the photon is emitted it will be emitted in the direction of a half-silvered mirror. If the photon is reflected away, the cat will live; if the photon gets through the half-silvered mirror, it will strike a sensitive detector and the cat will be electrocuted.

Schrödinger's claim was that if von Neumann is right, then one can think of this closed system as being in a superposition of states of the form $(1/\sqrt{2})$ live cat $+(1/\sqrt{2})$ dead cat, and this is uninterpretable, isn't it? Something must be wrong with the theory. (In my one conversation with him, Einstein raised a very similar objection. Einstein said, 'If this theory is right, then my *bed* jumps into a definite state when I come into my room and look at it.') Well, I am not going to agree that the superposition is uninterpretable. I am going to take the heroic stance of assuming that the theory is right, and that one can have superpositions even of macroscopic states. Now, many people say that this is a tremendous extrapolation, an extrapolation to systems with many, many degrees of freedom, and this is where the theory is going to turn out to be wrong. Maybe they are right, but even if they are right there is still a possible world in which the present theory is true, and as a philosopher I am interested in giving the correct interpretation of quantum mechanics for that possible world.

Since I have taken this heroic stance, let me suppose that our technology becomes so perfect that we are able to manufacture macroscopic systems in pure states. So we actually bring into existence Schrödinger's cat-system, the satellite containing the cat and so on. We even manufacture large numbers of identical copies. ('Identical', of course, means the same pure state. Doubtless this is impossible, but I want to describe a certain thought experiment.)

So, let us suppose we manufacture a large ensemble of these Schrödinger cat-systems, and we examine each one at the pre-set time and see if the cat is alive or dead. Then classical physics and quantum mechanics both predict: you will find 50 % of the cats are alive.

Now, suppose this is not the measurement we make. Suppose that instead we make a measurement to determine if the system is in a superposition. This means that we have to find some observable O (and there always is one) such that if the thing is in the superposition predicted by the theory then that observable has the definite value one, and instead of looking to see if the cat is alive or dead, what we do is measure *this* observable O in each one of these systems. If the system does not spontaneously go out of the superposition when a macro-observable is involved, then we shall find the value *one in each case*. But, as I said a moment ago, assuming that the predicted value would be discovered is extrapolating quantum mechanics to systems with very very many degrees of freedom. If quantum mechanics ceases to hold when so many degrees of freedom are involved; if, for some reason, the ensemble spontaneously becomes a mixed one so that half the satellites are in one state and half the satellites are in a different state (or, perhaps, so that many, many different states are exhibited by members of the ensemble after the pre-set time), then O-measurement will not yield the single value *one* in every case, but instead we will find a smear of O-values, and that is how we will know that there is no longer a superposition.

If the prediction of quantum mechanics (as formalized by von Neumann) is correct, and when we measure the observable O we get the value *one* in every case, then after we have measured O we will not be able to find out whether the cat *was* alive or dead before the O-measurement. The O-measurement and the cat-being-alive-or-dead measurement are measurements of incompatible observables, in the sense that making either measurement precludes making the other, on the standard interpretation of quantum mechanics. Perhaps the O-measurement disperses the entire system, so that the cat is *now* definitely dead, whether or not it was alive before the O-measurement, and so that there is no way to recover the information about the state of the cat's health before the O-measurement. And if we try to *first* measure the state of the cat's health and *then* measure O, we disturb the system by the first measurement, so that we cannot tell what the result of the O-measurement would have been if the system had not been disturbed, which was what we wanted to know.

The point to keep in mind is that on von Neumann's view one can *either* regard the cat as an observer, in which case half of the cats are alive at noon and half of the cats are dead – i.e., the ensemble is 'mixed' – or one can regard the outside person who measures O as the observer, in which case the ensemble is a 'pure' one, and all the systems are in a superposition of the form $(1/\sqrt{2})$ live cat $+ (1/\sqrt{2})$ dead cat. It all depends upon where you put the cut between the observer and the system. There is no objective truth *about the metaquestion* of whether there is a determinate answer to the question 'Is the cat alive or dead?' It depends upon where you cut.

Analysis of quantum mechanical measurement

According to the quantum mechanical definition of measurement, there should be a certain kind of correlation of properties between the system M and the system S after M performs a measurement upon S. This 'correlation' requirement is mathematically expressed as a requirement about the form of the state of the combined system $M + S$ after the measurement interaction, treating that interaction as time evolution in a single closed system.

(Note how the 'relativity' we have been talking about plays a role in what was just mentioned: we look at the interaction between M and S as if it were *not* a measurement, i.e., we consider it from the 'outside' perspective, in which it is an interaction in the single closed system $M + S$. If this interaction results in a state of the kind I am about to describe, then we say that the same interaction may also be viewed from an 'inside' perspective, the perspective of M, as a measurement performed by M upon S. This moving back and forth between perspectives happens in every quantum mechanics text, but von Neumann is one of the few writers to make it explicit.)

The requirements that the state of $M + S$ must fulfill for the interaction to count as a measurement – rather, the requirements that the state of $M + S$ *in the perspective in which that state is the result of time evolution in a single closed system* must fulfill for it to be legitimate to 'put the cut between M and S' and view the state of S alone as the result of a quantum jump induced by the measurement performed by M – are easy to describe.

Imagine that we wish to measure a particular 'observable', i.e., a particular physical magnitude, say total energy, in S. The measurement is to tell us which of a number of intervals $d_1, d_2, \ldots, d_n$ the energy lies in. The measuring system M contains a meter, or something of that kind, and we are going to find out which interval the measured observable in S (the energy) lies in by examining the meter and seeing which of the intervals $e_1, e_2, \ldots, e_n$ the meter needle lies in (of course the idea that the registering observable, as I shall call it, is a meter needle is only an example; any macro-observable whose values can be split up into the appropriate number of disjoint 'intervals' – mathematically, Borel sets – will do).

Let us call a possible state of $M + S$ a *determinate state* (from the point of view of this particular measurement, defined by the choice of an observable to be measured – energy, in the example – a registering observable, a set of possible disjoint intervals that the value of the observable to be measured can lie in, and a set of corresponding disjoint intervals that the value of the registering observable can lie in) if the state is one in which the possible values of the observable to be measured lie in some interval d_i and the possible values of the registering observable lie in the *corresponding* interval e_i. (The 'possible values' of an observable when a system is in a state Ψ are the values that have a non-zero probability of being obtained if that observable is measured when the system is in the state Ψ. The mathematical postulate of quantum mechanics that we mentioned earlier, the projection postulate, determines which these are. If the possible values of an observable in Ψ are $r_1, r_2, \ldots, r_k, \ldots$ *then* Ψ itself can be thought of as a superposition of states or conditions in which the observable has the definite values $r_1, r_2, \ldots, r_k$.)

Suppose that we start out with an M and an S which are not interacting, and we determine that state of $M + S$ at the end of an interaction by using quantum mechanics and treating the interaction as time evolution in the single closed system $M + S$. If the state of $M + S$, calculated in this way, is a *superposition of determinate states*, then the interaction can also be viewed as a measurement of the relevant observable in S by means of the registering observable in M; if the registering observable in M is found to have a value in the interval e_i (where 'found' just means *by looking* – recall that the registering observable is a macro-observable), then, in this perspective, the interaction caused S to 'jump' into a condition in which the possible values of the energy (or whatever the observable was that we were measuring) lay in the corresponding interval d_i.

Since a superposition of states is mathematically represented by a linear combination of vectors, we can also express this mathematically by writing

$$\Psi_{M+S} = \sum_i c_i \Psi_i, \tag{1}$$

where for $i = 1, 2, \ldots, n$, Ψ_i is a determinate state in which the possible values of the two observables lie in d_i and e_i respectively.

In (1) the states are all states in the Hilbert space of $M + S$, the number of summands may be infinite or even continuous (so that the sum may actually have to be an integral); and there may have to be a 'slop term', a small additional term of very low amplitude, corresponding to the fact that perfect correlation is strictly impossible.

The criterion I have just given for a measurement, represented by the formula (1), reflects the fact that one can look on a measurement as *either* throwing S alone into an eigenstate of the observable measured *or* as throwing $S + M$ from a superposition of determinate states into exactly one of them: yet another example of the pervasive 'relativity' I have been describing.

Incompatibility

Following von Neumann, we shall use the term *proposition* to mean any statement of the form: 'observable so-and-so has such-and-such a value' (or a value in such-and-such an interval). (Von Neumann speaks of '*experimental* propositions', to emphasize that he is concerned with whether the propositions will be found correct or incorrect upon a measurement, not with whether they are true or false in some realist sense when we aren't looking.) It can happen that there is only one state Ψ (up to multiplication by an arbitrary complex scalar, since, in quantum mechanics, vectors that are scalar multiples of each other have the same experimental significance) which assigns probability *one* to a particular proposition p, i.e., only one state such that it is *certain* that p will be found to be true if the system is in that state; such a proposition is called a *maximal* proposition (in quantum logic, which we shall describe below, the maximal propositions are the logically strongest contingent propositions). For any proposition p, the vectors Ψ which represent the states relative to which p has

255

probability *one* (i.e., the states or conditions such that it is certain p will be found to be true if the system is in that state) form a *subspace* of the Hilbert space (the linear space used mathematically to represent states or conditions).

It can happen that two propositions p, q are such that no state Ψ simultaneously assigns probability *one* to both of them; i.e., if a state is such that either p or q is certain, then the other is uncertain. For example, according to the famous 'uncertainty principle',

$$\Delta q \cdot \Delta q \geqslant h/4\pi,$$

where Δp and Δp are the uncertainties of momentum and position, respectively.

No state can be such that position and momentum are both determinate; in fact, if the position is extremely determinate (i.e., the 'most probable' values of position in that state lie in a small interval Δq), then the uncertainty principle says that the momentum must be correspondingly indeterminate.

There are two cases in which it can happen that two propositions are related in this way; obviously it can happen if p and q are contraries or contradictories in classical logic. For example, no state can assign probability *one* to the statement that a particle is in one place and also assign probability *one* to the statement that it is in a different place. We shall refer to this as a *Boolean incompatibility*. But the incompatibility between the proposition that the particle has a definite momentum and the proposition that it has a definite position is evidently not of this classical Boolean kind. (Mathematically, both kinds of incompatibility correspond to the fact that the intersection of the subspaces of the Hilbert space corresponding to the two propositions is the O-subspace. But in the case of 'quantum mechanical incompatibility', as opposed to Boolean incompatibility, the projection operators onto these subspaces do not commute. For this reason, quantum mechanically incompatible propositions, such as the proposition that X has such-and-such a definite position and X has such-and-such a definite momentum, are also sometimes called 'non-commuting'.)

The received view about the experimental significance of quantum-mechanical incompatibility (i.e., of the relation between 'non-commuting propositions') is that if p and q are incompatible, then they cannot both be *known* to be true by any measurement or combination of measurements that an observer could carry out. Incompatible propositions are such that their truth values cannot be simultaneously known. (Here and below we are only concerned with the non-Boolean kind of incompatibility; for in the Boolean case, if one knows one of the propositions is true, by a measurement, then one also knows the contrary proposition is *false*; so the truth values of propositions of this kind can be simultaneously known.)

Another view, more of a minority view, but one which has been around for a long time, is that the truth values of incompatible propositions *can* be simultaneously known, but it is just that the knowledge cannot have predictive value. The classical argument for this minority view is the *time-of-flight* argument. As set out, for example, by Margenau and Park (1968), the argument runs as follows: emit a particle at a definite time t_0. Determine the time and place at which the particle hits a screen. From the distance between the positions at the two times, which is known, and the difference between the two times, which is known, one can determine the momentum of the particle while it was in flight. Also, by straight-line extrapolation, one can determine its position at times between t_0 and the time it hit, t_1. So one can know its *simultaneous* position and velocity; however, this knowledge has no predictive value, since the velocity is disturbed in an unpredictable manner when the particle hits the screen at t_1.

For many years I rejected the minority view just described because it seemed to me that the argument (the 'time-of-flight' argument) offered in its defense imported too many assumptions from *classical* physics (e.g., that the particle has a straight-line *trajectory*). (Although it is undeniable that time-of-flight measurements of velocity are in fact made.) Then I observed that *it follows from just the quantum mechanical criterion for measurement itself* that the 'minority view' is right to at least the following extent: simultaneous measurements of incompatible observables *can* be made. That such measurements cannot have 'predictive value' is true, because a measurement of any observable must disturb that observable unpredictably, according to quantum mechanics, unless the Hamiltonian of the interaction between M and S (i.e., the operator corresponding in quantum mechanics to the Hamiltonian function of classical physics) stands in an appropriate mathematical relationship to the operator corresponding in quantum mechanics to the observable to be measured, and the operators corresponding to observables which do not 'commute' cannot *both* stand in the mathematical relationship in question to the Hamiltonian. Thus, a measurement which determined the values of two 'non-commuting' observables would have to disturb at least one of them, and so could have predictive value with respect to only one of the two observables.

It is wrong, however, to use this fact as a reason for *dismissing* measurements of 'non-commuting' observables, i.e., to think that measurements which disturb the value of the observable to be measured are of no scientific significance. Many measurements are made not to predict the future course of the system being examined, but to *test theories*; the system being examined is frequently *destroyed* in such experiments (so they certainly have no 'predictive value' in the sense described); but such experiments are of great scientific importance. (The two-slit experiment itself is one in which the particle being measured is destroyed by the experiment.)

Measurement of non-commuting observables

Since the possibility of measuring non-commuting observables is of great importance for the interpretation of *quantum logic*, about which I shall speak below (it clears up a problem which hung me up for nearly twenty years), I shall describe a case in which one can show – without appeal to 'time of flight', or any assumptions from classical physics – that incompatible propositions can be determined to be true.

Imagine a source of light inside an absorbing box. A very small shutter is opened at t_0 for a brief time. If a photon is emitted at t_0, then (since the space–time extent of the open shutter aperture is small) the position of the photon at t_0 is extremely definite. (Visualizing the photon as a wave bundle, one may say that the wave bundle is 'packet like', i.e., concentrated in a tiny region, at t_0.) One may arrange the intensity of the light source so that the probability that a photon is emitted during the brief interval that the shutter is open is exactly $\frac{1}{2}$. The state of the system at t_0 may, thus, be thought of as a superposition of two states: 'photon emitted at t_0' and 'no photon emitted at t_0'. Mathematically, we can represent it in the form:

$$\Psi_{M+S} = \frac{1}{\sqrt{2}} \, \Psi_{\text{photon emitted}} + \frac{1}{\sqrt{2}} \, \Psi_{\text{no photon emitted}}. \tag{2}$$

(The states are all represented in the Hilbert space of $M+S$, where M, the measuring apparatus, is described below. Strictly speaking there is an additional term of small amplitude corresponding to the possibility that *two or more photons* are emitted at t_0: we shall regard this as part of the 'slop' term that will appear in (1) anyway, when we apply the criterion (1) for measurement.)

In what follows I shall employ a conceptual trick due to Heisenberg; it is not essential to the argument, but it simplifies exposition. This is as follows: instead of saying that, in time evolution, the *state* changes, one can, alternatively, think of the state as staying the same, and the rule coordinating observables to states (i.e., determining the possible values of observables in states, the expectation values for the result of each measurement in a given state, etc.) as changing. This trick is known as 'Heisenberg representation'.

In Heisenberg representation, the form of the state Ψ_{M+S} does not change through the time evolution. (In the other, more conventional, representation, the states in the sum change, but the state of the system remains a sum of the two states, one of which arises from the case in which no photon was emitted.)

As a measuring device we shall employ a *spherical* emulsion, with the shutter at its center. Let t_1 be the time at which a photon emitted at t_0 will hit such an emulsion, if it is emitted at the center of the sphere.

The state $\Psi_{\text{no photon emitted}}$ in the expansion (2) corresponds to the situation at t_1 in which the emulsion is blank (no 'hits') and whatever photons were emitted by the light are still inside the absorbing box. The state $\Psi_{\text{photon emitted}}$ corresponds to a situation at t_1 in which there is a mark on the emulsion (a 'hit') at an uncertain place.

I propose to regard this experiment as a measurement to determine whether or not a photon is emitted at t_0. (We might, for example, want to test our prediction that a photon will be emitted half the time.) The registering observable is the presence or absence of a mark on the emulsion after t_1.

Notice that this is, in fact, how any physicist would regard this experiment. Of course, the presence of a mark at t_1 shows a photon was emitted at t_0 (I assume there is no other source of light). I am not making a 'proposal' here, but describing what the physicist actually does and the inferences he unhesitatingly makes.

A proposition, in the sense in which I am using the term (a statement to the effect that an observable has a value in a definite interval), can include such a statement as 'A photon was emitted at t_0'. (In fact, there is an 'idempotent', or two-valued, observable which has the value 1 if a photon was emitted at t_0, and 0 if no photon was emitted.) With this in mind, we see that the expansion (2) has the form (1): $\Psi_{\text{photon emitted}}$ is a *determinate state* at t_1 in which the observable being measured (whether or not a photon was emitted at t_0) has the value 1 and the registering observable (whether or not there is a mark on the emulsion) has the value 1, and $\Psi_{\text{no photon emitted}}$ is a determinate state at t_1 in which the observable being measured has the value 0 and the registering observable has the value 0. What

(2) says is that the state of the combined system $M + S$ is just a superposition of these two determinate states. By the quantum mechanical criterion for a measurement, it follows that we may view the situation at t_1 (when the mark has appeared or failed to appear on the emulsion; before t_1 the states are not determinate, because the registering observable does not have a value restricted to an interval excluding o in the state $\Psi_{\text{photon emitted}}$) as a *measurement*. If the mark is on the emulsion at t_1, then, in the perspective in which the 'cut' is between M and S, a photon was emitted at t_0; if no mark is on the emulsion at t_1, then no photon was emitted at t_0. And, as already emphasized, this is how any physicist would interpret the presence or absence of a mark on the emulsion at t_1. If one does *not* accept (2) as an instance of the quantum mechanical criterion for a measurement (1), then one cannot give any *quantum mechanical* reason for concluding from the fact that a photon hit the emulsion at t_1 that a photon was emitted at t_0.

But the state $\Psi_{\text{photon emitted}}$ is itself a superposition. The relevant superposition is easiest to see if we think about the situation at t_1. Divide the emulsion into disjoint tiny regions $R_1, \ldots, R_n$. The uncertainty concerning where the mark is at t_1 corresponds to the fact that $\Psi_{\text{photon emitted}}$ is itself a superposition of states Ψ_i in which the mark is inside the region R_i and the photon hit inside the region R_i. Mathematically:

$$\Psi_{\text{photon emitted}} = \sum_i c_i \Psi_i, \tag{3}$$

where the c_i are suitable complex numbers, and the i are as just described.

Substituting this expression in (2) we get:

$$\Psi_{M+S} = \sum_i c_i \Psi_i + \Psi_{\text{no photon emitted}}. \tag{4}$$

The expansion (4) *also* has the form (1); Ψ_i is a determinate state (if we think of ourselves as measuring the *position* of the impacting photon, if one struck). The registering observable is whether or not there is a mark on the photographic plate and which of the regions R_i the mark is in. In the state Ψ_i, the registering observable has a value in an interval which corresponds to there being a mark in R_i and the measured observable has a value which corresponds to the photon having hit in the region R_i. (4) says that the state Ψ_{M+S} may also be viewed as a superposition of determinate states in *this* way. If a mark is in the region R_i at t_1, then, in the perspective in which the 'cut' is between M and S, a photon hit in the region R_i at t_1; if no mark is in any of the regions R_i at t_1, then no photon struck the emulsion at t_1. And again, any physicist would accept *this* interpretation of the experiment.

If we view the experiment in the first way, then finding a mark on the photographic plate throws S into the state 'photon emitted at t_0' (i.e., S is in this state before its interaction with M); if we view the experiment in the second way, then finding a mark on the photographic plate in, say, the region R_{17}, throws S into the state 'photon at the position R_{17}' just before t_1. But these are incompatible states (as is easily seen from the Heisenberg representation in which they are just $\Psi_{\text{photon emitted}}$ and Ψ_{17}, respectively). (Strictly speaking, $\Psi_{\text{photon emitted}}$ and Ψ_{17} are states of $M + S$ and not of S alone; but they correspond to *incompatible mixed states* in the subspace of just S.)

One might propose to rule out the first way of viewing the experiment on the grounds that the macro-observable used (presence or absence of a mark on the emulsion) does not 'code' *all* the macroscopic information we have (we also know the *location* of the mark). But, besides being *ad hoc*, this leaves us with no way of knowing that a photon was emitted at t_0, which we clearly *do* know. There is nothing *wrong*, after all, with either interpretation of the experiment; all that is wrong is the orthodox remarks about it being impossible to measure incompatible observables in quantum mechanics.

Instead of using the Heisenberg representation, in which the states stay the same and the observables change their representation, we can also use the conventional representation, in which the states change. In this representation, the statement that a photon was emitted at t_0 does not correspond to the statement that the state is $\Psi_{\text{photon emitted}}$ at t_1, but rather to the statement that the state at t_1 is $U(\Psi_{\text{photon emitted}})$, where U is a certain unitary transformation. But $U(\Psi_{\text{photon emitted}})$ and $U(\Psi_{17})$ (this corresponds to a photon striking in the region R_{17}) are incompatible states in the conventional representation, since a unitary transformation preserves all relations of incompatibility.

We have written as if a measurement performed by M upon S throws S into a definite state of the observable measured *just before* the interaction; but this is not essential for our discussion. All that matters is that the two observables, *photon emitted at t_0*, and *photon located at the position R_{17} at t_1* are incompatible by the criteria of incompatibility standardly used in quantum mechanics. And one and the same experiment can determine both of these incompatible propositions to be true.

It is, of course, perfectly correct that no *state* can assign the definite value 1 (or 'true') to both of these propositions. There is no state in which both of these propositions have the probability 1. But it does not follow, as is usually thought, that no *measurement* can assign truth to both of these propositions; the error lies in supposing that a measurement can throw a system into only one state. *Relative to a particular way of analyzing an experiment*, the experiment can throw S into only one state; but an experiment may admit of more than one analysis at the same time.

In my view, this extends rather than conflicts with the perspectival character of quantum mechanics so stressed by von Neumann. We had a case before (the ensemble of Schrödinger cat systems) in which the 'inside' observer (the cat) assigned one state ($\Psi_{\text{live cat}}$) and the 'outside' observer assigned a different state

$$\frac{1}{\sqrt{2}}\,\Psi_{\text{live cat}} + \frac{1}{\sqrt{2}}\,\Psi_{\text{dead cat}}.$$

This was the case in which the outside observer measured O.

If the outside observer chooses *not* to measure O, but rather to open the satellite at some time after the pre-set time and see if the cat is alive or dead, then he does not have to view the system as 'jumping' from $(1/\sqrt{2})\,\Psi_{\text{live cat}} + (1/\sqrt{2})\,\Psi_{\text{dead cat}}$ into either *live cat* or *dead cat* when he looks (this is the interpretation that so distressed Einstein, in our conversation); rather, he can view the so-called 'quantum jump' as not a *physical* jump at all, but simply another expression of the relativity of truth to the observer which it was von Neumann's concern to advocate. When we choose to measure the 'mortality condition' of the cat (*alive* or *dead*), we choose to institute a frame *relative to which* the cat *has* a determinate property of being alive or a determinate property of being dead *and the measurement finds out which*; we are, so to speak, 'realists' *about the property we measure*; but we are not committed to realism about properties *incompatible* with the ones we measure. Relative to *this* observer *these* properties are 'real' (i.e., there to be discovered); but relative to a different observer different properties would be 'real'. There is no 'absolute' point of view.

What made it seem as if there was a *physical* 'jump' was the idea that we could not *retrodict* and say that the cat was alive before our looking. And it looked as if we could not say this because this would *conflict* with the assumption that before our looking the satellite was in the condition we prepared, which was (by hypothesis) $(1/\sqrt{2})\,\Psi_{\text{live cat}} + (1/\sqrt{2})\,\Psi_{\text{dead cat}}$. But if a system can have more than one state at a time relative to the same observer (provided only one has predictive value), then this argument collapses, and, indeed, the retrodiction that the cat was alive *before* we looked is just as correct as the retrodiction that a photon was emitted at t_0.

Quantum logic

Von Neumann's book also contains the first hint of his idea of interpreting quantum mechanics with the aid of a non-standard logic (see also von Neumann & Birkhoff, 1936). Apparently he did not regard this as incompatible with the perspectival view I have been stressing; but it is my purpose to explore this connection beyond the brief hint he gives in the book. (This is the remark that quantum logic has to do with the fact that propositions may not be *simultaneously* testable.)

The logic von Neumann proposes is based on orthomodular lattices (the ones of physical interest are isomorphic to the lattice of subspaces of the Hilbert space of the system being talked about).

I shall not give any technical details in the present paper. The key idea, in a contemporary formulation (see, e.g., Bub, 1974) is that one is not allowed to conjoin 'non-commuting' propositions. (Von Neumann himself did allow one to conjoin them, but treated all such conjunctions as identically false, i.e., like conjunctions of propositions whose incompatibility is Boolean. Today it seems more perspicuous to treat conjunctions of 'non-commuting' propositions as not even well formed.)

Perhaps the best way to think of quantum logic is this: in quantum logic, the rule of conjunction-introduction (from p, q to infer the conjunction $p \& q$) is restricted to *compatible* propositions p and q.

In my example in the previous section, the two statements 'The photon was emitted at t_0' and 'The photon struck in the region R_{17}' are statements that have no conjunction. The two statements cannot be conjoined without violating the restrictions of quantum logic.

To recapitulate: in quantum logic there is a new semantical relation of *incompatibility* (over and above the classical notion of incompatibility, 'p entails not-q'). One is not allowed to conjoin propositions which stand in this semantical relation to each other. The problem is, evidently: how is this relation, the quantum-mechanical relation of incompatibility, to be understood?

When I wrote 'The logic of quantum mechanics' (1968), I shared von Neumann's view that incompatible propositions *cannot be known to be true* (by the same observer). In view of the example, this is wrong. If p is 'The photon was emitted at t_0' and q is 'The photon struck in the region R_{17}', then I can know both of them to be true; but within quantum logic there is no way I can conjoin those two pieces of information. What that *means* we shall discuss shortly. But it doesn't mean what I once thought it meant.

What I once thought it meant was based on the orthodox view that one cannot measure non-commuting observables at the same time. What turns out to be the case is that one can know that p and one can know that q (where p and q are the two statements in the example) but one is not allowed to have *a single text* in which one says both p and q.

What this means, of course, is that one is renouncing a certain cognitive ideal. The ideal is that one should be able to visualize knowledge, or, at any rate, *ideal* knowledge, as one text. (Ignoring error, ignoring the fact that people make mistakes:) all the things that anyone knows anywhere should just be able to be conjoined.

So far we have two failures of this: there is the original failure pointed out by von Neumann, which I explained in terms of the population of Schrödinger cats; the statements by the cats (think of a milder version than Schrödinger's, in which the cats are not killed, but only tickled) and the statement by the outside observer who measures O cannot be conjoined; and in the case of the consequence that I pointed out of the quantum mechanical definition of measurement, two statements known to be true by one observer at one time cannot be conjoined.

Well, what *does* it mean that these two statements are incompatible if they can both be known to be true by one observer at one time? What, for that matter, is the interpretation of the uncertainty principle?

It does turn out, as we have already mentioned, that when one has two pieces of knowledge which 'violate the uncertainty principle' in this way – or one has one interaction which can be read as a measurement in two ways, so that the two resulting pieces of knowledge cannot be conjoined – that they cannot both have predictive value.

But, as I pointed out above, many measurements in quantum mechanics have 'no predictive value' in this sense: one doesn't know anything about the photon, or whatever, henceforth, because it is destroyed in the interaction. But, as I also pointed out, such measurements should not be dismissed; they are of great importance in physics.

So we have this situation: we can make measurements of non-commuting observables, but at least one of those measurements has no future value as far as that very system is concerned.

I have also mentioned how we represent this fact in quantum logic: we allow ourselves to conjoin statements that lie in a common Boolean sublogic of the whole big quantum logic (that is what 'commuting' comes to, in logical terms), but not to conjoin statements that do not lie in any common Boolean sublogic. So we get a *lot* of texts. Even one observer may have a lot of texts. Only one of those texts at any given time will have predictive value (i.e., *direct* predictive value, predictive value about the objects upon which he performed the measurements). Other texts may have predictive value for other observers.

So far I have only said that we do not *allow* the conjunction of certain statements in quantum logic. Is that just a perversity? Is it just that we have an idiosyncratic preference for writing p, q in certain cases and not p & q (pq for short)? Perhaps we just don't like the word 'and'?

In effect, not allowing ourselves to conjoin all the statements we know to be true means that we have what amount to two different kinds of conjunction: one amounts to asserting statements in two different 'frames', as I shall call them (different Boolean sublogics); and the other, for which we reserve the *and*-sign, is conjunction of statements which lie in a common frame. Well, what is this ceremony for?

The fact that this isn't a classical logic because we *don't* allow all the statements that we know (or that anyone knows, or could know) to be conjoined doesn't show that this couldn't be *embedded* in a classical logic. But the question of whether this could be embedded in a classical logic was closed some years ago by Kochen and Specker (1967). (See pp. 49–51 above for details.)

We recall that the example of Kochen and Specker involved formulas
$$(\bar{p}_{i(1)}p_{i(2)}p_{i(3)} \vee p_{i(1)}\bar{p}_{i(2)}p_{i(3)} \vee p_{i(1)}p_{i(2)}\bar{p}_{i(3)})$$
which assert that exactly one of the squared spin components in the directions $i(1)$, $i(2)$, $i(3)$ is a one and the other two are zeroes (for $i = 1$, 2, ..., 63). The conjunction of all sixty-three of these formulas is contradictory in classical propositional calculus.

Quantum logic itself has been interpreted both in verificationist and in 'realist' ways by different authors. The interpretation which is ruled out is to think of quantum logic as a fragment of classical logic. Quantum logic is *essentially* non-classical. Each of the statements
$$(\bar{p}_{i(1)}p_{i(2)}p_{i(3)} \vee p_{i(1)}\bar{p}_{i(2)}p_{i(3)} \vee p_{i(1)}p_{i(2)}\bar{p}_{i(3)})$$
is true in the case described by Kochen and Specker, and their conjunction is likewise true (since the statements are compatible, it

is legitimate to conjoin them); but the *distributed* form of this conjunction is a contradiction! Something which is a contradiction in classical logic is true in the quantum-mechanical universe, namely, the above conjunction in its undistributed form.

The interpretation of quantum logic which I now favor is a 'verificationist' one but not an 'operationist' one.† The notion of *correctness* (idealized verification) in the logic on this interpretation is this: a statement is correct if it is verified by a measurement in the sense explained above (idealizing so that we can make perfect measurements and so on). More precisely: a statement is verified by performing a measurement in which one of the determinate states lies in the subspace corresponding to the statement, under the canonical correspondence between propositions and subspaces of the Hilbert space provided by the von Neumann theory and observing a value of the registering observable that lies in the interval corresponding to that same determinate state. Notice how this differs from the 'verificationism' associated with *intuitionist* logic. In that 'verificationism', the correctness of a compound statement is a function of the correctness of its parts in the case of disjunctions and conjunctions (though not of implications); in the 'verificationist' interpretation of quantum logic, we specify a test condition for a disjunction as a whole in such a way that a disjunction may be correct even though neither disjunct is correct‡ (for the relevant observer at the relevant time).

---

† The use of the word 'verificationism' here is in opposition to the use I made of this word in Putnam (1975*d*, *e*) where it was virtually synonymous with *operationism*. Since the appearance of those volumes, Michael Dummett has convinced me that one may hold the theory that truth is (an idealization of) justification without being committed to the view that statements about sense data are more basic than statements about material objects, and without being committed to reductionism of any kind. Indeed, as Dummett points out, reductionists only renounce the correspondence theory of truth for the statements they want to *reduce*; for statements in the *reducing* class they typically retain the views that (1) truth and justification are independent; (2) that truth is determinate and bivalent; (3) that there is, in the ideal limit anyway, just *one* true and complete description. In short, *reductionism is a form of subjective idealism* (when the reducing class is the class of sense datum statements); whereas the 'verificationism' or 'non-realism' espoused by Dummett and myself does not deny the reality of any of the objects of scientific or ordinary discourse, or construe some of these objects as constructions out of others, but consists rather in a renunciation of these three assumptions about truth itself. If there is a species of idealism here, it is a 'transcendental' idealism and not a subjective idealism.

‡ This comes about because a state may be such that all possible values of a magnitude lie in either the interval D_1 or the interval D_2 although they do not all lie in D_1 or all lie in D_2. This happens whenever the vector representing the state lies in the span of the subspaces of the Hilbert space representing the statements 'the value of M lies in D_1' and 'the value of M lies in D_2'. It is because the span of two subspaces is not their set-theoretic union that there can be states in which a disjunction is 'correct' but neither disjunct is 'correct'.

Two statements are *incompatible* in quantum logic if no state is a determinate state which lies in the subspace corresponding to each or, more simply, if these two subspaces are disjoint. As pointed out above this means that no one measurement can verify both statements *under the same analysis of the measurement* (choice of a registering observable and of a correlation between values of the registering observable and values of the observable to be measured). Thus, in the case of conjunctions, there is a difference between verifying *each* conjunct and verifying the conjunction, which explains the fact that one can sometimes know incompatible propositions even though one has not 'verified' their conjunction in the sense just explained. As mentioned previously, the decision not to conjoin statements which are incompatible is a way of making the distinction *in the logic itself* between cases in which both of the statements we know have predictive value and cases in which only one of the statements has predictive value after the measurement.

On this interpretation, quantum logic gives rise to an interpretation of quantum mechanics which resembles one version of the highly ambiguous 'Copenhagen interpretation'.

Michael Gardner (1971)† has argued that one should not bother with quantum logic, or, indeed, with any of the other proposed interpretations of quantum mechanics, but one should just stick to what he calls 'the minimal statistical interpretation'. That amounts to saying, quantum mechanics just gives one the results of various measurements. It says nothing about how observables behave when we don't measure.

The interpretation of quantum logic and of quantum mechanics itself that I am proposing differs from this 'minimal statistical interpretation', and from the Copenhagen interpretation (if that can be distinguished from the minimal statistical interpretation) in several ways. First of all, I now believe that the only notion of truth that makes coherent sense is the so-called 'non-realist' view that sees truth as an idealization of rational acceptability, rather than as 'correspondence to reality', where correspondence is thought of as a *non-epistemic* relation (which is why whether a statement could be justified and whether it is true are regarded as *independent* questions

† On pp. 523–25 Gardner pointed out that the resolution of the paradoxes I offered in Putnam (1968) doesn't work precisely for the reason that the statement that a particle has a definite position at t_0 is incompatible with the statement that it has a definite position at t_1 ('for any non-trivial source'). The present interpretation overcomes Gardner's objection by allowing one to *know* both of these statements without *conjoining* them. The two-slit paradox is now explained by the non-classical character of the conditional probability, which in turn is connected with the logic (Putnam & Friedman, 1978).

by metaphysical realists). On a 'non-realist' view, it is not unnatural, I think, to regard it as a deeply important question whether the verification of one statement never in principle precludes the verification of another (as was believed in Newtonian physics), or whether, on the other hand, the world is such that to verify one statement sometimes makes it impossible in principle to perform the experiment that would verify or falsify another (or makes it impossible to perform such an experiment without bringing it about that one or the other statement ceases to have any predictive import).

Someone who feels that truth should be linked to *verifiability* (or at least to idealized verifiability), might well be led on *a priori* grounds to consider quantum logic once he realized propositions might be 'incompatible' in the sense just described. I don't mean that this is the only way in which one can be led to consider or even accept quantum logic; and it is empirical that there is such a relation of incompatibility in our world. But this illustrates the fact that even if we decide to accept quantum logic, we might be led to do so partly for *a priori* reasons.

In contrast, advocates of the Copenhagen interpretation have always insisted upon classical logic. (I have seen a transcript of a discussion between von Neumann and Bohr in which Bohr said, 'But the whole point of the Copenhagen Interpretation was to avoid changing the logic.') This is what makes the Copenhagen interpretation so peculiar; on the one hand, the whole thrust is 'don't talk about unmeasured phenomena'; on the other hand, the Copenhagen interpretation *requires* a distinction between measured values and unmeasured phenomena, because classical logic is retained. This means that the Copenhagen theorist *has* to talk about unmeasured phenomena, if only to say, 'we can't conceive them with our classical minds'.

Secondly, the minimal statistical interpretation, and likewise the Copenhagen interpretation, take measurements to yield information only about *present* values. Since they do not envisage or allow our 'quantum-mechanical time-of-flight' argument, they cannot say when the photon hits the screen that it must have succeeded in getting through the opening when the shutter was open at t_0. But then it seems that many inferences that physicists do make (e.g., in determining *velocities* of particles from the locations of successive *collisions* in a cloud chamber) cannot be accounted for at all. By broadening the notion of 'measurement', I hope to have allowed and justified the practice of retrodicting past values from later data. This also allows us to regard observables we measure as having had values just *before* the measurement, and to say that the measurement *discovered* the value instead of *creating* it; although, as remarked above, the 'quantum jump' reappears as a relativity of what is 'real' in this sense to the particular observer or frame.

Thirdly, whereas the Copenhagen interpretation and the minimal statistical interpretation seem to assume an operationalist view (according to which one doesn't need quantum mechanics, but only the so-called 'pre-theories', to say what a measurement is), the interpretation I propose *loops back*: quantum mechanics is interpreted with the aid of the notion of measurement, and if one asks 'what is a measurement?' the answer is given by quantum mechanics. One has to understand the theory in terms of verification, and one has to understand verification in terms of the theory.

The metaphysical realist interpretation of quantum logic, which I would no longer defend because I would no longer defend metaphysical realism, says, 'No, this isn't a theory about measurement. This is a theory about what is true and false.' I don't know how to account for the new relation of incompatibility on such a view, but I'm sure some metaphysical realist could find a way. 'You just live in an Escher world', the metaphysical realist might say, 'a world in which, because we have Boolean minds – i.e., the representations in our minds or on paper are themselves a commuting family of observables – we cannot possibly know how all the partial truths which Boolean minds can know can possibly fit together.'

Although the interpretation I have proposed is not realistic in the sense of assuming a copy theory of truth (metaphysical realism), or even in the sense of assuming that all observables have determinate values, it is *internally* realistiç in the sense that *within the interpretation* no distinction appears between 'measured values' and 'unmeasured values'. Even if one interprets the logic in a verificationist way, that does not mean that one takes the theory to be *about* measurements. What discourse is about is a different question from whether the concept of truth associated with that discourse is realist or non-realist. I think that I am here in agreement with the theses of Professor Süssmann, especially with theses (6) and (8) which affirm that the micro-entities spoken of in quantum mechanics are as 'real' as any entities knowable by us ('Quantum mechanics is the universal ontology'), while rejecting 'Einstein's idea of the detached observer'. There are real entities; *but which they are is relative to the observer*.

If one does not wish to stick one's neck out on such difficult and paradoxical questions, however, then it seems to me that the safest position is *not* the 'minimal statistical interpretation', but one I might call the *minimal quantum-logical interpretation*. This would be to accept quantum mechanics as reconstructed within quantum logic at face value while pushing the whole dispute about 'metaphysical realism' back to *philosophy*. It is possible to have either a realist or a non-realist conception of truth in classical physics too; if either conception is untenable, it is for philosophical, not physical, reasons.

15

Vagueness and alternative logic

Logic and metaphysics

Michael Dummett (1975) has argued that logic and metaphysics are intimately connected. While Dummett's arguments are based upon considerations from the philosophy of language, rather than upon the actual history of logic and metaphysics, I believe that the history of these subjects suggests that Dummett is right. G. E. L. Owen has pointed out† that the notion of a 'property' was neither an evident nor a simple one for either Aristotle or Plato. We can say of a man that he is a 'white man'; but if we ask whether the man is white *in the way* that a white wall is white, we shall have to answer 'no'. What 'white' *is* is not specified, Aristotle thought, until we say what sort of thing we are predicating it of, taking as the standard, or whatever. But what if the term we use to answer *this* question has the same relativity?

(Modern logic teachers would probably tell their students: 'in Logic we assume – or pretend – that all terms have somehow been made precise'. According to Owen, Aristotle – and even Plato – worried about this pretense. Is it a pretense that we have done something that we – or some conceivable cognitive extension of ourselves – could in principle do? Or a pretense that we have done a 'we know not what it would be like'? And who is truly more sophisticated: the modern logic teacher, for whom this is no problem, or the founders of the subject?)

Even the schema $\sim(Px \ \& \sim Px)$ becomes problematic if this relativity cannot somehow be avoided when we wish. Aristotle thought (this is the burden of Owen's interpretation) that this relativity does not arise when P is a *substance* term: something is not at the same time (fully) a man and not (fully) a man; nor is something (fully) a man *in a respect*; the being of substances is not *relative* in Aristotle's metaphysics. So substance terms – man, rabbit – can be used to pin down the respects in which predicates which do display relativity of signification are predicated in given contexts. (So, I

† I am reporting a lecture Owen gave at Harvard in 1980 entitled 'Negation and the origins of logic'.

271

suppose, can genus terms: 'tall for a Greek'; but I imagine that Aristotle would reply that genera are dependent on substances.) Thus (if Owen is right) we get at the very beginning of logic, a metaphysics accompanying it and conditioning it. In time the picture of substances and their predicates became the standard metaphysical picture of a world of fully determinate particulars characterized by their fully determinate properties. (This picture Aristotle himself resisted, however; consider, for example, his well-known doubts about the principle of bivalence for contingent statements about the future.)

Dummett uses the term 'realism' for a view which:

(1) assumes a world consisting of a definite totality of discourse-independent objects and properties;
(2) assumes 'strong bivalence', i.e., that an object either determinately has or determinately lacks any property P which may significantly be predicated of that object; and
(3) assumes the correspondence theory of truth in a strong realist sense of 'correspondence': i.e., a predicate corresponds to a unique set of objects, and a statement corresponds to a unique state of affairs, involving the properties and objects mentioned in (1), and is true if that state of affairs obtains and false if it does not obtain.

Dummett contends that the principle of bivalence ($p \lor \sim p$) seems evident because it reflects the fundamental assumptions we have made about states of affairs.

What happens when metaphysical realism becomes dubious? Philosophers who reject metaphysical realism (Kant, Peirce, and in the present period, Dummett, Goodman, and myself, to name just a few 'specimens') typically argue for a conception of truth as (idealized) justification or rational acceptability. (Kant does speak of 'correspondence of the judgment to its object', but by the 'object' he means the object for us, and this belongs to 'appearance'. This is more like what Goodman calls 'fit' than it is like the metaphysical realist notion of correspondence to a mind-independent world.) But very roughly, and without explanation, a statement is true if it could be justified, on the non-realist view. Brouwer saw a consequence of this that Kant would probably have found most unwelcome: *it is not at all evident that bivalence is correct on such a view of truth* (see Dummett, 1977). For many values of p, we simply do not know if it is the case that either p could be justified or $\sim p$ could be justified. ($p \lor \sim p$) (understood, as Dummett says, as asserting that p is either determinately true or determinately false) is hardly a 'tautology', on this notion of truth, which is why Brouwer gave it up in intuitionist logic.

Today we know that there is more than one possible logic based on a 'non-realist' view of truth,† but the philosophical point stands: if the metaphysical picture that grew up with and conditioned classical logic is wrong, then some of the 'tautologies' of classical logic may have to be given up.

Vagueness

Metaphysical realists do not appear to recognize just how puzzling vagueness is (or should be) on their view. To spell this out: assume a definite totality T of all states of affairs. Assume a relation R (the metaphysically singled-out relation of *correspondence*) such that a sentence is true if and only if the sentence (as used on the particular occasion) corresponds under R to a member of the totality T which actually obtains. *States of affairs* are, of course, to be thought of as non-mental non-linguistic entities which determinately obtain or do not obtain no matter what we think or say. Now, in the definition:

S *is true* if and only if $(\exists X)$ (X *belongs* to T. $R(S, X)$. X *obtains*) *only non-vague terms appear on the right*. R, recall, is a relation ('correspondence') between sentences (including, if you like, sentences and sentence-analogs 'in the mind') and objects, and thus belongs itself to the realm of *objects*. An object *does or does not* bear a relation (another, higher type, sort of object) to an object (e.g., a state of affairs); there is no such thing as an object's 'vaguely' bearing a relation to another object, on this picture. On the metaphysical realist view there are vague conceptions, vague ways of talking, but not vague *objects*. T is a set of states of affairs; these are, again, part of the realm of objects, and so determinate. A member of T does or does not stand in the converse of the relation R to a sentence S, and a member of T obtains or it doesn't. So there is a 'fact of the matter' as to whether a sentence S is true or not, which is just what sometimes fails to be the case with vague sentences!

Remark 1. There are a number of possibilities we could discuss here. For example, S (a vague sentence) might bear R to more than *one* member of T, even as S is used in a particular context. (This would be the case with *ambiguity*.) Secondly, one of these states of affairs

---

† In fact, *classical* logic is compatible with a non-realist view of truth, on some interpretations of the connectives (and of the speech act of assertion). See Putnam (1978, Part I, Lectures II and III) and chapter 14 of this volume.

may obtain and at least one may fail to obtain. (If all the states of affairs to which S bears R obtain, then S is clearly true, in spite of the ambiguity and, if they all fail to obtain, then S is clearly false.) This possibility calls for a suitable convention – say, saying that S is neither true nor false in this case – which would involve complicating the definition given above, but this would not affect the point just made.

Remark 2. If the so-called 'convention (T)' is correct for natural language (on a suitable, say Davidsonian, analysis of natural language), and
      'John is bald' is true if and only if John is bald
then 'true' itself must be as vague as 'bald' (as Davidson has pointed out). If metaphysical realism is right, we have just seen that truth *cannot* be vague. So one should not be a metaphysical realist *and* accept the convention (T) for vague sentences.

In fact, however, almost† no philosopher I know of (realist or not) does maintain that there is a *determinate* boundary between true sentences and sentences which are not true (either false, or neither true nor false) when those sentences contain vague predicates such as 'bald', 'heap', etc. So something seems to be wrong with metaphysical realism.

The 'what me worry' response

Quine has suggested that it really doesn't matter if ordinary language is vague (or even locally inconsistent), as long as we can think of ourselves as approximating a scientific language which is free of these defects. Thus, 'Ordinary language is only loosely referential, and any ontological accounting makes sense only relative to an appropriate regimentation of language. The regimentation is not a matter of eliciting some latent but determinate content of ordinary language. It is a matter rather of freely creating an ontology-oriented language that can supplant ordinary language in serving some particular purpose one has in mind.' (Quine, 1977, p. 195)

In Quine's view, statements in ordinary language *aren't* true or false; they are only true or false relative to a translation scheme (or 'regimentation') which maps ordinary language onto an ideal language, and there is no fact of the matter as to which is the 'right'

† See, however, Israel Scheffler, *Beyond the Letter*, London, Routledge and Kegan Paul, 1979. Scheffler urges us to 'hold fast to classical logic' and reject the very possibility of 'semantic indecision'. Such a course seems to me heroic but misguided.

translation. 'Ordinary language is only loosely factual, and needs to be variously regimented when our purpose is scientific understanding. The regimentation is again not a matter of eliciting a latent content. It is again a free creation.' (Ibid., pp. 191–2)

On such a view, all we are normally doing when we talk is making *noises*. (But why isn't it the case, on Quine's view, that even if we were to employ the 'regimented language', the only sense in which some of our sentences would be 'true' is that they would be elicited from scientists by certain stimuli?) Quine's view abandons the idea that our utterances are *about* something more than I am able to find coherent; but this is not a lecture about Quine. What Quine's view does bring into high relief is the problem with a very standard move: the move of saying that it is all right if there is no determinate truth or falsity in ordinary language, because we could 'in principle' rationally reconstruct ordinary language, i.e., replace it by an ideal language. (The 'what me worry' move.)

This move amounts to saying that sentences in ordinary language are true or false *relative to* translations (or 'reconstructions') into the ideal language. And Quine sees and faces the problem (even if his solution is one I find unacceptable): the problem of the status of the translation itself.

To spell this out: if the translation is 'reasonable', is *this notion* 'reasonable' *itself a notion in the ideal language or only a notion in ordinary language*? If the latter, then we have answered the challenge, 'In what sense can a sentence which employs vague notions be *true*?' with an answer which uses a vague notion. The problem is similar to the problem of avoiding 'relative' notions – notions which change their signification as the context changes – that Aristotle and Plato faced at the beginning of the subject; but they at least saw that replacing one unstable relative notion by another would be no solution.

Of course, if one is not a metaphysical realist; if one thinks that language which is 'vague' in the sense of not having the unimaginable precision that the realist's ideal language would have, can be philosophically, ontologically and metaphysically kosher; then one may throw the challenge back with the counterchallenge: 'Why *should* it be possible to account for ordinary language in a perfectly precise language?' This is, indeed, the stance I would myself take. Since I don't think that *any* objects are totally mind-independent (or theory-independent), I would add that, on my view, *objects* and *properties* are, in general, vague too. Or, as Michael Dummett (1979*b*) has put it, 'One cannot give a complete description of the world in terms of hard facts alone.' But vague facts and vague properties are *not* ontologically kosher for a metaphysical realist. He cannot ignore the challenge.

A little reflection will convince one that the problem is serious (if one is a metaphysical realist). Thus, (i) if 'reasonable' refers to a bivalent notion, then there is an acceptability predicate for ordinary language, namely, *true under at least one reasonable translation scheme*, which is also bivalent. (ii) If 'reasonable' refers to a *definite set* of bivalent notions, then there is again a bivalent acceptability predicate for ordinary language, namely, *true under at least one translation which has at least one of the kinds of reasonableness in the set*. (iii) If 'reasonable' refers to a bivalent *comparative* notion, then we can define a qualitative notion: *more reasonable than not* in terms of it, and argue as under (i). (If it refers to a definite set of comparative bivalent notions, we form the corresponding qualitative notions and argue as under (ii), of course.) (iv) If the metaphysical realist says that 'reasonable' does not *now* refer (in the sense of the 'correspondence' *R*) to any definite set of metaphysically real properties or relations, but 'it could be identified with one', then we should ask: 'Do you mean it could *reasonably* be identified with one? And in what sense of "reasonably"?'

The response of Unger and Wheeler

Unger and Wheeler have tackled cases like the following (which were originally employed by Max Black in his writings on vagueness). We take a chair apart one molecule at a time. (Fix a particular order for the sake of definiteness. As Rohit Parikh pointed out in the discussion of the present paper when it was read before the Boston Logic Colloquium, instead of taking away one molecule at a time, taking away a piece just below the visible threshold in size, would make the same point and would be technically feasible.) Is there a definite *N* such that when I have taken *N* molecules (or minute pieces) away the object is still a chair, but such that after I have taken *N* + 1 it is false (or neither true nor false) that it is a chair? (One might also ask, is there a definite *N* such that it is *more reasonable than not* to say the object is a chair when I have taken *N*, but not when have taken *N* + 1 molecules away?) They argue (correctly) that there is no such *N*. But, instead of abandoning metaphysical realism, they conclude that 'chair' is an *inconsistent notion* and hence that *there are no chairs*. In effect, they take the position that all atomic sentences which contain 'vague' (not *perfectly* precise) predicates are *false* (see Unger, 1979; Wheeler, 1975, 1979).

This position is incoherent. For one thing, the very language used to state it abounds in vague predicates ('analytic', 'self-contradictory notion', for that matter 'sentence' and 'word' themselves). For another, if ordinary language lacks significant truth, then why is the language of science, or any theory stated in that language, better off? Such terms as 'electron', 'charge', and 'mass' have themselves a certain vagueness. And even if they did not, why should we *accept* any theory which contains these terms? Because the theory is a good *explanation* of certain *phenomena*? But (on the Unger/Wheeler view) there are no 'explanations' and no 'phenomena'! ('Explanation' and 'phenomenon' are vague words too.) If ordinary language cannot be used to say anything significant, then it cannot be used to invent or justify a *better* language.

My concern in this paper is not with Unger's view or Wheeler's views, however. Unger and Wheeler are to be commended for this: they have seen how difficult it is to give a metaphysical realist account of vagueness. The heroic lengths to which they are prepared to go dramatize the problem.

Truth, vagueness and disquotation

My primary concern is with vagueness as a problem for metaphysical realists, but it may be helpful to glance aside at the responses of philosophers who reject one or another of the assumptions of metaphysical realism. Donald Davidson, for example, would reject the picture of truth as defined in terms of a single, antecedently-singled-out, relation of correspondence. Truth can be formally defined in terms of a correspondence relation (satisfaction) and, in a meaning theory for a language, truth conditions for sentences must be recursively specified by a procedure which exactly resembles a 'truth definition' (Davidson, 1967). But *philosophically* it is correspondence that depends on truth, and not vice versa. That is, according to Davidson, there is no single relation of 'reference' or 'correspondence' between words and things.† Rather, *any* relation (with the right formal properties) which enables us to recursively characterize truth in such a way that the correct truth conditions are forthcoming for whole sentences is admissible. (There are infinitely many such relations.)‡ Not only is truth philosophically prior to correspondence; truth, Davidson emphasizes, cannot help but be a vague notion (when there are vague terms in the language).

† See Davidson's remarks on the 'empty reference theory' at the Storrs colloquium (printed in *Synthese*, vol. 27, 1974).
‡ For a formal proof, see the appendix to Putnam (1981).

Correspondence, being implicitly defined (non-uniquely) in terms of truth, is then likewise a vague notion. We are not, Davidson has said (in conversation), going to say everything we want to say without using vague language. Coupled with Davidson's repeated claim that the idea of comparing a conceptual system and the world is senseless, this amounts to a total rejection of the assumptions (a ready-made world with a wholly precise structure and a determinate relation of correspondence) which make vagueness a problem for a certain traditional kind of realism.

Another, and still more radical, way of rejecting the assumptions which give rise to the problem is to adopt a disquotational view of truth. On such a view, 'is true' does not ascribe a *property* to a sentence; rather 'is true' is to be thought of as a syncategorematic expression which we use in such a way that an arbitrary sentence of the form '*S*' *is true* is equivalent to the corresponding quoted sentence *S*, or, in a generalization of this theory, to the translation of *S* in the language of the speaker. '*Snow is white*' *is true* is just another way of saying *Snow is white* on such a theory. Although there has been much confusion on this point, such a theory is *incompatible* with Davidson's view. On Davidson's view, truth is a 'substantial' notion; i.e., truth is a property which sentences have or lack depending on two things: what they mean and how the world is. '"Snow is white" is true if and only if snow is white' states that the sentence 'Snow is white' has the property of truth (and this is the property with respect to which speakers and hearers usually evaluate statements) just in case snow is white, and this is a significant fact about the way this sentence is used in English. In contrast, '"Snow is white" is true if and only if snow is white' only says that *snow is white if and only if snow is white*, if the disquotational view is right.

It may seem strange that vagueness is a problem for Quine, since Quine appears to accept a disquotational account of truth. However, Quine operates with *two* notions, not one: the notion of truth and the notion of *fact*.

According to Quine, we have an evolving notion of what is and is not a 'fact'. Today the only reasonable view is that what is a fact is just what can be expressed in the language of an ideal *physics*. In that language, bivalence is true in much the sense a metaphysical realist thinks it is: i.e., when I say $S \lor \sim S$, I mean that either S is a *fact* or that $\sim S$ is a *fact* (see Quine, 1981). Anything expressed in ordinary, non-ideal, language is only true or false *relative to* a translation into the language of physics. In effect, Quine accepts a fundamental asymmetry between his own (ideal) language and any other language, ideal or not; with respect to his own (ideal) language he is a 'robust realist'; with respect to any other language, a sort of Machian positivist. The disquotational account of truth is 'transparent' in the case of my own language, Quine says.

Philosophers who accept a disquotational account of truth still owe us an account of what a speaker's understanding of his language consists in. If they say, with Quine, that it consists in a schedule of conditioning, then they leave us puzzled as to how there can be any normative notions of *rightness* and *wrongness* connected with language. If they say, as is more usual, that it consists in a mastery of justification procedures, then they owe us an account of these. It is not clear either that justification procedures *can* be associated with all the sentences of a language in a recursive way,† or that a *single* justification procedure can be given for a typical sentence (say 'There is a chair in my office'), mastery of which is either necessary or sufficient for understanding the sentence.

Moreover, even if the use of a language could be described in terms of the notion of justification (confirmation/infirmation, in the case of empirical sentences), such a description would appear to suffer from a fundamental kind of incompleteness. Such a theory tells us of one way in which the sentence 'It will snow next year' can be (normatively) *right*: namely, it can be confirmed (relative to the present experience and memories of a speaker); but this is not what it is for the sentence to be right in the sense of being *true*. To give an account of the language without mentioning truth and then to add 'Oh, by the way, to say a sentence *S* is true is just to reaffirm *S*' is not to *provide us with any substantial notion of rightness which was not previously used in that account*. If the only notion of rightness used in the account is the notion of a kind of rightness (high degree of confirmation) which depends on my *present* memories and experiences, and not on what happens in the future, then telling me that to say, '"It will snow next year" is true' is to reaffirm 'It will snow next year', will inform me that whatever kind of rightness (degree of confirmation/infirmation) is possessed by 'It will snow next year' is also possessed by '"It will snow next year" is true'; but it will not tell me any more than this. If I view my utterances as noises which are to be appraised at each instant for some kind of rightness and wrongness which depends *only* on my experiences and memories at

† For example, no one has found a way to assign probabilities to *state descriptions* in a way that yields a successful inductive logic. (Carnap tried to do this for the last 20 years of his life.)

279

that instant, then I am perilously close to being a solipsist of the present instant.

I am not arguing that we have to go back to metaphysical realism after all. In my view, truth is idealized justification (the true is what would be justified under optimal conditions, where optimal conditions depend on the particular assertion, context, and interests in complex ways). Such a conception makes 'is true' somewhat vague; but metaphysical realism, I have argued elsewhere (Putnam, 1976), is not just vague but incoherent. I agree with Davidson that we are not going to succeed in saying all we want to say without using vague language; this doesn't mean that we have to wallow in vagueness, but it means that what is and what is not vague in the pejorative sense ('*too* vague') depends on our purposes – as John Dewey long ago told us – and not on expressibility in some chimerical 'ideal language'. A view which makes truth dependent on what could be justified and which allows that truths are not all translatable into some one ideal language is not metaphysical realism, but it does preserve a central insight of realism: that truth is a substantive property of assertions, and one which depends on facts which in general go beyond the present memory and experience of the speaker.

A theory of truth which is often confused with the disquotational view is Tarski's 'semantic conception' (Tarski explicitly distinguishes it from the disquotational theory). In the 'semantic conception' truth *is* a property: or rather, an improper totality of properties, one for each language. (There is no proper totality of 'all languages', because of the paradoxes, which is why there is no proper totality of 'all truth predicates'.)

One example of a property which could be the 'truth predicate' for a very simple language (one with just two sentences; this sort of example is due to Carnap) is the following: the property which an expression has if that expression is identical in syntactic shape with 'Schnee ist weiss' and snow is white or if that expression is identical in syntactic shape with 'Der Mond ist blau' and the moon is blue. This property has a feature which is a feature of *all* 'truth predicates' in the Tarskian sense: *whether or not something has this property depends on the world (whether snow is white or whether the moon is blue), but it does not depend on the meaning of the sentence.* For this reason, a truth predicate never coincides in any way with 'true' in the intuitive sense; 'truth predicates' are *coextensive* with 'true' (restricted to a particular language), but that is all.

Some philosophers would say that, in the 'semantic conception', the *meaning* of 'true' is not elucidated by the truth predicate for the particular language, but rather by the 'Convention (T)': the disquotation scheme which all 'truth predicates' must satisfy. Since the truth predicates *do* satisfy the Convention (T) *without* agreeing with 'true' in meaning (for the reason just given) it is hard to know what this claim means; it seems to be a way of saying that 'is true' *does* stand for a property – otherwise we don't have an account of what 'is true' means with quantifiers – but *nevertheless* the 'disquotation theory' *does* tell us the meaning of 'is true'. To the extent that I can understand this, it falls to the objection previously made to the disquotational view as an account of truth.

My purpose in this paper is not to defend a particular account of truth, however. What many philosophers have come to agree upon, in spite of various disagreements in their positions is that: (1) truth *is* a substantial property of assertions, one which depends upon both what the assertions mean and upon the world, and not simply a syncategorematic notion which functions to raise the level of language (i.e., purely disquotational accounts are inadequate); (2) truth cannot simply be justification (relative to the present experience and memory of the speaker); (3) the conception of the truth as a 'copy' of reality is incoherent. If this is right, then there is a significant philosophical problem (one not solved by Tarski's work, valuable as that work is as a contribution to technical logic) connected with elucidating the notion of truth. Vagueness is of philosophical interest because of its connection with the problem of truth.

Vagueness and verdicts

When logicians reflect upon the problem of vagueness, they encounter a problem which involves the actual *use* of language – something their training does not prepare them at all to deal with – and their instinct is to simplify the situation. Several logicians of my acquaintance (including Rohit Parikh, who commented on the present paper before the Boston Logic Colloquium) have considered very simple models for vagueness – say, situations in which all the 'speakers' are in one room at one time, and the sentences under consideration are of the form 'This is red' or 'This is the same color as that'. The speakers are asked to deliver 'verdicts' of a standardized form – say 'I am positive this is red', or 'This is something I would call red, but I'm not positive', and, with the aid of various simplifying assumptions,† one tries to define an extension, a complementary extension, and a vagueness range for the predicates 'red', 'same color as', and so forth.

† For example, Parikh proposed that one might assume that if one speaker is *positive* that x is red, then no speaker is *positive* that x is *not* red as such a simplifying idealization.

The technical problem of a *logic* for language containing vague predicates will be discussed in the final section of this paper. I don't wish to criticize the use of simplified models of the kind described when the purpose is to illustrate and test formal solutions to this technical problem; but there is a danger that such illustrations will be taken to resolve the *philosophical* problem, and one must be very clear that this is not the case.

The philosophical problem arises because we do have a substantial notion of truth, a notion which is not explained by Tarski's technical work or by disquotational theories, either separately or in some kind of attempted combination, and because the assumptions of metaphysical realism are of perennial attraction. (The central assumption – a world of hard 'facts', describable in some sort of ideal language with respect to which one has total bivalence – even attracts some non-realists, such as Quine, as we have seen.) Oversimplified models of our language fail to do justice to the situation because operationalism fails to do justice even to the so-called 'observational' vocabulary.

The two classic difficulties with operationalism were: (1) the need for subjunctive conditionals; and (2) the interanimation of theory and observation. Both arise in connection with the idea that one can take the extension of 'is red' to be the class of things that speakers give some kind of verdict on (either the verdict 'This is red', or the verdict 'This is red and I'm positive', or that some of them give one of these verdicts on and that none of them give 'This is not red' on, etc.).

(1) *The problem of subjunctive conditionals*

Many philosophers recognize a vagueness in the subjunctive conditional itself. In the most familiar theory of subjunctive conditionals, the Stalnaker–Lewis possible worlds semantics, this enters through the fact that there is no one fixed metric which determines which possible worlds are more and less similar to a given possible world. Even if we suppose that what a 'possible world' is is *itself* free from vagueness (a large assumption, needless to say), the fact that the 'similarity metric' depends on interests and context (it can even be different for different counterfactuals with the same antecedent, as Lewis recognizes), make it no more than a reflection of intuitive judgments which are certainly not free of vagueness.† This vagueness is just the vagueness that Nelson Goodman pointed out many years

† One thinks of such well-known examples as the pair of counterfactuals 'If Caesar had been the commander of the UN forces in the Korean war he would have used atomic weapons' and 'If Caesar had been the commander of the UN forces in the Korean war he would have used catapults'. A different example is given in chapter 3.

ago under the heading of 'cotenability': the vagueness in what 'relevant circumstances' could be supposed to hold *if* the antecedent were true, in addition to those explicitly included by the speaker in his formulation of the antecedent itself. Yet, as soon as we pass from model situations, in which all the speakers make 'verdicts' about all the objects, to the actual situation, in which no object is seen by *all* speakers, let alone judged by all speakers, and in which speakers do not even speak one language, let alone make all their judgments in one standardized form, we shall have to talk about what verdicts speakers '*would* accept *if*', rather than in terms of some closed set of verdicts they actually do make, and this will import all of the vagueness of the counterfactual into the 'verdict semantics' itself.

(2) *The interanimation of theory and observation*

Imagine that the room contains a white object which is made to look red by the fact that a concealed red light is shining on it. (Perhaps speakers can't move the object, because of a glass wall.) Then even if *all* the 'verdicts' are 'This is red', it still isn't *true* that the object is red. One can say that conditions aren't 'normal', and that speakers would give a different verdict if the conditions were 'normal'; but then an indefinite amount of theory (just how complicated we know from the work of Land) may have to enter to specify what 'normal' conditions *are*. (If instead of a red light shining on the object one had electromagnetic radiations which altered the perceptions of the viewers, one might also get unanimity of false verdict; to rule out such a case one would have to have a theory of the nervous system and of the influence of radiation on the nervous system!) If one tries to define 'normal conditions' in *observational* language, then one gets into the problem which sunk attempts at phenomenalist reductions of thing language: no matter how long the definition becomes, it doesn't rule out all possible 'abnormal situations', because (as Sellars has pointed out) there just aren't the kind of *laws* in observational language that there would have to be if an observational condition were to rule out all possible abnormal background conditions. (In addition, counter-factuals will enter, of course.)

What (1) and (2) together bring out is that a semantics for vague language in terms of *verdicts* cannot establish the requisite connection with *truth* (the 'extension' defined in terms of verdicts isn't in all cases the class of things the predicate is *true* of); and, apart from this, that it only gives us what we have anyway: a semantics for vague language in a vague metalanguage. But what the metaphysical realist wants is an account of vague language that uses no vague terms.

The logic of language containing vague terms

If 'vague' language – language which cannot be translated into 'ideal' language in some way which is itself singled out uniquely – is legitimate and unavoidable, then the question: *What is the best logical system for schematizing inferences that involve vague terms?* becomes an important one. Even if it is impossible to have a *perfectly precise* truth predicate (or, more vaguely, a *perfectly precise* acceptabilty notion, i.e., a notion of 'reasonableness', or 'correctness', or 'justification') for ordinary language, that does not mean that the *logical syntax* of correct inferences involving such predicates cannot at all be 'regimented'. Ordinary language, or at least language containing terms which are not 'perfectly precise', is the only language we are ever going to have: *philosophy cannot forever confine itself to theories of the logical structure of make-believe languages.* Several approaches have been suggested: (1) The supervaluation approach. Typically this assumes a *precise* set of admissible structures with respect to which the language is interpreted. If this is more than a pretense, it already runs into the objection that this would make *minimal acceptability* (truth in at least one admissible structure) an absolutely sharp notion. There would be a *definite N* such that when one has taken N molecules away the statement 'This is a chair' is still minimally acceptable, but such that when the $(N+1)$st is taken away, the statement loses minimal acceptability. (2) One could keep the supervaluation approach as a method of giving the validity concept for the language, however, while recognizing that the 'set' of 'admissible structures' is only a kind of regulative ideal. But this has some untoward consequences. For example, if one says that

'*John is bald or John is not bald*'

is a tautology (because it is true in every admissible valuation), even though neither *disjunct* is determinately true when John is in the 'vagueness range' of bald, then what will one do in the *metalanguage* about

'*John is bald*' *is true if and only if John is bald* ?

If one uses classical logic justified by a supervaluational semantics in the metalanguage, not only does 'John is bald or John is not bald' come out true, but so does

'*John is bald*' *is true or* '*John is bald*' *is not true.*

But if we think that 'John is bald' has, in fact, *no* determinate truth value, then how are we to express this? (It cannot be the aim of logic to create a language in which the fact that some of our terms are vague is *inexpressible*, after all.)†

---

† After writing this paper I learned that this point has been made by Saul Kripke in his seminars at Princeton.

It seems to me that the whole 'speak as if every sentence had a determinate truth value' approach to logic cannot be the right one when we wish to honestly face the fact that there are sentences which have no determinate truth value (and the fact that there is not even a determinate *set* of admissible valuations). (3) An intriguing approach, proposed by Parikh, is to reconstruct language with vague predicates as a *locally consistent but globally inconsistent language*. In such a language, proofs which are *short enough* never lead to a contradiction (or a falsehood, when we started from true premises), but long proofs cannot be trusted. This is an elegant idea, but again I don't think we can accept it as our final solution. (It is too much a Final Solution.) We cannot simply give up and admit that all our beliefs are ultimately inconsistent, after all. Perhaps Parikh would reply that one could accept the kind of formalism he proposes and *ban long proofs*, where 'how long is "long"' depends on the context and the particular predicates involved. I hope that Parikh will develop his ideas further. (4) An idea that has occurred to me, but that I cannot claim to have thought through, is the following: treat vague predicates (e.g., 'bald') just as undecidable predicates are treated in intuitionist logic. This means that one would accept the classical proof that from

(1) (n) (*If a man with n hairs is bald, then a man with $n+1$ hairs is bald*)

and

(2) *A man with 0 hairs is bald*

it follows that

(3) (n) (*A man with n hairs is bald*)

and hence that one must conclude that (1) is false (I assume that (2) is true and (3) false).

Hence one accepts (as in classical logic)

(4) $\sim(n)$ (*If a man with n hairs is bald, then a man with $n+1$ hairs is bald*)

but one *rejects* (since one is using intuitionist logic) the step from (4) to

(5) $(\exists n)$ (*A man with n hairs is bald. A man with $n+1$ hairs is not bald*)

as involving the rejected inference pattern

$$\sim(n)\,Fn \supset (\exists n)\,(\sim Fn)$$

and also involving the rejected classical rule $\sim(p \supset q) \supset (p \,\&\, \bar{q})$. (Instead one has the intuitionist rule $\sim(p \supset q) \supset (\sim \sim p \,\&\, \sim q)$. Note that not-not-'John is bald' ('John is not not-bald') could be used to deny that 'John is not bald' without committing oneself to 'John *is* bald'.)

By contrast, Parikh would *accept* (1), and accept the inference:

 (i) *(n) (If a man with n hairs is bald, then a man with n + 1 hairs is bald)* (Assumption 1)

 (ii) *A man with o hairs is bald* (Assumption 2)

 (iii) *A man with 1 hairs is bald* ((i), (ii), instantiation, modus ponens, and $o + 1 = 1$)

 (iv) *a man with 2 hairs is bald* ((i), (iii), instantiation, modus ponens, and $1 + 1 = 2$)

$$\vdots$$

$(m + 2)$ *A man with m hairs is bald* ((i), $(m + 1)$, instantiation, modus ponens, and the appropriate equation from arithmetic).

provided m is not too large. But this inference would be rejected by Parikh when *m* is 'too large', and so would be the proof of (3) '*(n) (A man with n hairs is bald)*' using (i), (ii), and mathematical induction.

My proposal *keeps* mathematical induction, even for 'vague' predicates, but distinguishes between saying 'it is false that *all n* are such that ——' and saying 'There exists an *n* such that not ——'.

16

Beyond historicism*

Hegel contributed two great and formative ideas to our culture, ideas between which there is some tension. On the one hand, he taught us to see all our ideas, including above all our ideas of rationality, our images of knowledge, as historically conditioned. After Hegel it was, for example, no longer possible to see Descartes' solipsistic methodology as a pure idea, a thought anyone might have had at any time (even if that is the way we still *teach* Descartes); the connections between individualism in methodology and the replacement of the whole hierarchical world view of the middle ages by the individualistic and competitive world view of early capitalism have been a subject for reflection ever since Hegel (not just since Marx). On the other hand, Hegel postulated an *objective* notion of rationality which we (or Absolute Mind) were coming to possess with the fulfillment of the progressive social and intellectual reforms which were already taking place. In the subsequent decades many accepted this idea of a new, a modernist, conception of rationality, while refusing to identify it with Hegel's system. Hegel's system has, indeed, been regarded as something preposterous. But the positivist conception of scientific rationality as the specifically modern product which is fated to replace older notions once and for all (and to replace the sequence of 'determinate negations' with a steady progressive evolution, an eternal self-improvement of 'the scientific method') owes much to the Hegelian conception.

Indeed, the first positivist, Auguste Comte, was a thorough going historicist. Writing not very long after Hegel's vision of history had begun to make itself felt (and Comte has often been compared to Hegel, although he seems to have arrived at his ideas alone) Comte presented his own version of history as a series of negations of which the determinate end product is 'positive science'.

Thinkers who accept the first Hegelian idea, that our conceptions of rationality are all historically conditioned, while rejecting the idea

* This paper was given as a 'conference inaugurale' at the Albi colloquium on 'Knowing and believing', 27 July 1981.

of an end (or even an ideal limit) to the process, tend to become historical or cultural relativists. A certain oscillation between historicism and positivism has been a central feature of late nineteenth-century and twentieth-century thought. Whether it is Nietzsche versus Mill, or Kuhn and Feyerabend versus Carnap and Popper, or Foucault and Rorty versus Quine, the theme has been history versus science, or rather broad, endlessly changing, *historical* conceptions of rationality versus inflexible adherence to such ideas as the idea that *there is no rational method except the scientific method* and the idea that *science is an instrument for predicting stimulations of our nerve-endings.* The debate has, I think, become boring; yet we seem doomed to repeat it (like a neurotic symptom), unless, perhaps, we can step back and offer a better (and deeper) diagnosis of the situation than the competing diagnoses of historicism and positivism.

One complicating factor in the situation is the self-refuting character of (total) relativism. In our beginning philosophy courses, we all teach that total relativism becomes self-refuting (mentioning Plato and Protagoras). For this reason, it comes to seem impertinent to remind one another of this fact. I myself am fascinated by the *different* ways in which relativism is incoherent or self-contradictory. I think they are worth careful study by epistemologists, not just by beginning students, because each of the refutations of relativism teaches us something important about knowledge. Perhaps the shortest, though not the least profound, has been wittily phrased by the Californian philosopher Alan Garfinkel. Speaking to his relativist students in their own jargon, he says, 'I know where you're coming from, but, you know, Relativism isn't *true-for-me*'.

If the incoherence or inconsistency of relativism is widely appreciated, the incoherence or inconsistency of positivism has been almost forgotten. The classical objection, that the verifiability theory of meaning is itself neither empirically testable nor mathematically provable was supposed to be turned aside when it was conceded that the 'theory' is actually a *proposal*, and as such, neither true nor false. But proposals presuppose ends or values; and it is essential doctrine for positivism that the goodness or badness of ultimate ends and values is entirely subjective. Since there are no universally agreed upon ends or values with respect to which the positivist 'proposal' is *best*, it follows that the doctrine itself is merely the expression of a subjective preference for certain language forms (scientific ones) or certain goals (prediction).

To see the situation more clearly, imagine the Roman Catholic conception of knowledge and justification to be formalized (including confirmation and infirmation rules), and imagine this to be done in such a way that when publicly testable prediction is concerned, the methods of science are to be employed. (I choose Catholicism simply because it is a worked out, rationally elaborated, conception of rationality clearly antithetical to the positivist one.)

Such a formalization would doubtless be sketchy and incomplete; but the positivists were the first to admit that their formalization of their own conception of knowledge and justification was and had to be sketchy and incomplete (especially with respect to the confirmation and infirmation rules). Let L_{RC} be the Roman Catholic formalized language, and L_P be the positivist formalized language. Then 'God exists' would be a confirmable (justifiable) well-formed sentence in L_{RC}. If the positivist rejects L_{RC} itself, then on his own showing it is for subjective reasons. Philosophy (including theology or anti-theology) becomes pure subjective choice!

The positivist might reply, 'I agree that "God exists" is true in L_{RC}, *provided* the Roman Catholic admits that all that this sentence *means* in L_{RC} is that the sentence itself is vacuously confirmable (i.e., without the use of sense data) according to the theological "rules" of L_{RC}.' (Compare Hans Reichenbach's reply to the cat worshipper in *Experience and Prediction*.) But this reply assumes what is not the case, that the connection between *meaning* and *method of verification* is itself something objective, i.e., applicable to all language systems.

That the meaning of a sentence is its method of verification is not a conceptual truth in ordinary language. A linguist could not verify from the rules of English or French that the meaning of a sentence (in English or French) is its method of verification, or that anyone who denies this 'misuses' the words 'meaning' or *signification*. This identification of meaning with method of verification is *itself* a 'proposal', a part of the total positivist proposal. In L_{RC} 'meaning' is not defined as 'method of verification'. Perhaps it is a theoretical primitive, subject to other rules than in the positivist language (rules probably in better accord with 'ordinary usage', as a matter of fact). There is no reason for the Roman Catholic, speaking *his* language, to 'admit' that 'God exists' *means* what the positivist says it means; in fact, this is *false* in L_{RC}.

The positivist will now say that the primitive concepts of L_{RC} are not 'clear'. But 'clear', too, is being *persuasively redefined* by the positivist. (In an ordinary-language sense of 'clear', the expressions 'God', 'set of sets', and 'space–time' are alike: they are 'clear' enough to use, but not 'clear' enough to be free of paradox!)

What the positivist really thinks, of course, is that the term 'God' is *nonsensical* (as used in theology, for a totally transcendent Cause of everything that is metaphysically contingent). And he *really* thinks that there is a fact of the matter about what is and isn't *nonsense* but, on his own view, if he is consistent, he has to admit that there *isn't* a fact of the matter: Roman Catholic theology is only 'nonsense' *relative to* the choice of prediction (or prediction-plus-simplicity) as the sole aim of knowledge. If the Roman Catholic says, 'I have an additional aim: to serve God', what can the positivist say? That this aim isn't expressible in the positivist's language? It *is* expressible in L_{RC}; and L_{RC} is 'understandable' even in the positivistic sense, that we can learn its confirmation and infirmation procedures. The positivist needs an *objective* standard of what is 'nonsense', and his own system provides him with only a subjective one.

We have the strange result that a completely consistent positivist must end up as a kind of relativist. He can avoid inconsistency (in a narrow deductive sense), but at the cost of admitting that *all* philosophical propositions, including his own, have no rational status. He has no answer to the Garfinkel-like philosopher who says, 'I understand your view, but, you know, positivism isn't *rational in my system*'.

Epistemic reductionism

Positivism and historicism are both attempts to reduce epistemic notions to non-epistemic ones: syntactical ones, in the case of positivism; anthropological ones (e.g., 'structuralist' ideas) in the case of historicism or relativism. But such reductions are much more problematical than is commonly appreciated. In a sense, this is the burden of this paper: that we should see positivism and historicism as heroic attempts to do the impossible, to *reduce* epistemic notions to non-epistemic notions. The 'next stage' in philosophy must begin, I think, by frankly acknowledging the impossibility of such a reduction. There is a certain duality in our ideology that we are not going to get rid of. If we are not going to get rid of it, let us accept it and proceed from it, I suggest, instead of continuing the attempt to breathe life into failed intellectual positions.

Let me now try to describe the problem in an abstract way. No philosopher would maintain nowadays that epistemic predicates are semantically or conceptually reducible to non-epistemic predicates. We know about the naturalistic fallacy, and we are all aware that the claim that an epistemic predicate is semantically or conceptually equivalent to a non-epistemic one commits a form of this fallacy. What naturalistic philosophers believe nowadays is that epistemic predicates are ontologically or metaphysically reducible to naturalistic predicates, not that they are conceptually reducible. But what *is* ontological reduction?

The standard example of ontological reduction is the reduction of temperature to mean molecular kinetic energy (of translation). *X has temperature so-and-so* does not have the same meaning (is not analytically equivalent to) *X has mean molecular kinetic energy blah-blah*, even when 'blah-blah' is the value of the mean molecular kinetic energy that corresponds to the value 'so-and-so' of the temperature, yet the property of having the temperature *so-and-so* simply is, as a matter of contingent empirical fact, the property of having the mean molecular kinetic energy *blah-blah*. As physicists have long put it, temperature has been 'reduced' to mean molecular kinetic energy.

This sort of reduction is explained by many philosophers in the following way: before the development of statistical thermodynamics, the term 'temperature' was understood to be a term for a property which was responsible for certain effects and (approximately) obeyed certain laws. We intended the term temperature to 'designate rigidly' whichever property was in fact responsible for those effects, etc. We found out that as a matter of empirical fact mean molecular kinetic energy accounted for the effects and obeyed (approximately) the laws that temperature was supposed to account for (respectively, obey) in phenomenological thermodynamics. This is what it means to say that temperature is synthetically identical with mean molecular kinetic energy of translation.

The key notion here is the notion of discovering that a property is 'responsible for' effects which we use quite another concept to explain, i.e., that the presence of a property *explains* certain effects. Ontological reduction itself, synthetic identity of properties itself, is always made clear using some such notion as 'explains', 'is responsible for', or 'accounts for' in just the way I have indicated. But, I wish to argue, *explanation* is itself an epistemic notion. The notion of explanation is very much in the same ballpark as the notion of *coherence* that Professor Sosa has talked about (unpublished).

My reasons for holding that explanation is an epistemic, or more broadly an intentional, notion are reasons that I wish to postpone giving for a few moments. Before presenting them, I want to say what follows if I am right in this contention, and explanation itself is, at least in part, epistemic or intentional.

(Here I can't resist digressing, and saying something about the semantic notion of *reference*, which has concerned me so much in recent years. Donald Davidson has argued, correctly in my opinion, that *truth is prior to reference* in the following way: a speaker's understanding of the reference of individual words consists in his grasping the truth conditions for sentences which contain those words. Here Davidson builds on and reinterprets Frege's insight that sentence meaning is prior to word meaning. Although formally reference appears to be prior to truth, in that logicians define truth in terms of reference, philosophically it is the other way around. What a speaker learns when he learns his native language is the truth conditions for its sentences, or for a subset of its sentences. If this speaker's knowledge of truth conditions is at least in part a knowledge of *justification conditions*; if a speaker cannot be said to know the truth conditions of the sentences of his language unless he knows the justification conditions for at least some of them, at least partially – and I do not see how one can deny this – it follows that reference itself is partly an epistemic notion. In any case, no one will deny that reference is an 'intentional' notion; in fact, for Brentano it was the paradigm case of an intentional notion. While there are some people today who hold that reference itself is reducible to physicalistic properties and relations, this claim too involves precisely the problems I am going to describe.)

Imagine a philosopher who says that explanation is ontologically reducible to some non-epistemic relation. He might, for example, be a logical positivist who says that explanation should be thought of as a relation between sentences rather than as a relation between facts, and that a sentence S explains a sentence T just in case S stands in a certain syntactic or semantic (in the sense of Tarski) relation to T: or he might be a poor soul who has been driven mad by reading too much sociobiology, and who thinks that an event or fact A explains an event or fact B just in case taking A to explain B (however he explains *that*) is 'conducive to inclusive genetic fitness'; or again, he might be a physicalist who holds that an event A (imagine that he thinks of an 'event' as a space–time region together with its contents) explains an event B just in case A stands in some 'complex physicalistic relation' to B. What any one of these claims comes to, when interpreted as an ontological reduction, is the claim that a certain complex phenomenon (perhaps a certain kind of human practice, or the success of certain kinds of practice) is itself *explained* by the fact that (respectively) a certain sentence stands in a relation R to another sentence, or that a certain practice is conducive to inclusive genetic fitness, or the fact that a certain event stands in a complex physicalistic relation R to certain other events.

I shall confine attention to the claim that explanation is ontologically reducible to (is 'synthetically identical' with) a syntactic or semantic (in the sense of Tarski) relation between sentences, since the discussion is exactly the same no matter which reductionistic theory is involved.

If the statement that explanation *is* the syntactic-semantic relation R is construed as an 'empirical identity claim', so that it *itself* means, in part, that the fact that certain sentences stand in the relation R to other sentences is what *explains* the success of certain human explanatory practices, or whatever, then we can formulate a sentence EP stating this last fact (that the human explanatory practices are successful, or whatever), and a sentence $R(S)$, possibly in the metalanguage, stating that the 'certain sentences' stand in relation R to the 'other sentences', and then according to the 'empirical identity theory' itself, the claim that *Explanation is the relation R* will be *made true* (at least in part) by the fact that the metalanguage sentence $R(S)$ stands in the relation R to the sentence EP about human explanatory practice.

In short, the claim that explanation is 'empirically identical' with R reduces to the claim that certain such sentences as $R(S)$ stand in the relation R to such sentences as EP, since this is what it comes to (on the theory, itself) to say that the facts we use the intuitive notion of explanation to account for (the success of the practice) are explained by the metalinguistic facts about sentences standing in the relation R to other sentences.

The problem is now this: since explanation is not *conceptually* reducible to the relation R (it is not self-contradictory, a violation of the rules of the language, a misuse of ordinary language, or whatever, to *deny* that explanation is the relation R); since there will undoubtedly be intelligent, well-informed, sophisticated philosophers who *reject* the claim that explanation *is* the relation R; we have to ask just what is being *asserted* when it is said that explanation is synthetically identical with R?

We may suppose that intelligent, sophisticated, well-informed opponents of this identity theory are aware of all syntactic facts. In particular, what they are denying when they deny that explanation is synthetically identical with R (is ontologically reducible to R) is *not* that the sentence $R(S)$ stands in the relation R to EP. Knowing full well that the sentence $R(S)$ stands in the syntactic-semantic relation R to the sentence EP, such a philosopher denies (without linguistic impropriety, conceptual confusion, self-contradiction) that R just *is* explanation in the way in which mean molecular kinetic energy of translation just *is* temperature.

As already remarked, if we are asked what we mean when we say that temperature *just is* mean molecular kinetic energy, then we can say what we mean in the fashion I indicated by using the notion of explanation, where 'explanation' is taken to be an available, shared, methodological notion. The question is whether we can do the same thing *informatively* when the thing said to be synthetically identical to something else *is explanation itself*.

Let Jones be the reductionist in this dispute and let Smith be his opponent. Smith will now say to Jones, 'I know perfectly well that $R(S)$ stands in the relation R to EP (*or whatever the relevant naturalistic fact may be, depending on which reductionist theory Jones is defending*). But from the fact, I don't see that it follows that explanation is synthetically identical with R. Of course, if I agreed with you that the truth of $R(S)$ is what *explains* the truth of EP then I would have some reason to believe that explanation *is R*. But from the fact that $R(S)$ *stands in the relation R to EP* it doesn't follow that the truth of $R(S)$ is what *explains* the truth of EP unless I *already* concede that R is the relation of explanation, and that's what's at issue. It seems to me, in fact, that your argument is totally circular.'

Jones will, of course, reply that he's not claiming that it's a *conceptual* truth that explanation is just relation R, or even that it's a conceptual truth that if $R(S)$ stands in the relation R to EP then explanation is synthetically identical with R. Jones will explain again that what he is saying is that the fact that a sentence S stands in the relation R to a sentence T is what *makes it true* that the truth of S explains the truth of T. In particular, the fact that $R(S)$ stands in the relation R to EP is what *makes it true* that the truth of $R(S)$ *explains* the truth of EP. But what is this relation of 'making true'?

Jones' claim amounts to just the claim that (in old-fashioned language) it is the essence of explanation to be R. But there is no place in naturalism, itself, for this sort of essentialism. What we have is not naturalism, but an incoherent mixture of naturalism and twelfth-century essentialism.

Jones has to concede that the statement that the relation R *is* explanation is one that cannot be justified to anyone who does not accept it as intuitively evident once he learns that $R(S)$ stands in the relation R to EP.

Jones cannot even claim that it is *irrational* not to accept it that explanation is synthetically identical with R upon learning that $R(S)$ stands in the relation R to EP. Or, if he tries to say that it *is*, he will have to claim that *rationality* is 'synthetically identical' with a disposition to, *inter alia*, make this philosophical leap. *This* claim will reduce to a claim that such a disposition is what *explains* certain facts, i.e., to a claim that another sentence V stands in the relation R to a sentence W (or to sentences $W_1, W_2, W_3, \ldots$). At every point, the inference from the undisputed non-epistemic fact, that certain sentences stand in the relation R to certain other sentences, to the claim that certain facts *explain* certain other facts, will proceed by an argument which is flagrantly circular.

We will keep coming back to the unexplained claim that the relation *R just is* the relation of explanation, or that the fact that $R(S)$ stands in the relation R to EP 'makes it true' that R is explanation, independently of whether that claim can be justified or not. The fact is that the use of the concept of synthetic identity in this context is unintelligible. The claim that a naturalistic relation *really is* synthetically identical with the relation of explanation is one that we cannot *understand* at all. It is as if someone, having built a certain mindlessness, a certain neutrality, (as we have done for centuries) into the notion of nature, then proceeded to tell us *without explanation* that nature has 'built-in' epistemic properties. No intelligible philosophical claim is really being made.

The same error, the error of supposing that a notion of *synthetic identity* which is explained using intentional notions such as *explanation* or *reference* can be used to say something philosophically informative about explanation or reference themselves, occurs in a recent review of my work by Michael Devitt.

I pointed out in chapter 1 that there are infinitely many admissible models of our language, i.e., infinitely many models which satisfy all operational and theoretical constraints. If the entities that these models consist of are thought of as mind-independent discourse-independent entities, then the claim that just one of these models is the unique 'intended' model becomes utterly mysterious. Each of these models corresponds to a reference relation. So there are infinitely many admissible reference relations, $R_1, R_2, R_3, \ldots$ Someone who believes that just one of these, say R_{17}, *really is* the unique *real* reference relation, *the* reference relation, believes that the word 'reference' is attached to R_{17} (and not to $R_1, R_2, \ldots$) with *metaphysical glue*.

Criticizing this argument, Devitt replies that the 'true' reference relation, R_{17}, is something he calls 'causal connection'. And he asserts that the word 'reference' is attached to R_{17} not by metaphysical glue, but by causal connection.

This is flagrant violation of the theory of types. There is, in fact, no relation which contains in its extension an ordered pair one of whose members is that relation itself (i.e., which is such that something bears that relation to the relation itself). But even if we change our logic so that this is possible, then even if it is the case that the word 'reference' is connected to the relation R_{17} by R_{17} itself, it will also be the case that the word 'reference' is connected to the relation R_1 by R_1 itself, to the relation R_2 by R_2 itself,... Michael Devitt will now reply that the word 'reference' is connected to R_1 by R_1 itself, but the word 'reference' is not connected to R_1 by R_{17} (not connected to R_1 by 'causal connection'). On Michael Devitt's view, it is not the formal fact that R_{17} is in its own converse domain that matters; rather, it is this formal fact *plus* the fact that R_{17} *really is* reference (really is 'causal connection'). It is the belief in this additional 'fact': the, as it were, self-identifying nature of the connection between R_{17} and the name 'reference' (or the name 'causal connection') that I described as tantamount to the claim that R_{17} is connected to the word 'reference' (or the phrase 'causal connection') by metaphysical glue. It is not that there aren't various naturalistic connections between the word 'reference' and R_{17}; it is the idea that one of these *declares itself* to have the honor of making R_{17} *be* the relation of reference independently from all operational and theoretical constraints that is entirely unintelligible.

Just as one can explain the notion of synthetic identity using the notion of *explanation*, one can also explain it (though less informatively) using the notion of *reference*. One can say that *temperature is synthetically identical with mean molecular kinetic energy* in case what we are *referring to* when we use the word 'temperature' (whether we know it or not) is mean molecular kinetic energy. But if someone says that reference *is* R_{17}, then the meaning of *that* statement cannot be informatively explained by saying that the word 'reference' *refers to* R_{17}; for if that very theory is true, then the fact that the word 'reference' refers to R_{17} just *is* the fact that the word 'reference' bears R_{17} to R_{17}, and what hasn't been *explained* at all is what it means to say that the fact that the word 'reference' bears R_{17} to R_{17} *is the same fact* as the fact that the word 'reference' refers to R_{17}.

My argument, however, depends upon the claim that explanation itself is epistemic, or at least intentional. Why do I think this?

Explanation shares with *justification* the characteristic of being action-guiding (in a wide sense of 'action', including the acceptance of statements and accounts as a kind of 'action'). If I say that a statement is 'justified' in a strong sense, I am *expressing approval* of the acceptance of the statement in the context. (Some philosophers believe that action-guiding properties are 'ontologically queer'; by this criterion, all epistemic properties are 'ontologically queer'; but that only shows that there's more on heaven and earth than dreamed of in physicalist philosophy.) We have seen that no non-action-guiding property is associated with *justified* as the descriptive condition for its application by the rules of the language (at least not by rules which are conventional and do not require a prior notion of rationality to interpret). If we say that some naturalistic property just *is* justification (just is the property whose presence makes justification claims *true*), this is precisely the claim we found unintelligible, the claim that something is at one and the same time action-guiding and built into nature. The possibility of this kind of epistemic naturalist fallacy argument in the case of both *explanation* and *justification* turns on the similarity between the notions. I am saying, by the way, that the naturalist fallacy is *more* of a fallacy in the case of epistemic words than in the case of *ethical* words; the claim that 'good' is ontologically reducible to a natural property is not senseless, although I think it is false, while the claim that explanation or justification is so reducible is *senseless*.

Explanation is not just a matter of formal-semantical relations between *explanans* and *explanandum*, as Hempel has maintained. The fact that the Empire State Building casts a shadow of a certain length (when the sun subtends a fixed angle in the sky) is nomologically connected to the fact that the Empire State Building is the particular height that it is; but the length of the Empire State Building's shadow does not *explain why* the Empire State Building is the height that it is, Hempel's valiant defense of his explication notwithstanding. Explanation is interest-relative and context-sensitive. We expect an explanation of a fact to cite the factors that are *important* (where our notion of importance depends on the reason for asking the Why-question). We also expect an explanation to support counterfactuals and, on contemporary theory, the truth of a counterfactual depends on what we take to be the most *similar* hypothetical situations to the actual ('similarity of possible worlds'). An example of a kind used by Alan Garfinkel (1981) is the following: if we are asked to explain why the unemployment rate in England is 11 %, one possible answer of an 'individualistic' kind might be to *conjoin* the 'local' explanations of the facts that John didn't get a job, Betty didn't get a job, ... (For each individual x who didn't get a job we simply have a sentence, as a conjunctive part of the total explanation, which says why the various employers whom that individual approached gave the job to someone else. We also add the fact that the other people have jobs and the number of people in the two groups.) From this conjunction one can indeed deduce what the percentage of unemployed people in England is. Moreover, this 'explanation' does cite factors which *caused* the particular people who are unemployed to be unemployed, and which therefore caused 11 % of the English workforce to be unemployed. Yet this is no answer to the question 'Why are 11 % of the English workforce unemployed?' For it is not the case that *if* the *explanans* had not been true, then 11 % of the English would not have been unemployed. What is true instead, is that if this 'explanans' had not been true, then a *different* 11 % of the English workforce would have been unemployed. Of course, if the question had meant 'Why are this *particular* 11 % unemployed?', then the explanation might have been acceptable.

These factors of importance relative to the Why-question asked and counterfactual supporting power (what counterfactuals our theories would support assuming they are true), seem to me to be an essential part of what Professor Sosa refers to as 'coherence'. In any case, unless one thinks that 'similarity of possible worlds' is built into the universe, it seems to me to be true without question that both *importance* and *similarity of possible situations* are intentional properties, and that explanation is thus (at least partly) an intentional notion.

Nomothetic and ideographic

There is a tendency in European thought in the twentieth century which seems to me to have an indirect connection with the topics we have been discussing. This is the tendency to draw a sharp line between the so-called 'nomothetic' sciences, such as physics, and the so-called ideographic or hermeneutic sciences, such as history. In Max Weber, this tendency was developed to a very modest degree. The only special 'method' of the sciences of man, the 'Verstehen-methode', was limited to the historian's sensitive intuition of the desires and beliefs of various historical persons and 'ideal types' on the basis of historical evidence. (In this sense I myself think that there *is* such a thing as *Verstehen*: Isaiah Berlin has it to an exceptional degree! Indeed, Donald Davidson's well-known paper 'Mental events' might be construed as a defense of 'Verstehen' in Max Weber's sense.) Whether an agent is or is not rational is determined, according to Weber, by asking whether (1) his means-ends beliefs are in accord with the means-ends relationships established by nomo-thetic science; and (2) whether he acts on those means-ends beliefs in the way which is most likely to achieve his goals. These, the goals themselves, cannot be subjected to rational criticism. As Apel has recently put it, Weber thought that 'a rigorous and sincere thinker had to accept the following insight: human progress in the sense of "rationalization" had its complement in giving up the idea of a rational assessment of last values or norms in favor of taking recourse to ultimate prerational decisions of conscience, a pluralism, or as Weber put it "polytheism" of last norms or values.' Recently Habermas has suggested that, contrary to Weber, there can be a rational assessment of values themselves, and has connected this idea with the idea of hermeneutic rationality by suggesting that rationally supported values can be derived from the idea of an ideal dialogic situation.

These attempts clearly represent a recognition of what I might call the *nihilism* that lies behind positivism; the unsupportable suggestion that there is nothing at all to the ideas of insight, intuition, wisdom, except in so far as intuition and wisdom issue in laws and mathematical results which can be publicly verified. The desire of both Weber and Habermas is to defend the existence of better and worse judgments in areas in which what is better and worse cannot be 'inter-subjectively' demonstrated in the positivistic sense. But the method seems to me to be the wrong one.

The price of taking the Weber–Habermas approach is to concede that the positivists have given essentially the right description of the natural sciences, the so-called 'nomothetic' disciplines. This, it seems to me, we cannot and should not concede. The fact is that, contrary at least to Habermas, the method of verification in natural science does not consist simply in deriving testable predictions of the form If you do A, then you get result B, and carrying out experiments. In the first place (although it is surprisingly rarely discussed) it is possible to think of an infinite number of mutually exclusive strongly falsifiable hypotheses which are compatible with background know-ledge. Without some informal notion of *plausibility* or *rationality* it would be impossible to decide *which theories it is rational to test at all* and *which theories it is rational to refuse to even test*. There would be no such thing as scientific rationality. (Notice that such a decision falls into *neither* the positivist 'context of discovery' *nor* their 'context of justification'.) If we admit that this is so, as Carnap did, and seek to find a 'prior probability metric' that underlies the intuitive judgments of scientists that some theories are sufficiently plausible to test and others are not, then we will quickly realize that rationality in the 'nomothetic' sciences is just as vague and just as impossible to formalize as 'Verstehen'. If we deny it, as Popper does, and insist that all there is to scientific rationality is the systematic testing of certain 'if-then' statements (and the rejection of theories which imply false ones), then we give a totally distorted picture of the nomothetic itself.

Secondly, even when a theory has survived attempts to falsify it, it is quite easy to think of an indefinite number of other theories that lead to the same practically testable predictions as that theory. A historic example of this is the case of Poincaré's theory of relativity and Einstein's theory of relativity, which were proposed in the same year, and which led to the same predictions that could actually be tested. Without methodological criteria which rule out certain theories on grounds of (lack of) simplicity, (lack of) coherence, postulating unnecessary entities, postulating entities which are insufficiently observable, and so on, there would never be any choice of a scientific theory on the basis of experiment. Once again, the idea that what Habermas calls 'means-ends rationality' is a cut and dried thing is totally mistaken.

Finally, there are scientific theories which are not accepted on the basis of testable predictions at all, scientific theories which are in a sense 'historical', although they do not involve hermeneutics, i.e., the ascription of beliefs or desires to human agents. An example is the Darwinian theory of evolution by natural selection, which implies no testable predictions, but which is accepted precisely on the grounds of the coherence of the explanation it affords for speciation, and the fruitfulness of the questions to which it has given rise. As Monod has put it,

The selective theory of evolution as Darwin stated it required the discovery of Mendelian genetics, which of course was made. This is an example, and a most important one of what is meant by the content of a theory, the content of an idea – a good theory or a good idea will be much wider and much richer than the inventor of the idea may know in his time. A theory is judged precisely on this type of development, when more and more falls into its lap, even though it was not predictable that so much would come of it.

In sum, the desire to recognize that rationality is much wider than the intolerably narrow (in fact, self-refuting) positivistic conception of it is highly laudable; but, one cannot achieve a correct conception of rationality by pasting together a positivistic account of rationality in the 'nomothetic' sciences and a vague account of rationality in the 'ideographic' sciences. A better approach would be to begin by recognizing that interpretation, in a very wide sense of the term, and value are involved in our notions of rationality in every area. I do think that our notion of coherence is closely connected with our image of an ideal speculative intelligence, and that this is in turn connected with our idea of total human flourishing. To this extent, I think that Habermas is pointing in the right direction. But I see no gain in trying to derive our whole conception of human flourishing from one human activity, however important and central that human activity may be, even as central an activity as human dialogue.

Conclusion

One might sum up what I have been saying by saying that, on the one hand, the attempt to deny the objectivity of reason leads to self-defeating irrationalisms, while the attempt to explain the objectivity of reason leads to nonsense, at least if our paradigm of explanation is the familiar reductionist one. Of course, there is a good deal of philosophical work that philosophers who do not seek any sort of reductionist theory of rationality have been doing and will continue to do. We have many beliefs about truth, about explanation, about counterfactuals, about coherence and simplicity, about belief and desire, and philosophers are engaged in discussing and describing these beliefs and their function in our life. Some of the beliefs we have about *truth*, for example the belief that *speakers' beliefs about certain kinds of topics tend to be true*, and that *speakers are more likely to attain their goals when they act on true beliefs*, play an important role in interpretation, as Donald Davidson has taught us. The beliefs that we have about belief and desire and their connection with action (in an idealized way, these are described in rational preference theory) also play an important role in interpretation. All these beliefs together: our general beliefs about truth, our beliefs about belief, our beliefs about desire, form a kind of informal system, an overarching mentalistic theory, which gives material content to such notions as truth, reference, belief, and desire, as a number of philosophers have argued.

Attempts at a grand synthesis in epistemology, a theory of coherence, simplicity, warranted assertibility and so on, that would make the structure of reason evident to reason itself, have been less successful.

Perhaps the deepest cause of this is that our notion of coherence has proved to be extremely topic relative. It is not very informative to say that we tell whether or not there is a bittern in a bush (to use a famous example of John Austin's) by asking whether or not the belief that there's a bittern in that bush 'coheres' with our total system of factual beliefs. In fact, it's not just uninformative to say this, it's desperately vague. What counts as justifying the belief that there's a bittern in the bush depends on a whole system of interrelated concepts that one has to be more or less of a birdwatcher to acquire. Generally, what counts as justification is learned as one learns the individual concepts that one uses in a particular enterprise. Of course, we sometimes criticize our inherited traditions; and when we do this, or when our inherited traditions conflict, more abstract notions of coherence may indeed play a role in our thinking. To make our knowledge of all this into anything like a 'science' seems today like a hopeless dream.

If the discovery/justification distinction does not do the work it was supposed to do (ruling the considerations that make it rational to *entertain* a theory, as opposed to accepting it, out of epistemology altogether), then a successful science of epistemology would have to survey human creativity, human conceptual innovation itself; and if there is anything we *have* learned from historicism, it is that there is no external place, no Archimedean point, from which we can do this.

Yet the kind of work that John Rawls (1970) has done indicates that giving up the dream of totalistic epistemology is not the same thing as giving up the dream of philosophy. Rawls' *A Theory of Justice* does not pretend to provide a 'foundation' for ethics in an ultimate sense. Yet, while it begins by deliberately accepting certain of our ideals and values without question, while it refrains from asking certain ultimate metaphysical questions about truth and justification, it is by no means a narrow or trivial exercise. Even if we cannot survey all cognitive activity, all justification, there is no reason why we cannot seek to do what philosophers have always done: order and criticize the beliefs and methods on which various departments of human life depend.

What philosophers like Donald Davidson and David Wiggins have been telling us is that we should stop worrying about the problem of dualism. We are not committed in any case to a substance dualism, but only to a property dualism, and the kind of property dualism we are committed to, the irreducibility of the intentional and the epistemic, is not a dualism that contradicts any of the claims of *physics*. In a way, it is the kind of dualism that Kant acknowledged; we are not able to overcome what Kant called the 'dualities of experience'. We are stuck with having to use intentional language, normative language, mentalistic language, epistemic language as well as 'descriptive' language, scientific language, naturalistic language.

But saying this is not, I think, saying quite enough. I wish I knew what would be saying enough. In philosophy, as in everything else, we are at the beginning of a post-modernism. The great rejection of everything 'traditional', and the great hope that by rejecting the tradition we would make possible either a utopian future for man (optimistic modernism) or a final recognition of the grandeur and terror of life, a final immediacy which scientism and progressivism robbed us of (quietistic modernism), are both beginning to look very tired.

The problem is this. Analytic philosophy claimed to be piece-meal philosophy. It gave up, or said it gave up, the dream of an integrated view, which is so characteristic of what people refer to as continental philosophy. This was always somewhat of a pretense. The logical positivists had very much an integrated view, and Quine has very much an integrated view. The 'motor' of analytic philosophy was logical positivism (and, earlier, logical atomism); not because all analytic philosophers were positivists, but because the arguments pro-and-con positivism were what kept analytic philosophy in motion. Analytic philosophy has already begun to lose shape as a tendency with the disappearance of a strong ideological current at its center. The desire for integration is so central to philosophy, I think, that no philosophical tendency will long endure without it. On the other hand, every attempt at integration which has been too grand has collapsed. The incoherence of the attempts to turn the world views of either physics or history into secular theologies have not yet been entirely exposed, but the process is, I hope, well under way. As philosophers, we seem caught between our desire for integration and our recognition of the difficulty. I don't know what the solution to this tension will look like. But Etienne Gilson was right when he wrote that 'Philosophy always buries its undertakers.'

Bibliography

Austin, J. L., 1961. 'A plea for excuses', in his *Philosophical Papers*, Oxford, 175–204.

Ayer, A. J., 1936. *Language, Truth and Logic*, London.

Barwise, J., 1971. 'Infinitary methods in the model theory of set theory', in R. O. Gandy and C. E. M. Yates (eds.) *Logic Colloquium 69*, Amsterdam, 53–66.

Boyd, R., 1980. 'Materialism without reductionism: what physicalism does not entail', in N. Block (ed.) *Readings in the Philosophy of Psychology*, Cambridge, Mass., 67–106.

Bruner, J., 1976. 'Psychology and the image of man', in H. Harris (ed.) *Scientific Models and Man: The Herbert Spencer Lectures 1976*, Oxford.

Bub, J., 1974. *The Interpretation of Quantum Mechanics*, Dordrecht.

Burret, C. (ed.), 1967. *L. Wittgenstein: Lectures and Conversations*, Berkeley.

Canfield, J., 1975. 'Anthropological science fiction and logical necessity', *Canadian Journal of Philosophy*, v, 467–79.

Carnap, R., 1967a. *Pseudo-problems in Philosophy*, Los Angeles.

1967b. *The Logical Structure of the World*, London.

Cavell, S., 1969. *Must We Mean What We Say?*, New York.

1979. *The Claim of Reason*, Oxford, 86–125.

Davidson, D., 1967. 'Truth and meaning', *Synthese*, XVII, 304–23.

1970. 'Mental events', in L. Foster and J. Swanson (eds.) *Experience and Theory*, London, 79–101.

1974. 'Belief and the basis of meaning', *Synthese*, XXVII, 309–22.

Dummett, M., 1959. 'Wittgenstein's philosophy of mathematics', reprinted in his *Truth and Other Enigmas*, London, 1978, 166–85.

1975. *What is a Theory of Meaning? I*, Oxford.

1976. *What is a Theory of Meaning? II*, Oxford.

1977. *Elements of Intuitionism*, Oxford.

1979a. 'What does the appeal to use do for the theory of meaning?', in A. Margalit (ed.) *Meaning and Use*, Dordrecht, 123–35.

1979b. 'Comments' on Putman's 'Reference and understanding', in A. Margalit (ed.) *Meaning and Use*, Dordrecht, 218–25.

Evans, G., 1973. 'The causal theory of names', *Aristotelian Society Supplementary Volume*, XLVII, 187–208, reprinted in Schwartz (1977).

Feyerabend, P., 1975. *Against Method*, London.

Field, H., 1972 a. 'Tarski's theory of truth', *Journal of Philosophy*, LXIX, 347–75.

1972 b. 'Theory change and the indeterminacy of reference', *Journal of Philosophy*, LXX, 462–81.

1974. 'Quine and the correspondence theory', *Philosophical Review*, LXXXIII, 200–28.

1978. 'Mental representation', *Erkenntnis*, XIII, 9–62.

1980. *Science Without Numbers*, Oxford.

Finkelstein, D., 1963. 'The logic of quantum mechanics', New York Academy of Sciences, section of *Physical Sciences Review*, 621.

Fodor, J., 1975. *The Language of Thought*, New York.

1979. 'Methodological solipsism considered as a research strategy in cognitive psychology', *The Behavioral and Brain Sciences*, 63–109.

Gardner, M., 1971. 'Is quantum logic really logic?', *Philosophy of Science*, XXXVIII, 508–29.

Garfinkel, A., 1981. *Forms of Explanation*, Yale, ch. 3.

Goldman, A., 1978. 'What is justified belief?', in G. S. Pappas and M. Swain (eds.) *Justification and Knowledge*, Cornell.

Goodman, N., 1947. 'The problem of counterfactual conditionals', *Journal of Philosophy*, XLIV, 113–28.

1977. *The Structure of Appearance*, 3rd edition, Amsterdam.

1978. *Ways of Worldmaking*, Indianapolis.

Grice, H. P. and Strawson, P. F., 1956. 'In defence of a dogma', *Philosophical Review*, LXV, 141–58.

Grünbaum, A., 1970. 'Space, time and falsifiability, part 1', *Philosophy of Science*, XXXVII, 469–588.

Huxtable, A. L., 1981. 'Is modern architecture dead?', *New York Review of Books*, 16 July, 17–22.

Kant, I., 1933. *The Critique of Pure Reason*, London.

Kochen, S. and Specker, E. P., 1967. 'The problem of hidden variables in quantum mechanics', reprinted in *The Logico-Algebraic Approach to Quantum Mechanics*, vol. 1, 1975, 293–328.

Kripke, S., 1971. 'Identity and necessity', reprinted in S. Schwartz (ed.) *Naming, Necessity and Natural Kinds*, 1977, London, 66–101.

1972. 'Naming and Necessity', in D. Davidson and G. Harman (eds.) *The Semantics of Natural Language*, Dordrecht, 254–355.

Kuhn, T., 1962. *The Structure of Scientific Revolutions*, Chicago.

Lewis, D., 1969. *Convention*, Cambridge, Mass.

1973. *Counterfactuals*, Oxford.

1974. 'Radical interpretation', *Synthese*, XXVII, 331–44.

1976. 'Survival and identity', in A. D. Rorty (ed.) *The Identity of Persons*, Berkeley, 17–40.

Mackie, J., 1974. *The Cement of the Universe*, Oxford.

1977. *Ethics, Inventing Right and Wrong*, London.

Margenau, H. and Park, J. L., 1968. 'Simultaneous measurability in quantum theory', *International Journal of Physics*, I, 211–83.

Matson, W., 1967. *The Existence of God*, Ithaca, New York.

Meehl, P. and Sellars, W., 1956. 'The concept of emergence', in H. Feigl and M. Scriven (eds.) *Minnesota Studies in the Philosophy of Science*, I, Minneapolis, 239–52.

Minsky, M., 1975. 'A framework for representing knowledge', published as part of his *The Psychology of Computer Vision*, New York.

Monod, J., 1975. 'On the molecular theory of evolution', in R. Harré (ed.) *Problems of Scientific Revolution: Progress and Obstacles to Progress in the Sciences*, Oxford, 11–24.

Mycielski, J., 1963. 'On the axiom of determinancy', *Fundamenta Mathematicae*, LIII, 2.

Plantinga, A., 1974. *The Nature of Necessity*, Oxford.

Putnam, H., 1962a. 'The analytic and the synthetic', reprinted in Putnam (1975e), 33–69.

    1962b. 'Dreaming and "depth grammar"', reprinted in Putnam (1975e), 304–24.

    1962c. 'It ain't necessarily so', reprinted in Putnam (1975d), 237–49.

    1965. 'How not to talk about meaning', reprinted in Putnam (1975e), 117–31.

    1968a. 'The logic of quantum mechanics', reprinted in Putnam (1975d), 174–97. Revision of Putnam (1968b).

    1968b. 'Is logic empirical?', in R. Cohen and M. Wartofsky (eds.) *Boston Studies in the Philosophy of Science* v, Dordrecht, 216–41.

    1970a. 'On properties', reprinted in Putnam (1975d), 305–22.

    1970b. 'Is semantics possible?', reprinted in Putnam (1975e), 139–52.

    1975a. 'The meaning of "meaning"', reprinted in Putnam (1975e), 215–71.

    1975b. 'Language and Reality', in Putnam (1975e), 272–90.

    1975c. 'Philosophy and our mental life', in Putnam (1975e), 291–303.

    1975d. *Mathematics, Matter and Method: Philosophical Papers, Volume 1*, Cambridge.

    1975e. *Mind, Language and Reality: Philosophical Papers, Volume 2*, Cambridge.

    1976. 'Realism and reason', reprinted in Putnam (1978), 123–38.

    1978. *Meaning and the Moral Sciences*, London.

    1979. 'Reference and understanding', in A. Margalit (ed.) *Meaning and Use*, Dordrecht, 199–216.

    1981. *Reason, Truth and History*, Cambridge.

Putnam, H. and Friedman, M., 1978. 'Quantum logic, conditional probability and interference', *Dialectica*, XXXII, 305–15.

Quine, W. V., 1936. 'Truth by convention', reprinted in P. Benacerraf and H. Putnam (eds.) *The Philosophy of Mathematics*, Englewood Cliffs, New Jersey, 1964, 322–45.

    1951. 'Two dogmas of empiricism', reprinted in his *From a Logical Point of View*, Cambridge, Mass., 1953, 20–46.

1957. 'The scope and language of science', *British Journal for Philosophy of Science*, VIII, 1–17.

1960a. 'Carnap and logical truth', *Synthese*, XII, 350–74.

1960b. *Word and Object*, Cambridge, Mass.

1966. *The Ways of Paradox*, New York.

1969. *Ontological Relativity and Other Essays*, New York.

1970. *The Philosophy of Logic*, Englewood Cliffs, N.J.

1975. 'On empirically equivalent systems of the world', *Erkenntnis*, IX, 313–28.

1977. 'Facts of the matter', in R. Shahan and K. Merrill (eds.) *American Philosophy from Edwards to Quine*, Oklahoma, 176–96.

1978. Review of Goodman's *Ways of Worldmaking*, *New York Review of Books*, 25 November, 25.

1981. 'What price bivalence?', *Journal of Philosophy*, LXXVIII, 90–5. Reprinted in his *Theories and Things*, Cambridge, Mass.

Rawls, J., 1970. *A Theory of Justice*, Oxford.

Reichenbach, H., 1938. *Experience and Prediction*, Chicago.

1958. *The Philosophy of Space and Time*, New York.

Rorty, R., 1980a. *Philosophy and the Mirror of Nature*, Oxford.

1980b. 'Pragmatism, relativism and irrationalism', *Proceedings and Addresses of the American Philosophical Association*, 53,

Russell, B., 1912. *The Problems of Philosophy*, London.

Scheffler, I., 1979. *Beyond the Letter*, London.

Schilpp, P. (ed.), 1963. *The Philosophy of Rudolf Carnap*, La Salle, Ill.

Schwartz, S. (ed.), 1977. *Naming, Necessity and Natural Kinds*, London.

Smart, J. J. C., 1965. 'Conflicting views about explanation', in R. Cohen and M. Wartofsky (eds.) *Boston Studies in the Philosophy of Science*, II, New York, 157–69.

Stalnaker, R., 1968. 'A theory of conditionals', in N. Rescher (ed.) *Studies in Logical Theory*, Oxford.

Strawson, P. F., 1979. 'Universals', *Midwest Studies in Philosophy*, IV, 3–10.

Stroud, B., 1965. 'Wittgenstein and logical necessity', *Philosophical Review*, LXXIV, 504–18.

Tarski, A., 1933. 'The concept of truth in formalized languages', reprinted in his *Logic, Semantics, Metamathematics*, Oxford, 1956, 152–278.

Tversky, A. and Kahneman, D., 1982. *Judgement under Uncertainty*, Cambridge.

1975. 'Judgement under uncertainty: heuristics and biases', *Science*, 185, 1124–31.

Unger, P., 1979. 'Why there are no people', *Midwest Studies in Philosophy*, IV.

von Neumann, J., 1955. *Mathematical Foundations of Quantum Mechanics*, Princeton.

von Neumann, J. and Birkhoff, D., 1936. 'The logic of quantum mechanics', *Annals of Mathematics*, XXXVII, 823–43.

Wheeler, S., 1975. 'Reference and vagueness', *Synthese*, XXX, 367–74.
   1979. 'On that which is not', *Synthese*, XLI, 155–73.
Wiggins, D., 1976, 'Truth, invention, and the meaning of life', *Proceedings of the British Academy*, LXII, 331–78.
   1980. *Substance and Sameness*, Oxford.
Will, F. L., 1974. *Induction and Justification*, Ithaca, New York.
Wittgenstein, L. W., 1953. *Philosophical Investigations*, Oxford.

Acknowledgements

The author and publisher would like to thank the following for their permission to reprint material in this volume: the Association for Symbolic Logic for 'Models and reality' from *Journal of Symbolic Logic*, 1980, XLV, 464–82; Clarendon Press for 'Philosophers and human understanding' from *Scientific Explanation, Papers based on Herbert Spencer Lectures given in the University of Oxford*, ed. A. F. Heath, 1981; 'Giulio Einaudi Editori for 'Equivalence', 'Possibility and necessity' and 'Reference and truth', which appeared in *Enciclopedia* as 'Equivalenza', V, 547–64, 'Possibilità/ necessità', X, 976–95, and 'Referenza/verità', XI, 725–41; the Foster–Wills Committee and the Oriel Press for '"Two dogmas" revisited', from *Contemporary Aspects of Philosophy*, ed. G. Ryle, 1976; D. Reidel Publishing Co. for 'There is at least one *a priori* truth', from *Erkenntnis*, XIII, 153–70, and 'Quantum mechanics and the observer', from *Erkenntnis*, XVI, 193–219, copyright © 1978 and 1981, by D. Reidel Publishing Company, Dordrecht, Holland; the University of Minnesota Press for 'Analyticity and apriority: beyond Wittgenstein and Quine', from *Midwest Studies in Philosophy*, vol. IV, ed. P. French, copyright © 1979 by the University of Minnesota; the editor and publisher of *Profiles: An International Series on Contemporary Philosophers and Logicians*, D. Reidel Publishing Co., for 'Computational psychology and interpretation theory' to appear in the volume on *Donald Davidson* edited by M. Hintikka and B. Vermaezen; the editor of *Journal of Philosophy* for 'Reflections on Goodman's *Ways of Worldmaking*', from *JP*, 1979, LXXVI, 603–18; the editor of *New Literary History* for 'Convention: a theme in philosophy', from *NLH*, XIII, no. 1 (autumn 1981).

Index